The History of Ochiltree

Village & Parish
(Including Drongan, etc.)

Other books by Dane Love:

Scottish Kirkyards
The History of Auchinleck – Village and Parish
Pictorial History of Cumnock
Pictorial History of Ayr
Scottish Ghosts
The Auld Inns of Scotland
Guide to Scottish Castles
Tales of the Clan Chiefs
Scottish Covenanter Stories
Ayr Stories
Ayrshire Coast
Scottish Spectres
Ayrshire: Discovering a County
Ayr Past and Present
Lost Ayrshire
The River Ayr Way
Ayr – the Way We Were
The Man Who Sold Nelson's Column
Jacobite Stories
The History of Sorn – Village and Parish
Legendary Ayrshire
The Covenanter Encyclopaedia
A Look Back at Cumnock
A Look Back at Girvan
A Look Back at Ayrshire Farming
Ayr Then and Now
Ayrshire Then and Now
The History of Mauchline – Village and Parish
The Galloway Highlands
Ayrshire's Lost Villages
A Look Back at Dalmellington
Scotland's Lost Villages
A Look Back at Irvine
A Look Back at Stirling

www.dane-love.co.uk

The History of Ochiltree

Village & Parish
(Including Drongan, etc.)

Dane Love

CARN PUBLISHING

© Dane Love, 2021.
First Published in Great Britain, 2021.

ISBN - 978 1 911043 10 2

Published by Carn Publishing Ltd.,
Lochnoran House,
Auchinleck, Ayrshire, KA18 3JW.

www.carnpublishing.com

Printed by Bell & Bain Ltd,
Glasgow, G46 7UQ.

The right of the author to be identified as the author of this work has been asserted by him in accordance with the Copyright, Designs and Patents Act 1988.

All rights reserved. No part of this publication may be reproduced, stored, or transmitted in any form, or by any means, electronic, mechanical or photocopying, recording or otherwise, without the express written permission of the publisher.

Contents

List of Illustrations	6
Introduction	9
1 Early Times (before 1700)	11
2 Parish Life	28
3 Roads and Transport	78
4 Estates and Landowners	87
5 Ecclesiastical	150
6 Education	198
7 Health	218
8 Industry	222
9 Commerce	251
10 Agriculture	259
11 Recreation	270
12 Sons and Daughters	290
Appendices:	
Farms and Small Lairdships	304
Coal Mines	338
Bibliography	341
Index	346

List of Illustrations

1.1	Cinerary Urn found at Mote Hill *(Author's Collection)*	13
1.2	Stone-Age axe head found at Mote Toll *(Author's Collection)*	14
1.3	Cinerary urn found at Stewart Avenue site *(Author's Collection)*	16
1.4	Sketch and profile of urn found at Stewart Avenue site *(Author's Collection)*	16
1.5	Bronze spear-head found near to Ochiltree Moat *(Hunterian Museum)*	17
1.6	Work in progress excavating at the Witch Knowe *(Alastair Hendry)*	18
1.7	Pit A within the Witch Knowe *(Alastair Hendry)*	18
1.8	Witch Knowe *(Alastair Hendry)*	19
1.9	Ochiltree parish area as depicted in Joan Blaeu's *Coila Provincia*, 1654	24
1.10	Market Cross around 1900 *(James Brown)*	25
1.11	Market Cross today *(Dane Love)*	26
2.1	Sundial on wall of house in Burnock Street *(Dane Love)*	28
2.2	Ochiltree parish area from Captain Armstrong's Map of 1775	31
2.3	Rev David Grant's Gravestone, old kirkyard *(Dane Love)*	33
2.4	The House with the Green Shutters *(Author's Collection)*	35
2.5	Ochiltree Cross, with Mill Street to the left and Burnock Street to the right *(Author's Collection)*	36
2.6	Burnockholm House *(Author's Collection)*	37
2.7	Burnockholm House *(Dane Love)*	38
2.8	Smiddy Brae, Ochiltree *(Author's Collection)*	40
2.9	Robert Johnstone's Gravestone *(Dane Love)*	43
2.10	Hawthorn Villa *(Dane Love)*	44
2.11	Main Street with the House with the Green Shutters on the right *(Author's Collection)*	48
2.12	Ochiltree Cemetery *(Dane Love)*	48
2.11	Burnock Street *(Dane Love)*	49
2.13	Private George Brown's military gravestone, Ochiltree cemetery *(Dane Love)*	52
2.14	Unveiling of Ochiltree War Memorial *(Author's Collection)*	56
2.15	Ochiltree War Memorial *(Author's Collection)*	57
2.16	New council housing in Broom Crescent *(Author's Collection)*	59
2.17	War Memorial on new site *(Dane Love)*	61
2.18	Ochiltree Community Hub *(Dane Love)*	63
2.19	Taiglum Rows *(Author's Collection)*	65
2.20	Tom and Susan Ross at Taiglum Rows *(Jo Stewart)*	67
2.21	Drongan Resource Centre *(Dane Love)*	70
2.22	Alex Linwood *(Author's Collection)*	76
3.1	Old Burnock Bridge *(Author's Collection)*	80
3.2	Lugar Bridge *(Author's Collection)*	82
3.3	Ochiltree Railway Station *(Author's Collection)*	84
3.4	Drongan Railway Station *(Author's Collection)*	85
4.1	Colville arms *(Author's Collection)*	88
4.2	Stewart of Ochiltree arms *(Author's Collection)*	101
4.3	Cunningham of Glencairn arms *(Dane Love)*	114
4.4	Ochiltree House from South East *(Author's Collection)*	115
4.5	Ochiltree House from North East *(Author's Collection)*	118
4.6	Ochiltree House on 1856 Ordnance Survey map, showing ruined wing of old castle *(Author's Collection)*	119
4.7	Ochiltree House from North East *(Author's Collection)*	120

4.8	Auchencloigh Castle *(Dane Love)*	122
4.9	Drongan Castle *(Dane Love)*	123
4.10	Drongan House in 1920s *(Author's Collection)*	131
4.11	Polquhairn House *(Dane Love)*	138
4.12	Bonnyton House, South front in 2020 *(Dane Love)*	141
4.13	Bonnyton House, East front in 2020 *(Dane Love)*	143
4.14	Lord Skerrington in 1910 *(Author's Collection)*	145
4.15	Campbell of Barquharrie and Sornbeg arms *(Author's Collection)*	146
5.1	The former Manse, 2019 *(Dane Love)*	164
5.2	Communion Token from 1762 *(Author's Collection)*	165
5.3	Ochiltree Parish Church *(Author's Collection)*	168
5.4	Architect's drawing of Ochiltree Church Hall *(Author's Collection)*	172
5.5	Ochiltree Parish Church in 2019 *(Dane Love)*	173
5.6	Communion Token from 1699 *(Author's Collection)*	174
5.7	Ochiltree Free Church *(Author's Collection)*	175
5.8	Rev A. Gordon MacLeod *(Author's Collection)*	181
5.9	Rev Angus MacLeod's gravestone *(Dane Love)*	183
5.10	Ochiltree Free Church *(James Brown)*	184
5.11	Schaw Kirk *(Author's Collection)*	187
5.12	Schaw Kirk in 2020 *(Dane Love)*	188
5.13	Hardwicke Hall in 2020 *(Dane Love)*	194
5.14	St Clare's R.C. Church *(Dane Love)*	196
6.1	William Simson's Monument in the old kirkyard *(Dane Love)*	204
6.2	Architect's drawing of school *(Author's Collection)*	205
6.3	Quintin Stewart's gravestone, old kirkyard *(Dane Love)*	206
6.4	Ochiltree Public School *(Author's Collection)*	208
6.5	Ochiltree Primary School *(Dane Love)*	210
6.6	Sinclairston School class *(Author's Collection)*	212
6.7	Sinclairston School football team, 1922 *(Jo Stewart)*	214
6.8	Drongan Primary School *(Dane Love)*	216
7.1	Ochiltree Convalescent Home from the South East *(Author's Collection)*	219
7.2	Ochiltree Convalescent Home from the West *(Author's Collection)*	220
8.1	Gravestone of James Findlay, hook maker *(Dane Love)*	223
8.2	Ochiltree Mill *(Author's Collection)*	224
8.3	Ochiltree Mill *(Author's Collection)*	224
8.4	Old Coal Pit, Coalhall *(Author's Collection)*	232
8.5	Drumsmudden Pit plan *(Author's Collection)*	238
8.6	Killoch Colliery under construction *(Author's Collection)*	242
8.7	Killoch Colliery *(Author's Collection)*	243
8.8	Drongan Miners' Memorial *(Dane Love)*	247
9.1	Drongan shops in Mill of Shield Road *(Author's Collection)*	253
9.2	Commercial Inn *(Dane Love)*	255
9.3	The House With the Green Shutters *(Dane Love)*	256
9.4	Gateside Inn *(Dane Love)*	257
9.5	Toll Bar, Drongan, 2020 *(Dane Love)*	258
10.1	Lease of Carston farm from Earl of Glencairn to Hugh Murray, 1757 *(Author's Collection)*	262
10.2	Harvesting Ryegrass Seed at Clydenoch *(Author's Collection)*	263
10.3	Knockshiffnock farm in 1966 *(Author's Collection)*	267
10.4	Carston farm in 1966 *(Author's Collection)*	269

11.1	Ochiltree Curling Club's Morton Rink (left to right: William, Hugh, David and John) *(Mungo Howat)*	271
11.2	Ochiltree Curling Club Eglinton Jug winners *(Mungo Howat)*	272
11.3	Ochiltree Schoolfellows' 4th Reunion, 1871 *(Mungo Howat)*	275
11.4	Ochiltree Schoolfellows' 100th dinner *(Mungo Howat)*	276
11.5	Ochiltree Schoolfellows' 100th dinner speakers *(Mungo Howat)*	277
11.6	Ticket for Glasgow Ochiltree Reunion *(Mungo Howat)*	283
12.1	George Douglas Brown *(Author's Collection)*	290
12.2	George Douglas Brown's gravestone, Holmston Cemetery, Ayr *(Dane Love)*	292
12.3	George Douglas Brown's plaque, Ochiltree *(Dane Love)*	293
12.4	James Morton, painted by T. Corsan Morton *(Royal College of Physicians and Surgeons of Glasgow)*	297
12.5	David Rowan Baillie as depicted in 'The Baillie' *(Author's Collection)*	299
12.6	Brass Plaque from engine manufactured by David Rowan *(Author's Collection)*	299

Introduction

It is basically a century since the last detailed history of the parish and village of Ochiltree was published. *Ochiltree, its History and Reminiscences*, was written by Alexander Murdoch and was published in 1921 by Alexander Gardner of Paisley. Today it is a rare and much sought-after book. In the intervening years much has changed in the village, and the present writer feels that a new look at the interesting past of this rural Ayrshire parish is long overdue. Though mainly pastoral, Ochiltree has many connections of note throughout its history, from associations with Robert Burns, the Tennant family of Glenconner, John Knox and other notable folk from the past, to more recent times, being the birthplace of Johnny Cymbal, a noted singer and pop-star in the sixties!

Alexander Murdoch, in his first chapter, notes that Ochiltree's position makes it 'the centre of gravity' of Ayrshire, and as such, its history has been influenced by all aspects of county history. However, in many aspects, the history of the parish spilled into the national scene. Some of the early owners of the barony were closely involved with the royal family, sometimes to their benefit, at other times to their cost.

Every aspect of history in between is recounted in this book, from churches and Covenanters, schools and scholars, to farms and castles, pits and peoples. Hopefully all Ochiltree residents, or sons of the parish resident elsewhere, will find much to interest them in these pages.

Within the parish are a few other communities, in some cases, like Drumsmudden, now lost and returning to nature, in other cases, like Coalhall and Sinclairston, developing into small villages of their own, and in the case of Taiglum, redeveloped as a new community named Drongan, eclipsing Ochiltree in size and importance.

Within the text, the use of italic years indicates a year that was known, but is not necessarily terminal. Dates written as c.1660 are approximate, whereas years in Roman type, eg, 1771, are confirmed.

Dane Love
Auchinleck, 2021

Acknowledgments

In the writing of this book, I have consulted hundreds of individuals who have freely given their time and information. This has been gathered over a number of years, perhaps originally for some other project. To list them all would be impossible. However, I feel I must acknowledge the following for particular contributions: James S. Brown for some of the pictures, Rob Close for various notes, and Alastair Hendry for notes and pictures. For odds and ends that all add to the bones of the book, I also wish to thank Terry Andreucci, Neil Dickson, Bill Gibson, Anne Hope, and Isabell Montgomerie.

CHAPTER ONE

EARLY TIMES (before 1700)

DESCRIPTION OF PARISH

The parish of Ochiltree extends to 18,401 acres (7,447 hectares) and is bounded by the parishes of Auchinleck, Old Cumnock and New Cumnock to the east, Dalmellington to the south, Coylton to the west, and Stair and Mauchline to the north. It is located in the central part of Ayrshire, known as Kyle. The parish measures around eight miles from north to south, by five miles at its widest. The parish of Stair was at one time part of Ochiltree parish, but this was disjoined by the Commissioners of Teinds on 9 July 1673, supposedly because the Earl of Stair found it inconvenient to travel from Stair House to Ochiltree kirk! The church was suffering during the Covenanting struggles at the times, and it was not until 22 July 1690 that an Act of Parliament ratified this decision. Nevertheless, even after Stair was separated, many properties in that parish still had to contribute to the stipend of the Ochiltree minister. Part of what is now Ochiltree parish was also included in a disjoined section of Stair parish, around Schaw, but this was transferred back to Ochiltree when the authorities were tidying up parish boundaries and doing away with enclaves and detached sections.

A rural parish, much of the land is used for grazing, though here and there crops are grown, though not so regularly as in the past. The parish has quite extensive woodlands within it, mainly shelter belts and ornamental woodlands in the north, but to the south the higher and rougher ground has in more recent years been planted as part of the Kyle Forest. Previously, this ground was open moorland, grazed by sheep. A few small lochs exist in the district - Belston Loch at Sinclairston, the almost-gone Plaid Loch (it measured around 8 acres in extent in the 1850s), and the Trabboch lochs. There were formerly others, but these have been drained over the years as part of the agricultural development of the countryside. Lost lochs include the Shield Loch (or Loch of the Scheel), near to Shield, and Loch of the Hill, which was located somewhere around Watston. In more recent years, a few stretches of open water have been created as a result of abandoned opencast mines, and these exist at Belston, near to the Belston Loch itself, and Auchencloigh.

Ochiltree village is located at the east side of the parish, near to the confluence of the Burnock and Lugar waters. Originally little more than a long main street stretching up the Hill of Ochiltree, today the village is slightly larger, there being a scheme of council-built houses at the top of the hill and private houses beyond this and others erected in Mauchline Road.

Writing in 1927, Frances H. Walker describes the location of the village thus:

> It sits on a rocky eminence commonly called The Brae and near the confluence of two rivers, one of which so much surpasses the other in size and importance that it is always known as the river. At the foot of the Brae and near the 'Meeting of the Waters' stands a relic of the hoary past, the 'Big Hoose' built in the fifteenth century, which brings the people of [Ochiltree] into spiritual contact with some of the more notable figures who have helped to make the inspiring pages of Scottish history. Its ancient Cross stands like a world-old sentinel in the middle of the village and not far removed from the Cenotaph, which was but lately erected in memory of the brace young men who were killed in the Great War. There are also the beautiful gardens – a dream of apple blossoms – which in early Summer transforms the old village into a wondrous vision of pink and white.

The name Ochiltree is quite difficult to explain. Old maps spell it as 'Uchiltre' or 'Uchletree'. This may be an ancient British word meaning 'high place' or 'the high house'. John Smith, in *Prehistoric Man In Ayrshire* (1895), states that the name 'is thought to take its name from a camp and a tree', before agreeing that it probably means 'high house'. Uchle is said to be the Gaelic for camp, with the English word tree added, making this an unlikely tautological hybrid. Another Gaelic derivation that was put forward in the *New Statistical Account* in 1837 is *O' Chaaltearan*, or *O'chailtearan'*, meaning a wooded countryside. The 'High House' has been claimed to refer to the original Ochiltree Castle, located on the banks of the Lugar Water across from Auchinleck Castle, whereas the camp refers to the area of the village known as the Camp, located off Mill Street.

POPULATION

The population of the village and parish has grown steadily over the years. According to the Census, which is usually taken every ten years, and other accounts, the population of the village, parish and the community of Drongan was as follows:

Year	Village	Parish	Drongan
1755		1,210	
1792		1,144	

1801		1,308	
1811	500	1,548	
1821		1,573	
1831	642	1,562	
1841		1,601	
1851		1,787	
1861	709	1,676	
1871	699	1,656	
1881	523	1,493	
1891	499	2,062	
1901		1,932	
1911	661	2,024	350
1921	726	2,102	
1931		2,023	
1941	*No Census due to war*		
1951	900	2,794	480
1961		5,187	
1971		5,053	
1981			
1991	758	4,238	2,910
2001	693	4,553	3,012
2011	1,046	4,862	3,205
2016	1,060		3,180

STONE AND BRONZE AGES

There are no major sites with surviving relics of prehistoric man's life in this area, but many smaller items have been discovered over the centuries indicating that he was here. Some of these have long-since been lost again, or are unidentified in museum collections, but a few still survive and are known about.

Near to Drumbowie farm a celt of clay stone was found sometime in the nineteenth century. This was highly polished and had a sharp cutting edge. It was in the possession of historian, James R. Wilson of Sanquhar, who exhibited it to the Glasgow Ochiltree Association's thirtieth meeting in 1890.

1.1 Cinerary Urn found at Mote Hill *(Author's Collection)*

Sometime prior to the year 1838, during some excavation work at Mote Hill, just west of the village, workers unearthed a cinerary urn. This was a particularly fine example of a Bronze Age urn, and it was able to be removed from the ground in its entirety. It was examined and found to have been manufactured from a coarse light-coloured clay. It measures seventeen inches in height. The mouth of the urn is 14½ inches in diameter and the base is five inches in diameter. The sides of the urn are a full inch in thickness. It was noted that these dimensions were amongst the largest found in urns of this type. The opening of the urn is slightly oval and there is a prominent overhanging rim, highly decorated with scored chevrons and lines. The bevelled edge of the top rim is also decorated with zig-zag lines. Below the outer rim is a substantial concave belt. The largest circumference of the urn measures 48 inches. When discovered, the urn was half-filled with calcined bones. The urn was presented to the museum of Ayr Mechanics' Institution in 1865 by the representatives of Dr Charles F. Sloan, F.S.A. (Scot) of Ayr. When that museum was closed, the urn was moved to 'a small dark apartment in the Town's Buildings, along with the misecellaneuos collection of articles of which it had formed a part'. The urn is now preserved in a glass case on the first-floor landing at the Carnegie Library in Ayr.

According to the *New Statistical Account*, at Mote an urn containing calcined bones was unearthed a few years prior to 1837. This probably refers to the same urn as that just mentioned, but that cannot be now confirmed.

A stone-age axe was found near to the Mote Toll sometime in the nineteenth century. The axe measures approximately 7¾ inches in length. It is 3½ inches thick and the diameter of the hole for the shaft is 2¼ inches on the face, but slightly smaller in the centre. In the centre of the axe the circumference measures around 13 inches. The axe weighs 4¾ pounds. The stone is thought to be micaceous quartz porphyry. The actual location where the axe was found cannot be determined, but James Macdonald, in 1882, wrote that 'It has been kindly lent me by Miss Sloan, and was in the small collection of Ayrshire antiquities formed by her brother, the late Dr Chas. F. Sloan,

1.2 Stone-Age axe head found at Mote Toll
(Author's Collection)

Ayr, some of which were described in a former Volume of the "Collections." In the course of professional visits that he had occasion to make a good many years ago to Ochiltree, he observed it lying on the window-sill of a cottage near the Moat Toll, a short distance west of the village. After passing it several times, as he used humorously to tell, he could "thole" it no longer, and one day made bold to stop and ask the mistress of the house if he might be allowed to carry it off. Her reply was that she could not give him permission to do so without first consulting her husband, "as he had put it there." Next time he was at Ochiltree the woman came out and cheerfully presented it to him.' This Dr Sloan appears to have been some character, for he is referred to in the *Archaeological and Historical Collections relating to the Counties of Ayr and Wigton*:

> To those who were privileged to spend an occasional hour with Dr Sloan when his leisure permitted, the Ochiltree urn was a familiar object. For years it lay in a corrner of his consulting-room, carefully placed in a box made for its reception. In many respects Dr Sloan was a superior man. To a thorough knowledge of his profession, and a most genial disposition, he added intellectual gifts that made him a valuable friend and agreeable acquaintance. His store of information on general subjects was large, and on none did he dwell with greater enthusiasm than on the natural history and antiquities of his native county, more especially when he found a sympathetic listener. In the progress and prosperity of the Mechanics' Museum, as calculated to promote a taste for such studies, he took a warm interest, and had he lived longer its fate might have been different. To the great regret of a wide circle he was cut off in the very midst of his years and his usefulness. To those who knew him will not, I feel sure, deem this brief tribute to his memory out of place in the present volume; and others may excuse it on learning that to him we owe the preservation of nearly half of the 'urns' to be noticed in this paper as being still in existence.

A number of stone arrow or spearheads or darts were discovered on the farm of Laigh Tarbeg. They had been separated and passed into the ownership of different people, and their whereabouts are no longer known. To the south-east of Darntaggart farm, near to Skares, a flint scraper was discovered. Little more is known about it, or its current whereabouts.

On Monday 26 September 1955 James Wallace, Hilltop Cottage, Mauchline, and workmen digging drains for the new council houses at the top of the village discovered a cinerary urn in the ground. It was located in an oval enclosure, formerly covered in trees, that lay to the south of the Pool path. This former wood appeared to be planted on a low mound, around 450 feet above sea level, which measured about sixty feet in diameter and which latterly was about two to three feet higher than the surrounding fields. Its shape and the fact that the urn was discovered within it, hinted that the mound was probably a Bronze Age burial cairn. The subsoil was sandy, but there was a layer of stones which appeared to extend under all of the mound's extent.

The urn had been recognised by James Wallace as being of antiquarian significance, and it was carefully removed. The site was visited by James L. Davidson of the Ordnance Survey Archaeology Division. The urn had been buried around three feet below the ground height at the time, in an inverted position. It contained a large quantity of calcined bones. Near to the urn, around four feet below the surface, a large quantity of black wood-ash was discovered. The urn broke soon after its removal, but was sent to the Hunterian Museum in Glasgow where it was restored.

1.3 Cinerary urn found at Stewart Avenue site
(Author's Collection)

Later in 1955 the site was re-exained by Edward Henderson of Cumnock, who excavated a trial pit in the centre of the mound. He discovered a layer of charcoal, but nothing else of any significance. A survey of the mound took place in 1956. The site of the possible burial cairn is now occupied by the eastern cul-de-sac of George Douglas Brown Avenue, and partially within the garden of 26 Stewart Avenue.

1.4 Sketch and profile of urn found at Stewart Avenue site
(Author's Collection)

The urn measures eleven inches in height, 8½ inches in diameter at the open end, and 4½ inches in diameter at the base. It has an incised pattern around the rim, typical of cinerary urns from across the United Kingdom. It was subsequently sent to the Carnegie Library in Ayr and thereafter to the store at Rozelle House, Ayr.

A bronze spear-head was found in Ochiltree parish sometime in the nineteenth century. According to the attached label, it was found at Ochiltree Moat, and as it was in the collection of the Old Hunterian Museum, this places the donation sometime between 1807-1870. It was a Class IV type spear-head, meaning that it has two loops on it for binding it to the shaft. It measures around five inches in length and a flat point, though the tip may have been broken off at some time. The spear-head is preserved at the Hunterian Museum of the University of Glasgow.

1.5 Bronze spear-head found near to Ochiltree Moat
(Hunterian Museum)

Perhaps discovered at the same site, at the same time, is a bronze axe hammer. Little more is known about this item, and its whereabouts is now unknown.

There is also scant references to a Bronze Age burial cairn that once existed on the farm of Lessnessock. This was located near to Cairnford, hence the latter's name. In 1890 it was noted that the site of the cairn only ever became obvious when the field was ploughed, for the crops that grew thereafter were more luxuriant on the circumference of the monument.

NORMAN PERIOD

Probably the most significant survivor from this period is the Witch Knowe, located out Mauchline Road, at the back of the field beyond the cemetery. This was in fact a motte hill, thrown up by Norman settlers as a place of defence. These mounds of earth often incorporated natural lumps, to reduce the labour required. They were crowned with a wooden structure, which would form the Norman baron's home, and the mound was usually surrounded by a wooden fence or palisade, creating a bailey. Depending on the size of the bailey, other dwellings were erected within it, home to the baron's servants and retainers. No remnants of a bailey are noted at the Witch Knowe, but this was probably destroyed over the centuries by ploughing and other agricultural works. The mound at the Witch Knowe measures around 80 feet in diameter at the widest point of the summit. The minor axis measures 55 feet, resulting in an elliptical surface. The sloping sides expand to around 110 feet in diameter at the base. This is surrounded by a moat

1.6 Work in progress excavating at the Witch Knowe *(Alastair Hendry)*

1.7 Pit A within the Witch Knowe *(Alastair Hendry)*

or ditch to the south and west, 60 feet wide and seven feet deep, whereas to the north-east the steep banking down to the riverplain at the side of the Lugar Water forms a greater means of defence. The ditch has probably partially filled in over the years. The mound comprises of a sandy soil, in which can be found a number of large boulders, the upper surface of which is around three feet or so higher than the surrounding fields. In 1964 some trial excavations took place at Witch Knowe by Thomas Alastair Hendry and members of a University of Glasgow Extra Mural Class in Archaeology. A few small pits were dug across the mound, but no major finds were discovered, and no trace of a defensive palisade nor walling. On the summit of the mound two large sub-circular pits, measuring around four feet deep were found. Some traces of burning were unearthed.

1.8 Witch Knowe *(Alastair Hendry)*

The Mote or Moat Toll is named after another motte hill that existed at one time. Speaking in 1890, James R. Wilson recalled that part of the moat hill was removed when he was a boy at school, the material used for road metal.

ROMAN OCCUPATION

For a period, between 79 AD and 118 AD, the mighty Roman empire extended north of Hadrian's Wall, into lowland Scotland, as far as the Antonine Wall. In 82 AD Cnaeus Julius Agricola came to scotland and pushed into Ayrshire and Galloway where he subdued the local Novantae tribe. Ochiltree, lying as it does with the rest of Ayrshire, between the two great frontiers walls, must have felt the presence of Roman occupation at this time. Again, between 138 AD and around 154 AD, the southern part of Scotland was occupied by the Romans under Q. Lollius Urbicus. A further period of occupation took place between 160-163 AD and, for the final time, in 185-207 AD.

There is little in the parish to indicate their presence, indeed, little in Ayrshire as a whole, but camps at Girvan and Hunterston, as well as Roman roads up Nithsdale and to Loudoun Hill, indicate that they were certainly in the immediate vicinity. An old tradition claims that the Romans had an outpost at the Mote Toll area, associated with a camp that was claimed to have existed at the Gallowlea, at the top of Ochiltree Main Street. This is referred to in Murdoch's *Ochiltree*, but there is no evidence of this today.

During a survey of the moorland south of Auchencloigh and Polquhairn prior to proposed opencast coal mining, an old roadway was discovered which the archaeologists ascribed to the Roman period. This was later questioned as being unlikely. The roadway measured 37 feet in width and comprises of a mound of yellow boulder clay with a single layer of cobbles.

OCHILTREE CAMP

A circular earthwork at one time existed at the lower end of the village, between Mill and Burnock Streets. Old Ordnance Survey maps of the mid-nineteenth century onward indicated a 'Camp'. Adjacent to the earthwork, in Mill Street, stood 'Camp Cottage'. Of the history of this camp there is no record, and suggestions as to its date are few. Whether it was a prehistoric fortified camp, or the remnants of a motte hill cannot be ascertained. The site of the camp was in recent years obliterated by the council houses of Mill Place. Alexander Murdoch, in *Ochiltree*, claims that the camp only dates from 1789, that being the place where the military occupation of Ochiltree took place. However, if that was the case, the Ordnance Survey would not have indicated it as an antiquity only sixty years later. Perhaps the ancient camp site was used again in the late eighteenth century, explaining Murdoch's reference.

EARLY REFERENCES

There are few references to Ochiltree as a village before the 1500s. Perhaps there was just a castle, kirk and estate, the latter comprising of small farms across the parish. Only here and there can we unearth any indication of parish life to try to indicate what was happening in that period.

It is claimed that there was once a great battle held on the lands of Laigh Tarbeg, and around the old motte hill that once stood at Mote Toll. Indeed, some old accounts state that Laigh Tarbeg was also known as Dirthole, or Darthole, after the many darts, or spear heads, that were unearthed there over the years.

Sometime during the reign of King Robert the Bruce (which was from 1306 until 1329), but before the date 1321, Eustacia de Colvil, widow of Sir Reginald de Cheyne, and daughter of Sir William Colvil of Ochiltree, granted the church and church lands at Ochiltree to the monks of Melrose Abbey. This grant was confirmed by Robert de Colvil of Oxnam (Roxburghshire) and Ochiltree.

The lands remained their property until the Reformation in 1560. Granting of lands to cathedrals or abbeys was a popular act at the time, and many local parishes were similarly gifted. This meant that the church lands came under the direct control of the abbeys, and they appointed priests to carry out all church duties in the parishes.

At the time of the grant to Melrose Abbey, the head abbot was one Abbot Roger. It is thought that he sent some of his relatives to Ayrshire to manage the lands, said to explain the arrival of some familes surnamed Roger to the district. The family remained in the parish for many centuries thereafter. In the first volume of the *Commissariat Register* of Glasgow, the will of Alexander Roger in Ochiltree is recorded, made in 1549/50. This will indicates Roger's wealth as a substantial farmer in the parish, his inventory including, 'one horse, three mares, four oxen, eight cows, two stirks [young bullocks], nineteen sheep, forty bolls of oats, five and a half bolls of barley, and household goods to the value of fity pounds.' In his will, he left fourpence towards the building of St Kentigern's church in Glasgow.

Sometime around 1498 Sir WIlliam Colville of Ochiltree and his tenants were granted an exemption by King James IV from the jurisdiction of the Sheriff of Ayr, Hugh Campbell of Loudoun, because of a feud which existed between the families.

In 1513 Sir Robert Colville of Ochiltree marched with King James IV to the Battle of Flodden. The king led an army of about 20,000 men south into Northumberland, along with seventeen cannon, 'as goodly guns as have been seen in any realme'. The two sides met at Branxton Hill, north-west of the village of Flodden, on the afternoon of 9 September 1513. The Scots' left-hand side, led by Lord Hume, managed to disperse their opponents, but the right, led by the earls of Argyll and Lennox, were routed and fled. The middle battalion, under the direct command of the king, forced its way into the English troops, James coming close to defeating the opposite leader, the Earl of Surrey. However, an English soldier managed to kill the king. Some of the remaining Scots fought on until night-fall, only prolonging the defeat. The king lay dead on the field, along with eight of the 22 Scots earls, and numerous bonnet-lairds. The battle, against the English, was a disaster for the Scots, and they were totally defeated. Sir Robert Colville was one of hundreds of lairds who died on the battlefield, and many local lairds fell with him, including Thomas Boswell of Auchinleck and Sir David Dunbar of Cumnock. After the battle, forces from England entered Ayrshire and it is said that the 'strong houses of Cumnock and Uchletree were both violently taken possession of; their owners having fallen on Flodden field.'

The Craufurd of Drongan family appear to have been involved in a number of feuds and squabbles in the sixteenth century. Gavin Ros, a Ayr lawyer at the start of the sixteenth century, records one of these feuds in *Legal Practice in Ayr and the West of Scotland*:

> On 10th November, 1520, John Craufurd of Drongane passed to the Parish Church of Dalmellington, with a mind to enter it in a peaceful manner, in order to count the sum of 100 merks and to pay the same to Margaret Craufurd, relict of the late William Hebburn of Lowis, upon the high altar of the church, for the redemption of certain lands, with letter of tack of the lands for two years after redemption. There appeared no safe access to the church for him to

carry this out, because Bartholomew Craufurd of Kerse, his enemy with William Cathcart, son of the creditor, and others, to the number of sixteen persons, armed with weapons, straitly guarded the church and graveyard and the entrance thereto and prevented his entrance, while one of them shot an arrow at him. In these circumstances he counted the 100 merks in presence of the notary and witnesses in a place near to and immediately adjoining the graveyard and tendered it and a letter of tack to the lady, who was personally present, and requested her to receive them; but this she declined to do, as the sum was not offered to her on the high altar of the church in terms of the letter of reversions. John Craufurd then left the money in the hands of the notary, and protested that his non-entry to the church to count and deliver the money should not prejudice him. Margaret Craufurd, on the other hand, offered and affirmed that she was ready to receive the money and the tack in the church on the high altar, and declared that she did not cause Bartholomew Craufurd of Kerse to come to the church to hinder John Craufurd's entrance. Bartholomew Craufurd next asserted that he was willing to permit John Craufurd of Drongane to enter the church to count and pay the money, and offered to deliver his two brothers in-surety to Craufurd that he might have entry and exit-to and from the church without bodily injury. He also declared that he did not come to the church that day by occasion or by the persuasion of Margaret Craufurd but of his own motive. This was probably correct, as he had a dispute with John Craufurd regarding the Church of Quiltown or Coylton, which was referred to arbitration a few days after this occurrence, and he may have taken this means of bringing their difference to a point.

On 1st April of the next year, 1521, at Ochiltree, Margaret Craufurd gave notice to John Craufurd requiring him to pay her the 100 merks for redemption of the lands with tack for two years, and offered him the evidents of the lands which were in her hands. Craufurd on the other hand declared that the sum with the tack had been delivered to sure keeping for her.

This was, in fact, a minor dispute between two branches of the Craford family, arising over the payment of an outstanding debt. The dispute appears to have been extended over a period of time for the sole purpose of providing amusement for the more powerful Laird of Kerse.

The great Scottish Reformer, John Knox, visited Ochiltree a number of times in the sixteenth century. One of these occasions took place on his travels in 1556. He had lost his first wife, and at Ochiltree met the young daughter of Lord Ochiltree,

Margaret Stewart. In March 1564 Knox, aged 51, married Margaret Stewart at Ochiltree, the bride aged only seventeen. Apparently Knox had originally had designs on Margaret's elder sister, but she spurned him. A local tale claims that Mary, Queen of Scots, attended the wedding.

Andrew Stewart, 1st Baron Castle Stuart (1560–1629), and a member of the Ochiltree family, was appointed Warden of the West March by King James V. He only held the appointment for five months, but in that time 'he hangit and slew three score, with the more notable thieves and kept the country in great quietness and order all this time'.

The sixteenth and seventeenth centuries in Scotland was a period of witch-hunting. This was promoted by the king, James VI, who wrote a book entitled Daemonolgie, in which he explained his full belief in magic and witchcraft, and aims to both prove the existence of such forces. He also set out to determine what sort of trial and punishment these practices merit, which, in James's view, was death. In the accounts of various witches we find reference to Janet Wallace, from Ochiltree, who was tried on 9 August 1630 for witchcraft. A commission was given to Sir William Cuninghame of Caprington and others to try Wallace.

The kirk session minute books from a variety of surrounding parishes give some glimpses of life in seventeenth century Ayrshire, and Ochiltree in particular. A few examples can be quoted. In Dundonald in 1611 Adam Fleiming in Corsbie is reputed to have 'Bessie Thomsoun with bairn, quho is now in Ochiltree'. Similarly, on 14 July the same year, 'Adam Flemeing in Corsbie, compeirand, confessit his fornicatioun with Bessie Thomsoun, now in Ochiltree, aleging that it was lykvyis under promeis of mariage. The Sessioun ordeined that scho be brocht before thame to declair hir mynd thairintill that thairefter order may be tain with thams as effeiris'.

In 1654 the Dutch cartographer, Joan Blaeu, published *Theatrum Orbis Terrarum Sive Atlas Novus Pars Quinta*, the most detailed map yet published of Europe. The Scottish maps were based on the earlier work of Timoth Pont, who surveyed the country between 1583 and 1610. His Ayrshire survey may have taken place between 1604-8, when the Cunningham description was compiled. Notes by W. Camden accompanied the maps, and writing in 1607 he mentions Ochiltree:

> On the former's [i.e. Lugar Water's] bank also is Ochiltree Castle, the seat of the Stewarts of the Royal Family, and likewise progenitors of the Dukes of Albany, who are from it Barons of Ochiltree; from this family was that Robert Stewart, who was the inseparable companion of the Prince of Condé and was slain in battle with him in France.

Blaeu's map indicates the various farms and important buildings within the parish, many of them appearing for the first time in print. Some of the spellings are now

1.9 Ochiltree parish area as depicted in Joan Blaeu's Coila Provincia, 1654

classed as archaic, and a number of places no longer exist, even their existence being long-forgotten. At the confluence of the Burnock and the Lugar, the map indicates Uchiltre Cast[le] and Uchiltre K[irk]. There is also a mill shown nearby, indicating the Ochiltree Mill is of considerable vintage.

Names of farms or houses from the map that no longer exist within the parish include: Knocklery, Lesslumnochshill, Wallacestoun, Mosed, Windyhill, Welleyes, Barnhill, Coogs, Glengabyr, Lit[tle] Craigoch, and Jockstoun.

BURGH OF OCHILTREE

In 1669 Ochiltree was raised in status to a burgh, in favour of the Earl of Dundonald. The creation of burghs was something that local lairds were keen on, for it brought them considerable prestige, and helped them to develop their estates. At Ochiltree

1.10 Market Cross around 1900 *(James Brown)*

the charter seems to have been quite ineffective, for the village didn't grow much at all, and it is debatable whether any market of standing was established here. One thing that may have arisen following the creation of the burgh was the erection of a market cross. It is possible that an older cross of sorts was in the village, for Sir Robert Colville of Ochiltree raised the king's standard here in 1513 prior to his part in the Battle of Flodden.

1.11 Market Cross today *(Dane Love)*

The present mercat, or market, cross in Ochiltree is located at the centre of the village. An ancient pillar, it was used to mark the place where markets could be held. The cross was also the focal point of the village, for here throughout history numerous meetings and gatherings have been held. It is possible that the cross was rebuilt in 1836. The cross was broken on a number of occasions, and in 1897, to mark the Diamond Jubilee of Queen Victoria, a group of Ochiltree sons based in Glasgow arranged for its restoration. One of the committee, William Murdoch, appeared at a committee meeting of the Glasgow Ochiltree Society 'to collect subscriptions for the re-erection of the Old Cross at Ochiltree village. He explained his mission and the members freely subscribed'. Financial assistance was also received from Sir Charles Tennant and his sister, Marion Wallace, wife of Rev R. Wallace. The three flagstone steps were added at this time, using Arbroath stone. An inscription commemorating the restoration was added to the bottom step of the cross to mark this.

The cross has been damaged by vehicles on a number of occasions. In July 1967 it was knocked down by a brewer's lorry. It was damaged again by a car in 1972 and it had to be restored. In 1977, to mark Queen Elizabeth's Silver Jubilee, the cross was restored once more by Cumnock and Doon Valley District Council.

John Graham, Viscount Claverhouse, the persecutor of the Covenanters, visited Ochiltree on many occasions. He was to marry Jean Cochrane, third daughter of Lord Cochrane of Ochiltree, on 10 June 1684.

A number of old customs survived into the modern era. Beltane was a Celtic festival which was held on either the 1 or 3 of May. Ministers felt that it had pagan origins, and thus were keen to suppress any form of celebration held at that time of year. However, writing in *A General View of the Agriculture of Ayrshire*, in 1811, William Aiton noted that in Ochiltree parish bonfires were still being lit just before the May Fair and near to Beltane. These attracted large numbers of revellers who 'on the evening preceding the fair, the herds were in use to collect whins, broom, coals, &c. and kindle fires after dark, which were attended by great numbers of the inhabitants'.

CHAPTER TWO

PARISH LIFE

1700-1800

In the second half of the eighteenth century the village of Ochiltree was considerably redeveloped by the Earls of Glencairn. Many of the original leases date from 1785, being offered for 999 years. In 1787 houses were erected in Burnock Street, the date surviving on a sundial which was rebuilt and preserved in a later house. A number of new houses were erected in Mill Street in 1789. Kelburn, 74 Main Street, was erected in 1793 following a lease issued that year. In 1795 Lady Glencairn wrote to Rev William Thomson regarding his complaint regarding the poor condition of the manse and the minister's desire to change the arrangement regarding the building. The letter makes reference to the development of the village at the time, 'with regards to the grounds you wish to take, I am extremely well pleased, if they in no way interfere with the plan of the building in the village that's carrying on.' In 1809 some houses were erected in Mill Street on feus which were to be held on a 999-year lease from Whitsunday that year. A single-storey thatched cottage in Main Street was let for 999 years from Martinmas 1800. Another was let for 995 years from Martinmas 1805.

The proprietor of the estate, Lady Glencairn, who usually resided at Coates House, Edinburgh, often wrote to the minister at Ochiltree with suggestions for him to improve the conditions of the parishioners. A number of these letters have been transcribed:

2.1 Sundial on wall of house in Burnock Street *(Dane Love)*

Revt. Sir,

When I saw you in Edr. I then mentioned how glad I wd be to show some distinction to those most remarkable for Filial Piety. I've had much enquireys on ye subject with regard to Wheels, but nothing has answered my expectations, I am now told there's a Wheel made can admit 12 children working from 5 years old & upwards; this, with proper attention shown to other branches, such as knitting and sewing, by a woman of pious principle, of good life and conversation, I think may be very usefull in your town, assisted by the schoolmaster in Reading and Writing. Samson tells me he has a room in one of his houses wd answre & be ready in a short time. I must beg your assistance in this matter. Will you be so good as send me ye dementions of the lloom, & one for ye Mistress, & the price of the House Rent, yt I may order ye wheel to be ready and sent when yr prepared for it? The most important matter is ye Teacher. Do you know any you could recommend who would teach them their prayers, questions, and Hyms, & attend the rest of their operations? I propose after they have payed me for the Lint, the future produce of their Labours should the one half go for premiums to the most distinguished in their different branches, ye other layed up as a fund for marriage, such as buying clothes or Furniture, or any missfortune of inability, as every stage of ye human existence is liable to miserable accidents. We must have some person of generous humanity, who will volunteer himself as our treasurer and actor in disposing of our Yarn and buying our lint, for if he be not very moderate in his demands he may encroach on Funds, Charity and Goodwill to our fellow-creatures, which we must look on as sacred. Pray write me directly if you have any woman in view; she should be 40 I think, or thereabouts. Ye wheel shall be ordered immediatly on hearing you have a room fite to receive it. The woman's wages from £5 to 6 pds a year during my life, to be payed by me - her room's rent and the school's. But at this distance, without yr countenance & frequent visits to give approbation to piety for their soul's good, and cleanliness for their bodies, I'll have but little credit and comfort in my scheme. I must therefore beg of you, sir, to take a fatherly interest in my plan.

Would G. Colvil be fit for, and accept freely, being our treasurer.

Again I recommend myself and Family to yr prayers, and am, Revt. Sir,

Your most Humble Servant,

E. GLENCAIRN.

7th Janr. '89, Coats.

Lady Glencairn finds by this day's post the spinning machine is to be here the Eleventh, so she begs Mr. Grant wd please order any one he's fixed on for Mistress, to attend here yt day, that she may receive instructions from the maker, will enable her to teach the way and method to the children. John Samson seemed to wish to be perfectly ascertained of the dimensions of the wheel, yt his room may bo layed out accordingly as wd best answer to accommodate the children. So, if you please, he may be informed, and ho said he wd see the wheel safe to her destination, where I trust to your very tender interest in this concern, all shall answer to yr comfort and my wish, to be of real service in leading the young mind to that industry which is virtue's friend.

March 2nd, '80, Coats.

We can get a small glimpse of life at the end of the eighteenth century from the report in the *Statistical Account*, compiled in 1792. At the time there were around 1,150 people living in the parish. This figure appears to have fallen from the total of 1,210 which was calculated in Rev Dr Alexander Webster's account in 1755. Births amounted to around 37 per annum. The minister reckoned that there were around 220 families in the parish, of which 67 lived in the village of Ochiltree itself. The average number of people in each family was computed to be 5, but Rev Thomson noted that this was more likely to be six in a farming family, and four in a village family. He also reckoned that there were around 560 men and 590 women.

Smallpox struck the parish on a number of occasions. The disease claimed the lives of many, and the old parochial registers list those who died from the disease. Amongst these were John Black, a child of fourteen months, living in Ochiltree, who died on 21 February 1791. Edward Bryden died on 28 January 1791, aged eleven months, the second son of John Bryden. Older folk suffered too, such as Margaret Wyllie, daughter of William Wyllie of Watston, who died on 30 December 1790 aged fifteen years and five months. Janet Weir died on 16 February 1791, the daughter of William Weir. Marion Walker, daughter of Thomas Walker a tailor in Ochiltree, died on 15 April 1791. To help out parishioners who had fallen on ill times, the Ochiltree Benevolent Society was formed to help, existing in 1795.

The maintenance of the poor in the parish was something that occurred over the years. For example, in March 1796 the factor to the Dowager Countess of Glencairn, several farmers and others in the parish subscribed nearly 100 bolls of oatmeal to be sold to the poor at a reduced price of 1 shillings per peck. In 1792 there were twenty poor folk who were in receipt of a regular monthly supply. The church collected around twelve shillings per week towards the cost of this, in addition to the special collections made on sacramental occasions, totalling around £9 per annum.

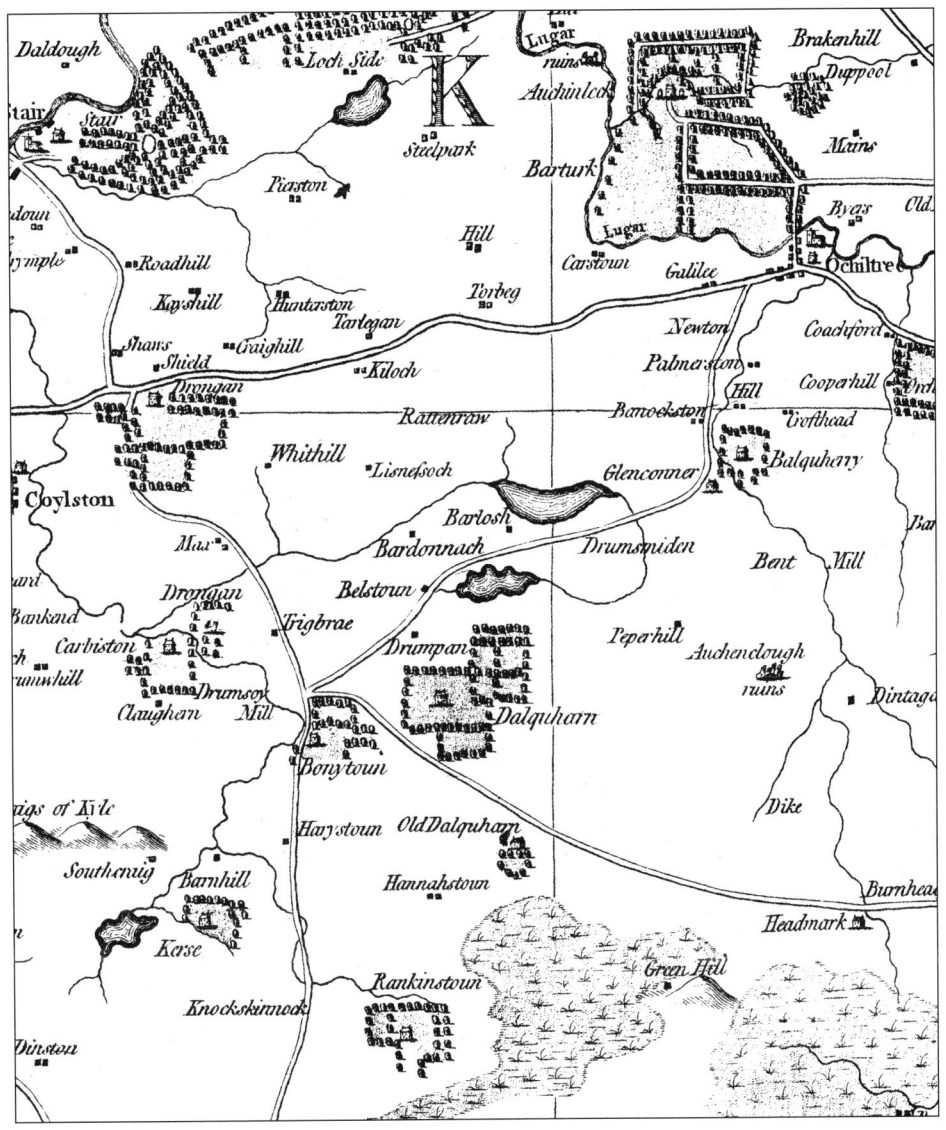

2.2 Ochiltree parish area from Captain Armstrong's Map of 1775

Colonel William Fullarton's *General View of the Agriculture of Ayrshire* noted that the parish had ten proprietors owning estates in the parish. The greatest part of the parish was arable, with only four grazing farms. The annual collection for the poor was £36.

The old kirkyard, once the parish church had been demolished, became quite neglected and in 1796 it was decided to rebuild the kirkyard walls.

In September 1797 the introduction of the Militia Act resulted in a number of young men rioting in the village against it. As a consequence of the French Revolution it was feared that there would be an attack on Britain, and the first form of compulsory military service was introduced. When, in November 1798, the recruiting officers arrived in Ochiltree to make up a list of all men in the parish between the age of eighteen and thirty-five years the womenfolk acted in defiance. Originally, the schoolmasters of each parish were charged with making the list, which had to be checked off by a Justice of the Peace. It was determined that this would take place in one of the inns in the village, but the women of the area were determined against it. They gathered large boulders and stones which they prepared for the situation. As Patrick Simson was making his way to the inn, a woman named Jenny Brown stepped between the schoolmaster and the door. Grabbing a hold of his arm, she directed him further down the street. The justices, which included Alexander Boswell of Auchinleck, on observing this kidnap, came to his aid, whereupon they were rained on with stones.

The ensuing melee was referred to as 'The Siege of Ochiltree'. To ensure that peace returned, a company of the 94th Highlanders was sent from Ayr to the village, under the command of Captain James MacKay. He knew the area, and as he arrived at the west end of the village, near Finlaystone road-end, he ordered his men to stop, load their muskets, and prepare to march down the Main Street. They met no resistance, and were able to set up camp in the space between Ochiltree House and Burnock Street. A barn belonging to George MacLelland was requisitioned as the guard room. Whilst based in the village, the soldiers had little to do, and it is said that some of them passed their time by carrying on some of the trades that they had as careers, some even working at the mill or farms.

Nine women who had been regarded as the principal instigators in the disruption were arrested. Six of them were set free after a serious warning and being bound over to keep the peace. Three women were sent to Ayr jail on the back of a cart. Two of these women were strong farmers' daughters and they managed to work free from their bonds and leapt to their freedom from the cart as it made its way into Coylton, disappearing over hedges and into woodland. The only woman who remained, known as Mal Lockie, reached the jail where she spent a couple of nights in the cells before being liberated.

Robert Burns, the national poet, had many associations with Ochiltree. Some of these are recounted elsewhere in this book. The minister of the time, Rev David Grant, was referred to by the bard in *The Kirk's Alarm* as 'Davie Bluster'. Burns described him in a letter to Lady Elizabeth Cunninghame as, 'A designing, rotten-hearted Puritan.' Burns was told by his friend, John Tennant of Glenconner, that he had a false impression of the minister and arranged a meeting between the two. Burns met Grant, and the two became friends. Grant died on 16 July 1791 and is buried in the old kirkyard.

John Tennant was the farmer in Glenconner farm. He had been born in 1726, the son of William Tennant, farmer in Mains, Bridgend of Alloway, and his wife, Agnes Reid. John Tennant was asked to sign the baptismal register when Robert Burns was baptised in 1759, though this may have been another John Tennant, smith in Alloway. He also advised the poet when he took the lease of Ellisland farm, near Dumfries. It is quite significant that, when Burns' father died in 1784, John Tennant loaned a pony to assist in carrying the coffin from Lochlea to his last resting place in Alloway kirkyard. The pony was taken to Lochlea by James Tennant.

2.3 Rev David Grant's Gravestone, old kirkyard *(Dane Love)*

John was appointed as factor to Lady Glencairn on her Ochiltree estates in 1769, and served as such for the next eleven years. He also tenanted Glenconner farm from 1769 until his death on 28 April 1810. He was married three times.

John's brother, David Tennant, was to become a teacher at Ayr Academy. He had taught a young lad who had some potential to be a teacher, John Murdoch, and it was in his school that Burns attended at the age of six. David Tenant was later to enter the navy and fought against the French. In one affray he lost his right hand. It is said that he was offered a knighthood by George IV, but he turned this down. When asked by his brother why he did not accept it, he replied, 'Deed, Jamie, I just considered it little better than a nickname'.

Old Glenconner's eldest son, James, was sent some epistles by Robert Burns. He was later to tenant Ochiltree Mill.

A story is told that Burns went to Glenconner with his collection of poems prior to them being published. He recited many of them that night, and the farmhouse was filled with friends enjoying the evening. There being a scarcity of beds, it was determined that the womenfolk should repair to Barquharrie, at the time the property of Rev George Reid. However, the women managed to take the manuscript with them, and sat up for most of the night reading it, before returning it to the poet early in the morning, perhaps before he had noticed it was missing.

Rev William Tennant LLD (born around 1758) was educated in Ochiltree school and followed this by attending the University of Edinburgh. He became Chaplain to Colonel Fullarton's regiment in the East Indies. In India, he was a campaigner for the establishment of schools there. He was a writer of some note, compiling four volumes on *Indian Recreations*, published in 1803. In it he proposed that schools should be established across the sub-continent and thus be a method in which Christianity could be spread in the country. He also wrote *A New Year's Gift to Tom Paine*. Another work was a political ballad which gained some popularity at the time, the first line beginning, 'There was a lad cam' frae the North'. When he died in 1813, he was interred in the old kirkyard of Ochiltree.

John Tennant Jr. was the tenant farmer at Auchinbay. He later moved to the larger farm of Girvanmains, to the north of Girvan.

Charles Tennant was born on 3 May 1768. He was originally a weaver, hence Burns referring to him as 'Wabster Charlie'. However, he was to achieve a considerable fortune as the proprietor of the St Rollox Chemical Works in Glasgow. These were established in 1800 and grew to be the largest chemical works in the world at the time. Tennant had taken out a patent for bleaching liquor in 1798 and a second patent for bleaching powder in 1799. The works were famed for the manufacture of these bleaching liquids and powder, as well as other soaps and cleaning materials. Located to the north of Glasgow city centre, the works was famous for its massive chimney. From this family sprung a number of descendants who were to become famous nationally. Edward Tennant was raised to the peerage in 1911, taking as his title Lord Glenconner, in honour of the family home. His sister, Emma Alice Margaret (or Margot) Tennant, was to marry Herbert Henry Asquith, leader of the Liberal party and Prime Minister from 1908-16.

Lord Glenconner purchased Dryburgh Abbey and presented it to the nation. He also purchased the estate of Glen, near Innerleithen in Peeblesshire, where he erected a large neo-baronial castle. He died on 1 October 1838. Glen House remains the property of the present Lord Glenconner, Cody Tennant, 8th Lord.

The St Rollox family continued to thrive for many years. Charles was succeeded by his son John (1796-17 April 1878), who doubled the size of the factory and opened a second at Hebburn on the River Tyne.

George Reid of Barquharrie was friendly with Burns. He was the son-in-law of John Tennant of Glenconner, having married Agnes Tennant (1764-1787). When Burns was invited to Edinburgh in 1786, he borrowed a pony from Reid to allow him to travel there. In 1787, to repay the favour, Burns presented Reid with a copy of the first edition of his poetical works.

Another friend of Burns, but more associated with Kilmarnock, was Thomas Samson, seed merchant in that town. Samson was born in Ochiltree's Main Street, where his father ran a nursery opposite the parish church. Tam's brother, John, is remembered for returning the horse Burns borrowed to take him to Edinburgh. John Samson is also buried in the old kirkyard.

1800-1900

The village continued to expand by new development in the nineteenth century. As before, new feus were laid out westward along Main Street with similar leases to those offered previously. In 1911 the houses on Main Street occupied by William Walker and John Mathieson were offered for sale. They had 29½ falls of ground and paid a rent of £7 10s. The 999-year lease ran from Whitsunday 1809. The House with the Green Shutters occupied a plot extending to 1 rood, 2 falls and 29 yards in extent and was also on a 999 year lease.

2.4 The House with the Green Shutters *(Author's Collection)*

In 1807-8 new houses were erected in Burnock Street for John Samson. Starting at the Cross, the first building has a curved gable facing the cross, built over two storeys and harled. The ground floor of the corner building was to be used as commercial premises. Adjoining this are two other blocks. One of these has the Cunninghame coat of arms over the doorway. It is known locally as the Noble House. It is thought that this may originally have been proposed to be a new inn for the village, but whether it ever served as such is unknown. When first built there was a stone slab incorporated which bore the following lines, written by Patrick Simson:

> This is the Noble House of Ochiltree,
> Built by John Samson, miller here.
> Although he's not a miller now,
> He'd gone to farm and hold the plough;
> A better fellow ne'er did steer:
> See how he builds, and spends his gear.

This stone disappeared during later alterations to the building prior to 1920.

In all Samson is reckoned to have erected thirteen houses, replacing old single-storey thatched buildings with new double, or storey and a half, sandstone houses with slate roofs. On one of the houses in Burnock Street, a second stone slab bore the incised lines:

2.5 Ochiltree Cross, with Mill Street to the left and Burnock Street to the right *(Author's Collection)*

> This is Samson Square, the property of John Samson, farmer in Cooperhill, consisting of 1 ac., 2 roods, and 31 falls, on which he has built 13 houses, 9 of them in 15 months. Long may he live to do good, and die in the fear of the Lord. 1808.

Samson was to celebrate the purchase by the Earl of Dumfries of eight lots of Ochiltree estate in 1809. He was 'so overjoyed at the event, that he caused a large bonfire to be made, and a tub of twelve gallons capacity to run over with Toddy, at the Cross of Cumnock, where he was joined by a number of the respectable inhabitants of the place; the Rev Dr Miller, Minister of Cumnock, honouring the occasion with his presence for some time; when the following toasts were drunk, as proposed and arranged by Mr Samson: - 1. Lord Dumfries, long may he live to enjoy his Lands. 2. The Laird of Borland. 3. The Marquis of Bute. 4. The Lord Dumfries's Tutors and Factors. 5. The KING. 6. The parishes of Ochiltree and Cumnock. 7. A Good harvest.'

In 1811 William Aiton reckoned that there were fourteen proprietors in Ochiltree parish, a larger number than neighbouring parishes, indicating that Ochiltree estate had been divided quite considerably by then.

Burnockholm, built immediately across the Burnock Bridge from the village, was erected in the first half of the nineteenth century – one estimate says around 1830. On the first Ordnance Survey map of 1857 it is named Burnock Cottage, but by 1895 was renamed Burnock Holm House. One theory is that it may have been erected for a member of the Crichton Stuart family, who owned Dumfries House. Another claim is that Burnockholm was probably erected just before 1843 by Thomas Cuthbert (1793-12 February 1870), cheese merchant in the village. He was the son of Thomas Cuthbert (d. 1793 aged 29). He may have moved into the new house around 1844, for in March that year he was letting his property in the village, which comprised of a dwelling house, front and back shop and cheese store. The *Ayrshire Directory* of 1851 also lists him as being the village postmaster at that time. Burnockholm was later the property of Hugh Morton, builder (23 June 1823-2 November 1891).

Thomas Cuthbert supplied information to Poor Law Inquiry Commission for Scotland, dated 14 November 1843. The full transcription of the Ochiltree sections reads:

2.6 Burnockholm House *(Author's Collection)*

[Cuthbert] Is a native of Ochiltree, and has resided there almost all his life. Has frequently had an opportunity of seeing the poor people on the parish roll in Ochiltree. A number of the houses where paupers have dwelt, and where some still dwell, belong to witness; and he has had frequent opportunities of seeing the people in them. They live in a very poor condition. Their bedding is very thin and very middling. Most of the houses are free from damp in the floor.

2.7 Burnockholm House *(Dane Love)*

They are very cold in winter. The session pays the rent, and it is a very poor rent they will give. There are very few strangers in the parish of Ochiltree, and the poor being nearly all natives, there is a very kindly feeling towards them, and the people assist them. In this way they generally get tolerably well through. Sometimes they must be ill off. He has known several families within these last two or three years who were sometimes very poorly off; but for the assistance the poor get from private charity, they could not exist. The parish allowance would not do at all. He is very well acquainted with the poor in the country part of the parish of Ochiltree, as well as those in the village. They are all very much in the same condition. The poor are badly off for fuel; but for the coals given them in winter, they could not get through. There is an annual collection for supplying them with coals; and witness having had the duty of distributing them, he, in this way, had an opportunity of becoming acquainted with the poor and their condition. That he knows that in the parish of Auchinleck the poor are in a still worse condition than in Ochiltree. In Cumnock they are in a better condition than in Ochiltree. This is owing to private charity given by the family of Bate, who also give a little in Ochiltree parish; but Cumnock being the parish of their residence, the poor there are more immediately under their observation. Witness knew the history of the man who died in being removed lately from Ochiltree to Cumnock. He had been an industrious man in his time, but having got a sore in his leg, he was unable to work, and took to begging, and had come into the parish of Ochiltree for years occasionally. Prior to his removal he had been living in the farm house of South Palmerston, where James Robb is tenant, who is a humane man, but being the time of harvest, he could not get the pauper attended to, he therefore wished the session to provide some person to wait upon him at his house. The session-clerk, who is an old man of very little judgment, thought it proper to remove him, and he died immediately after reaching Cumnock. He has known several cases of people coming in carts with passes from other parishes, and forwarded through Ochiltree, when, from their diseased state, they were not fit to travel. Witness states that there is a fatuous person of the name of William Aird, residing in Ochiltree, and a native of the place, who conveyed the property left him by his father to the session, or to some person for behoof of the session, and they now take charge of him. On Tuesday the 7th instant witness went into the house where he is kept, with two constables. They found him lying in an out-house, the floor of which was very dirty. His bedding was very poor and filthy. There was no fire in the house, and the man himself was quite emaciated. Mr Pettigrew of Tarshaw went with witness afterwards to see that pauper. He asked the man who had charge of him, why he had not a fire in the room. The man said he had applied several times to a member of the session for coals, but that he had not got them. Mr Pettigrew ordered a cart of coals to be procured immediately, and a fire to be lighted. According to the statement of the neighbours, too, the treatment of the pauper by those having charge of him is not at all what it ought to be. He is not properly taken care of, but is treated in some respects with harshness. This person is bed-ridden, and is quite incapable of doing anything for himself, being altogether insane. The session give to the man who takes care of this pauper the dwelling-house and a four-loomed shop, which belonged to the pauper, rent free; and 3s. per week for taking care of him and boarding him.

Rev James Boyd also gave evidence to the same commission. He noted that the parish population was 1,601 at the time, of which 27 were belived to be paupers.

In 1842 £142 was distributed amongst them. He noted that an infirm person, who could not work, was given about eight shillings per month. One who was bed-ridden was given twelve shillings. First applicants are usually given four shillings. There were no beggars in the parish, but some from surrounding villages, or Ayr, often passed through.

Some of the first commercial directories appeared early in the nineteenth century. Pigot and Company's *National Commercial Directory of Scotland*, published in 1826, gives half a page to Ochiltree. In the description, its states that Ochiltree 'is a small but pleasant village'. Among the industries listed, it states that 'weaving of cotton goods for the Glasgow market gives employment to several hands.' A number of women, particularly younger girls, found employment in sewing muslin. It also notes that the manufacture of snuff boxes is carried on to a limited extent. There was a 'considerable manufactory' for shearing hooks.

In 1837 it was reckoned that there were an average of twenty people on the poor roll. They were paid an allowance of 4 to 8 shillings per month, depending on their circumstances. They also receive some money towards the rent of their houses. A further number received occasional aid in either cash or in coal. This

2.8 Smiddy Brae, Ochiltree *(Author's Collection)*

latter fund distributed around £114 per annum. This figure was funded from church collections (around £62), hiring of the mortcloth for funerals (£2), and contributions from heritors (£50).

With a growing demand for knowledge, and with improvements in education, in 1836 a subscription library was established in the village. A Free Church Library was established in August 1844 with around 250 books, all of a 'highly moral and religious tendency'. In 1863 a reading room and library was presented to the parishioners by Lady General Vassal.

In 1845 a new act of parliament established Parochial Boards to run various services in each parish. Thus, Ochiltree had its first form of local control. Looking after the poor was taken away from the church, and the Parochial Board appointed Inspectors of Poor. Among those holding this position was Andrew Smith, Inspector of the Poor in Ochiltree parish in 1869.

Up until the end of the nineteenth century, Ochiltree had two annual fairs, officially named Fast Days, when the schools were closed for the day. The minister would conduct sermons on such days, usually assisted by clergy from neighbouring parishes. Services in the kirk would dispense communion, and in the kirkyard and adjoining street the rest of the parishioners, and other visitors, would await their turn by singing hymns and enjoying the festival. The spring fast day, or Spring Fair, had a cattle show associated with it, precursor to Ochiltree Cattle Show. Originally this took place on the second Wednesday of May. The Winter Fair took place on the first Tuesday in November. At the fairs horses and black cattle were sold. It was also when servants were engaged for the following term.

Emigration has taken place in a number of cycles over the years. In the 1860s a number of locals emigrated to New Zealand to take up opportunities in industry there. Many of these people settled happily, establishing themselves in that country. One who was less fortunate was David Guthrie, who emigrated from Drumsmudden farm. He was seriously injured on 28 September 1874 in a landslip at the Black Lead, Charleston Nelson, and died of his injuries in hospital two days later. He was 31 years of age.

William Murdoch left Ochiltree in 1831 and settled in the United States. He was the eldest son of Alexander Murdoch, builder in Ochiltree, and his wife, Helen Peden, of Knowe farm, Auchinleck. He was born in November 1811. At the age of twenty Murdoch emigrated to the United States where he set up in business as a builder, being responsible for a number of notable buildings in Charlestown, South Carolina, and August, Georgia. He moved into building railroads, and was responsible for many bridges, indeed, one American newspaper claimed that he built more railway bridges than any other man in America. He then started an ironworks in Chatham County, producing iron for the Confederate Government. At the overthrow of the Confederacy he lost his business and the works were closed. His fortune was lost and he was virtually penniless. Murdoch, however, rebuilt his business. He died in Salisbury, North Carolina, on 30 December 1893.

Some other businessmen, if that is not too grand a title, from nineteenth century Ochiltree are known. John MacCall was a shoemaker who lived in Mill Street. He was deaf and dumb, but had a high intelligence level. When he died the villagers erected a memorial over his grave which bears the inscription: *Erected by a few friends to the memory of John MacCall, Shoemaker, Ochiltree, who died*

September 16th 1865 aged 70 years. Though deaf and dumb, he won the admiration and esteem of all who knew him, by the development of qualities honourable alike to the head and heart of man. Other shoemakers from the mid nineteenth century include James Fisher, and Messrs MacClelland and Colville.

In 1831 the Census found the population of the parish to be 1,562, a drop of 26 from the previous Census, compiled ten years earlier. The 1831 figure could be broken down as follows: 320 families, living in 271 dwelling houses. There were 739 males and 823 females. Of the total, 642 people lived in Ochiltree village. With 920 living in the rest of the parish. Over the past seven years there were an average of 34 births, 13 marriages and 27 deaths. Other more obscure data compiled noted that there were an average of four children per family, that there were 10 insane and fatuous persons, one deaf person and two blind. There were 118 families whose principal income was from either trade, manufacture or handcraft. Within the three years up to 1837 there had been seven illegitimate births in the parish.

In the mid ninetenth century the average resident of the parish was fed on oatmeal. In the *New Statistical Account*, it is noted that:

> The food of the peasantry is generally oatmeal porridge and milk to breakfast, broth, with butcher-meat and potatoes to dinner, and porridge or potatoes with milk for supper. In addition to these articles, they often use, at their meals, milk with cakes of oatmeal, or a mixture of oatmeal and bear meal, made into scones. In the families of most mechanics, tea is used, generally twice-a-day, but the practice does not prevail amongst farm-servants to any extent.

In the early 1850s Andrew Murdoch erected a large house for himself at what was the western extremity of the village. Gallowlea was built on the northern side of the road, next to the access roadway into the Gallowlea Well. The house was built of random rubble, with a slate roof. Andrew Murdoch was the local stonemason and quarrymaster, responsible for many buildings in the parish, including the Lugar Bridge and Ochiltree gasworks. Andrew Murdoch was known as 'the strongest man in Ayrshire'. He had a number of sons, including Alexander Murdoch, author of *Ochiltree – Its History and Reminiscences*. Andrew Murdoch sold the cottage in 1881 to Flora Campbell Whiteside, wife of the Ayr solicitor Charles George Shaw, who converted it into a convalescent home.

Andrew Murdoch was born in Ochiltree and trained as a 'cork' mason. Around 1860 he obtained the lease of the the Coalburn Quarries (New Cumnock) from the Marquis of Bute, moving from Ochiltree at that time. Stone from these quarries was used to build Glaisnock House, Old Cumnock Parish Church, St John's R. C. Church, Cumnock, and many buildings in Glasgow and elsewhere. He died on 14 July 1906, aged 90 years, and was buried in Ochiltree.

In 1862 Lady Boswell of Auchinleck sent £10 to purchase coals, which 'the farmers in the parish cart gratuitously'. This figure was sufficient to supply one cart each to fifty families. Lady Boswell at the time also granted £5 to the Female Industrial School in the village. In 1865 General Stuart, guardian to the Marquis of Bute, gifted £4 for coals for the poor of the parish to Rev Walker.

In 1879 a new book about Ochiltree was published, written by David Rowan. *Memorials of Ochiltree and Neighbourhood in a Letter to a Friend*, was published by Aird and Coghill and became popular. David Rowan was born in 1822 and originally worked as a slater with his father. He later moved to Glasgow where he worked for various businesses, including Dixon's ironworks. He was to set up his own business in Clydeside in 1866. David Rowan died in 1898 and his business was taken over by his son, also David Rowan.

2.9 Robert Johnstone's Gravestone *(Dane Love)*

The Robert Johnstone Bursary was endowed by Robert Johnstone, a native of the village. Alexander Murdoch refers to him as 'the recognised teller of Ochiltree stories'. His gravestone in the old kirkyard reads: 'In grateful remembrance of Robert Johnstone, founder of the Robert Johnstone Bursary. Born at Ochiltree 11th March 1831, died at Glasgow, 12th March 1892.'

On 15 January 1870 the village was supplied with a public water supply from the springs at Netherton, which was piped to a reservoir at Townhead. This was regarded as being capable of holding twice the amount of water required. From this reservoir, the water was piped through cast iron pipes. Initially, there were eight water pumps located around the village from where water could be drawn. These were located at Burnock Street (on the inside corner); half-way down Mill Street, on the left-hand side (known as the Broom Spoot); in front of the Commercial Inn; at the Smiddy corner; in Main Street – half-way between the church and the cross; in front of the church; opposite the school; and opposite the Crown Inn. The works were constructed by Mr MacIlwraith.

The water supply had been given free by the Marquis of Bute, arranged by

2.10 Hawthorn Villa, Ochiltree *(Dane Love)*

his factor, Charles G. Shaw, although there were a few residents who opposed the scheme. Most, of course, were in favour. To celebrate, a large bonfire was constructed at the Cross and the dignitaries involved had a meal in the Commercial Inn, after which 400 buns were given out to the children.

In December 1878 there was considerable flooding in the district, when heavy rain, compounded with melting snow, caused the rivers to burst their banks. The mill dam at Ochiltree was severely damaged, resulting in the lade being starved of water and the mills idle.

In one quarter of 1882 there were 17 births in the parish, 11 deaths and 3 marriages, according to the Registrar General's Quarterly Return.

In 1883 a very short-lived newspaper appeared on sale. *The Mauchline and Catrine Advertiser and Tarbolton and Ochiltree Reporter* appears to have closed within a few issues of its maiden copy.

A few larger villas were erected in Ochiltree in the late 1880s. Glenhead and Hawthorn villas were built in Mauchline Road, in the corner of a field backing onto the Dyer's Wood. Glenhead was occupied by Andrew Jamieson. Hawthorn was occupied by Graeme Ramage, former hotel-keeper from Cumnock's Black Bull Hotel, who died in 1919.

In 1891 the Boundary Commission looked at parishes across Scotland were there were detached portions, often of small size, located within surrounding parishes. These tended to be a historical anomaly, existing due to having been owned by particular estates whose main seat was elsewhere. Ochiltree was one such parish to be considered, for there was a sizeable detached part of Stair parish within it, comprising the lands of Drongan estate. Accordingly, this fragment was transferred to Ochiltree parish, from which it had been detached at the creation of Stair parish in 1673. To compensate the parish of Stair, the lands of Trabboch were detached from Ochiltree and appended to that parish.

Soon after the parishes were realigned, in 1894 an act of parliament replaced the old Parochial Boards with new Parish Councils. This replaced the work of the heritors to a considerable degree, and the elected councillors were responsible for arranging local services including looking after the poor, improvements to the village, and other works, including paying the Inspector of Poor and Medical Officer for the Parish. The board in Ochiltree also sent a representative to the Kyle Union Board, which ran the poorhouse in Ayr. An election was held, costing over £16 to run, and councillors were duly appointed. Jacob Sloan in Clydenoch (1849-1913) was appointed as chairman.

In 1889 the new Local Government (Scotland) Act was passed which established county councils which required councillors to be appointed to represent local communities. At the first elections, James Pettigrew Wilson of Polquhairn (1829-1899) was selected to represent Ochiltree.

Incidents in the history of the village crop up in various places. Around the year 1816 a wandering beggar, named John Greer, fell from the Coachford Bridge into the stream below. He died, and his corpse was found a couple of days later by the local farmer, Robert Steel of Orchardton. The death was reported to the church, and the beadle, Peter Kennet, was sent to collect the body. This was later laid on the floor of the church, where a thorough investigation was made into all of the pockets and bags associated with the deceased. The event appears to have been open to the public, and subsequently the kirk session and minister were decried for the method in which they dealt with the body. A local weaver, John MacGregor, wrote a poem lampooning the members of the kirk session, some of the verses of which are as follows:

> Johnnie Greer, Johnnie Greer, ye have bred a' the steer
>   They laid you longside of a pew
> After cuttin' your rags, and rippin' your bags,
>   They buried you juist like a soo.
>
> Billy Lees, Billy Lees, ye're a saunt on yer knees,
>   I ha'e heard ye mysel' at the Book,
> Graun' visions ye saw, but ye fell clean awa',
>   An' snored like a dog in the neuk.

Other incidents would have been the subject of much tittle-tattle at the time, many of which have become forgotten. William Wilson, an engineer on the steamboat *Fingal*, was killed instantly as a result of an incident in Belfast Lough on 27 November 1830 at the age of 47. He was a son of James Wilson of High Tarbeg.

On 16 July 1873 John Gallon, of Ponteland, Newcastle-on-Tyne, was drowned when he was leading the Barskimming otter hounds alongside the Lugar Water, near to Slatehole. He was cheering on the hounds when he fell over a precipitous rock, falling into the river below. His body was recovered after a search lasting two hours. Aged 59, he left a wife, Margaret, and a daughter, Margaret Jane. He was buried in Elsdon churchyard, Northumberland.

A drowning of an Ochiltree son took place in the Bristol Channel on 27 January 1884. William Morton, aged 25, was on board the *Hornet* when the vessel foundered. He was the son of Andrew Morton (1816-1885) and his wife, Elizabeth. Similarly, William George Strathearn, chief engineer, was drowned at sea on 7 December 1919.

There appear to have been a fair number of drownings taking place across the parish. Robert Wilson, who lived at Cooperhill farm, was drowned in the River Ayr on 11 December 1841 at the age of 35. On 4 January 1866 there was a double tragedy when George Anderson, farmer at Mill of Shield, and his wife were crossing the Water of Coyle at Barbieston. Both were carried away in the raging flood and both were drowned. George was 52 years old, his wife, Mary Ferguson, being 46. They were both interred in the old cemetery at Coylton, where their gravestone notes that 'they were kind and obliging neighbours, beloved and respected by all who knew them.' On 28 August 1844 a boy of around one year of age, son of David Gemmell, Muirston, was drowned when he fell into a horse pond.

Alexander Kay was killed by a falling tree on 3 February 1838. Kay, who was 65 years old at the time, was cutting the tree down. Similarly, Agnes Green was killed by a tree on 24 April 1846. She lived at Ochiltree Mill.

On 16 February 1836 David Bryden, a weaver who lived in Ochiltree, was returning home from a visit to his brother, William Bryden, who lived in Newmilns. He was almost home when he died near to Drumfork farm, on the Five Mile Cut, near Auchinleck estate. His body was found in the Dippol Burn, near to the road.

In 1862 the house of Robert Wilson was burned to the ground.

1900-1914

At the turn of the century, in the declining years of Queen Victoria, the country had been at war in South Africa for a year. A number of sons from the parish served in the army during what was known as the Boer War. Corporal Philip MacArdle, Royal Scots Fusiliers, was killed in action at Pieter's Hill. Two soldiers had greater luck, and when they returned to Ochiltree in June 1901 they were feted at the Cross. Bugler Hugh Brown (1883-1942) had been born at Laigh Garleffan in Old Cumnock but had later moved to live with his widowed aunt, Anne Brown, at Ochiltree Mains. Lance-Sergeant Adam William Montgomerie (1873-1955) moved to Lessnessock with his parents from Hall of Caldwell in Renfrewshire. On their arrival back in Ochiltree, each was given a gold pocket watch with a suitable inscription. They had signed up with the 17th Company (Ayrshire and Lanarkshire) of the 6th (Scottish) Battalion of the Imperial Yeomanry. They set sail from the Clyde on 23 February 1900 on the SS *Carthaginian*, arriving in South Africa almost four weeks later.

Sons of the parish can turn up in some rather strange places. In 1903 advertisements in various newspapers across Great Britain, such as the *Essex Newsman* of 28 March 1903, refer to John Meggatt, a miner, of Drongan, who 'suffered from indigestion for eight years. Pain after every meal, sleeplessness, and gradually decreasing strength were the symptoms. His blood became impoverished, and when he sustained a cut or bruise in the course of his work, it festered and was bad for a long time. He underwent a course of Bile Beans, and in a few weeks was not like the same man! Now, he says, he is in the best of health, can enjoy hearty meals, and "is in fine condition".

In August 1912 a tablet was erected in the vestibule of the parish church in memory of William Lyons. He was a soldier with the Royal Scots Fusiliers but had died whilst sailing across the Indian Ocean in 1910. All of Lyons' family had emigrated to Canada by this time, but there was nowhere in that dominion that was deemed a suitable place to commemorate him, so it was decided to do this back in Ochiltree. The tablet comprises a white marble scroll, on which lead letters read:

> Sacred to the memory of Sergeant William Lyons, 1st Batn. Royal Scots Fusiliers, born at Ochiltree, 15th Sept. 1875, died at sea, 9th Oct. 1910, en route from Rangoon to South Africa. This tablet is erected by the Members of the Sergeants' Mess and Officers, N-C Officers and Men of F Company and Regimental Signallers.

Proposals to improve the supply of water through the village had been made for a number of years before anything was ever done about it. In 1865 it was rumoured that Lady General Vassal was considering piping water from the Gallowlee Well down through the village. However, it wasn't until 1906 that Ayr County Council improved the water supply when a new large water tank was erected at the head of Main Street, next to the Convalescent Home, and a second by the side of Ayr Road, immediately below. These reservoirs were needed to compensate for the lack of water in the public supply.

In 1901 the telegraph reached Ochiltree, the poles carrying the wires being connected from the national network to the post office.

2.11 Main Street with the House with the Green Shutters on the right *(Author's Collection)*

In 1925 the Ayrshire Electricity Board, based in Kilmarnock, announced that it would like to supply electricity to other communities across the county. The people of Ochiltree approached the board, requesting that a supply be brought to Ochiltree, but the company turned this down, reckoning that the sale of electricity would not meet the costs of getting the main supply to the village.

Within the village there were a number of improvements being made to the housing stock. In 1910 there were still some thatched buildings in the village, for

2.12 Ochiltree Cemetery *(Dane Love)*

2.11 Burnock Street (Dane Love)

in that year we find that the old Toll House and 'Sick House' were re-thatched. In 1927 the roof of the old 'Sick House', which comprised thatch over timbers, partially fell in. It was agreed by the council that the remainder of the roof should be demolished.

A number of the houses in the village were sold off on 999 year leases at the turn of the twentieth century. An example was the House with the Green Shutters, offered on a 999-year lease in April 1904, previously the property of William Smith, Burnside, Drongan. The house was put up for sale again in February 1913. Its plot extended to 1 rood, 2 falls and 29 yards, the tack duty 11s 3d.

New red sandstone houses were built in Burnock Street in 1908.

Ochiltree Parish Council continued to run various local services in the new century. The council chamber was located in a building in Burnock Street in 1912. In February 1915 the architect A. C. Thomson drew up plans for a new office, board room and house for the parish council and school board of Ochiltree. A variety of locals served as chairmen of Ochiltree Parish Council, such as Robert Montgomery of Lessnessock, John MacCaig, Archibald Andrew MA, and Alex Green JP.

The Inspector of Poor from 1894-1907 was Adam Urquhart (1861-1907). Others who have served as Parish Clerk and Inspector of Poor include Robert Hay (1874-1923), who served from 1907 until 1923. Hay was also clark to the school board and in 1913 he was elected as president of the Scottish Junior Football Association. He was a notable man in football at the time. Robert Hay was replaced by William M. Watson in 1923. In 1912 it was calculated that the gross rental of

Ochiltree parish stood at £20,209 18s 7d.

The councillors representing Ochiltree parish on Ayrshire County Council in the new century were Robert Montgomery in Lessnessock (until 1904) and James Montgomerie in East Tarelgin (from 1904).

Every New Year at the turn of the twentieth century a quantity of coals for the poor was distributed by the locals. The Marquis of Bute gifted £5 in 1904 and Thomas Pettigrew Wilson of Polquhairn £2 towards the cost.

In September 1903 the parish council commissioned the Ayr architect, Allan Stevenson CE, to visit the district and make recommendations on where to establish a new cemetery, the old kirkyard by the side of the Lugar Water being overcrowded. Three possible sites were identified by Stevenson – the south-west corner of a field at Ochiltree Mains, the west corner of Burnockholm, and a field between the old and new roads to Ayr, adjacent to the old access road to Finlayston. Of the three sites, the first at Ochiltree Mains was picked, and it was planned to fence off one and a half acres of land, erect a wall and railings alongside the road, and railings on the other three sides of the cemetery.

The original site for the cemetery was not developed, and in May 1904 a different site of one and a half acres was acquired from the Marquis of Bute on Mauchline Road, at Hill of Ochiltree farm. At the time the number of burials within the parish was noted as being 1898 – 26; 1899 – 22; 1901 – 27; 1902 – 24; 1903 – 24. The new cemetery was opened in November 1905, the walls and gates being designed by Allan Stevenson, the work being carried out by George Reid of Catrine.

A police station was established in Ochiltree, existing for a short period of times. Located at 10 Burnock Street, constables in the village included Alexander Home (in 1909; he died in 1951 aged 82); Constable Thomson (until c. 1920), William Cameron (until 1925), Constable Gardiner (from 1925) and John Dalrymple (around 1930-1940). A number of early crime statistics are worth recording, for example, in 1901 there were 43 instances of crime reported to the police. The constabulary station was closed on 1 August 1970.

A second police station in the parish was located at Coalhall. It existed in 1940. This was superseded when a new police station was opened in Drongan.

In May 1921 *Ochiltree, its History and Reminiscences* was published. Written by Alexander Murdoch BA (Lond.) FEIS, the book was subtitled 'At Ochiltree Langsyne'. In it he looks back to his childhood days in the village, and gives details of Ochiltree House, the landowners, description of the parish, churches, Burns connections, place names and biographical details of many older residents.

Alexander Murdoch was the son of Andrew Murdoch, mason. He was born at Gallowlea, Ochiltree, and educated in the village school. He trained to be a teacher and taught at Ladybank in Fife, Lesmahagow in Lanarkshire, then became a master at the John Neilson Institution in Paisley from 1876. He retired from teaching in 1913, but had settled at Meikleriggs in Paisley, where his house was named Gallowlea after his birthplace. During the Great War he returned to teaching, retiring again in 1922. He died at his Paisley home on 10 July 1929 at the age of 82.

A notable character in the village at the start of the twentieth century was James Reid, who was known locally as 'The Provost'.

At Ochiltree dam a new salmon ladder was installed in July 1910 to allow the passage of fish. The design of the ladder was advised by the Fishery Board.

A number of tragic accidents occurred in the village and its vicinity, often as a result of drowning in local watercourses. Among those accidents that are recorded were George Fleming, who was drowned in the Lugar Water on Friday 3 May 1907 at the age of three years. His body was found one week later at Slatehole farm. On 8 August 1909 Daniel MacLean was drowned in the Lugar Water near to Ochiltree. At Creochill farm in October 1882, George Sloan, the tenant, and his daughter were bringing in crops when the horse pulling the cart took fright and bolted. Mr Sloan was on the cart at the time, and jumped off, but the cartwheel appears to have run over his daughter, Janet Sloan, aged 34, and she subsequently died.

In March 1900 a child of four years, William MacArdle, knocked over a pail of hot water at his home in Drongan Rows. He was severely scalded, causing his death. His father, Corporal Philip MacArdle, Royal Scots Fusiliers, had been killed in action at Pieter's Hill.

FIRST WORLD WAR

The outbreak of the Great War, or World War I as it was later to be known, caused considerable unrest in the local communities. Many hundreds of men signed up to serve in the army, leaving behind their wives and families. In many situations, women had to step in to take over their jobs, and on many farms the Land Army of women had to carry out harvesting and other work. In the parish council chambers in November 1917 Mrs Findlay Hamilton of Carnell Castle gave a talk on the importance of recruiting women to serve on the farms, but pointed out that in most cases the bothies used by farm labourers were unfit for women.

Many of the men from Ochiltree parish who signed up failed to return, losing their lives in the defence of the country and for the freedom of others. Of Ochiltree sons, the following paid the ultimate sacrifice:

- Private Harry Allison (A/7179), 1st Battalion Royal Scots Fusiliers, died 31 July 1916. Buried at Etaples Military Cemetery, France.
- Lieutenant Robert Edward Angus, Ayrshire Yeomanry, 64th Squadron Royal Flying Corps, killed in France on 20 November 1917 aged 23. Son of James Angus JP and Elizabeth Angus of Ochiltree House. They previously lived at Craigston House, Lugar. R. E. Angus

PARISH LIFE

lived at Hill House, Leckhampton, Cheltenham, Gloucestershire. He is commemorated at Arras Flying Services Memorial and also in Auchinleck kirkyard, Lugar War Memorial and Monkton War Memorial.
- Private Robert Austin (22314), 10th/11th Battalion Highland Light Infantry, died 11 April 1917 aged 25. Son of Robert Austin, 28 Castle Street, Maybole. Born in Kilmaurs. Commemorated at Arras Memorial, France.
- Private John Blane (or Blain) (240993), 1st/5th Battalion Royal Scots Fusiliers. Born in Rankinston and lived in Drongan. Died 1 October 1918. Commemorated on Vis-en-Artois Memorial, France.
- Private George Brown (200275), Ayrshire (Earl of Carrick's Own) Yeomanry, killed on 27 April 1917 at the age of 24. A military gravestone marks his grave in Ochiltree Cemetery. He was the youngest son of William MacTurk Brown, Lochhead, Mochrum, Wigtownshire. He married Agnes Gray Little of Rosebank Cottage, Ochiltree.
- Private Hugh Brown (7337), 1st/5th Battalion Royal Scots Fusiliers. Killed 16 August 1915. Commemorated at Helles Memorial, Turkey.
- Sergeant Robert (or Bertie) Brown, Ochiltree Mains, Ayrshire Yeomanry, killed 26 March 1918 aged 25. He was the son of John Brown of Garleffan, Old Cumnock, and had taken over the management of Ochiltree Mains.

2.13 Private George Brown's military gravestone, Ochiltree cemetery *(Dane Love)*

- Private John Carruthers (35914), 8th Battalion Royal Scots Fusiliers, died 2 October 1918 aged 24. He was the son of John and Susan Carruthers of Airth, Stirlingshire, but was a native of Ayrshire. Buried at Kirechkoi-Hortakoi Military Cemetery in Greece.
- Private William Cassidy (5712), 2nd Battalion Royal Scots Fusiliers, died 3 May 1918. Buried at La Clytte Military Cemetery, West-Vlaanderen, Belgium.
- Private David Purdie Clement (1579), 14th Battalion Australian

Infantry, died 19 May 1915 and buried at the Shrapnel Parish Cemetery in Turkey. He was the son of James and Jane Clement, Hollybush, but was a native of Ochiltree.
- Private James Clement (4005), 9th Battalion Highland Light Infantry. Died 15 July 1916. Buried at Thiepval, France.
- Private James Colville, Royal Scots Fusiliers. Commemorated on Prestwick War Memorial as Sapper James Colville (156241), 173rd Tunnelling Company, Royal Engineers. Born in Tarbolton, miner from Drongan, lived at Campbeltown. Son of H. Colville, Glenburn, Prestwick. Died 15 December 1916. Commemorated at Noeux-les-mines Communal Cemetery, Pas de Calais, France.
- Corporal Allan Scott Cuthbertson (53583), 1st Battalion Royal Scots Fusiliers/Ayrshire Yeomanry. Died on 3 May 1918 aged 26. He is buried at Pas de Calais, France. He was the son of James and Jane Cuthbertson, Mark farm, Pinwherry, and was married to Margaret Cuthbertson, Killochside.
- Bombardier William Dickson (7176), D (Howitzer) Battery, 147th Brigade, Royal Field Artillery, died 25 June 1916. He was the husband of Maria Dickson, Main Street, Ochiltree. He is buried at Louvencourt Military Cemetery, France.
- Private Hugh Douglas (8170), 5th Battalion Royal Scots Fusiliers. Lived in Coylton. Died 14 July 1915 and buried at Lancashire Landing Cemetery, Turkey.
- Private Ralph Douglas (S/10810), 1st Battalion Black Watch Royal Highlanders. Died 30 August 1916 aged 19. Son of Ralph Douglas, Main Street, Ochiltree. Commemorated at Thiepval Memorial, Somme, France.
- Private Thomas Haggart (or Huggart) (7430), 1st/5th Battalion Royal Scots Fusiliers. Born Dalmellington, lived at Drongan. Born 13 January 1891 in Dalmellington, died 12 July 1915 in the Balkans. Commemorated on Helles Memorial, Turkey.
- Artificer James Hall, Royal Navy (M/14767 CH), died 6 April 1916 on Royal Navy ship HMS *Comus*. Buried at Polmont Churchyard.
- Private John Hodge (15804), 2nd Battalion Royal Scots Fusiliers. Born at Laigh Coylton, lived in Drongan. Died 1 October 1915. Commemorated at Loos Memorial, Pas de Calais, France.
- Private John Jamieson (511894), 1st/14th Battalion, London Scottish Regiment. Killed in action in France, 28 November 1917, aged 31. Commemorated on the Cambrai Memorial at Louverval, Nord, France, and in Auchinleck.
- Private Henry Knox (1747), Ayrshire Yeomanry. Native of Coylton.

Died at sea, 15 October 1915. Commemorated at Helles Memorial, Turkey.
- Private George Lindsay Lyle, or Lyell (42473), Royal Scots Fusiliers and 9th Battalion Cameronians (Scottish Rifles). Died 25 April 1918 aged 17.
- Private Lachlan MacEwan (4558), 58th Company Machine Gun Corps, died 8 July 1916. Commemorated at Thiepval Memorial, Somme, France.
- Lieutenant Archibald McCallum Mackie, 3rd Battalion Royal Inniskilling Fusiliers. Previously served with 14th Battalion Highland Light Infantry. Raised to Second Lieutenant on 22 March 1918. Son of James Mackie, Drongan Mains.
- Private Archie Mair (43144), 1st Battalion Cameronians (Scottish Rifles). Born at St John's Town of Dalry, Kirkcudbrightshire, lived at Craigbrae, Drongan. Died 26 September 1917 aged 19. Buried at Sunken Road Cemetery, Boisleux-St Marc, Pas de Calais, France. Also commemorated on war memorial at St John's Town of Dalry.
- Lance Corporal David Millar (27043), 2nd Battalion Highland Light Infantry. He died on 16 April 1917 aged 30. The son of James and Isabella Millar, Laigh Mains, Drongan. Graduated from Glasgow University with Master of Arts Honours degree. Buried at Aubigny Communal Cemetery Extension, Pas de Calais, France.
- Private James Morris (7317), 1st Battalion Royal Scots Fusiliers. Died on 16 September 1915 aged 39. He was the son of the late John and Annie Morris, of Craigstonholm, Lugar, Ayrshire; husband of Cathrine R. B. Bell Morris, of 68 Dunard St. North, Kelvinside, Glasgow. Served in the Sudan (1898) and the South African Campaigns, with Seaforth Highlanders. Commemorated at the Menin Gate, Ypres, Belgium. He is also listed on the war memorial at Lugar.
- Private John Murchie (9494), 2nd Battalion Royal Scots Fusiliers, killed in action in France when he was shot in his back, 12 March 1915, aged 27. His parents were John and Mary Murchie, of Main Street, Ochiltree. Commemorated at Le Touret Memorial, Pas de Calais, France.
- Saddler Private Adam Purdie (05594), 37th Company Royal Army Ordnance Corps. Died at Calais on 2 February 1919 aged 35. Buried at Les Baraques Military Cemetery, Sangate, Pas de Calais, France. He was the son of James and Elizabeth Purdie, Ochiltree.
- Private John Purdie (S/7531), 2nd Battalion Black Watch Royal Highlanders. Born in Govan, he was killed on 17 May 1915. Commemorated on the Le Touret Memorial, France.

- Private William Purdie (7654), 1st/5th Battalion Royal Scots Fusiliers, died 18 September 1915 aged 26 years. Commemorated at Helles Memorial, Turkey.
- Private William Reid (S/12234), 9th Battalion Black Watch (Royal Highlanders), killed in action on 9 April 1917. Commemorated on Arras Memorial, Pas de Calais, France.
- Private Alexander Russell (12286), 2nd Battalion Royal Scots Fusiliers. Died 12 March 1915. Commemorated on Le Touret Memorial, Pas de Calais, France.
- Lance Corporal William Sargenson (196014), 12th Battalion Royal Scots Fusiliers. Died 31 October 1918 and buried at Harlbeke New British Cemetery, West Vlaanderen, Belgium. Lived at Trabboch.
- Private John Semple (6968), 1st/5th Battalion Royal Scots Fusiliers. Died 19 September 1915. Commemorated at Helles Memorial, Turkey.
- Corporal Archibald Barr Thomson (158693), 4th Canadian Mounted Rifles Battalion, died 30 November 1918, aged 21. Born in Ayrshire, he was the son of James Thomson, St Catherones, Ontario, Canada. He was buried at Valenciennes (St Roch) Communal Cemetery, Nord, France.
- Private James Walker (34923), 6th/7th Battalion Royal Scots Fusiliers. Born in Glencairn, Dumfriesshire but lived in Ochiltree. Died 8 February 1917. Buried at St Sever Cemetery Extension, Rouen, France.
- Private James Wallace (8184), 1st/5th Battalion Royal Scots Fusiliers. Educated in Cumnock, signed up in Drongan. Died of wounds received at Gallipoli, 20 July 1915, aged 37. Commemorated on Helles Memorial, Turkey. Son of Mrs Robert Wallace, Glespin. Married to Margaret Wallace, Kirkconnel.
- Private Hugh Reid Wilson (2697), 11th Battalion Australian Infantry. Born at Auchencloigh and emigrated to Australia at the age of nineteen. Killed in action on 25 July 1916 aged 32. Commemorated at Villers-Bretonneux Memorial, France.
- Sergeant John Wither, or Withers (56312), 52nd Battalion Machine Gun Corps, died 27 August 1918. Born Tarbolton, lived in Drongan. Buried at Wancourt British Cemetery, France.

The only casualty of the First World War to be buried in Ochiltree New Cemetery was Private George Brown.

Fortunately, not all of the men from Ochiltree who served in the forces were killed. Some were given military honours. Sergeant Robert MacNeil of the 1st

Battalion, Royal Scots Fusiliers, was awarded the Distinguished Conduct Medal in January 1916 for his conspicuous gallantry. In 1918 Corporal David Thomson, of the Canadians, was awarded the Military Medal for taking Hill 70 on the Western Front that year. He had been brought up at Belston, near Sinclairston, but moved around 1912 to Canada.

A number of Ochiltree soldiers suffered imprisonment, such as Private Douglas Smith, held as a prisoner of war in 1918. He was the son of Mrs Smith of the Crown Inn.

The war effort back in the village was primarily made up of fund-raising and collecting of materials to make the life of the soldiers at the front more comfortable. A Ladies Work Party made shirts and socks for the soldiers. When they sent their second parcel to the Red Cross, it contained 93 pairs of socks, 17 pairs of mittens, 8 pairs of cuffs, 26 shirts, 13 hospital sleeping semmits, 5 suits of pyjamas, 6 helmets, 2 lumbago belts, 7 pillow slips, 6 pillows, 4 blankets and 31 mufflers. Schoolgirls were also drafted in to help with the knitting. Around the local farms egg collections were made to feed the wounded soldiers.

In December 1915 a War Relics Exhibition was held in the village using objects gathered by T. MacWhirr. It raised £50 for the relief of local soldiers.

During the war Ochiltree House was requisitioned by the war office and it was used to accommodate Belgian refugees. When the refugees moved on, the house was abandoned.

2.14 Unveiling of Ochiltree War Memorial *(Author's Collection)*

2.15 Ochiltree War Memorial *(Author's Collection)*

On 11 November 1918, when the Armistice was signed, the people of Ochiltree celebrated with a huge bonfire, the flames of which leaped forty feet in the air.

To commemorate the sacrifice of the soldiers from the parish who died in the war, a committee was established to collect funds and arrange for some form of permanent memorial. In April 1919 a public hall was proposed, but it was soon realised that the cost of this was prohibitive. Instead, a war memorial cross was proposed.

In 1921 Ayr County Council granted permission for a site for the memorial to the victims of the First World War. The memorial was erected at the junction of Main Street with Ayr Road. The memorial was unveiled on Sunday 1 October 1922 by Sir Charles Fergusson, 7th Baronet of Kilkerran, Lord Lieutenant of Ayrshire. A church service was conducted by the two ministers, followed by a march to the memorial. In the procession were Auchinleck Pipe Band, James Brown MP (1862-1939), Adam W. Montgomerie of Lessnessock, Col. William Houldsworth (1874-1960), Colonel John Douglas Boswell of Auchinleck and Major J. C. Kennedy, the last two representing the Ayrshire Yeomanry. Sir Charles unveiled the memorial when he dropped a Union Flag. This was followed by three volleys in the air and the playing of the Last Post. The memorial has two polished granite panels bearing the names of 38 who died. James Brown MP gave a vote of thanks, as well as addressing those who had not been in the services. The memorial takes the form of a Celtic cross fifteen feet in height. In 1924 an iron railing was erected around the memorial.

In June 1920 a tablet was unveiled in the vestibule of the parish church in memory of Archie Barr Thomson, was had died in France. This reads:

> Erected by his father, mother, brothers and sisters, and his uncle William Hunter, late of Ochiltree, now of St Catherine's, Ontario, Canada, in loving memory of Corporal Archie Barr Thomson, 4th C. M. R. Canadians, who died in France of influenza, 30th November 1918, in his 21st year, after nearly three years in the trenches. 'Until the day break and the shadows flee away'.

1918-1939

Between the wars was quite a depressed time in the area – it took many years for the economy to build up after the First World War, and only in the 1930s were things beginning to look better when the Second World War broke out. In the meantime, many folk were encouraged to emigrate, and there were various campaigns made by Canadian authorities. For example, in 1928, there was a 'cinematograph display' of Canada held in the Crown Inn Hall, with a lecture informing interested villagers of the potential in that country.

The years of strikes resulted in considerable hardship for many of the miners within the parish. In the 1926 miners' strike many parish councils offered relief to families, children being fed and vouchers issued. At Ochiltree this occurred for a period, before it was suspended as being unaffordable. The residents from Drumsmudden and Drongan marched to the parish inspector's office in Ochiltree where they held a mass meeting in the recreation ground. Two prominent local Labour men, James Brown MP and Alex Sloan, were among those who addressed the crowd.

Street lighting was slow in coming to Ochiltree. In November 1923 three new petrol storm lamps were erected in the village to aid seeing at night. These were positioned at the war memorial, cross and church.

On Tuesday 31 October 1933 Ochiltree was connected to the national grid and an electricity supply was switched on for the first time. Many householders were aware that the supply was coming and had purchased electrical goods in readiness for it, so that when the main supply was connected they soon had electric ovens, lights, and other appliances running from it.

A series of articles in the *Kilmarnock Standard* occurred in the 1920s, written by Frances H. Walker. These told of Ochiltree's history, and they were keenly read by locals and those interested in the history of the village. In 1927 the articles were revised and issued in book form. *About 'The Old Place'* relates some tales recalled by Walker. The book was illustrated with a few photographs by Frances L. Walker, who lived in Canada. Frances H. Walker was also the author of *Vignettes from Scottish Parish Life and Morning Musings: On Things New and Old in Scottish Life* (published in 1929).

Ayr County Council started a programme of house building across the county and in Ochiltree the first council houses were erected in 1928. The first phase comprised of twelve three-apartment houses built in Mill Street. Built in a typical county council style, they occupied three blocks, with two upper and lower flats in each. These were offered to let in September 1928 with a proposed rent of £17 per annum.

2.16 New council housing in Broom Crescent *(Author's Collection)*

Further council housing was erected at Gallowlea, creating the start of Broom Crescent. By the time the Second World War started a total of 21 council houses had been built in the village, but the war brought work to a close. In June 1939 plans were passed for the erection of new council houses on land at Watston farm.

The county council was also responsible for many other improvements in the area. One of the most advantageous was the surfacing of the main road through Ochiltree with tarmacadam. This took place in 1925, the route from Ayr to Cumnock being completed, aiding transport considerably.

In July Ayr County Council proposed that the streets in Ochiltree should be officially named for the first time, and that houses would be suitably numbered.

Events and incidents in the parish and villages occurred over the years. In March 1932 William Ross, aged 56, was knocked down by a fellow cyclist as they made their way along the Littlemill-Drongan road during the early hours of the morning. Ross died in Ayr County Hospital. In May 1937 there were a series of events to mark the coronation of George VI. Surplus funds from this were used to hold an old folks' party, which took place annually for many years thereafter.

In August 1924 a boy was drowned in the Water of Coyle at a deep hole located between Tobergill and Orchard.

WORLD WAR TWO

The outbreak of the Second World War on 1 September 1939 led to more disruption in the village, and again a number of residents signed up to fight.

The former Free Church in Ochiltree was used as a centre for Land Army girls, who worked on local farms and estates when most of the menfolk were serving in the forces. The church was also utilised by the local Home Guard, the captain of which was William Watson.

In September 1940 a major flood caused some disruption and damage in the village. The level of the Burnock and Lugar waters rose considerably, and the Lugar Bridge was unable to cope with the deluge. The water passed over the Mill Holm and flooded the ground floor of the Meal Mill. At the Saw Mill the water rose three feet above ground level, flooding the mill and adjoining cottage.

In March 1945 three escapee prisoners of war from Pennylands Camp, near Auchinleck, gave themselves up at the house of John Drever, headmaster of Sinclairston Public School. They had escaped earlier that morning, but had suffered from cold and hunger. Two of the prisoners of war were from the German air force, the other an army soldier.

When peace had returned to the world, the names of eight more residents of Ochiltree were added to the granite cross. These were:

- Leading Seaman Charles Arthur (D/JX 143166), HMS *Diamond*, Royal Navy. Son of James and Jeanie Arthur, Ochiltree. Died on 27 April 1941. Commemorated on Plymouth Naval Memorial, Devon.
- Private Thomas Campbell (3132087), 7th Battalion Argyll & Sutherland Highlanders, killed in action 11 August 1944 aged 26. Buried at Ranville War Cemetery, Calvados, France. Son of Thomas and Mary McCrae Campbell.
- Able Seaman John Kirkland Clark (D/JX 142269), Royal Navy. Died 9 April 1942 on HMS *Hermes*. Commemorated on Plymouth Naval Memorial.

2.17 War Memorial on new site *(Dane Love)*

- Gunner Ralph MacMorland (1790965), 181 Field Regiment, Royal Artillery. Son of Andrew and Jessie MacMorland, Drongan. Died on 25 June 1944 and buried at Brouay War Cemetery, Calvados, France.
- Sergeant John Robert Pyper (564567), 57th Squadron, Royal Air Force. Died 18 February 1943, aged 19. He was the son of Archibald and Christina Pyper. Married to Lorna Pyper, of Worksop, Nottinghamshire. He is commemorated on the Runnymede Memorial, Surrey.
- Private John Reid (14698659), 2nd Battalion, Gordon Highlanders. Killed in action on 27 August 1944 aged 20. Son of David Harkness Reid and Isabella Reid, Ochiltree. He is buried at Tilly-sur-Seulles War Cemetery, Calvados, France.

- Lance Bombardier Joseph Cumming Smith (913915), 130 Field Regiment, Royal Artillery. Died 20 April 1944 aged 23. Son of Thomas Davidson Smith and Agnes Craig Smith, Ochiltree. Buried at Taukkyan War Cemetery, Myanmar.
- Sergeant Air Gunner Robert Wilson (1597046), 153 Squadron Royal Air Force Volunteer Reserve. Born in Drongan. Died 13 March 1945 aged 20. Son of John and Helen Wilson, husband of Sarah Wilson, Ochiltree. Buried at Tranebjerg churchyard, Samso island, Denmark.

In the summer of 1962 proposals were made to have the War Memorial relocated, its site at the corner of Main Street being regarded unsuitable due to the increasing traffic. Different sites were considered, including the cemetery, but nothing happened.

The war memorial was damaged in 1971 and again the local community started to identify other suitable sites. The site of the former South Church came on the market and the council valuer assessed the site and set a value of £100 on it. However, the retaining wall along the road side was regarded as being in a poor condition, needing repairs, so a figure of £20 was suggested as a suitable offer.

The war memorial was relocated to the site of the church in 1973 and a dedication service was conducted there by Rev John Heron on Sunday 9 September.

HISTORY 1945-2021

In 1951 the *Third Statistical Account of Scotland* was published, compiled by John Strawhorn and William Boyd. Of the village of Ochiltree, they noted that it had just over 100 houses, divided into 75 ordinary houses, 10 cottages, 10 villas and 7 two-storey houses. They noted that there were several new Swedish-type houses recently occupied, and that four new blocks of houses were being built by Ayr County Council. The council built blocks of housing in various stages throughout the 1950s. Despite water being brought to the village from the Afton Reservoir, it was recorded that many households still had to draw their water from the five pumps which still survived.

Shortly after the war a number of old properties in the Main Street were demolished, leaving gap sites for a number of years. Some were never rebuilt on. With further demolitions threatened, most of the older part of the village was declared a Conservation Area by the District Council in 1974.

In the late twentieth century and early twenty-first century a number of new private housing developments were erected on the edges of the village. Houses appeared along much of the north-east side of Mauchline Road, the houses extending as far as the cemetery. A line of fourteen private bungalows were erected in Glebe Crescent, off Mauchline Road. A second cul-de-sac was created on the opposite site of the road, forming Hazelbank Crescent of seven homes. In a field

2.18 Ochiltree Community Hub *(Dane Love)*

that originally belonged to the Free Church Manse, Hope Homes Ltd of Drongan, developed Manse Brae - fifteen homes, four of which faced onto Mauchline Road. To the west of Broom Crescent, Hope Homes (Scotland) Ltd built new private houses in a staged development called Highfield and Barony Crest, comprising of 71 houses. This created the streets of Knowe View and Highfield Place, developed 2001-2006. In 2010-12 an additional development to the north of this, called Langdale Park, was built, comprising 26 houses. This forms the street named Langholm View.

The old public school in Ochiltree, which had been used by the council as a store since its closure in 1976, was sold to Hope Homes Ltd in 2005. The sandstone building was restored, being converted into six houses. In what was the playground to the rear, two blocks of four flats were erected, also by Hope Homes. Developed 2007-9, the flats were styled Coyle House and Burnock House, but the street was named Old School Wynd. The Hope Homes Ltd. business was founded in 1990 by Ian, Anne and Scott Hope and by 2020 they had built over 1,000 houses, mainly across Ayrshire.

Mains gas was piped into the village in 1992 as part of a scheme to extend gas supplies across parts of Ayrshire. Soon many business premises and houses converted their heating from coal fires to gas boilers.

In March 2016 the Community Centre was closed by East Ayrshire Council and the building was demolished in October the same year. The residents of Ochiltree had formed a local committee in May 2013 and started proceedings towards erecting a new community facility, named The Hub. The former post office was taken over in June 2016 as an office and coffee shop, opened by Provost Jim Todd in August. In 2017 they proposed a new community centre in Main Street, designed by Anderson Bell and Christie of Glasgow. The building was to contain a community café, library, large hall with stage, and various meeting rooms.

Work on the new Hub building started on 16 July 2018. A donation of £40,000 came from the Minerals Trust and £958,000 from the Big Lottery Fund. The hub opened to the public on 22 July 2019 and was officially opened on Friday 4 October 2019. It had cost £1.84 million to erect.

When the Free Church library closed, Ochiltree lacked library provision for a number of years. Eventually, in the late 1940s, a library was opened in a room within a private house at 94 Main Street by Ayr County Council. In 1974 a new library was opened at 79 Main Street. The library was closed by East Ayrshire Council on 24 March 2016.

The former farm buildings of Netherton were acquired by Spark of Genius (Training) Ltd in 2008 and converted into a children's residential home. This has accommodation for six young people, living at the home and either being educated on site or at nearby schools.

The 2011 Census gives some statistics on the parish. Ochiltree had 468 houses within it, of which 361 were owner-occupied. There were 67 council houses, and forty other houses, mainly privately rented.

In April 1979 John MacLean, of Lane Crescent, Drongan, was one of seven people killed in a train crash at Paisley's Gilmour Street Station.

TAIGLUM & DRONGAN

The coal pits sunk on Drongan and neighbouring estates required miners to work in them, and consequently houses had to be built for them to live in. In 1841, when the *New Statistical Account* of Stair parish was written (in which parish Drongan was located at the time), it was noted that there was 'a collection of houses, affording accommodation for fifteen or sixteen families.' Most of the families were incomers, miners often being peripatetic in their search for work.

On Drongan estate itself, the first row of houses specifically erected for miners to live in was probably that erected at Taiglum, north of the Taiglum Burn and south of the Toll Road (later named Watson Terrace). This row of houses was certainly in existence by 1857, when the Ordnance Survey made their first detailed maps of the area. Here, one row of houses was erected on the west side of the road, originally having eight houses in it. Each of these was a single-end house, the room inside measuring twelve feet square. To the rear were extensive gardens, each house having its own area of ground for growing vegetables and potatoes. The front doors of each house opened directly onto Littlemill Road, and on the opposite side of the street were three buildings that served as privies for the families. At the north-western end of the row a large building was used as a smithy, with a smith's house attached, again having its own garden area.

On the triangle of land between the Taiglum Burn and a small stream were another two rows of six houses, one on each side of the road. These were single-apartment houses, and were known as the Wee White Row. The occupants of these houses had to walk up Littlemill Road a few hundred yards to a roadside well, from where they could draw water. The houses on the east side of the road had fair-sized gardens, whereas those on the west side of the street didn't appear to have any.

2.19 Taiglum Rows *(Author's Collection)*

Between the single row and the Wee White Row was Taiglum coal pit, located on the west side of the road, just south of the single row. This had a building on the surface of the pit, and a small headframe which lowered the miners into the ground. To the south-east of this pit, on Mill of Shield Road, were a few limekilns, but these were indicated as being disused by the 1857 survey.

In April 1863 a collier from Taiglum, James Wilson, disappeared, only for his partially decomposed body to be discovered at the mouth of Ayr Harbour around six weeks later. It was reckoned that he had been drunk and fallen into the harbour.

Messrs Merry and Cuninghame took over the lease of the Drongan coal pits around 1870 and it was they who erected more houses at Taiglum, considerably extending the community. Life in the rows could be hard, and a few examples of incidents can be related here. In April 1871, James Whyte, grandson of one of the miners residing at Taiglum, was sent to prison for setting fire to a belt of woodland on Drongan estate. The damage extended to half an acre of woodland; the fire being extinguished by the residents. In July 1889 John Wilson and James Harkins were sentenced to four months' imprisonment for breaking into a cottar's house at Drongan and stealing a watch and other articles.

In 1890 Ayr County Council noted that there was no syvor in front of Drongan Rows to the south side of Lane Burn. In 1890 the county surveyor recommended that a wooden footbridge should be erected at the Millmannoch ford across the Water of Coyle at Cairnston.

The Ordnance Survey updated their maps in 1894, and by this time Taiglum had five new rows of miners' houses. Opposite the smithy, which was still in operation, seven houses were erected in a terrace, but these houses were of unequal sizes. They were all double-apartment houses, but it was noted that the rooms were so small that the floorspace was little more than single-apartment homes. The houses were constructed of stone and had slate roofs. They had gardens to the rear. The house at the northern end of the row appears to have been larger than the rest, with its own wash-house in an enclosed garden. Across the road from the old Single Row was another row of houses, nine in number, with gardens to the rear.

At the northern end of the Single Row a new building was attached, forming a new house for the blacksmith. This building also doubled as the post office for a time, certainly serving as such in 1894. The Wee White Rows now had a new well from where water was obtainable, located immediately to the side of the Taiglum Burn, upstream from the Taiglum Bridge. The Wee White Row west row by this time had gardens to the rear.

Prior to 1894 the final three new rows of houses had been erected at Taiglum, located along the west side of Littlemill Road. Known variously as Drongan High Row, or Drongan Cottages, there were eight houses in each of the farthest blocks, all of which were two-apartment. The terrace nearest to Taiglum Burn Bridge was longer, and had seventeen houses in it. There were privies for these cottages, most located to the rear, where there were small gardens. Most cottages only had rear gardens, but in the case of the long row, there was one to the front, and another to the rear. Drongan Cottages were built of stone had had slate roofs. Along the ridge were chimney stacks, and each house had a single Georgian-paned window to the front. The rows were set back slightly from the public road. It was stated that the coal company threw up these houses as quickly as possible, and that the sloping site and poor drainage meant that they suffered from damp and subsidence. In 1914 the population of Drongan Cottages, or the High Row, was 208.

A supply of clean water was brought to Drongan in 1912 when water from Loch Bradan was piped across much of the county. The water scheme was instigated by

2.20 Tom and Susan Ross at Taiglum Rows *(Jo Stewart)*

Troon Burgh Council and the pipe from Loch Bradan came by way of Littlemill and Tarbolton, thus passing through the parish. A number of cast iron pumps were installed at various points.

At the start of the First World War there were 65 houses at Taiglum, 48 of which were of two apartments, and seventeen were single-apartment. The rent for single-apartment homes was 1s 5d and for double-apartment houses was 2s 10d. The population at the time was reckoned to be around 350.

In 1919 Taiglum village was put on the market as part of the sale of Drongan estate. In addition to the farms, the store was offered for sale, as was the post office and 67 houses.

In 1926 new houses were erected at Taiglum's northern end by Ayr District Council. Woodend Cottages were built to form a small cul-de-sac, and the houses were notable in that they were the first houses to be built in the community to have bathrooms.

A village hall was erected in 1903 at Taiglum in Lane Road (later to be Mill of Shield Road). Known as the Iron Hall, from the material from which it was clad, the hall was used for numerous social events, including meetings, dances, lectures, and clubs of different sorts. This was demolished in April 1960. Alexander Mathieson had a large hut that served as a shop and billiard saloon. In 1940 he had a site where he proposed erecting a new saloon and shop, but war restrictions prevented its erection.

From 1935 onwards, the sub-standard miners' houses at Taiglum were slowly replaced by new county council houses. As the occupants of the old Taiglum rows were rehoused, the rows were demolished. The first council houses in Drongan were those erected to form 1-36 Watson Terrace, and 1-51 and 2-36 Lane Crescent. The former was named after John Neill Watson JP (1876-1958) of East Tarelgin, the latter after the farm on which most of the village was to be built.

The Second World War intervened, when no building took place, but by 1951 Ayr County Council had erected 75 house and 11 prefabricated homes, or 'prefabs' as they were affectionately known. Most of the houses were of the four in a cottage style, often used by the county council, with two homes upstairs, and two downstairs. Unfortunately, by 1951 these houses showed signs of cracking due to mining subsidence.

After the Second World War, plans were being drawn up to create a new town at Drongan. New Towns were created across Scotland to rehouse families who had been relocated from inner-cities. These were established at Glenrothes, East Kilbride, and Irvine. Originally, there had been plans to develop Coylton as the new community, but this was changed to Taiglum, where the proposal for a New Town at Drongan was made in 1946 by Joseph Westwood, Secretary of State for Scotland, under the New Towns Act of that year, but a development corporation was never established.

The community was expected to cover the area between the Sinclairston to Drongan road (Drumjoan) and the Mill o' Shield to Kersepark road, extending from Taiglum in the north, south to include Littlemill and Rankinston. The area covered would remove 22 dairy farms. The name Taiglum was dropped at this time, the name for the new community to be Drongan, from the local estate on which much of the village was to be erected. As new houses were being constructed, the old rows were evacuated and gradually pulled down.

The proposal for a new town at Drongan was to satisfy the demand for homes for miners who were expected to come in to the area to work in the new super pit at Killoch. Initially, the plan was for a large town with a population between 30,000-35,000

Work on building new homes in Drongan started apace, but in 1948 these were slowed down, as work at Killoch had still not progressed. As late as 1949, however, assurances were still being given that the plan for a new town was on track. It envisaged that the population of the town would now reach 19,000, with 1,100 miners from Killoch living there. By 1952 300 houses had been erected and 110 were nearing completion. By the time Killoch Colliery opened in 1953, Drongan New Town was dead in the water, and instead it was planned simply to create a small village with a population of around 6,000-10,000. This figure was never to be reached.

Writing around 1950, following three years of survey work across Ayrshire, the compilers of the *Third Statistical* Account of the county were less than flattering on their description of the village:

> The young people no longer seek to entertain themselves now that they can buy their entertainment. Female youth has been demoralised with fine dresses, cigarettes, cosmetics, dancing and the cult of the glamour girl depicted in the films and illustrated magazines. Their elders are no better. Nobody to-day thinks of walking even a short distance. If a bus is not available it is a common practice to hire one of the local taxis, even for long distances like the run to Ayr. And more money has meant more gambling. In time, no doubt, things will right themselves. It is not easy for the ordinary man or woman to get the best out of life in a scottered district like the Drongan area. It is not only housing that is inadequate, but social facilities. Apart from the school at Sinclairston, there is only a single meeting hall available for public gatherings, a corrugated iron hall in Drongan village, and a single inn at Coalhall.

In December 1953 there was considerable flooding in Drongan, resulting in families being evacuated from 200 homes when the burn overflowed.

By 1958 Ayr County Council had erected around 400 houses on the lands of Lane farm. An additional 200 had been erected by the Scottish Special Housing Association. An additional 120 were still at the planning stage. However, it was reckoned that a further 1,500 houses would still be required to house the miners expected to work at Killoch Colliery. Hannahston Avenue was erected in 1954. By November 1960 the Scottish Special Housing Association had completed 312 houses.

The growing village at Drongan was in need of community facilities, and in 1951 the old canteen at Shieldmains Colliery – Carston pit, was converted into a hall and institute by the Miners' Welfare Commission and then taken over by Ayr County Council. The Drongan Working Men's Club was erected in Lady's Walk in 1965.

In 1959 a new community centre was built in Millmannoch Avenue, after which the old centre was closed. This contained a large meeting hall, kitchen and ancillary rooms. It was built in a typical Ayr County Council style, with flat roof, steel-glazed windows and rough-cast panels between brick pillars. Many organisations and events were held in the hall, including bingo, Scouts, dances, exhibitions and shows. In 2011 the centre was closed by East Ayrshire Council and subsequently demolished.

The new cemetery was passed by the council in 1960 and work on laying out the pathways and erecting the walls commenced. The first interment in the new cemetery took place on 8 April 1964.

Rowantree Court was erected in Glencraig Street in 1976-77 by the council as a sheltered housing complex, to cater for elderly residents. It includes eighteen one-bedroom flats for elderly guests, who can use the dining room, lounge, activities room and other facilities, all with on-site care staff. The cost was £250,000.

A police station was erected in Drongan in 1962 at a cost of £8,865 14s 7d. Police constables who worked in Drongan for longer periods include David R. Morgan, who served from 1945-1964.

2.21 Drongan Resource Centre *(Dane Love)*

A new Drongan resource centre was erected in the village by Ayrshire and Arran Health Board and East Ayrshire Council at a cost of around £1.2 million. The centre was built to replace outdated community facilities, and incorporated a new health centre run by Ayrshire and Arran Primary Care N. H. S. Trust, two G. P. consulting suites, community police station, and council offices. It was designed by Wren Rutherford AustinSmith:Lord architects and erected by William MacClure & Sons. Located in Mill of Shield Road, work started on site in June 2001 and it was completed the following June. The centre was officially opened on 10 February 2003 by Andy Kerr MSP, Minister for Finance and Public Services.

Councillors who served the Drongan area in local councils included Tommy Farrell, who served for 22 years. He also sat as Chairman of Drongan Community Association for eleven years. Farrell Crescent was named in his honour. Joe Hodge JP was councillor for many years, and Hodge Crescent was named after him. Councillor William Reid was honoured by the naming of Reid Place.

When Drongan Junior Secondary School opened in 1960, a new public library was annexed to it, serving the community. This continued until August 1978 when a new library building was erected in Mill of Shield Road. Built in typical council 1970s style, it had facing-brick walls, vertical windows and a flat roof with bargeboarded eaves. The new facility had a lending department, plus an audio section and a small reference room. The library building was closed in 2017. In 1992 the village was connected to the natural gas main for the first time.

A new community centre, incorporating an Early Childhood Centre was erected by East Ayrshire Council and opened in February 2017 by Corri Wilson, MP for Ayr, Carrick and Cumnock. The new building was erected at a cost of £1.2 million adjoining Drongan Primary School. It includes a new community hub and library.

On 14 November 2008 Michelle Stewart (aged seventeen years) was murdered in the street at the shops in Drongan when she was stabbed ten times by ex-boyfriend John Wilson. He was later found guilty and served ten years in prison. The family appeared on television programme 'Judge Rinder's Crime Files' in 2020 as part of a campaign to prevent murderers returning to where they had lived.

A number of private housing developments were erected in and around Drongan in the 1980s onwards. The first stage of Craufurd Drive was started in 1997. Local business, Hope Homes, were to build Pettoch Road, Hodge Crescent and Byres Road from 1997. Ailsa Craig View and the rest of Pettoch Road date from 1999-2001. Truesdale Crescent, Arran Court and Corrie Place dates from 2000 onward. In 2004-5 Farrell Crescent, Craufurd Drive and Torrance Drive were built. They developed Lomond View and Lomond Crescent from 2005-6. Hope Homes also carried out a number of smaller developments, including Cairnston Court (four flats), Whitegables Court (14 homes), and buildings in Glencraig Street (four homes) and Watson Terrace (8 homes). Milestone Developments erected 12 semi-detached double-storey houses forming Shanter Crescent.

COALHALL

The hamlet of Coalhall owes its origins to the sinking of small coal pits on Drongan estate. Coalhall itself was originally the name of a few cottages at the junction of the Trabboch Road with the main Ochiltree-Ayr Road. It is named on Thomson's *Atlas of Scotland* in 1832. In 1856 the Ordnance Survey indicated that there were five houses there – a row of three, a detached cottage and a single cottage across the road, in the corner of the road junction. To the east of this, next to an old cottage, was another dwelling, and to the rear of this was an old coal pit, disused by 1856. Drongan Pottery comprised of a group of buildings formed round a courtyard, with kilns and other buildings making up the group. To the north-west of the kiln was a clay pit. The only other part of Coalhall as we know it today was Gateside, a row of four cottages plus the building that had still to be converted into an inn.

By the next survey in 1894, the cottages at Coalhall proper had been reduced to two, that in the corner of the road being demolished, as well as two of the terrace. At the old pit, the long cottage appears to have been divided into two. The buildings at Drongan Pottery were converted into eight houses, occupied by miners who worked in the local pits. The Gateside Inn was by this time operational. And the terrace adjoining it now comprised of five homes. A well at the junction of the Drongan road was used for a supply of water.

In 1914 the miners' union inspectors visited the houses at Drongan Pottery and reported on their condition. At the time there were five single apartment houses here, plus three two-apartment homes. They were arranged to form three sides of a square. 'On one side there are 4 single apartment houses, on the other side one house of two apartments, and in the middle row there are two houses of two apartments and one house of one apartment. Most of the houses are built of stone, and have thatched roofs. We measured one single apartment house, and its dimensions were 12 feet by 13 feet. The roadway in front of the houses is unpaved, and pools of water and mud were at every door.' The houses were owned by the Countess of Hardwicke, being part of Drongan estate. The inspectors' report continued: 'There is one earth closet and open ashpit for the whole property, and this provides for a population of 48. The open ashpit is about 40 feet from the nearest door. The closet has no door, and, in fact, has not been built with the purpose of providing a door. Human excretion is littered about for yards round the entrance to the closet. This is probably due to the children not having sufficient accommodation inside. The stench was abominable, and originates round the closet and ashpit which are within 40 feet of the nearest house. No outhouses of any kind have been provided, and the people store their coals below their beds.' One of the single-apartment houses had six occupants in it, and in another was a family of four plus a lodger. At the time, the rent payable on a single-aprtment house was 1s 5d per week; that for a double-apartment house being 1s 8d.

In August 1956 three men were killed in a road traffic accident outside the Gateside Inn. Around thirty miners were waiting on the bus to take them to work at Sinclairston when a lorry collided with a bus and then ran into the men. Nine other men were injured, the remainder of them managing to jump to safety. The lorry ran into the façade of the inn, causing considerable damage. Some of the cargo of magnesium lime fell from the lorry, covering some of the men. The three dead were William Dykes, aged around 56, of Coalhall Pottery; William Taylor, aged around 50, from Joppa, and John MacGinn, 68, of Windmillhall, Coalhall.

A petrol filling station and associated garage was established at Coalhall in 1952 to supply fuel and facilities for motorists. Known as Darwin Garage, it was operated by John Keenan. The garage was later taken over by Keenan Coach Hire as a depot for their buses. This firm was founded around 1960 by Jack and Anne Keenan. Their three sons assisted, and eventually the youngest Jamie Keenan and his wife took over.

In more recent years Coalhall has had new bungalows erected at it, forming a development known as Evergreen. By the Census of 2011, Coalhall had a population of around 100 people.

SINCLAIRSTON

The small clachan of Sinclairston was built on the roadside on the farm of Sinclairston, all part of Drumjoan estate. In 1855, when the Ordnance Surveyors visited to make the first detailed maps of the area, they described the village as comprising 'a few cottages, one storey, slated and in good repair. The property of Robert Campbell [of Drumjoan].' One of the buildings also housed a small school. Some houses were subsequently built on what was Polquhairn estate, including Beechbank. The Ordnance Survey map of 1858 only shows five homes, plus Sinclairston farm itself and Beechland, perhaps three cottages joined together, located on Drumjoan road.

In the middle of the nineteenth century Sinclairston had a small shop, which sold a multitude of items (in 1851 the proprietor was Alexander MacCrindle), plus a tailor's shop and a shoemaker - James Lees (1809-1887). In 1870 Jean Finlay, who ran the grocer's shop, was fined for selling porter to local masons in contravention of the Public House act. When the railway came this way, a few buildings in the village were demolished to allow it to pass through. In 1862 Sinclairston Mutual Improvement Society was founded by some young men in the area.

By 1894, when the Ordnance Survey map-makers compiled their next edition, one of the houses at Beechland was demolished, and Sinclairston farm had fallen into ruins. The school had been erected and a schoolhouse had been erected next to it. A third edition of the Ordnance Survey map appeared in 1908, by which time only one cottage survived at Beechland, now renamed Beechbank. Sinclairston Cottages were rebuilt, one older house being replaced with four smaller homes.

The Polquhairn Coal Company Ltd. built some new cottages at Sinclairston in 1908-12, designed by Murdoch and Lockhart, architects, Ayr.

A public water supply was introduced to Sinclairston in 1912 when the Loch Bradan watermain was led into the village. A cast-iron water pump was positioned centrally in the village to serve the small community. Previously, a well in the small wood adjoining Sinclairston Cottages was used.

Most of the original Sinclairston Cottages were demolished in the twentieth century, leaving only Bellview. Numbers 1 and 2 Craigview were erected to the north of this. By 1977 it was reckoned the village had nine houses and a population of 26.

In recent years, a number of private houses were sporadically erected at Sinclairston, mainly to the south-west of the original hamlet, to either side of the railway, which had become disused. The old school was closed and converted into three houses. In a small field opposite the original Sinclairston Cottages, six private houses were erected to form a cul-de-sac known as St Clare's Court. At Polquhairn road-end, Craigness, Sinclairston House, Pineview, Chestnuts, Taiglum Bank and Hillside were built. By 2020 there were 23 houses in the hamlet.

DRUMSMUDDEN

Drumsmudden is the name of a lost community of miners' rows that were built (mainly on the farm of Drumjoan) to house colliers employed at Drumsmudden Pit, which operated from 1882 onwards. Although the land was owned by Lord Skerrington, the colliery and rows were sold to the Dalmellington Iron Company.

The Drumsmudden Row was built adjoining the pit, six houses in a terrace. It was often referred to as 'Number 2 Row'. The front doors faced northwards, overlooking gardens towards the woods and shelterbelts on the knoll occupied by Crawsland. Running along the northern side of the gardens were two railway sidings from the colliery, meaning that pugs and coal carriages often drew along in front of the houses.

The rear of the row had projecting wings on each of the houses, and between these wings were outside toilets. These homes were the better quality of the two rows, being larger in size. Here the pit manager and other 'gaffers' lived.

A second, much larger, row of houses existed at Drumsmudden, officially named Skerrington Row but often referred to as Number 1 Row. The row had fourteen houses in total. This was located at right angles to the road linking Drongan with Sinclairston, near to where the four houses of Drumjoan Terrace stand today. The front of the houses looked to the south-east, the rising field blocking distant views. Along the front of the houses was a track, running the length of the row. To the rear the houses also had a projecting wing, but the houses were different in layout to the other row. Here the houses were either L- or T-shaped, repeating alternately, the buildings fitting together in a rather strange way, a bit like a tessellated pattern. These homes simply comprised of a room and kitchen.

The kitchen measured around 21 feet by 13 feet, doubling as a sleeping area, there being two large built-in beds located along one side, and a press, or cupboard just inside the door. Within the 'room' there was a further set-in bed.

Linking the two rows was a track across the field. By the side of this path was the source of water for the village. The 1894 Ordnance Survey map indicates this as a pump, whereas by 1908 it was shown as a well. The supply of water to the rows always appears to have been something of a problem, for this pump often dried up. When this happened, the residents had to walk a mile and a half to a former test bore, the 'Diamond Bore', from which water flowed continually. Another source of water that was used when possible was the water tank at Belston railway junction. This was normally used to fill the tanks of the steam engines, but it could be made to overflow and run into the burn that flowed past the rows. The men of the community would then scoop the water up and fill the barrels that stood by the rows to collect rainwater from the roofs.

The rows at Drumsmudden, although fairly new and of better quality, became surplus fairly quickly. By the start of the First World War in 1914, of the twenty houses there, thirteen were sitting empty. The Drumsmudden Row had three tenants – Mrs Bennet, a widow, and two workers' families. These were James MacGarvie, labourer, and John Rodger, pitheadman. In Skerrington Row there were four houses occupied, one of them by Mrs Kernachan, widow. The other three were lived in by John Wilson, James Wilson and William Hodge, all miners.

To try to improve the quality of life at Drumsmudden, and encourage new tenants, in 1918 new drainage, water closets, coal-houses and sinks inside the sculleries were constructed at the High Drumsmudden Row. Previously there had only been two dry closets for the full row of fourteen houses. Dirty water was poured from the basins in the houses and closets into the small stream that flowed to the back of the rows. To keep the 'sheugh' as free-running as possible, a young man was sent from the pit every Saturday and he had to brush it clean.

One of the families who lived at Drumsmudden was an old Irish couple known as John and Katie Bell. Every 12 July they travelled back to Ireland to take part in the festivities. The Bells were known for their pet monkey, but most locals were frightened of it, for when you approached it, it bared its teeth in a threatening manner.

A social spirit thrived in the rows of the district. The Coylton Drumsmudden Friendly Society existed for a number of years, providing a means of saving and boosting the welfare of its members. In August 1895 the president of the society, Thomas Watters, was presented with a mantelpiece clock 'for his long and faithful services, having acted as president for the last eighteen years'. Members of the society paid around threepence per week from their wages. Should the wage-earner turn ill, the society would pay the family an income for around five to six weeks.

In 1921 Ochiltree Parish Council agreed to rent 2½ acres of land on Whitehill farm as a recreation ground for the residents. This was located east of the Bardarroch Road between the railway and the small burn that drained the nearby fields, as well as the rows' drains.

The field was noted for being rather rough, but it didn't stop the local children from playing on it. One who used the field often was Alexander, or Alex Linwood, born in the rows on 13 March 1920. At the age of fourteen he, like most other boys of the time, went to work in the pits, but his love of football led him to sign for Muirkirk Juniors in 1938. He was to become a notable player, signing for St Mirren in October later the same year. In 1943 the club won the Summer Cup, beating Rangers by one goal to nil in the final – the boy from Drumsmudden scoring the only goal. Linwood's cousin was at the controls of a Lancaster bomber when news of the win came through. Local tales claim that he raised his arms to celebrate, causing the bomber to plummet several hundred feet before he regained control! Alex was signed by Middlesbrough, followed by Hibernian, Clyde and Morton. In November 1949 Linwood was picked to play for Scotland against Wales, his only peacetime cap, but he managed to score. He retired from football in 1955, living in Renfrew, before he died on 23 October 2003.

Life in the rows could be hard. During the General Strike of 1926 there was much hardship for many of the miners living there. Ochiltree parish council offered relief to families, children being fed and vouchers issued for a time, before it was suspended as being unaffordable. The residents from Drumsmudden and Drongan marched to the parish inspector's office in Ochiltree where they held a mass meeting in the recreation ground. Two prominent local Labour men, James Brown MP and Alex Sloan were among those who addressed the crowd.

When the colliery at Drumsmudden was closed, the rows no longer had any real need to be there, so the Dalmellington company leased the houses to the Coylton Coal Company, and miners employed by them were able to stay there, though they had to travel further to their work.

2.22 Alex Linwood *(Author's Collection)*

By 1951, when the *Third Statistical Account* of Scotland was written, Drumsmudden's houses were 'much overcrowded'. The community of Drongan was then being developed by Ayr County Council to rehouse miners from Trabboch and other communities, and gradually the residents of Drumsmudden were given new homes there. The old rows were demolished in 1958, so that today there is little to indicate their former existence. Even the pit bing was partially removed and landscaped when a firm dug away much of the mound to make it into bricks.

In 1951 four new semi-detached cottages were built near Drumsmudden, named Drumjoan Terrace. These were erected by Ayr County Council, initially for agricultural workers.

HAYHILL

New workmen's houses were erected at Hayhill from 1920 by Ayr County Council, being available to let from February 1922. These houses were designed by the Ayr architect, Allan Stevenson and comprised fourteen semi-detached cottages, positioned alongside the north side of the road, opposite what had been Hayhill cottage.

Hayhill remained little changed for almost a century. In 2017-2019 twenty new semi-detached houses were erected on the south side of the road, next to Hayhill House, forming a development known as Bryden Way. Designed by Lawrence MacPherson Associates, architects, of Ayr, the houses were built by Hayhill Developments. In 2020 plans were submitted to the council for a further 21 houses in the same area.

CHAPTER THREE

ROADS AND TRANSPORT

The first proper roads in Ayrshire were not constructed until the first few decades of the eighteenth century. The earliest known road in the county was perhaps constructed in the 1730s, when the 4th Earl of Loudoun laid one out across his estate. By 1768, the roads laid out were still of a very poor condition, and Alexander Montgomerie of Coilsfield noted that 'the great roads leading through [Ayrshire are] next to impassable for six months in the year.'

One of the earliest detailed maps of Ochiltree parish was that produced around 1750 by General William Roy. At a scale of about one inch to one mile, Roy's Military Survey was drawn up following the Battle of Culloden to assist the British Army should any future uprisings take place. At this time there were few roads in the parish, and those travelling from farm to farm or to church would journey across country by whichever route they wished, there being few fences or hedges. Roads in the parish that appeared on Roy's survey existed from the Old Cumnock parish boundary, travelling west into Ochiltree, continuing westwards by a rather more meandering route than the present A70 road, towards Bell's Brae and the ford across the Water of Coyle, at the Coylton parish boundary. A second road is shown heading north-west from Ochiltree, following virtually the same route as Mauchline Road, as far as Rodenloft and Barskimming estate.

In 1767 the Ayrshire Road Act was passed, allowing trustees to create turnpike roads across the county and to charge a toll for passing along them. The act provided for the construction and improvement of many miles of roadway, as well as associated bridges and other civil engineering works. The 1767 Act resulted in the formation of two toll roads in Ochiltree parish. The principal one was the road from Cumnock to Ayr, which passes through Ochiltree village, as well as Coalhall. This was almost seven miles in length. A toll gate was set up at the Mote Toll in order to charge fees from those using the road. These fees were used to maintain the road surface and other improvements. In October 1767 reference is made to the proposed route of the roadway being surveyed. Although a route existed from Ayr to Cumnock previously, the act was seen as an opportunity for the road to better laid out, straightended or levelled. Accordingly, James Bruce, the factor to the Boswells of Auchinleck, who owned considerable lands in the parish of Ochiltree, met with Robert Crozier and planned the best way through the parish from the Waggon Ford to the vicinity of Drongan. They were joined by Adam Smith of Drongan who gave advice on the best location for a new bridge to replace to old Waggon Ford.

The second road created under the 1767 Act was that from Irvine to Dalmellington. This was a rather strange route, making its way through Dundonald and Tarbolton to Stair. The road entered Ochiltree parish at Windmillhall and headed south to Coalhall. A dogleg at the Cumnock-Ayr road allowed the road to strike south through Drongan and Littlemill before heading over the hill and moorland country above Rankinston to Dalmellington. Tolls were established at Bonnyton and Drongan. In Drongan, or Taiglum, the toll cottage was located at the corner of the Main Road with Toll Road, or Watson Terrace as it became. Bonnyton Toll was located at the juntion of the road with that heading east towards Hayhill and Sinclairston. This road extended to around three and a half miles within Ochiltree parish.

Bonnyton Toll was located at the junction of the road from Drongan towards Littlemill with the road to Sinclairston. In 1846 Margaret MacBurnie lived there. Toll-keepers at the Mote Toll included Miss Johnstone (before 1883).

The minister of Ochiltree in 1794, Rev William Thomson, did not agree with the rules of the period which stated that all of the money raised in a parish was to be spent solely on the turnpike road through that parish. He felt that this took funds from the maintenance and creation of other roadways in the parish. In the *Statistical Account* he wrote:

> The parish might be much more improved, were there any roads through it; but at present there is not one made road, excepting the turnpike road to Ayr formerly mentioned, and another small portion of road, that crosses a corner of the north west side of the parish. It would be much for the interest of the proprietors, to attend to the state of the roads, and to the funds allotted for that purpose, there being £60 annually collected, of which £20 goes to the repair of the toll road to Ayr. The rest is otherwise applies, but unfortunately not to roads within the boundaries of this parish.

An additional account in a later volume dealt with the roads in more detail. Thomson noted that the rateable valuation of the parish was £5,213 Scots, therefore the road repair tax would be £65 3s 3d Sterling, based on a rate at threepence per pound. In addition each family, apart from paupers, paid three shillings towards the upkeep of roads. At the time there were around 8 ½ miles of turnpike road in the parish. The main road was, as now, that from Ayr to Cumnock. The toll bar was located in the middle of Ochiltree.

In 1774 the Ayr Road Act proposed converting the road from Barskimming Bridge to Coalhall to a toll road. The road went by way of Crosshill, Trabbochburn and Schaw.

Additional roads appear on Armstrong's map of Ayrshire, published in 1775. In addition to the Ayr-Cumnock road, and the Irvine-Dalmellington road (via Bonnyton), two other roads appear on maps for the first time. One of these is a roadway from near Ochiltree heading south-west past Netherton, Finlayston and Holehouse to Glenconner, and thence westward by way of Plaid and Belston to Bonnyton.

3.1 Old Burnock Bridge *(Author's Collection)*

The second roadway shown was probably never properly surfaced or laid out formerly, and was perhaps little more than a drove route. This is shown on Armstrong's map as going from Bonnyton across country by Old Polquhairn and Headmark to Burnston, near Dalgig, to join the main road at Bank House, west of New Cumnock.

In 1780 the road from Barskimming Bridge, near Mauchline, to Ayr, was converted into a turnpike road, of which around two miles passed through Ochiltree parish. From the amount collected in the parish towards the upkeep of the turnpike roads, there was a surplus, but this was spent elsewhere. Thomson complained that it should perhaps have been used to improve, or at least maintain the other country roads in the parish, which were more or less left to the locals to repair as they felt desirable.

Around the 1790s, the road from Ochiltree to Barskimming was laid out, passing by the farms of Laigh Carston and Auchinbay. William Lees of Auchinbay and John Tennant of Girvanmains were appointed to value the lands taken over the by the roadway. There was a dispute regarding the values, and John Colville of Bardarroch was asked to settle the dispute.

The road from Ochiltree towards Ayr underwent some upgrading in the early 1800s. A new bridge crossing the Water of Coyle was proposed on 19 April 1809. The plans for this show a bridge with a fairly level deck, the arch spanning 35 feet and the width of roadway being 30 feet. This was sent out for tenders, the road trustees signing it – John Grierson, William Ramsay, John Hamilton and John MacDougall of Polquhairn.

Improvements were made to the road from Ochiltree to Auchinleck in 1818-19. A new stone Lugar Bridge was erected below Ochiltree dam, replacing what had been a ford and adjoining timber bridge, the latter being washed away in a flood in 1819. The new bridge was paid for by subscription. Comprising a single hump-backed arch, the bridge remained in use until 1866.

By the time John Thomson's *Atlas of Scotland* was published in 1832, the parish was criss-crossed with public, estate and farm roads, the result of enclosing fields and improving estates.

At the turn of the nineteenth century horse-drawn carriages made their way from town to town, some of them passing through Ochiltree. In 1837 the coach named 'Independent' passed through Ochiltree. The market coach arrived at Andrew Edgar's inn each Tuesday and Friday morning at eight o'clock from Cumnock, and continued to Ayr. Travellers could return by the same coach, which stopped at Edgar's on the same days at six o'clock in the evening.

In 1837 there were seven miles of turnpike road in the parish, being the roadway linking Ayr with Cumnock. In 1838 the roadway east of the village was relaid, along with a new Burnock Bridge.

In addition to the turnpike roads, there were an additional sixteen miles of public roads in the parish linking smaller communities and farms. These were maintained by statute labour converted into money, totalling £75 per annum. In 1833 it was proposed that the old by-road from Killoch through Creoch and Tenpoundland to Plotcock be closed off to the public, having been superseded by the new road lately made from Moat to Mauchline, 'as the road was in such a state of disrepair as to be quite impassable, and moreover, of no further use to the public'

The steep Main Street had always been something of a problem for travellers between Cumnock and Ayr, and thus in 1838 it was decided to construct a new route avoiding it. Accordingly, a sweep was created from near to the Cross, passing alongside the head of Burnock Holm, and then taking a more gentle route towards Moat Toll. To facilitate the creation of this roadway, some property in the village had to be demolished, and some back gardens destroyed. Within a short period of time, a couple of cottages had been erected on the remainder of the back rigg attached to the demolished cottages.

At the same time the road from the Cross towards Cumnock was realigned at Burnock Cottage. The old bridge led the roadway past the west side of the building, whereas the new route created in 1839 lay to the east side of the cottage. The new bridge over the Burnock was erected in 1839, the masonic lodge from Cumnock, St Barnabas No. 230, being present at the laying of the foundation stone.

In May 1843 the old road passing through Glenconner, Holehouse and Finlayston was closed off as a public highway. In March 1844, the route 'having become useless to the public in consequence of the opening of the New Line to Ochiltree, and having also been used for the purpose of evading the Toll Bar at Moat, was in May last, ordained by judicial authority, to be shut up after the lapse of 6 months in terms of the Road Act, notwithstanding whereof, and of public notice by hand bills, various persons continued to use the road as formerly. The Trustees therefore found it necessary to bring an action against one of the aggressors who, having pleaded guilty, was fined in £3.'

3.2 Lugar Bridge *(Author's Collection)*

The old Lugar Bridge was replaced with a new one in 1866-67 at a cost of £600, £366 of which was granted by the County Road Trustees. Andrew Murdoch of Gallowlea constructed the twin-arched bridge, built of dressed stone. In July 1867, when the second arch was under construction, flooding in the river washed away the scaffolding and supports, resulting in the arch crashing into the water below.

Around 1893 James Hendry established a bus run from Ochiltree to Cumnock, Auchinleck and back. This operated for many years, known at times as the 'Ochiltree Express'. In 1923 James Hendry was succeeded in the business by his son, John Hendry, who continued to operate the Ochiltree bus on the same route. However, in 1924 the horse-bus service from Ochiltree to Cumnock was stopped.

In 1919 the bottom end of the village was improved when the wall at the bad corner was taken down and moved back a bit, easing traffic flow.

The Drongan Bridge was widened in 1920. By April 1923 the road from Craigbrae farm towards Bonnyton Toll junction was improved, the gradient of the steep hill at Craigbrae being reduced and Burnside Bridge widened.

The arrival of the motor car and diesel-engined lorries and other vehicles resulted in the establishment of petrol filling stations. These were often associated with hotels, replacing change-houses, but in time independent filling stations were established. Over the years there have been three filling stations in the parish – Darwin Garage at Coalhall and William Drain's Garage and the Toll Garage, both in Drongan. Ochiltree itself had a couple of petrol pumps, one operated by John Peden & Sons, Main Street, the other by Smith Brothers' Garage, also Main Street. There was a vehicle repair workshop at the Central Garage and a repair workshop at Mote Toll Garage.

The road from Ochiltree towards Auchinleck was realigned in the early 1960s, avoiding the circuitous route over the Lugar Bridge. The old bridge was declared unfit for heavy traffic, and a public order of June 1960 restricted it to vehicles under 12 tons. A new roadway, which was considerably wider than the old roadway, was formed, continuing in a straight line from Mill Street. The Lugar Water was crossed by a new steel girder bridge, erected in 1961-62. The roadway, by now in the parish of Auchinleck, then swings to the left and rejoins the old road. In total, 1,000 yards of new roadway was created. The contractors for the new bridge was Murdoch MacKenzie Ltd. of Motherwell, who were paid £59,694. The new bridge and approach roads were opened on Wednesday 11 April 1962. The old bridge was subsequently closed to traffic.

In the Autumn of 1994 the junction of the High Road at Tarbeg was closed off next to the Mote Toll. The Mote Toll Cottage had its porch extended in November 1996.

RAILWAYS

In the first half of the nineteenth century, there were great strides being made in the creation of railway lines across much of Britain. Different companies vied with each other to establish lines, complete with railway stations and other infrastructure, in order to profit from the transport of goods as well as passengers. Areas of the country that were not covered by the railways were in demand for extensions by the railway companies, and these were fought for competively in order to achieve acts of parliament to allow their construction.

Plans for a railway through the parish from Ayr to Cumnock had been mooted in 1845-6, when the Glasgow and South Western Railway Company had employed Edward Blyth (1825-1902), civil engineer, to survey a route. It was proposed to make its way via Blackhouse, Auchincruive and then cross the River Ayr half a mile above Overmills, and onwards to Belston. From Belston it would make its way through Joppa, Coylton and Drongan and then east to Cumnock, passing Ochiltree to the south by around a mile and a quarter. This route did not proceed to construction.

In June 1864 a public meeting was held in the Assembly Rooms, Ayr, where it was proposed to create a railway from Ayr to Douglas. This was to pass through Drongan and by Ochiltree towards Cumnock. The chair was occupied by Provost Andrew Paterson of Ayr (owner of Low Carston farm), and many of the local landowners attended, including James Pettigrew Wilson of Polquhairn. A government act was passed in November 1864 allowing construction work to start, but it took eight years before the line was to open. During construction temporary huts were erected for the labourers at Sinclairston. In February 1870 Catherine MacCulloch, wife of R. MacCulloch of the Railway Huts, was fined for selling ale to the workmen.

On 11 June 1872 the railway between Ayr and Cumnock and onward to Douglas was opened, initially just for cargo trains, in the main carrying coal to the harbour at Ayr. This passed through the parish to the south of the village. A station was formed on the Knockshiffnock road, though it was almost two miles from the village, and opened on Monday 1 July 1872. Stationmasters at the station included Thomas MacLeod, appointed when the line opened in 1872, who remained until he retired in July 1906. He died in 1917. He was replaced by David MacCardle, who had previously served at Auchincruive Station. In 1924 John R. Campbell left as stationmaster and was replaced by William MacLeod. The line was not busy for

3.3 Ochiltree Railway Station *(Author's Collection)*

passenger traffic, there only being two services heading eastwards each day, and two heading westward. The station was closed on 10 September 1951. The line remained for a number of years before being lifted.

3.4 Drongan Railway Station *(Author's Collection)*

A railway station was established at Drongan, located to the north of the village of Taiglum. The station had a single platform for the single-track line, but there were three sidelines where carriages or engines could be laid up. A station building was erected, accessed from the road from Gateside to Taiglum. The stationmaster for a time was Alexander Fowler (1840-1897), then Mr MacIver, who was replaced by Robert Glen (until 1909). Thomas Waugh was stationmaster before moving to Muirkirk in October 1939. He was badly wounded in the First World War. Like the station at Ochiltree, Drongan Station was closed in 1951.

A second railway line was constructed to the south-west of the parish, leaving the Ayr and Cumnock line at Belston Junction and heading past Sinclairston and Rankinston before joining the Ayr to Dalmellington line at the Holehouse Junction. Known as the Holehouse Branch, this railway was often used for transporting coal, but was never popular for passenger transport, the only station on the branch being at Rankinston. The line was laid around the end of 1872, and one source claims that it was made to allow waggons to bring iron ore from Cleator Moor in England to the ironworks at Waterside, though this may never have happened. This line was closed in 1951.

When Killoch Colliery was being sunk, a branch line was laid into the pit from Drongan. This line took as flat a route as was possible, to aid with the hauling of coal, and consequently followed a circuitous route around the low hillocks of the district. From Drongan the line swung round a low knoll south of Drongan House, then made its way across low ground towards West Tarelgin. The line passed under the main Ayr-Cumnock road by a bridge before swinging around another low knoll (which was to become the bing for Killoch, before arriving at the colliery to the north. Although Killoch Colliery is long-since closed, the branch railway survives, allowing open-cast coal to be transferred from lorry onto waggons at a coal disposal point.

CHAPTER FOUR

ESTATES AND LANDOWNERS

Ochiltree had three ancient castles within its present bounds - Ochiltree castle itself, Auchencloigh Castle and Drongan Castle. Prior to the separation of Stair parish, there was also the castle of Trabboch. At a later date a new Ochiltree Castle was erected adjoining the village, a fortified house with vaulted cellars. There also appears to have been a couple of other small places of defence – these being located at Waterton and Barquharrie. The following chapter gives details of the estates and ownership over time.

OCHILTREE CASTLE

In the twelfth century, King David I (reigned 1124-1153) granted feudal baronies to many of his loyal subjects. This was part of a scheme to keep the country in control, each baron being responsible for keeping the king's peace within their area, or barony. Ochiltree was one of the baronies created, and it was probably granted initially to the Colville family, though this cannot be confirmed. Certainly, the Colvilles have been noted as owners of the barony since the middle of the twelfth century. This family is reckoned to have come to Scotland in the early twelfth century, and in 1066 a Gilbert de Colleville, a Norman lord, arrived in England with William the Conqueror. His family are said to have originated from Coleville, a town near Caen in Normandy. Between arriving in England and settling in Scotland, the Colville appear to gained some English estates and titles.

Of the castle of Ochiltree, little can be accurately determined as to its extent, date, or style of construction. It is known that the original castle was located on a high headland above the Lugar Water, a mile and a half downstream from Ochiltree kirk. The exact site is no longer known, and old accounts often referred to the spot as comprising a few large stones, or occupied by some ancient trees.

PHILIP COLVILLE (fl. 1154-1208)

The earliest reference we have to an owner of the Barony of Ochiltree is Philip de Colville, the 'de' gradually being dropped. He is also noted as being the proprietor of the estates of Oxnam and Heiton in Roxburghshire, which had previously belonged to the Percies. He also had property in Ayrshire, and we may safely assume that this included the Barony of Ochiltree. During the reign of Malcolm IV he witnessed a number of charters dated 1154 and 1160. He was still witnessing other charters during the reign of William the Lion. In 1174, at the Treaty of Falaise, Philip Colville was one of the hostages passed over. He was still alive in 1200, when his name and that of his son appears as witnesses in a settlement of dispute between William Comyn and the Bishop of Glasgow. He probably also witnessed an agreement between the monks of Melrose and Patrick, Earl of Dunbar in 1208.

THOMAS COLVILLE (d. 1219)

Philip was succeeded by his son, Thomas Colville. The earliest reference to him dates from 1181, when he walked round the lands which had been granted to Melrose Abbey. In a charter dated after 1200 he granted some lands in Ayrshire to Melrose Abbey. In 1210 there was a plot against King William and Thomas Colville was alleged to have been complicit in this. He was captured and imprisoned in Edinburgh Castle. However, after being locked up for six months, his innocence was proven and he was allowed to go free. In 1215 Thomas was sent as a hostage to the court of King John of England. As a result he was held in Corfe Castle in Dorset until 1216. Thomas Colville died in 1219.

4.1 Colville arms
(Author's Collection)

Thomas Colville was married to Amabilis, by whom he had three sons and four daughters. The eldest son, Sir John Colville, succeeded to most of his estates. The second son, William, was to be given the church of Ochiltree by Sir John. The third son, Thomas, was given the Barony of Ochiltree by Sir John. He died without any legitimate children, and the barony was claimed by his elder brother, William. Sir John objected to William's claim on the barony, and gave the patronage of the church of Ochiltree to the Preceptory of Torphichen. The two brothers disputed the matter for some years, eventually William agreeing to pay the preceptory an annual pension. However, he died soon after.

SIR JOHN COLVILLE

Sir John Colville was the initial heir to Thomas Colville, but as mentioned above, he was to pass some of the properties to his brothers. As they both died without heirs, the properties returned to him and passed to his son, William Colville. Of Sir John Colville, very little is known about him, other than he was proprietor of both Ochiltree and Oxnam.

WILLIAM COLVILLE (d. c. 1280)

William succeeded to the Barony of Ochiltree on the death of his father, Sir John. However, he had four aunts, sisters of Sir John, who were to contest his right to the barony. The names of these four women are not known, but it is known that three of them were to marry men surnamed Heron, Maitland and Marshall. The fourth sister was unmarried. William was married to a daughter of Sir John de Normanville, by whom he had a son and daughter. William Colville died around 1280 and was succeeded by his son, Sir Thomas Colville. William was to grant the Barony of Ochiltree to his daughter, Eustacia Colville, along with the patronage of the church. She was to marry Reginald Le Cheyne as his second wife. They had no issue, and she outlived him by many years. In 1296 Eustacia Le Cheyne is listed in the Ragman's Roll of lairds who paid homage to Edward I of England. On 18 July 1316 Eustacia granted the church of Ochiltree to the monks of Melrose. At the time of the grant, she sent a document charting the history of the connection of her family with the church.

SIR THOMAS COLVILLE (d. c. 1322)
Sir Thomas Colville succeeded to most of the Colville lands, including Oxnam, Gosford in East Lothian, and some lands in Dumfriesshire. On the death of Eustacia Le Cheyne, he became proprietor of the Barony of Ochiltree once more. In the year 1297 Sir Thomas lived in England and appears to have supported the English monarch. He was given various commissions to raise troops to fight the Scots, before and after the Battle of Bannockburn in 1314. In 1319, once peace had settled on the two kingdoms, Sir Thomas Colville returned to Scotland. Robert I (the Bruce) granted him the lands of Whitsome in Berwickshire in 1320. Sir Thomas died sometime between his receiving the lands of Whitsome and 1324. He left three sons, William, the eldest, who was granted the lands of Spindleston and Botel in Northumberland. He died without issue, leaving his properties to his younger brother, Philip. The second son was Robert, who succeeded to the majority of the estates. The third son was Philip, who was married to Agnes Mordington, daughter of Peter Mordington of that Ilk. Agnes outlived Philip, and she was remarried to Henry Haliburton. Philip and Agnes had no issue, and the lands passed back to Robert Colville. It was reckoned that Henry Haliburton and his wife did not inherit them as they were 'rebels'.

The Colville lairds at this early period are difficult to organise and confirm, and we only get snapshots of their names in official documents. Known lairds include the following:

SIR ROBERT COLVILLE
Robert de Colville of Oxnam and Ochiltree lived in the first half of the fourteenth century. In 1324 he issued a charter confirming the grant of the church of Ochiltree and all its pertinents to the monks of Melrose Abbey.

THOMAS COLVILLE
Thomas Colville of Oxnam and Ochiltree is referred to around 1384. It is possible that he formed one of the many Scots barons who attended Margaret of Scotland when she was married to Louis, Dauphin of France, in 1436.

ROBERT COLVILLE
Reference is found to Robert Colville of Oxnam and Ochiltree in 1390.

ROBERT COLVILLE
Robert Colville was given a charter to the lands of Barnweill and Symington, on his own resignation, on 20 May 1441. He had a charter to the Barony of Ochiltree on the same date, when his father resigned it. He was married to Margaret Colville, who appears to have had a charter from her son, Robert Colville, of the lands of Cralelgyn (perhaps Tarelgin) in the Barony of Ochiltree, dated 10 September 1441. Robert appears to have been married twice, for on 16 February 1451 he had a charter of the Barony of Ochiltree in his name, as well as that of his spouse, Christina Crichton, daughter of Sir Robert Crichton of Sanquhar. It is thought that he had at least two sons, Richard, who was killed by the Earl of Douglas for killing John Auchinleck of that Ilk in 1449, and Sir Robert, who succeeded to Ochiltree.

Tradition relates the story of a feud which developed between the Colvilles of Ochiltree and the Auchinlecks of that Ilk in 1449. The story of the Auchinleck/Colville feud is one that has been passed down over the years, and which may, in part, be apocryphal, but which explains the feud, and subsequent murders which occurred around this period.

During the life of Robert, the Colvilles of Ochiltree became friendly with their near neighbours, the Auchinlecks of Auchinleck Castle. Auchinleck Castle and Ochiltree Castle stood on cliff-tops on either side of the Lugar Water, the former a little bit further upstream. To save the two families the trouble of crossing the ravine and often deep waters of the Lugar, they had a rope joining the two buildings, along which messages could be sent by means of a basket hanging from a pulley. Something caused a misunderstanding between Robert and James Auchinleck, so the latter sent over the bare bones of a sheep's skull in the basket, well wrapped up. Colville, thinking that the gift was an act of repentance by Auchinleck, had the basket brought to his main hall and opened before him. When he saw the disgusting remains of the sheep his temper grew and he vowed to get his own back. He managed to force an entrance into Auchinleck Castle and kill James Boswell. The rest of the family escaped and enlisted the help of the Douglas clan, who attacked the castle of Ochiltree and set it alight. This fact is said to have been confirmed by the finding of pieces of charred oak where the castle stood, said to have come from the roof timbers. Colville escaped from the building and tradition states that he and his son were slain by Douglas at Polshill Burn, in the parish of

New Cumnock, within a few days of Auchinleck's murder.

SIR ROBERT COLVILLE

Sir Robert succeeded his father as his elder brother had been killed. On 9 March 1477 he was given a charter to various lands within the Barony of Ochiltree. He was married and had at least two sons – Sir William, who succeeded, and Robert Colville of Hilton, in the Barony of Tillicoultry, Clackmannanshire. This Robert of Hilton was married to Margaret Logan, and they held a charter to Hilton, dated 16 October 1483.

SIR WILLIAM COLVILLE (d. 1509)

Sir William Colville of Oxnam and Ochiltree lived around 1498, at which time he feuded with Hugh Campbell of Loudoun, Sheriff of Ayr. As the Sheriff had the advantage of the law behind him in all disputes, Sir William received a declaration from the king that he and all of his tenants were to be granted exemption from the Sheriff's jurisdiction. The Colville-Campbell feud continued for some years. In 1502 Robert and Henry Douglas were permitted to compound for 'art and part of the oppression done to Sir William Colville of Uchiltree, in occupying, labouring, and manuring his lands of Farnesyde and Hardane, and taking and keeping the house or pele in Hardane without any title of law; and, item for the theft of iij oxen from the said Sir William Colville, furth of Synlawis.' Also in 1502 John and William Douglas were convicted for their 'art and part of oppression and convocation of the lieges, and coming upon Sir William Colville of Uchiltree, Knt., at his lands of Hardane-hede, in the year 1502'.

Sir William was murdered around 1509. On 20 November 1510 George Haliburton was put to the horn for 'art and part of the slaughter of Sir William Colville of Uchiltree (Knt.) and Richard Rutherfurde.'

Sir William appears to have left no male heirs, but his eldest daughter and co-heiress, Elizabeth, had married Sir Robert Colville of Ravenscraig in 1509. In that year a charter was issued to Robert Colville of Hiltoun of half of the Barony of Ochiltree, upon the resignation of Elizabeth Colville, eldest daughter and one of the heirs of the late William Colville of Ochiltree, knight, with consent of her spouse, Robert Colville, son and heir of William Colville of Ravenscraig, 10 April 1509. The second daughter, Margaret Colville, was married to Patrick Colquhoun of Drumskeith. Patrick and Margaret Colquhoun had a daughter, Francisca, who was married to Robert Colville, a natural son of Sir James Colville of Easter Wemyss.

SIR ROBERT COLVILLE (d. 1513)

Sir Robert Colville of Hiltoun succeeded to the estate. He was appointed as Director of the Chancery at the accession of King James IV and Keeper of the Quarter-seal, or 'testimony' of the Great Seal, by letters dated 17 June 1488. At times he acted as Steward to James IV's consort, Queen Margaret, and was Master of the Household to James IV.

In 1513 Sir Robert raised the standard at Ochiltree Cross and led some men-at-arms in support of the crown. He went with King James IV to the ill-fated Battle of Flodden, where he was killed on the battlefield. He left Sir James, who succeeded, and two other sons, William Colville and Robert Colville. Robert Colville became Commendator of Culross Abbey, certainly by 1539. William Colville appears to have succeeded as abbot at Culross, and in 1544 was a Lord of Session (spiritual side). He was Comptroller from 1546-50. He joined the Reformers, and when the Confession of Faith was ratified in August 1560, he was one of the Lords of the Articles. He died in 1566.

SIR JAMES COLVILLE (d. c. 1540)

Sir Robert's son, Sir James Colville, succeeded to Ochiltree and Hiltoun. He spent much of his life in public service, being knighted for this. He served as Comptroller from 1525 and Director of Chancery in 1527. In 1530 Sir James Colville transferred the barony of Ochiltree to Sir James Hamilton of Finnart in exchange for the barony of East Wemyss and Lochoreshire in Fife. In 1532, upon the instruction of the College of Justice, he was nominated as one of the Lords of Session, taking as his title on the bench, Lord Easter-Wemyss. In this office he appears to have offered assistance and counsel to the Douglases, much against the King's pleasure. As a result he was deprived of his offices in 1539. On 21 August 1539 he was ordered to enter himself as ward, or prisoner, in Blackness Castle, but instead he left the country. He spent much of the time with the Earl of Angus and Sir George Douglas, but it appears that he died not long after. On 10 January 1541 a summons was executed against Margaret Forrester, his widow, and children, to see and hear it discerned that 'the said deceased James Colville, while he lived, had incurred the crime of lese Majestie, for his disobediences to enter himself in ward'. On 14 March 1541 his estate was forfeited and annexed to the Crown.

The Colville family, although they had exchanged the Barony of Ochiltree with Sir James Hamilton, retained an affection for the area, and when on 4 January 1651 Robert Colville of Cleish was raised to the peerage by Charles I, he took the title Lord Colvill (or Colville) of Ochiltree. He died in 1662 and was succeeded by his nephew, Robert Colville, 2nd Lord Colville of Ochiltree (died 1671). The 3rd Lord Colville of Ochiltree was the eldest son, also Robert. He was opposed to the Union of Parliaments in 1707. He died on 25 March 1728, when it is thought that the title became extinct. However, a distant relative, or so he claimed, David Colville, assumed the title. He died in 1782. His cousin, Robert Colvill, then claimed the title, but in 1788 it was proved that the two cousins were, in fact, not related to the original lords Colville.

SIR JAMES HAMILTON OF FINNART

Sir James Hamilton retained Ochiltree for just four years, before he transferred the ownership to Andrew Stewart, 3rd Lord Avondale, in exchange for the barony of Evandale or Avondale, in 1534.

ANDREW STEWART, 1st LORD OCHILTREE (d. c. 1548)

Andrew Stewart, 3rd Lord Avondale or Evandale, was the eldest son of Andrew Stewart, 2nd Lord Avondale, Lord of the Bedchamber to King James IV, and his wife, Margaret Kennedy, daughter of John, Lord Kennedy. The 2nd Lord Avondale was killed at Flodden in 1513. The 3rd Lord Avondale took the side of the Queen Mother during the minority of James V. The Queen Mother was to marry Andrew's brother, Henry Stewart, and he gained the title, Lord Methven. In 1525 Andrew received a pardon for his part in fighting against the Regent, John, Duke of Albany. With Andrew Stewart's affairs becoming rather too involved, he exchanged his lands of Avondale (around Strathaven in Lanarkshire) with Sir James Hamilton of Finnart's Ochiltree property. The change of property was confirmed by a charter under the Great Seal of 2 September 1534.

By an Act of Parliament of 15 March 1543, Andrew Stewart was created Lord Stewart of Ochiltree, or, more commonly, Lord Ochiltree. The act, in part, states that he is 'to be callit, he and his successiouris in tyme to cum, Lord Stewart of Oycheltree, and to haif vote and place in the parliament as utheris lordis of the realme aught and sould half in ye samin, haif and all honouris and dignities efferand thereto'. He was sometime prior to 22 August 1515 to marry Margaret Hamilton, 'filia notha' to James, Earl of Arran, one of his many illegitimate children. At the time of the wedding the couple had confirmation of the lands of Glengavel, in the parish of Avondale, Lanarkshire. By her he had three known children: Andrew, born about 1521, who succeeded as 2nd Lord Ochiltree; Walter Stewart, 'submersus'; and Isobel, who was the first wife of Duncan MacFarlane of that Ilk.

The 1st Lord Ochiltree is also thought to have had two illegitimate children – Sir Robert Stewart and William Stewart. Sir Robert Stewart received a charter under the Great Seal on 1 September 1542 making him legitimate. He is known to have fought in France on the side of the Huguenots, but was killed in battle. The other illegitimate son, William Stewart, is known to have 'went with Sir Andro Keth [Keith], the Lord of Dyngwell', perhaps to Sweden.

It may have been the first Lord Ochiltree who built the new castle of Ochiltree near to the present village. This would have been a fortified tower, the remains of which were still in existence in 1856 when the Ordnance Survey mapmakers visited the village. They noted that the ruins were adjoining the later Ochiltree House, and must have been roofless for many years, 'as there are large trees growing within it'. The ruinous walls were still standing to twelve feet in height in places, and the walls were about six feet thick. Internally, the building was divided into apartments, and it was noted that the remains of a vaulted roof survived.

The 1st Lord Ochiltree died about 1548.

ANDREW STEWART, 2nd LORD OCHILTREE (c. 1520-c. 1591)

Andrew Stewart succeeded as the 2nd Lord Ochiltree about the age of 27. He was known as a zealous reformer, and in 1533 he was accused before the Bishop of Glasgow of casting down images that he deemed unacceptable in the church of Ayr. For his devout support of the protestant cause he was often called 'the Good Lord Ochiltree'. He was married before 1549 to Agnes Cuninghame – the couple were given a charter to the lands of Pennymore in Ochiltree parish, dated 27 March 1549. Agnes, Lady Ochiltree, was mentioned in a charter concerning lands in Ochiltree in January 1557. In it she is stated to have been 'filia domini de Caprington', or sister to the laird of Caprington Castle, near Kilmarnock. She was the daughter of John Cuninghame, 5th of Caprington. Andrew and Agnes had five sons and two daughters.

Soon after inheriting Ochiltree Castle and estate, on 25 May 1549, Andrew, 2nd Lord Stewart of Ochiltree, was pursued by a few local landowners who were intent on murdering him. These were John Lockhart of Barr (Galston), his full brother, John Lockhart (who did have the same Christian name) and Charles Campbell of Skerrington in Old Cumnock. On 15 July 1550 the three perpetrators were denounced as rebels and put to the horn.

In 1555 Stewart is known to be one of Rev John Knox's staunchest supporters. He and the minister were to remain friends for the rest of their lives. When Rev John Knox was interviewed by Mary Queen of Scots at Holyrood, Lord Stewart was in attendance.

In 1559 Lord Ochiltree took part in the march to Perth by the Lords of the Congregation, of which he was one. This group was 2,000 strong, and they were there to negotiate with the Queen Regent, Mary of Guise.

Stewart opposed the marriage of Queen Mary to Lord Bothwell and for his protection fled to England. After the murder of David Riccio on 9 March 1566, which he was not involved with, but 'consented unto his death', Ochiltree returned to Scotland, taking part in the Battle of Langside, south of Glasgow, on 13 May 1568. He fought against Mary, Queen of Scots, suffering wounds, being 'sore hurt and in danger of his life … receiving his chief wound with a sword in his neck, given by the Lord Herri[e]s'.

Lord Ochiltree was close to the household of King James VI, becoming a member of the Privy Council and one of the Lords of the Articles in 1578. In later years he was decried as the father of the King's favourite, James, Earl of Arran, 'and some others of ill government. His own lyuinge and power of lyttle value.' For a time little is recorded about Lord Stewart, but in 1592 he is listed as Warden and

Lieutenant of the Borders. In 1593 he was patron of the parish church of St John's Town of Dalry in Galloway. The second Lord Ochiltree died about the year 1594.

At the Reformation, Andrew Stewart appropriated the church lands of Ochiltree for himself. He also obtained from David Crichton, vicar at the time, the patronage of the parish church, a charter of fee farming of the church lands of Ochiltree, excluding the vicar's glebe and garden. The grant was agreed to by the Commendator of Melrose Abbey and was later confirmed in a charter from the Great Seal of King James VI, dated 10 May 1567.

The 2nd Lord Ochiltree was married for a second time (sometime between August 1570 and February 1573) to Margaret Cunyngham or Cunningham, widow of John Wallace of Craigie Castle (he died August 1570). She was the daughter of Alexander Cunningham, 4th Earl of Glencairn, who died in June 1573, and his wife, Janet, daughter of James Hamilton, Earl of Arran. Margaret, Lady Ochiltree, died in 1574.

The 2nd Lord Ochiltree had a number of children. Andrew, his eldest son, was styled the Master of Ochiltree, but he predeceased his father in 1577. The second son, Captain James Stewart, originally styled 'of Bothwellmuir', was a favourite of the young James VI, and he was created the 1st Earl of Arran of a new patent on 22 April 1581. He was married to Elizabeth Stewart, daughter of the 4th Earl of Atholl, by whom he had five children. Arran was described as being 'profligate and audacious'. He became the Lord High Chancellor of Scotland and was instrumental in the execution of Regent Morton for his part in the murder of Lord Darnley. Lord Arran was making his way to Ochiltree on 5 December 1595 when he was approached by Sir James Douglas of Torthorwald (Dumfriesshire) and murdered. Lord Arran's eldest son, Sir James Stewart of Killeith was to become the 4th Lord Ochiltree.

The third son was Sir William Stewart of Monkton, who was given the barony of Carstairs in 1587. He was murdered by Francis Stewart, Earl of Bothwell, in Edinburgh's High Street in July 1588. The fourth son was Henry Stewart who was married about 1580 to Janet Reid, second daughter of Adam Reid of Barskimming. The fifth son was Robert Stewart of Pitheavlis, also known as Halltoun of Luncartie. Both he and his elder brother, Henry, were each granted 2,000 acres of land in Ulster in 1609. Robert Stewart was married in 1586 to Jean Ross, daughter of John Ross of Craigie. Their eldest son, William, was given a charter dated 2 April 1622 to the superiority of the lands of Easter Polquhairn.

On 2 July 1579, King James VI sent a letter to the Earl of Eglinton and Lord Boyd requesting them to use their endeavours to settle a controversy that existed between the sons of Lord Ochiltree and family of the deceased Charles Mowat.

The 2nd Lord Ochiltree also had a few daughters. The eldest, Isobel, is said to have been married to Thomas Kennedy of Bargany. The third daughter was named Bethia. There was also an illegitimate daughter, Elizabeth, who received legitimation papers on 31 March 1585.

The second daughter of the 2nd Lord Ochiltree, Margaret Stewart, was married as a young girl to Rev John Knox, the famous reformer. He was 59 years old at the time, and it is said that his enemies attributed her marriage to his skill in witchcraft:

> Rydand there with ane gret court, on ane trim gelding, nocht lyke ane prophet or ane auld decrepit priest, as he was, but lyke as he had been ane of the bluid royal, with his bendes of taffetie feschnit with golden ringis and precious stones, and, as is plainly reportit in the country, be sorcerie and witchcraft did sua allure that puir gentlewoman that scho sould not leve without him: whilk appears of gret probabilitie, scho being ane damsel of nobel bluid, and he ane auld decrepit cretur of maist base degree of onie that could be found in the countrie. Sua that sik ane nobel hous could not have degenerat sua far except Johann Knox had interposit the power of his maister the devil quha, as he transfigures himself sometimes into ane angel of licht, sua he causit Johan Knox appear ane of the maist nobel and lustie of onie that could be found in the countrie.

They also accused him of trying to get at the Crown in marrying a Stewart. The wedding took place in March 1564 within the old kirk of Ochiltree. Some accounts, however, claim that they were married in Ochiltree Castle, or House, at the bottom of the village. If this was the case, it would have been in the old tower that stood there prior to the later house which survived for many years. In the nineteenth century one of the rooms within the house was pointed out as being the chamber in which the wedding took place, but this was probably apocryphal. Lord Stewart is said to have given Knox, by way of a dowry, Pennymore farm, or, as some say, a bond upon the farm to the value of 800 merks. This was left by Knox in his will to his wife, or else to her three daughters, whom failing to return to Lord Ochiltree. Margaret was to marry for a second time, on 8 January 1574, to Sir Andrew Ker of Faldonside.

Rev John Knox and Margaret Stewart had three daughters – Martha (1565-1592), Margaret (b. 1567) and Elizabeth (1570-1622). Knox and Margaret's youngest daughter, Elizabeth, married Rev John Welsh, minister of Ayr, in 1594. She died at Ayr in January 1622. Rev John Knox died on 24 November 1572.

Andrew, the Master of Ochiltree, died before September 1578. He had been married to Margaret Stewart, daughter of Henry, 1st Lord Methven, sometime before 9 March 1567. Even although she did not officially become Lady Ochiltree, she seems to have been given the name by many others, perhaps being made official as she is referred to as this in a document from King James VI in which he grants her a pension of 700 merks. This was for having served his queen for thirteen years, from the time she arrived in Denmark to the time she moved to England. The document also states that it was for 'her carefull and duetifull attendance upon the late queene and thair royal children in thair young and tender age'. She was to marry for a second time, to Uchtred MacDowall of Garthland. She died on 1 January 1627.

Andrew, Master of Ochiltree, and his wife had eleven children. The eldest son, also Andrew, was to succeed his grandfather as the 3rd Lord Ochiltree. The second son, Josias Stewart, was a witness to a charter on 26 December 1587. He was probably given the lands of Bonnyton within Ochiltree parish, as he is referred to as being 'of Bonyngtoun'. In 1604 he was referred to as Josias Stewart of Wester Polquhairn. He was married to Mariota Finlayson, by whom he had at least one daugher, Margaret. She was to marry Thomas Kennedy of Bargany, but their married life was subject to numerous disputes, many of which were recorded in the Privy Council Register.

The Master of Ochiltree's third son was William Stewart, who appears to have lived in Ayr. He was married to Marion MacAlexander, certainly by 1614. In that year he witnessed a Procuratory of Resignation by the minister of Ayr, Rev William Birny, of the Blackfriars lands to the Burgh of Ayr. Another brother was John Stewart, who is referred to in a legal document in 1605. Margaret Stewart was married to John Stewart of Traquair, Peeblesshire. Anne Stewart was married on 20 October 1584 to Sir Andrew Kerr, 1st Lord Jedburgh (1565-1633). Marjory was married to Sir Roger Ashton, Gentleman of the Bedchamber to King James I. Martha Stewart was married to Nichol Rutherford of Hundalee at Jedburgh in Roxburghshire. Jean, or perhaps Anna, or Janet, was married on 6 January 1596 to Gilbert Kennedy, heir of Thomas Kennedy of Bargany. He died in 1601 and she died a widow at Stilton, on her way back north from London, in 1605. She was buried in the Kennedy vault at Ballantrae. Two other daughters known were Agnes and Susanna, the latter executor of her mother's will, 1627.

ANDREW STEWART, 3rd LORD OCHILTREE (1560-1628)

Andrew Stewart was born in 1560. He succeeded his grandfather, the 'Good Lord' Ochiltree, around 1593.

Andrew, Lord Ochiltree, was very much involved in the political struggles of the last decade of the sixteenth century. He was involved in the many feuds which resulted in the murder of the 'Bonny Earl of Moray' by the Earl of Huntly on 7 February 1592. Ochiltree had been sent to negotiate a truce between Moray and Huntly. He travelled to Darnaway Castle in Moray, where he persuaded the earl to return south with him. Moray agreed, and the two were in a party that made its way south to Donibristle House, on the southern shores of Fife. The earl remained there, whereas Ochiltree made his way to the royal court, informing the king that

Moray had submitted himself to the king's order (he had probably been offered a pardon if he did so). Word from the court leaked, and Huntly discovered Moray's whereabouts. He made his way to Donibristle, where he murdered Moray.

After the murder of Moray, Lord Ochiltree made suggestions that as he had not betrayed Moray's whereabouts, the king must have done so. The king was angry at this inference and denied it. To keep himself from further implication he silenced Ochiltree and had him imprisoned. To change the direction of anger, he ordered the homes of the Gordon lairds who were supposed to have assisted in the murder to be destroyed, commissioning Ochiltree to carry this out. Accordingly, he led a group of men to the north-east, where they burned a series of castles and homes. A later proposal to murder Huntly was thwarted when King James placed Ochiltree under house arrest. He also joined the side of Francis, Earl of Bothwell. King James 'had ever great favour and liking for the Lord Ochiltree, and used all means and occasions to persuade and draw the said Lord from the Earl of Bothwell's company'. In time, King James pardoned Ochiltree for his part in the murder.

Lord Ochiltree was close to the king, and served as a member of the Council, was First Lord of the Bedchamber, Governor of Edinburgh Castle, and General of the Ordnance.

Andrew, Lord Ochiltree, obtained a grant in 1601 of the church lands remaining in Ochiltree, known as the Vicar's Holm. With this he also obtained the 'advowson, donation, and patronage of the parsonage and vicarage of Ochiltree'. This was later confirmed in an act of parliament in 1606.

In 1608 Lord Ochiltree was appointed as the king's lieutenant over the Western Isles. He led an expedition to the Hebrides that year in a plan to overpower the clan chiefs. He was able to trick many of them into being arrested, and after a period in prison they agreed to attend a conference on the Island of Iona, at which they were subject to curbs to their power.

Lord Ochiltree's finances became seriously compromised, and he decided to settle in County Tyrone in Northern Ireland, on lands that had become escheated. These were granted to him by the king in 1609. With mounting debt, he consulted his son, daughter-in-law and his own wife, before deciding to sell the estate of Ochiltree in 1615 to his cousin, Sir James Stewart of Killeith, eldest son of the Earl of Arran. He also resigned the title of Lord Ochiltree to the king, who granted it to Sir James. The charter, dated 7 June 1615, names him as 'Domino Jacobo Stewart of Killeith, milit. et heredibus suis masculis'. Sir James was married and had an only son, William, who was to become the second Lord Stewart of this creation. However, he died in 1675 under age, and with him the title became extinct.

Lord Ochiltree in Ireland was granted 3,000 acres in 1609 by King James VI as a reward for his work in the Western Isles. He became one of the main planters of Ulster, and he settled there in 1611, living at Roughan Castle or Irry, later to be renamed Stuart Hall.

The original 3rd Lord Ochiltree was given a new title by James VI on 7 November 1619, Baron Castle Stuart, in the county of Tyrone, with remainder to the heirs-male of his body. He died in January 1628.

The 3rd Lord Ochiltree and 1st Lord Castle Stuart had been married to his cousin, Margaret Kennedy, daughter of Sir John Kennedy of Blairquhan. In 1600 she was appointed as governess to the newly-born Prince James, later to become King James VII. Lord Ochiltree and Margaret had at least six children. Sir Andrew Stewart, the eldest, was Master of Ochiltree, but did not become Lord Ochiltree as his father sold the title. He was created a Nova Scotian baronet in 1628 and was to succeed his father as 2nd Lord Castle Stuart. He received his education in France under Mr Welsh, son-in-law of Rev John Knox. He died in 1639. John Stewart was the second son, and in time became 5th Lord Castle Stuart. The third son, Robert, had a family who were eventually to become Earls Castle Stewart. There were three daughters, Margaret, who married George Craufurd of Leifnoreis in the parish of Old Cumnock (and latterly of Crawfurdsburn, County Down); Maria, who was married on 7 June 1615 to John Kennedy of Blairquhan; and Anna Stewart, who died unmarried.

SIR JAMES STEWART OF KILLEITH – 4TH LORD OCHILTREE

In 1615 the Barony of Ochiltree was purchased by Sir James Stewart of Killeith, a cousin of Lord Stewart, son of Captain James Stewart. Sir James was the eldest son of James, Earl of Arran. However, he failed to inherit the Earldom of Arran, due to his father's behaviour and the title being removed from him and restored to the Hamilton family. Instead, he purchased the title, Lord Ochiltree, becoming the 4th Lord. James VI wrote from Greenwich to the Privy Council on 27 May 1615, noting that he wished him to 'injoy all the honnouris, dignities, and privileges belonging to the Lordship of Uchiltree in als large and ampill manner as the said Lord might have done before his demission, to continew with him and his posteritie.' Accordingly, a charter was issued to Stewart on 7 June 1615.

In 1620 a charter from King James VI to James Stewart, 4th Lord Ochiltree, confirms the extent of the estate at that time:

> Terras et baroniam de Uchiltrie (viz. terras dominicales [lie Maynes] de Uchiltrie extendentes ad 7½ mercat. terrarum, cum castro, manerie loco, lie Dainholmes, molendino, lie Mylneholmes, piscationibus, urbe seu villa vocata Clauchantoun et ejus acris &c, 2 mercat. terrarum de Burnokheid, 2½ mercatas de Darntaggart et Hannaystoun, cum molendino vocato Newmylne, terris molendinariis &c, 4 mercat. de Knokschifnoches, 4 mercat. de Penstaninie, 4 mercat. de Croftheid et Barquharrie, mercatam de Palmerstoun, mercatam de Know, 23 sol. 4

den. de Brigmark, ½ mercat. de Burnemouth, 4 mercat. de Leflamnokis [vel Leflumnock], 4 mercat. de Auchincloiche et Bent, cum turre et manerie loco, 4 mercat. de Plaid, 4 mercat. de Burnokstoun, 3 mercat. de Fynlaystoun, 3 mercatas de Carbeg [vel Tarbeg], 3 mercatas de Lesnassok [vel Lesnessok], 3 mercatas de Claignoch, cum molendino, terris molendinariis &c, 20 sol. de Killoche, 4 mercatas de Terrelgin, mercatam de Clandiehill, 40 den. de Glenlurkan [vel Glenturkan], 20 sol. de Corslat, 20 sol. de Glencaber [vel Glengaber], 3 mercat. de Craigoch, 4 mercat. de Bartuok [vel Balturk], 4 mercat. de Pennymoir, 2 mercatas de Towquhallane [vel Cowquhallane], 1 mercatam de Meikle Jokistoun alias Newintak, 10 sol. 4 den. de Hill, 40 sol. de Gallilie, 2 mercat. de Auchinlin, 2 mercatas de Glenconner, mercatam de Rattounraw, 2 mercatas de Barlosche, 16 sol. de Gargowne, 2 mercat. de Auchinbay, mercatam de Plotcok, 10 sol. de Nether Craigoch, mercatam de Steill, 2 mercat. de Overglen, cum castris, maneriebus locis, molendinis, piscationibus, carbonibus, tenentibus &c, et advocatione beneficiorum, cum terris ecclesiasticis de Uchiltrie nuncupatis Vicarisholme, advocatione rectorie et vicarie ecclesie parochialis de Uchiltrie cum earundem decimis et devoriis), vic. Air.

Sir James Stewart served as Lord Chamberlain and Sheriff of Orkney. He also held a nine-year tack of the Earldom of Orkney, which brought him considerable wealth. It is said that he established a colony in Nova Scotia in Canada in 1629, but this was short-lived. In 1639 he was sentenced to life imprisonment for 'leasing making' - having accused the Marquis of Hamilton of an attempt at seizing the Scottish throne. The feud between Ochiltree and Hamilton had been long-standing. He was sent to Blackness Castle on the Firth of Forth, in 1631, where he was held prisoner for over twenty years. He was set free by the English in 1652, after the Battle of Worcester. However, during his twenty-one years' imprisonment he had lost his fortune and needed to sell all of his estates.

Sir James was married twice. His first wife was Katherine MacDowall, daughter of Uchtred MacDowall of Mondurk, and sister of John MacDowall of Garthland. She was the widow of Hew Kennedy, Master of Cassillis. Sir James' second wife was Mary Livingstone, aunt of George Livingstone of Gairdoch. On 25 January 1675 she received a pension of £14 Scots annually for life from the exchequer. She died in February 1683.

Sir James Stewart died in 1659. He had at least seven children by his two wives. The eldest son, William, Master of Ochiltree, predeceased him in 1645. He made his sister, Jean, executor of his will, in which he left his aunt Marie, 'good wife of Killeith', 1,100 merks Scots. Jean was married to a William Stewart, perhaps the

William Stewart of Corrogan, her cousin. A second daughter was named Doratie and a third, Isabel. There may also have been a daughter named Margaret.

By the second wife, Mary Livingstone, Stewart had a second William. He also had a daughter, Katherine, who was retoured as heir on 9 June 1696 to George Livingstone of Gairdoch, son of William Livingstone, her uncle. Another daughter was Anna, born on 10 April 1653. She was married on 6 January 1676 to John Murdoch, apothecary and burgess of Edinburgh. Anna had the 'especial advyce and consent of her said mother' to this marriage. There were also twins born to the 4th Lord Ochiltree and his second wife – Robert and Rachael – on 13 January 1656.

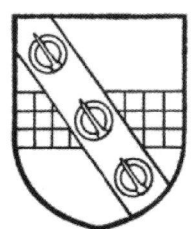

4.2 Stewart of Ochiltree arms
(Author's Collection)

It may have been Sir James Stewart of Killeith who built Ochiltree House during the period he was well-off and before he was sent to jail. The old building is thought to have dated from the early seventeenth century and was built in the fortified style common amongst lairds in Scotland at that time. Whether or not there was an older building on site is not known. The oldest part of the house formed a rectangle lying in a north-west/south-east alignment. At the south-eastern end, a wing extended to the north-east. The ground floor of the building was vaulted, indicative of its age. The western block had four vaults on the ground floor, reached from a common passage. The vaulted cellar at the southern extremity of the house was the original kitchen, the fireplace in its wide arch having a flue through the thick gable end. The wing was also vaulted, there being probably two vaults in this part of the house. In the re-entrant angle was a stair tower, though this was probably rebuilt at a later date.

The upper floor of the house was reached by the stairway, and here would have been a great hall and perhaps ancillary rooms. The stair continued to the second floor, where the main bedrooms were located, and on to the rooms located in the garret or roofspace. The walls of Ochiltree House were plain, being harled over, though the gables had corbie-steps, with ball finials on the uppermost one. The windows were gernerally small, but over the years they were probably widened. They had a simple roll-moulding around them. At one time there were dormer windows in the roof, over which were stone pediments, ornamentally carved. These were removed from the house at some period, probably in the late nineteenth century, and were left in a round flower bed. The carvings, whether of dates, initials or arms, were indecipherable in the 1930s.

WILLIAM STEWART, 5TH LORD OCHILTREE (1659-1675)

William Stewart, son of the second marriage of the fourth lord, was still a young man when he succeeded to the title. The lands of Ochiltree had been sold by this time. He was described as a 'very hopeful young man'. He attended the University of Edinburgh, but died there at the age of sixteen on 12 February 1675. He was interred the following day within the Abbey Kirk of Holyroodhouse. The title has remained dormant since.

Although unconnected with the parish of Ochiltree, it may be worth recording that in 1768 Andrew Thomas Stewart-Moore made a claim to the title. This failed, though he did manage to establish his right to be the 9th Baron Castle Stuart in the Irish peerage. In 1791-92 he claimed the peerage of Ochiltree once more, but this was not sufficiently proven for him to be recognised as such. In 1800 he was created 1st Earl Castle Stewart, and his descendants continue to bear that title.

SIR ARCHIBALD STEWART OF BLACKHALL

Ownership of Ochiltree estate passed through a number of hands over a short period of time. Sir Archibald Stewart 10th (or 11th) of Blackhall and Ardgowan (c. 1585-1665) acquired the estate of Ochiltree. He married, firstly, Margaret Blair, and secondly, Margaret Home. He succeeded to the properties of his father in 1612 and was knighted by Charles I around 1636. He sold the estate in 1647 to William Cochrane, who became 1st Lord Cochrane of Dundonald.

WILLIAM COCHRANE, 1st EARL OF DUNDONALD (1605-1685)

Ochiltree estate was acquired by William, 1st Lord Cochrane of Dundonald. He was a close friend of Charles I, having been knighted by the king in 1641, and on 26 December 1647 was raised to the peerage as the 1st Lord Cochrane of Dundonald. He actively raised soldiers across the county to form two regiments which took part in the 'Engagement', an attempt at restoring Charles I's authority by invading England on his behalf. In return, Charles I would accept Presbyterianism for Scottish church government, as demanded by the Covenanters, as well as introduce it to England on a three-year trial. The attempt failed, and for his part the presbytery of Ayr refused to allow Cochrane to renew the Solemn League and Covenant for his participation.

In 1651, when Charles II came to Scotland, Lord Cochrane was active in running the Scottish forces and also the coinage. He also raised men across Ayrshire and Renfrewshire for the king's army, and the monarch himself led at the Battle of Worcester. Cochrane was to purchase the lordship of Paisley from the Earl of Angus for £160,000 Scots in 1653, and he moved there to live. Cromwell fined him £1,666 13s 4d Sterling under an Ordinance of Pardon, however, Cochrane was also to contribute £20,900 to General Monck to assist in the restoration of Charles II.

Charles succeeded in reclaiming the crown in 1660. He appointed Lord Cochrane to the Privy Council and on 12 May 1669 he raised him in the peerage to the dignity of an earl – creating him Earl of Dundonald. Two lesser titles were also conferred on him – Lord Cochrane of Paisley and Lord Cochrane of Ochiltree. He was married (sometime before 1634) to Euphame Scott, daughter of Sir William Scott of Ardross and Elie (Fife), Director of Chancery. The Earl of Dundonald died in 1685 at the age of eighty. He was buried at Dundonald.

The 1st Earl of Dundonald and his wife had two sons and three daughters. The eldest son, William, styled Lord Cochrane, predeceased him in 1679/80 and was also buried at Dundonald. He had married Catherine Kennedy, daughter of John, 6th Earl of Cassillis, by whom he had John, who succeeded, William Cochrane of Kilmaronock, and three daughters – Margaret (married Alexander, 9th Earl of Eglinton); Helen (married to John, 16th Earl of Sutherland); and Jean (married to John Graham of Claverhouse, 1st Viscount of Dundee and subsequently to William Livingstone of Kilsyth).

Lord Dundonald was succeeded in the title and most of the estates by his grandson, John Cochrane. The lands of Ochiltree were given by the 1st Earl of Dundonald to his second son, Sir John Cochrane.

SIR JOHN COCHRANE

Sir John Cochrane was the second son of the 1st Earl of Dundonald. He was educated at the University of Glasgow, where his name appears on a roll of 1653. Sir John Cochrane was married in St Paul's, Covent Garden, in March 1656 to Margaret, daughter of Sir William Strickland, 1st Baronet of Boynton, Yorkshire, by whom he had four sons and two daughters. Strickland was one of Oliver Cromwell's Lords of Parliament. John Cochrane was gifted the estate of Ochiltree by his father. Cochrane was knighted in 1669 and soon after was elected as Member of Parliament for the county of Ayr.

Sir John was a devout Covenanter, and actively supported the cause of religious freedom. In June 1672 he and Ochiltree parish were fined 3,000 merks for non-conformity, the money to be paid to the curate. In 1678 he was one of a number of nobles and lairds who wrote to the Duke of Monmouth to complain of the miseries of Scotland at that time. In June 1679 Sir John Cochrane of Ochiltree and his son, John of Waterside, were denounced as fugitives and were put to the horn. He was active at the Battle of Bothwell Bridge in 1679, at which he narrowly escaped imprisonment. He and the Duke of Hamilton made their way south to speak with the king, hoping to persuade him to be more lenient on his Scottish subjects, but to no avail.

In 1679 Sir John is noted as joining a few other Ayrshire landowners, including Lords Loudoun and Cochrane, in denouncing the practice of holding armed conventicles in the area, at which preachers, many of whom were never proper ministers in the church, were said to instigate 'schism, separation and rebellion'.

Although a supporter of the Covenanters, a traditional tale links Cochrane with the death of Rev Richard Cameron. Sir John was granted ten thousand merks (about £550) for informing Sir Andrew Bruce of Earlshall about the Covenanters who were hiding on Airds Moss. Cochrane had been watching the movements of Rev Richard Cameron and passed word to Bruce where he was to be found. Bruce met the Covenanters at Airds Moss, in the parish of Auchinleck, and during a short battle, nine Covenanters were to be killed. It was 22 June 1680. The head and hands of Cameron were severed from his body in order to claim the reward that had been placed on them. Bruce was later to be given £500 for his victory. Ochiltree House mysteriously went on fire two days later. Tradition says that a burning cross came from the heavens and destroyed the building and most of its contents. It is reckoned that many ancient charters and artefacts were lost at this time. An old account reads, 'That morning wherein the house of Ochiltree took fire, about two in the afternoon; wherein furniture, plate and charters were all burnt to ashes (and so remains to this day) as twelve men were going to bring lime about break of day, they saw the likeness of a bloody fiery pillar, as the apprehended, about two yards in length: which made them conclude, that it was Mr Cameron's blood, and the blood of them that were killed with him at Airds-moss. The said laird of Ochiltree had given information to the enemy where they were to be found; for which, it was said, he received ten thousand merks, the price of blood.' The original part of the house was never rebuilt, the later Ochiltree House being erected alongside. Young John Cochrane is said to have told his father that 'This is the vengeance of Cameron's blood which you sold.'

Another strange tradition concerning the burning of the castle was long told by residents of the village. Apparently, prior to the house being consumed by fire, the rats which formerly occupied its cellars and holes in the walls left the building en masse. They made their way up Mill Street, looking for new homes. One rat was apparently blind, and it is said that it held a straw in its mouth, either end of which was held by rats which could see, thereby directing the blind rat to safety.

In 1682 Sir John Cochrane joined a number of fellow Covenanting lairds in a plan to acquire 12,000 acres of land from the king in Carolina, United States. These fellow Covenanters were Robert Baillie of Jerviswood (Lanark), George Campbell of Cessnock (Ayrshire) and Sir Hugh Campbell of Cessnock. They planned to establish a new Scots colony there, populated in the main by Covenanters – both transportees and voluntary emigrants. In a letter he wrote that he intended 'to bring over such a strength of people that according to the advice wee have had at London it will be our great advantage and greatly for the support of all that is there already planted'.

Cochrane was alleged to have taken part in the Rye House Plot in 1683, which planned the executuon of Charles II and his brother, James, Duke of York. The Johns Cochrane, father and son, were listed on the 'Porteous rolls' - names of folk implicated in this. Sir John wrote to the Chancellor claiming that he was erroneously listed, and boasted of his part in tracking down the Cameronians. John of Waterside had to flee to Holland for his own safety. In December 1684

Sir George MacKenzie of Rosehaugh was instructed to commence a process of forfeiture against Cochrane. He spent some time in Holland with other like-minded Covenanters.

On 8 April 1684, Sir John Cochrane and John Cochrane of Waterside were charged with having, in June 1679, joined Robert MacLellan of Barscobe (Galloway) and a party of rebels of five or six hundred, and having ridden with them, supplying them with wine and other provisions. On 9 April the Lords continued the process of forfeiture, till the second Monday of July. John of Waterside was indicted and witnesses adduced. John Black, smith in Duncanziemere (parish of Auchinleck), claimed that he saw Waterside with the rebels in Cumnock, at the Barrhill, but did not hear him speak to either Alexander Gordon of Earlstoun or MacLellan of Barscobe. Another witness claimed to have seem him walking with the rebels, carrying a small sword. The court found Waterside guilty of treason, and ordained to be executed and demeaned as a traitor when he was apprehended.

In 1684 proceedings were drawn up against Sir John Cochrane, his son, John of Waterside, James, Earl of Loudoun, and George, Lord Melville, for treason. In the document, there are various references to Ochiltree residents, such as 'William Gilchrist, sone to William Gilchrist, in Ochiltree, who was a pretended preacher, and frequented houses and field conventicles, a common and notorious traitor and rebell, who was actualy in the said rebellion, having thereafter returned, was recept, harboured, conversed and intercommoned with by the said Sir John Cochrane in his house of Ochiltree, and several days other places, gott lodging, meat, drink, and was otherwayes supplied and comforted by him.' Others named include 'Andrew Paterson in Ochiltree, Charles Colvil younger in Townhead, James Johnstoun sone to John Johnstoun in Ochiltrie, David Dune in Closs, Peter Murdoch near the Kirk of Ochiltrie, common and notorious rebells and traitors, who were actually in the rebellion, and were his [Sir John's] tenents before and after the rebellion'. Other Ochiltree witnesses included William Wallace, aged 50 years or thereby, who saw at the Calsay of Ochiltree, John of Waterside, William MacGhie, William Howie (a weaver in the village), James Muir, James Key, David Gillies and Thomas Reid. Archibald MacGhie, smith in Ochiltree, saw around twenty men gather in Ochiltree prior to the rebellion, where they were drilled by David Gillies and John Sinclair. John Paterson in Ochiltree (aged 50) saw some men, armed with 'bitts of forks, bitts of swords and halberts, and that they had a whyte cloath tyed to a stick for colours, and that he sawe John Cochran, of Watersyd, whom he knew, come out and speak with them, and this was some dayes before Bothwellbridge.'

In 1685 Sir John Cochrane returned to Scotland to take part in the abortive rising led by the Earl of Argyll. Sir John was instrumental in supporting Argyll's rising. He raised funds towards the cause, one interesting incident being the case of John Porterfield of Duchal Castle, Renfrewshire. Cochrane asked him to donate £50 towards the cause, but Porterfield refused. Porterfield was later taken to court for not divulging this request, and was sentenced to death as a result. Cochrane came with Argyll in his push on the west of Scotland, but had caused some friction in the ranks by demanding a second front was made on the Ayrshire coast. In Argyll's Rising, Cochrane was responsible for an attack on Greenock, but he was beaten back by the militia.

Sir John managed to escape and hid with a relative, Gavin Cochrane, in Renfrewshire. He was betrayed by Gavin's wife and subsequently captured, along with his son William Cochrane, and taken to Edinburgh on 3 July 1685. It is recorded that Sir John was led 'ignominiously' through the streets by the hangman, his hands bound behind his back, his head bareheaded (a mark of disrespect to him), into the tolbooth in the city, which was located near to the High Kirk of St Giles. Charged with high treason, Cochrane was sentenced to be hanged. His father, Lord Dundonald, intervened on his behalf, and with the aid of a sizeable bribe (perhaps £5,000) was able to persuade the authorities to pardon both him and William. Fountainhall stated that he 'turned approver' to save his head.

Another reason the Cochranes were so readily pardoned was the desire, 'ane itching curiosity to hear his discoveries,' that is, to gain intelligence from them, which would help convict other, more notable, participants in the plot against the king. However, the authorities were to gain nothing of import from Sir John, his past flitting from side to side meaning that neither political party were willing to trust him with any secrets. In 1685 Sir John's lands were annexed by the Crown for his Covenanting sympathies.

Sir John's daughter, eighteen year old Grizel, managed to intercept the mail carriage at Alnwick and acquired her father's death warrant. Thus he was saved, and it was a number of years before the truth was discovered. However, Sir John was not hanged and Grizel went unpunished. Grizel lived in the Borders, becoming married to John Ker of Moriestoun (died 27 September 1691), Berwickshire, on 18 February 1686. She lived until 21 March 1748.

Whilst Sir John and John of Waterside were held under the charge of treason, they spent their time under the threat of execution. All that was needed was a formal warrant from London.

According to Sir John Lauder of Fountainhall's *Decisions of the Lords of Council and Session:*

> July 9th. The English Packet coming to Edinburgh was twice stopped and robbed about Alnwick. Some conjectured it was Polwart's doing; others that it was by Sir John Cochrane's friends, lest there should have been any warrant from the King by these packets to have executed him.

A tradition is that the stagecoach with the death warrant was held up by Sir John's daughter, Grisel Cochrane. Aged about eighteen at the time, she intercepted the coach dressed as a man whilst the mailman had stopped at an inn near to Berwick.

In any case, no warrant was ever received in Edinburgh, and the two Cochranes were simply forfeited of their property. The Earl of Dundonald pleaded on his son and grandson's behalf. The estate of Waterside, in the parish of Auchinleck, which had been granted to John Cochrane, had been taken from him and granted to Lord Middleton. However, the Earl of Dundonald purchased this back for £6,000, even although it was reckoned that the estate was only worth one third of this.

John Graham of Claverhouse wrote about Sir John in one of his letters. Within it he writes that he is 'a mad man and lait him perish. They deserve to be damned would owen him'.

Sir John returned to Scotland from London (where he and his son had been detained) in 1687, being a member of a royal commission to negotiate a possible agreement regarding religious freedom.

Following the Glorious Revolution in 1689, Sir John's lands were restored to him by an act of parliament of 4 July 1690. By 1695 he was a Commissioner of Supply. He was appointed to collect the Poll Tax of 1695 but when the funds received did not match that due, and Cochrane's explanations being unsatisfactory, he was sent to prison. He survived until soon after 23 June 1707, when he was succeeded by his eldest son, William Cochrane of Ochiltree.

Sir John's niece, Jean Cochrane, daughter of his elder brother, William, Lord Cochrane, was to marry the persecutor of the Covenanters, Sir John Graham of Claverhouse. The marriage took place at Paisley Abbey on Tuesday 10 June 1684. The story is told that soon after the wedding ceremony took place, Claverhouse and his men rode off in search of Covenanters, not returning to his new bride until the 16th. This appears to have been a true story, for Claverhouse wrote a letter to the Lord President of the Privy Council on the Friday following his marriage:

To Sir David Falconer of Newton   Dundee
Paisley, 13 June 1684

My Lord, Upon the news of the conventicle near Blackloch, and that one hundred of them had passed Clyde, towards the moors in our quarter, I marched with the half of the Guards—which, by the way, are but twenty-two, when they ought to be fifty—and my Lord Ross's troop, and some dragoons, and thirty foot, and scoured all the mosses but one part towards Lesmahago, which I left Colonel Buchan to seek in his back-going. And he having ordered the foot to march on his right hand a mile or two, they fell on an ambuscade of two hundred rebels, seven of which, being off their body, fired on four of ours, and wounded one of them. They followed the rogues, and advertised Colonel Buchan; but before he could come up, our party had lost sight of them.

Colonel Buchan is yet in pursuit, and I am just taking horse. I shall be revenged some time or other of this unseasonable trouble these dogs give me. They might have let Tuesday pass [a reference to his wedding day]. I am, my Lord, your Lordship's most faithful servant.

A couple of days later he wrote another letter detailing his exploits, this time to General Thomas Dalzell. In this letter he makes mention of Ochiltree:

To General Thomas Dalyell
Kilbride, 15 June 1684

May it please your Excellency: I parted on Friday (13th) at twelve o'clock from Paisley, went by Kilmarnock and Mauchlin, but could hear nothing of these rebels. So, hearing Colonel Buchan was at the old castle of Cumnock, I took by Ochiltree, who sent an express to a tenant's house of his, near Airdmoss, and he brought certain notice that they had been at a meadow near his house the night before, to the number of fifty-nine, all armed.

Upon which I sent immediately to the Glenkens, to Captain Strachan, to march to Dalmellington, and to the Sorn, and to leave Mauchlin on the left hand, and Newmilns and Loudon-hill on the right, and so to this place, scouring all the suspected places as he came along. I sent to Dumfries, to Earlshall, to march by the Sanquhar, by the Muirkirk, the Whitrick, and the Ploughlands, and so to Streven.

Colonel Buchan, with twenty dragoons, and thirty foot mounted on horseback, marched round Cairntable, and by Lieburn and Greenock-head, and so down. My Lord Ross and I, with the horse, came through the hills more easterly, leaving Douglas and Lesmahago a mile or two on our right. We have left no den, no knowe, no moss, no hill, unsearched. There is a great drought, so [we] could go almost through all.

We traced them from the Boghead near Airdmoss to the Hakhill, within two miles of Cumnock town, and from that to Gap, towards Cairntable, but could never hear more of them. They are separated, as most believe, and gone towards the hills of Moffat. I am sure there is not one man of them within these bounds.

[Lieutenant Andrew Bruce of] Earlshall is not yet come this length, nor Captain Strachan. But they are, I am sure, near; for the last was at

Cumnock all night. The troops complain mightily of this march; and I know not what further can be done. So I have sent Colonel Buchan with the troops to Dalmellington, and the troops of Galloway to their quarters. I am your Excellency's most humble servant.

Claverhouse was killed in battle at Killiecrankie on 27 July 1689 and was buried in a burial vault at Old Blair, near Blair Castle.

Jean was to remarry, this time to William Livingston, 3rd Viscount Kilsyth. She was in Utrecht with her young child, William, on 16 October 1695 when she was killed. The roof of a building had collapsed, either by accident or design, and Lady Jean was killed by a blow to the temple. Her child was probably smothered in the arms of his mother. Lady Jean's body was embalmed and returned to Scotland, where it lay on view for many years within the mausoleum in Kilsyth kirkyard. The inscription there gives a detailed account of her story:

> Beneath this stone are deposited the remains of Jean Cochrane, Viscountess of Dundee, wife of the Honourable W. Livingston, of Kilsyth, and of their infant son. Their deaths were caused by the falling in of the roof, composed of turf, of a house in Holland. Mr Livingston was with difficulty extricated. The lady, her child, and the nurse were killed. This occurred in the month of October, MDCXCV. In MDCCXCV, the vault over which the church at that time stood having been accidentally opened, the bodies of Lady Dundee and her son, which had been embalmed and sent from Holland, were found in a remarkable state of preservation. After being for some time exposed to view, the vault was closed. This lady was the daughter of William, Lord Cochrane, who predeceased his father, William, first Earl of Dundonald. She married, first, John Graham, of Claverhouse, Viscount of Dundee, who was killed at the battle of Killicrankie, MDCLXXXIX; and secondly, the Honourable William Livingston, who succeeded his brother as third Viscount of Kilsyth in MDCCVI. Lord Kilsyth married, secondly, a daughter of MacDougall of Makerstoun, but dying under attainder at Rome in MDCCXXXII, without surviving issue, this noble family became extinct. This stone was erected by Sir Archibald Edmonston, of Duntreath, Bart., MDCCCL.

The incident when the mausoleum roof was opened and revealed the bodies of Jean Cochrane and her son was also reported in the press of the time. According to the Edinburgh Evening Courant of 27 July 1795:

The bodies of Lady Kilsyth and her infant son were discovered on 15th May, 1795. The shroud was as clean, and the ribbons as bright, and both as fresh as the hour they were laid in the tomb. There was not a single fold or knot of either discomposed, and scarcely a particle of dust on them. Both bodies were entire, the features distinct, and as placid and pleasant to look upon as if they had been only asleep. The infant was a peculiarly interesting and moving spectacle; with the smile of innocence upon its lips, fair and full of flesh, it arrested the attention of every beholder. The lady herself bore evident marks of a violent death. Upon the right temple there is still visible a large wound, covered over with a patch of black silk about the size of a crown, and her features have rather the marks of anxiety. Beautiful auburn hair and a fine complexion, with a few pearly drops, like dew upon her face, when uncovered, occasioned a sigh of astonishment and silent wonder.

An incision was made into the leg of the son and it was noted that the skin reacted as though it was fresh.

WILLIAM COCHRANE OF OCHILTREE (d. 1716)

William Cochrane successfully obtained a grant of the lands of Ochiltree in 1686, returning them to his family. He served as a commissioned officer in the militia raised to serve William of Orange, dated 30 March 1689. He was nominated a Commissioner of Supply for Ayrshire in 1686, 1689, 1690 and 1704. He was a Commissioner of Supply for Renfrewshire in 1704. At the Royal Proclamation of 30 March 1689 he was one of a number of local lairds who turned out at Ochiltree Cross with his retainers for the defence of the realm. He acted as a guardian of the young John Cochrane, 4th Earl of Dundonald.

William Cochrane was married on 19 April 1681 to Lady Mary Bruce, the eldest daughter of Alexander Bruce, 2nd Earl of Kincardine. At the time, she was heir to her brother in the earldom, but on his death in November 1705 she was unsuccessful in her claim to this. Apparently, the 3rd Earl had resigned the honours in her favour, but this had not been ratified by Crown Charter, though it was within the hands of the Crown at the earl's death, and it was eligible to be completed. The question of the earl's sanity had been raised, and with no pronouncement in her favour, the title passed to the nearest heir male - Sir Alexander Bruce of Broomhall. He became the 4th Earl of Kincardine, and whose descendants are now earls of Elgin and Kincardine. Lady Mary disputed the settlement at the elections of 1707, 1708 and 1710, but was unsuccessful in claiming the title. Lady Mary Cochrane died soon after 1739. William Cochrane died sometime after 24 December 1716, leaving nine sons and five daughters.

William Cochrane, Younger of Ochiltree, was the eldest. He was born in 1682 and baptised on 25 January that year. He was educated at the University of Glasgow. During the dispute his mother and father had against Sir Alexander Bruce over the Earldom of Kincardine, he acted as procurator. However, he died sometime between 1707 and 1716. He was never married. The second son, Charles Cochrane, became the next laird of Ochiltree.

The third son, John Cochrane, was born at Ochiltree on 20 August 1684. He served with the Royal Navy and rose to the rank of lieutenant on the *Eagle*, a man-of-war. However, the ship was lost off the Isles of Scilly under Sir Cloudesley Shovel on 21 October 1707. He was never married.

The fourth son was Alexander Cochrane, born at Ochiltree on 20 August 1686. He received a commission as a Cornet in Lord Stair's Regiment of Dragoons. He went with the army to Holland to raise recruits, but was drowned at sea on his way back, in either 1708 or 1709. He, too, was unmarried.

The fifth son was George Cochrane, born at Ochiltree on 5 June 1689. He served in the army, rising through the ranks to become a captain. He was killed in Spain in 1709. He was never married. The sixth son, James Cochrane, was to succeed to the estates of Ochiltree and Culross on the death of his elder brother, Charles.

CHARLES COCHRANE OF OCHILTREE (1683-1752)
William Cochrane of Ochiltree was succeeded by his second son, Charles, who was born on 25 January 1683 at Ochiltree. He received a sasine to the Barony of Ochiltree on 15 July 1717, which at that time included the lands of Trabboch, Carbolls, Achill and Clauchentown. He was later to inherit the estate of Culross from his mother in 1739. At this time he decided to sell Ochiltree estate. Charles was an advocate (becoming a member of the Faculty of Advocates in 1708), but he was never married and in 1749 had executed a settlement of his estate in favour of his brother James. Charles died at Culross on 19 September 1752.

JAMES COCHRANE OF OCHILTREE (1690-1758)
The sixth son of William Cochrane of Ochiltree was James Cochrane, and he was to succeed his elder brother, Charles, in 1752. He was born on 13 May 1690 and was commissioned as a captain in the 20th Infantry. He was to rise to become a Lieutenant-Colonel in the 15th Foot. On 26 April 1741 he was to become Lieutenant-Colonel in the 5th Marines. He was married to Margaret Hawkison. WIlliam died at Hampstead on 29 June 1758 – had he survived a further ten days he would have succeeded as the 8th Earl of Dundonald, a title acquired by his younger brother. James and Margaret left two daughters, Mary Anne Cochrane, who married Robert Sibthorne, by whom she had some children, and Elizabeth, or Betty Cochrane, who was married twice. Her first husband was Henry Carey

Hamilton of Holycross, the second, Lieutenant-Colonel Nathaniel Gould, whom she married on 3 June 1759.

James was succeeded to the estates of Ochiltree and Culross by his brother, the seventh son, Thomas. They had two other younger brothers, Robert, born at Ochiltree on 20 November 1692 and who died unmarried in 1721, and Basil. Basil Cochrane served in the army in the 44th Regiment of Foot. He was active at the Battle of Preston in 1745 where he was taken prisoner by the Jacobite army. He was later to become Depute-Governor of the Isle of Man. On 15 July 1761 he was appointed a Commissioner of Excise, and in May 1764 a Commissioner of Customs in Scotland. He never married, and died at Dalry on 2 October 1788.

There were five daughters of William Cochrane, sisters to the nine brothers. These were Henriette, born in October 1687; Euphemia, who was married to Colonel John Erskine, said to be the Colonel J. Erskine who was Depute-Governor of Stirling Castle; Mary, born at Ochiltree on 20 December 1694 and who never married; Elizabeth who was alive in 1759 and who died unmarried; and Anne, married in 1725 to Sir George Preston of Valleyfield, Baronet. Anne died at Valleyfield on 7 November 1770.

THOMAS COCHRANE, 8TH EARL OF DUNDONALD (d. 1778)
The seventh son of William Cochrane of Ochiltree, Major Thomas Cochrane, was to inherit Ochiltree and Culross on 29 June 1758. However, he was to succeed to a greater estate, for on the death of his cousin, the 7th Earl of Dundonald, on 9 July 1759, he was to become the 8th Earl. William Cochrane served as the Fort Major of St Philip in Minorca, as well as Captain of the 27th Foot. He was elected as M.P. for Renfrew in 1722 and was appointed as Commissioner for Excise in Scotland in 1730.

Cochrane was married twice, his first marriage being in 1721 to his cousin, Elizabeth Ker, daughter of James Ker of Moriestoun (or Morriston) and his wife, Grizel Cochrane, daughter of Sir John Cochrane of Ochiltree. Elizabeth died in 1743. By her he had a son, William, who died in 1730 aged eight, and a daughter, Grizel (b. 1727). He was then married on 6 September 1744 to Jane Stuart (died 21 May 1808), eldest daughter of Archibald Stuart of Torrance, Lanarkshire. They had six sons, the eldest, Archibald Cochrane, succeeded on the 8th Earl's death on 27 June 1778.

JAMES MacRAE (b. c. 1685-1740)
On 12 October 1739 Ochiltree estate was purchased by Governor James MacRae from the Cochrane family. He paid £25,000.

James MacRae was born in Ochiltree, but on the death of his father whilst still a youth he moved with his mother to Ayr, where she worked as a charwoman. The exact date of his birth is not known, but was probably around 1685. Some accounts claim his birthplace was, in fact, in Ayr, but this can not be confirmed. His mother was a woman by the name of Bell Gardner, long referred to as 'Widow MacRae'. James was described as being a restless child, and after an elementary education he ran off to sea. He eventually settled in India, where there is reference to him in 1720 as Captain MacRae. He was appointed as Governor of Fort St George in 1720. He became much admired, and amassed a considerable fortune by 1725, when he was appointed as Governor of the Presidency of Madras on 18 January 1725. He remained in this position for five years, being succeeded on 14 May by George Morton Pitt. On 21 January 1731 he decided to return to Scotland, which he had left forty years previously. His fortune was immense, for his annual income at the time was reckoned to be in the region of £25,000 per annum.

Arriving in Ayr, he found that his mother had died. He also discovered that in her old age she had been looked after by a cousin, Isabella Gardner. She was married to a carpenter, Hugh MacGuire, by whom she had one son and four daughters. To reward her, Governor MacRae paid for their children's education and on their marriage he presented them with estates. Hugh was presented with the farm of Drumdow, in Stair parish. His son, James MacGuire, was given the estate of Houston in Renfrewshire, on condition that he change his surname to MacRae.

Similar grants were made to the daughters. The eldest daughter, Elizabeth, was married on 6 August 1744 to William, 13th Earl of Glencairn. MacRae gifted her the Barony of Ochiltree. In addition to the lands, on the day that she was married, MacRae presented her with diamonds valued at £45,000.

The second daughter was married to James Erskine of Barjarg, in Colmonell parish. She was given the estate of Alva in Clackmannanshire. James Erskine was later to become a judge in the Court of Session, taking as his courtesy title, Lord Alva.

The third daughter is little-known, and it is not known what she received. She married Captain MacRae, 'a somewhat dubious character'.

The fourth daughter, MacRae MacGuire, was married to Charles Dalrymple, Sheriff Clerk of Ayr. MacRae presented her with the estate of Monkton, renamed Orangefield. Their son, James Dalrymple, was a friend of Burns.

James MacRae was presented with the Freedom of the Burgh of Ayr in 1733. In 1734 he presented a bronze statue of King William of Orange to the city of Glasgow, the monarch mounted on a horse. The statue is quite unique in that its tail was mounted so that it could move in the breeze.

James MacRae died at Orangefield House, near Prestwick, on 21 July 1744. He was buried in the kirkyard at Monkton. In 1750 a monument on a low hill at Monkton was erected in his memory by John Swan.

ELIZABETH CUNNINGHAM, 13th COUNTESS OF GLENCAIRN
(b. c. 1727-1801)

The 13th Earl and his Countess did not have a particularly happy marriage, and it was often said that the earl married Elizabeth just to gain the inheritance from MacRae, the Glencairn fortunes being much depleted at the time. Nevertheless, they had six children.

William, the eldest son, was born at Finlayston House, Renfrewshire, on 20 May 1748, assuming the courtesy title Lord Kilmaurs. He served as a cornet in the 3rd Dragoons and died unmarried at Coventry on 3 February 1768. James, the second son, was to succeed his father as 14th Earl of Glencairn in 1791. He was also born at Finlayston House, on 1 June 1749. He succeeded his father in 1775. He died unmarried in 1791, resulting in Robert Burns composing the lines, 'Lament for James, Earl of Glencairn':

4.3 Cunningham of Glencairn arms *(Dane Love)*

> But I'll remember thee, Glencairn,
> And a' that thou hast done for me.

The third son, John, became an officer and clergyman, serving as a minister in the Church of England. He was to succeed his brother in 1791 and was earl for five years until his death on 24 September 1796, aged 47. He married Isabella Erskine, daughter of Henry, 10th Earl of Buchan, in 1785. They had no issue, and John died at the Glencairn residence of Coates House, Edinburgh. The fourth son was Alexander, but he died in his youth.

There were two daughters. Lady Henrietta (or Harriet) was married in 1778 to Sir Alexander Don, 5th Baronet of Newton Don, a Borders estate near Kelso. She died in March 1801. They had a son, Alexander, born in 1779, who was to inherit the Ochiltree estates in 1801 (Sir Alexander died on 5 June 1815, after which the son became Sir Alexander, 6th Baronet). They also had two daughters who were to be drowned in the River Eden on 7 June 1795, along with a third girl, Agnes Wilson, daughter of Dr Wilson of Kelso. They had been trying to cross a swollen stream when they were carried away. The second daughter, Elizabeth, died on 6 August 1804 at Coates House. It was she who was the recipient of Burns' poem, the only child of the six who survived her mother.

On 10 September 1780, James Boswell paid a visit to Ochiltree House and was saddened to note that it was in a very poor condition. He wrote in his journal, 'Its ruinous rooms affected me with melancholy not unpleasing'. It must have been repaired fairly soon thereafter, for in 1792 Rev William Thomson lived there, the manse belonging to the parish church being 'entirely in ruins'.

Lady Glencairn died at her home of Coates, Edinburgh, on Thursday 25 June 1801, in her 77th year.

4.4 Ochiltree House from the South East *(Author's Collection)*

SIR ALEXANDER DON, 6th Baronet (1780-1826)

Ochiltree estate was inherited by Sir Alexander Don, 6th Baronet of Newton Don. He was a captain in the Roxburghshire militia in 1802 and subsequently spent some time living in France. He served as a Member of Parliament for Roxburghshire from 1814-26, and was a close acquaintance of Sir Walter Scott. He was married twice, firstly to Lucretia Montgomerie, second daughter of George Molineux Montgomerie of Garboldisham Hall, Norfolk, in 1809, but they had no issue and his wife died in 1815. He was married for a second time in August 1824 to Grace Stein, daughter of John Stein, Edinburgh, who was a Member of Parliament for Bletchingley. They had a son and daughter. He died of a stomach complaint at Newton Don on 11 April 1826.

Sir Alexander Don held the property at Ochiltree for twelve years, but in 1805 placed part of it on the market. According to the Caledonian Mercury of 12 December 1805:

> Sale of Lands in Ayrshire. To be Sold public roup, in the course of next Spring, and of which particulars be afterwards advertised, the following farms, part of the estate of Ochiltree, lying in the parish of Ochiltree and county of Ayr, viz. the farms of Townhead, Auchincloigh,

Auchlin, and Dykeneuck. Greenhill, Meikle Burnockhead, Little Burnockhead, Closs, Duntaggart, the whole containing upwards of 3,150 acres, the present rent of which is only £374, but at the end of the current leases a great rise may be expected. Apply to Archibald and John Tod, W. S. George Square, Edinburgh.

In 1809-1813 Sir Alexander Don decided to put the remainder of the estate for sale. The greater estate was divided into smaller portions, the larger part being acquired by the 3rd Marquis of Bute. Sir Alexander Boswell of Auchinleck bought a block of land, including various farms adjoing Auchinleck estate. David Limond of Dalblair purchased the remainder of the estate, comprising Ochiltree Mill, Carston, Pool, Finlayston, Nether Finlayston, Holehouse, Laigh Tarbeg, Moat, Lessnessock, Killoch, Clydeneuch, East Tarelgin, Killochside, MacQuittiston and West Tarelgin. He placed Ochiltree estate on the market in June 1844, at the time comprising 1,489 acres. Creoch was sold to John Tennant. The village feus were purchased by Captain John Johnstone, but on the death of his wife, were sold to Lady Griselle Boswell, dowager of Auchinleck.

The Don family did not survive much longer than the sale of the Ochiltree estate. The last of the line was Sir William Henry Don, 7th Baronet (4 May 1825-19 March 1862). He served in the guards and became an aide-de-camp to the Lord Lieutenant of Ireland. He retired from the army as a lieutenant in 1845 and became a theatrical performer. His wife was also an actress. Sir William Don died at Hobart, Tasmania, whilst on a tour of Australia. He was survived by his second wife, but not having any sons, the baronetcy passed to the Wauchopes of Edmonstone, becoming Don-Wauchope.

CAPTAIN JOHN JOHNSTONE
Little is known about Captain John Johnstone, who had acquired Ochiltree House and its immediate surroundings. He also purchased the right to the feus forming the village. On the death of his wife, which must have been around 1819, the property was sold to Sir Alexander Boswell of Auchinleck. Pigot's *Directory* of 1826 lists Mrs Elizabeth Johnstone as occupying Ochiltree House. A nephew, Lieutenant-Colonel William Johnstone CB of the 26th Foot (Cameronians), served in China and at the Battle of Corunna. He died at sea, coming back to Britain, on 19 October 1842. Lieutenant-Colonel Johnstone's eldest son, John William Johnstone, Captain in the 16th Regiment of Foot, died at Montreal, Canada, on 7 July 1854.

SIR ALEXANDER BOSWELL, 1st BARONET OF AUCHINLECK (1775-1822)
In 1819 Alexander Boswell of Auchinleck purchased Ochiltree House. He was born in Auchinleck House on 9 October 1775 and was educated at Westminster School followed by Oxford University. Like his father, the diarist James Boswell, Alexander

was interested in literary pursuits, though was more a poet than a diarist. His first published works appeared in 1803, entitled *Songs, Chiefly in the Scottish Dialect*, which included 'Jenny's Bawbee', 'Auld Guideman', 'Ye're a Drucken Carle', 'Jenny Dang the Weaver', and 'Taste Life's Glad Moments'. In the same year 'The Spirit of Tintoc' appeared, followed by 'Epistle to the Edinburgh Reviewers'. In 1809 he contributed five songs to George Thomson's collection of Welsh airs. In 1810, 'Edinburgh, or the Ancient Royalty' appeared, under the pseudonym 'Simon Gray'. 'Clan Alpin's Vow' was published in 1811, 'Sir Albyn' in 1812. He contributed seven songs to George Thomson's collection of Irish airs, 'Paddy O'Rafferty' becoming well-known, and in 1816 he wrote 'Skeldon Haughs, or the Sow is flitted', published by 'A. & J. Boswell'.

Alexander was married to Griselle or Grace Cumming on 26 November 1799. She was the fifth daughter of Thomas Cumming, a banker in Edinburgh, and representative of the ancient family of Erenside. They were to have four children, James, who succeeded as 11th Boswell laird of Auchinleck, Theresa, who was to marry Sir William Francis Eliott, of Stobs and Wells, Baronet, Grace Jane, who died at a young age, and Margaret Emily, who was married to General Vassal.

Alexander's influence grew across Ayrshire, and soon he was serving as one of the Road Trustees, a Commissioner of Supply, and Colonel in the Ayrshire Yeomanry. He kept a small pack of hounds on the estate, and would ride out with them in search of vermin. He was a keen curler and a member of the masonic lodge.

In 1816 Alexander was elected MP for Ayrshire. He contributed twelve songs to George Thomson's, *Select Collection of Original Scottish Airs* in 1817, of which 'Goodnight and Joy be wi' ye a', 'Jenny's Bawbee', and 'Jenny Dang the Weaver', became very popular. He was elected MP for Plympton in Devon in 1818, holding it until 1821 when he applied for the Chiltern Hundreds. He was later to be given a baronetcy, granted in August 1821.

In the political turmoils of the period, Sir Alexander was active with the Ayrshire militia in quelling various riots that took place across the county. He wrote letters to the newspapers and magazines, one of which resulted in him being challenged to a duel by James Stuart, younger of Dunearn. He accepted, and the duel took place at Balbarton farm, near to Balmuto Castle in Fife on 26 March 1822. Boswell was injured, and he died soon after. He was buried at Auchinleck.

At the time of Sir Alexander's death his heir, James, was still a minor, aged 15, and so continued to live at Auchinleck House with his mother. When he was married in 1830 his mother moved to Ochiltree House where she died in 1864. It was noted that Lady Boswell 'spent the remainder of her days in strict retirement', and following Sir Alexander's death she kept the windows in her room closed for many years.

4.5 Ochiltree House from North East *(Author's Collection)*

Although the Boswells remained in ownership for a number of years to come, the house and gardens were actually put on the market in September 1834. This included 'the mansion house of Ochiltree, offices, garden and grounds; as also all and whole the houses and yards in the village of Ochiltree which were feued or let on long leases by John Johnston Esq., Ochiltree, and his predecessors, with the feu-duties, tack-duties, and casualties, payable furth thereof (but subject to the burden of the feu-rights or long leases, in favour of the feuars or lessees), together with the teinds of the said lands, lying in the parish of Ochiltree and shire of Ayr. As also, the Dominium Directum of the said subjects.' The price expected for that listed was £2,454 5s 10d.

JOHN PATRICK CRICHTON-STUART, 3RD MARQUIS OF BUTE (1847-1900)

Ochiltree House and surrounding estate was acquired by the 3rd Marquis of Bute in 1868. He was a keen antiquarian, responsible over a period of years for restoring various castles and abbeys, as well as building new churches. He arranged for Ochiltree House to be repaired, and the grounds were noted for their 'beautiful, striking and charming appearance'. The Marquis of Bute also owned three houses in Burnock Street in 1875.

A few years before 1880 ('recently undergone renovation', according to the *Ardrossan and Saltcoats Herald* of 23 July 1881) the old ruinous part of Ochiltree

House was swept away. This had stood in ruins for many years, its walls covered with ivy. In *Memorials of Ochiltree* by David Rowan, written in 1879, he notes that the remains were 'recently removed', placing the demolition before that year.

Lord Bute did not require Ochiltree House for any major family member, his larger country house of Dumfries House being located nearby. Accordingly, the house was leased to a series of tenants.

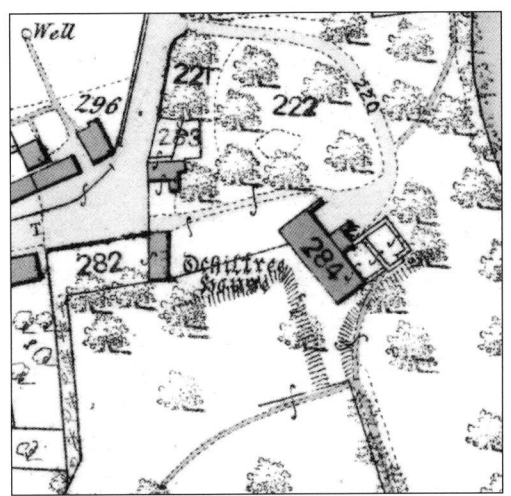

4.6 Ochiltree House on 1856 Ordnance Survey map, showing ruined wing of old castle *(Author's Collection)*

Around 1875-1883 Ochiltree House was let to the Hon. Richard Wogan Talbot, eldest son of James Talbot, 4th Baron Talbot de Malahide. He had married Emily Harriet Boswell on 26 June 1873, the daughter of Sir James Boswell, 2nd Baronet of Auchinleck. Richard Talbot succeeded as 5th Lord Talbot de Malahide on 14 April 1883. They left Ochiltree House in August 1884 to take up residence in Malahide Castle, the family seat near Dublin in Ireland. He died in 1921.

From around 1886-1891 Ochiltree House was occupied by H. G. Fallowfield and his wife. He retired from service in the 4th Battalion, Princess Louise's (Argyll and Sutherland Highlanders) in 1884 and must have taken on the lease of Ochiltree House soon after. He had served with the 91st Highlanders in the Zulu war of 1879 and was present in action at Gingindhloveu and the relief of Ekowe, being awarded a medal and clasp for this. Whilst at Ochiltree, they had a son, born on 27 April 1888. Captain H. G. Fallowfield had served with the 91st Highlanders in the Zulu war of 1879, and was present in the action at the Battle of Gingindlovu and relief of Eshowe (Medal with Clasp). In 1891 the house was altered to the plans of Allan Stevenson.

From around 1896-1908 Ochiltree House was occupied by James Angus JP, elder son of Robert Angus of Ladykirk, and his wife, Elizabeth They previously lived at Craigston House, Lugar. James was married to Elizabeth Jollie, daughter of Edward Jollie JP, of Patea, New Zealand, by whom he had one son. James Angus died at Ochiltree House on 17 December 1902, aged 38. James was a coalmaster, and was one of the proprietors of the Auchincruive Coal Company. In his will he left a personal estate of £48,673. Following Angus's death, Elizabeth Angus appears to have lived at both Ochiltree House and Hill House, Leckhampton, near Cheltenham. She later remained solely at Hill House. The coachman's house and stables at Ochiltree House were destroyed by fire on 21 October 1906.

The only son was Robert Edward Angus, who was born at Radcliffe in Northumberland on 27 May 1894 and was educated at St Ninian's School, Moffat, followed by Loretto School, Edinburgh. He left there at Easter 1914 and was set to attend Cambridge. He joined the Ayrshire Yeomanry at the outbreak of war and served at Gallipoli and Egypt as a Lieutenant with the Armoured Motor Car Service. He then transferred to the 64th Squadron Royal Flying Corps, becoming a Flight Commander, and was described by his commanding officer as the best pilot in the squadron. During a bombing raid over Germany he was reported as missing in action on 20 November 1917 aged 23 and subsequently confirmed as dead, although they have never found his body. He is commemorated on the war memorials at Monkton, Cumnock, Lugar, Leckhampton, Clare College, Cambridge, and the Arras Memorial. He is also commemorated on the Angus family grave memorial in Auchinleck kirkyard.

Ochiltree House was let to various other tenants after the Angus family moved on. These included Abel Girotti (around 1921). He was a restauranteur in Ayr, running the Athole restaurant at 11 Burns' Statue Square around 1906 and the King's Arms Hotel around 1920. On 6 November 1906 he received a Certificate of Naturalization from the British Government to replace his Italian birth. At the time he lived at 18 Beresford Terrace, Ayr.

From around 1925 the house was owned by Dumfries House Mountjoy Ltd, but remained empty. As a result, Ochiltree House fell into a dilapidated condition. It was demolished in March 1952. The site of the house was purchased by Gordon Anderson and a new double-storey house was built thereon in 1972.

4.7 Ochiltree House from North East *(Author's Collection)*

AUCHENCLOIGH CASTLE

At the southern edge of the improved ground in the parish are the broken and fragmentary ruins of Auchencloigh Castle. To the south of the castle the ground becomes rougher and turns into moorland. The castle was never very important, nor very large, and there is very little known of its history. The ruins occupy a very low mound, hardly projecting out of the surrounding landscape. There are few walls remaining in their original location, but most of the rubble that survives are blocks of masonry that have collapsed from the tower. Most of these have fallen outwith the floorplan of the building, making the ruins appear larger than the extent of the original castle. Most of the broken blocks of masonry now lie at odd angles, so that the random rubble beds that formed the stonework usually lie in strange positions. The appearance of the stonework hints that the castle is of an early period, perhaps dating from the fifteenth century. Some walls still stand around two to six feet in height, and in places are still several feet in thickness. In plan, the castle forms a rectangle, the interior of which was formerly divided into lesser apartments. The first Statistical Account simply describes the building as 'an old square tower', perhaps hinting that the walls were at that time much taller, but had little in the way of embellishments.

In 1855 the Ordnance Survey map-makers visited the site and in their Name Book made a few notes: 'All that now remains of this is a broken and irregular mass of stone and lime. To all appearance it has once been a quadrangular building, as the remaining portions of the walls indicate, which are from two to five feet high and about five feet in thickness. It stands in close proximity to Auchencloigh and a small portion of it has been converted into and is used as a sheep ree. To judge from the huge fragments which now remain it must have been a place of great strength, but there is no person in the neighbourhood can give any information as to when or for what purpose it was erected and though it is known by some as Auchencloigh Castle, by others it is asserted as having been nothing more than a farmsteading'.

The fragments of wall have been calculated to have contained a building of around 40 feet by 35 feet. The walls vary in thickness from around four and a half to five feet. The stone used for construction was whinstone, which was bonded in a random-rubble format with lime mortar. There are remnants of internal walls which were not so thick. At the south-eastern corner of the building there was probably a spiral staircase, built into the thickness of the wall. One of the large blocks of masonry that lies down contains a curved inner face, indicative of the stair. The incorporation of the stair within the wall thickness would have weakened the tower at that point. In plan, the tower would have been not unlike that at Newmilns in Ayrshire, or Kildonan on Arran, though whether Auchencloigh was as decorative at eaves level cannot be determined, there being no carved stones from this part of the tower surviving. The tower may also have mirrored some of the Border towers that exist across Selkirkshire and Peeblesshire, and like them may have been established to control reiving and freebooters in the upland areas.

4.8 Auchencloigh Castle *(Dane Love)*

As stated, the history of Auchencloigh Castle is almost forgotten. Who built it cannot be determined, but by 1610 we know that it formed part of Ochiltree estate, so the fact that it was subordinate to Ochiltree Castle perhaps meant that there was no great history attached to it. According to the charter issued by King James VI in 1620 to James Stewart, 4th Lord Ochiltree (replicated under Ochiltree Castle), Auchencloigh and Bent extended to four merks, and at the time there appears to have been a 'turre' or tower, and 'manerie', or manor house. The tower may have fallen into ruin soon after.

DRONGAN CASTLE

The earliest references to Drongan Castle date from the fourteenth century. A number of old charters from that period refer to the lands and their owners. In the early 1300s, the lands were divided amongst various members of the family of d'Aubigne, or Albini, of Ayr. Adam of Ayr owned Shield, Knockguldron and 'Antitigille'. John, his son, held the 'penny lands' of Nether Shield. The 'two-penny' lands of Shield were owned by Reginald, son of Reginald of Ayr, who was also a descendant of d'Aubigne. The name d'Aubigne has been spelled variously as Albini, Dobin or Dobney over the years.

In the latter part of the fourteenth century Alan Stewart bought Shield from John, son of d'Awbine, a descendant of Albini. Alan Stewart was the son of Alan Stewart, a cousin of the king. In 1377 he registered his coat of arms, which comprises of a standard Stewart shield – Or, a fess-chequy Azure and Argent, surmounted by a bend Gules charged with three buckles of the First, for Bonkyl of that Ilk. The heiress of Bonkyl was married to Sir John Stewart, second son of Alexander, Lord High Steward of Scotland, around 1294.

In the 1390s the lands of Shield, which included the Mill of Shield and the other properties of Alan Stewart, were granted by King Robert III to Roger de Craufurd of Dalleagles, in New Cumnock parish. Roger de Craufurd had a wife named Elizabeth. On the same day as acquiring Shield, Roger de Craufurd also received the resigned lands of Shield that belonged to Reginald d'Awbine. Roger de Craufurd also appears to have owned lands in Dalmellington, where he made an agreement with local landowner Sir Alan Cathcart.

4.9 Drongan Castle *(Dane Love)*

Roger de Craufurd was succeeded by his son, John de Craufurd. He is first mentioned on 17 September 1401 on a royal charter of Robert III, where he is named as 'John de Craufurd, filio Roger de Craufurd de Daleglis'. He is mentioned again in a charter of 16 November 1406, in which he concedes to John Shaw of Haly some lands in the Barony of Dalmellington. In this charter he is referred to as the 'Lord of Drongan'. In a charter of 24 July 1406, and later confirmed on 11 November 1425, John de Craufurd was granted the lands of 'Scheuylt', or Shield.

The main seat, or caput, of the Craufurd family was Drongan Castle, which stood to the south of the present Drongan Mains farm. A low oval-shaped knoll to the south of the farm contains some ancient masonry, reckoned to date from the early fifteenth century. The surviving portion of wall measures around 22 feet in length, and is about three feet in height. Built of rubble masonry, it is almost completely hidden by grass. When James Paterson wrote his *History of the County of Ayr* in 1847, he describes the castle as being larger in size than the old castle of Trabboch, and that 'the walls, until lately, were almost entire'.

After John Craufurd died, the estate passed to Roger de Craufurd. He may have been a son or brother to John de Craufurd.

The next owner of Drongan Estate was Robert de Craufurd. He was married to Isabella Campbell of Loudoun. In 1490 Sir William Colvill of Ochiltree sued Robert Craufurd of Drongan for £200. Robert de Craufurd died around 1499. The names of other landowners who may have existed around this time are unknown, and a complete genealogy is impossible to compile.

JOHN CRAUFURD OF DRONGAN (c. 1510 – c. 1535)

John Craufurd succeeded to Drongan. He was married to a very distant relative, Margaret Craufurd of Camlarg, only daughter of Duncan Craufurd of Camlarg, in the parish of Dalmellington, himself the third son of David Craufurd of Kerse. John Craufurd was very active in county politics, often being mentioned in the Ayrshire Criminal Records, the Ayr Sasines, and the Ayr Burgh Accounts. He appears to have served as Depute Sheriff of the county and also served as a councillor for the Royal Burgh of Ayr. As Depute Sheriff (under the Campbells of Loudoun, hereditary sheriffs) he is known to have served for at least twenty years, his name appearing in public records over that time.

In 1510-11 there were numerous feuds across Ayrshire and Galloway between some of the major landowning families. These often resulted in bloodshed, families avenging the murders of various members of their own clan. John Craufurd of Drongan was one of those who took part with his clansmen, the Craufurds of Leifnoreis Castle, which stood in the parish of Old Cumnock, until it was superseded by Dumfries House. William Craufurd, or Crawford, Younger of Leifnoreis, and John Craufurd of Drongan attacked Loch Doon Castle, at the time in the hands of the Kennedys. They were accompanied by Alan Cathcart of Clowlynan and five others.

On 10 November 1520, the Protocol Book of Gavin Ros makes reference to a dispute involving John Craufurd regarding property in Dalmellington:

> John Craufurd of Drongane passed to the parish church of Dalmellington with a mind to enter it in a peaceful manner to count the sum of 100 merks and to pay the same to Margaret Craufurd,

relict of the late William Hebburn of Lowis, upon the high altar of the church for redemption of the 3s. lands of Southir Barbiestoun and Knokcamour with letters of tack of said lands for two years after redemption; but there appeared no safe access to the church for him to do the above, because Bartholomew Craufurd of Kerse, his enemy, with William Cathkert, son of said Margaret, and others, to the number of 16 persons, with the intention of attacking John Craufurd straitly guarded with weapons the church, cemetery and entrance, nor could the said John have ingress, and one shot an arrow against him....

As access to the parish kirk and kirkyard was blocked, Craufurd offered to pay Margaret Craufurd the cash owed in front of the notary and other witnesses in the street outside the kirkyard, but she refused, stating that she would only take it if it was paid on the high altar within the kirk itself. She added that she had no part to play in the presence of the armed men who were blocking his way. A compromise appears to have been worked out, by which Bartholomew Craufurd would allow John Craufurd, the notary and two witnesses to enter the kirk. He also offered his two brothers in surety to make sure that no harm would come to Drongan whilst entering or leaving the kirk.

John Craufurd was also involved in the feud which resulted in the murder of the Earl of Cassillis at Prestwick in 1527. The assassination was orchestrated by Hugh Campbell of Loudoun, and Craufurd being his depute sheriff, was closely bound with Campbell in the political hostilities of the day. According to *Pitcairn's Criminal Trials*, 'Geo. Craufurd of Leifnoreis, and William his brother; John Campbell of Cessnock; Bartholomew Craufurd of Kerse; David and Duncan, his brothers; John Craufurd of Drongane; John and William, his sons,' with a great number of others found caution to underlay the law for this crime.' They were all summonsed to appear at the next court held in Ayr to receive their sentence.

In 1530 John Craufurd crossed the River Doon from Kyle and stole 125 oxen and cows from James Kennedy of Blairquhan Castle. Kennedy retaliated soon after, stealing 120 oxen and cows, 200 sheep and six horses and mares.

John Craufurd and Margaret Craufurd had three sons: John, who is thought to have predeceased his father; David, who was to inherit the estate of Camlarg; and William, who was granted Drumsoy Castle, which was located on the west side of the Water of Coyle from Drongan Castle itself.

John Craufurd the Younger was married to Janet Cathcart around 1517. The couple must have been fairly closely related, for in 1517 John and Margaret visited the priest in Cumnock for permission to marry, their degree of familial connection being within the disallowable degrees. As noted, John the Younger was also to be invloved in feuding with the Kennedys, in 1527 being a participant in the murder of the Earl of Cassillis. He appears to have died before 1530, for Janet Cathcart is described as a widow at that time.

John's brother, William Craufurd, is known to have been alive in 1551. He also had a sister, Egidia Craufurd, who was to marry Hugh Cathcart, son of John, 2nd Lord Cathcart, in 1517.

JOHN CRAUFURD OF DRONGAN (d. c. 1558)

John Craufurd succeeded his grandfather in the estate of Drongan. He was to marry Margaret Kennedy, a daughter of Alexander Kennedy of Bargany. In January 1552 there was a charter to the lands of Mains of Drongan and of the four merk land of Smithstown and the lands of Skeoch Hill, on a life-rent right, granted by John Craufurd in favour of his wife, Margaret Kennedy. John Craufurd also witnessed a sasine favour of M. Colville on 27 July 1552. In 1554 John Craufurd of Drongan had to find surety for resetting, intercommuning and supplying the Laird of Ballagan (Duncan Hunter) and others. John Craufurd died around 1558.

GEORGE CRAUFURD OF DRONGAN (c. 1550-1580)

Drongan estate passed to George Craufurd, who was still alive around 1580. As George was probably still a minor (of around eight years of age) at the death of his father, the lands of Drongan were held in ward by George Craufurd of Leifnoreis. This meant that Leifnoreis paid £300 for the ward of all of Drongan lands, including rents, etc. He was to draw all of the rents until such time as George inherited. On 10 January 1579/80 a charter was signed by George Craufurd of Drongan to William Craufurd of Leifnoreis, stating that in the event of George dying without issue, then the estate of Drongan would pass to Craufurd of Leifnoreis. George Craufurd of Drongan did indeed die without issue. There being no other close heirs, the estate of Drongan passed to the Craufurds of Leifnoreis.

Part of Drongan estate was broken away from the parent lands and was acquired by Alexander Craufurd of Balgregan, a scion of the Craufurds of Kerse. He was succeeded in these lands by John Craufurd of Balgregan. In 1584 he was served heir to Alexander Craufurd in the four-merkland of Over and Nether Drongan and twenty shilling lands of Hannayston in Carrick.

WILLIAM CRAUFURD OF LEIFNOREIS AND DRONGAN (fl. 1621)

William Craufurd of Leifnoreis inherited Drongan, but by this time it was but a subsidiary estate to his Leifnoreis property and other lands.

SIR GEORGE CRAUFURD OF DRONGAN (fl. 1621-1622)

Sir George Craufurd, Younger of Leifnoreis, may have occupied Drongan, or perhaps have been given the estate by his father. A charter under the Great Seal of 29 March 1621 confirmed the property:

> Apud Edinburgh, 29 Mar. Rex,—cum consensu etc. concessit D. Georgio Crawfuird juniori de Lefnoreis militi, heredibus ejus et assignatis quibuscunque, -terras et baroniam de Drownegane, viz. 8 mercat. terrarum de Drowngane nuncupat. Scheil-rankene, 2 mercat. terrarum dominicalium de Drowngane cum manerie loco, 2 mercat. terrarum de Chalmerhill, que fuerunt partes dict. terrarum dominicalium, cum molendino de Drownegane, mercatam de Skeochhill, 10 solidat. de Knokovir, 2 morcat. de Coquhaipill, 4 mercat. de Smeithstoun, mercatam de Barbeth, 10 sol. de Schirrinlawstoun, 2 mercat. de Knokcubine et Craigbrae, 10 sol. de Lokland, cum piscationibus et moris, in Kingis-kyill, vic. Air;—que, de rege tente per servitium warde, regi devenerunt ob alienationem absque regis licentia factam per Wil. Crawfuird seniorem de Lefnoreis vel per dictum Geo. ejus filium seu per aliquos eorum predecessores: —Test, *ut in aliis cartis* &c

He resigned Drongan to his brother, Matthew Craufurd, in 1622.

MATTHEW CRAUFURD OF DRONGAN (fl. 1622-1624)

Matthew Craufurd held Drongan estate from 1622 for just two years. He was married to Anne Kennedie, or Kennedy. The charter granting him the lands was Registered under the Great Seal on 20 December 1622:

> Apud Edinburgh, 20 Dec. Rex,—cum consensu etc. concessit M. Matheo Craufurd
> tunc de Drongane et Anne Kennedie ejus sponse in conjuncta infeodatione, et heredibus inter eos legit. procreatis, quibus deficientibus, heredibus et assignatis dicti Math. quibuscunque, irredimabiliter,— terras et baroniam de Drongane, extenden. ad 16 libratas 6 solidatas 8 den. terrarum antique extentus (viz. 16½ mercat. in proprietate et 8 mercat. in tenandria), cum turre, manerie loco, molendinis, piscationibus, cuniculariis, moris, tenentibus etc., in parochia de Uchiltrie, Kings-Kyle, vic. Air; — necnon dicto Math., heredibus ejus et assignatis quibuscunque, irredimabiliter, — 4 mercatas terrarum ant. ext. de Drumdow, cum moris etc., jacen. ut sup.;—quas D. Geo. Craufurd de Leifnoreis miles, frater germanus dicti Mathei, cum consensu Domine Margarete Stewart sponse sue et D. Gulielmi Cunynghame de Capringtoun militis resignavit: — Reddend. pro Drongane jura et servitia debita et consueta; pro Drumdow 50 sol. albe firme :—Test, *ut in aliis* etc.

WILLIAM CUNNINGHAME (fl. 1624-1657)

In 1624 the lands of Drongan passed to the Cunninghames. The first of this family to own the estate was William Cunninghame. A Charter under the Great Seal of Scotland was issued on 1 July 1624:

> Apud Halyruidhouse, 8 Jul. Rex, - cum consesu etc., - concessit Willelmo Cunynghame de Drongane, heredibus ejus et assignatis quibuscunque, irredimabiliter, - terras et baronian de Drongane, cum lavubus et carbonibus; - quas M. Matheus Craufurd de Drongane, cum consensu Anne Kennedy sponse sue, D. Georgii Craufurd de Leifnoreis militis fratris sui et Domine Margarete Stewart ejus sponse, resignavit; et quas rex de novo incorporavit in liberam baroniam de Drongane, ordinando maneriei locaum de Drongan principae for messuagium.

William Cunninghame, who may or may not be the same person, held sasine of the lands of Drongan on 9 October 1657. There is reference to the 'Laird of Drongan' being one of a number of disaffected people laid before the presbytery of Ayr in the time of the Marquis of Montrose's campaigns in 1645.

JOHN CUNNINGHAME OF DRONGAN

William had a son, John, who appears to have become the next laird. He was married to Helen Ross. She was given sasine of the lands on 29 April 1659 and again on 3 June 1660.

CHARLES CUNNINGHAME OF DRONGAN (fl. 1668-1689)

Charles Cunninghame was the proprietor of Drongan estate in 1668. He was a signatory to a charter registered by the Privy Council in 1668. During the time of the Covenanters he was one of several notables in the district who, in response to the Royal Proclamation issued on 30 March 1689, met with his followers at the cross in Ochiltree in support of William and Mary. Drongan Estate was sold to John Dalrymple, 1st Viscount of Stair, in 1698.

JOHN DALRYMPLE, 1ST EARL OF STAIR (c. 1648-1707)

Drongan estate was acquired by John Dalrymple, 1st Earl of Stair, adding it to his already extensive property around Stair House. He was a member of the Faculty of Advocates and became the King's Advocate in Scotland in 1687. He was one of three commissioners deputed to offer the Crown to the Prince and Princess of Orange in 1689. He was also responsible for ordering the massacre at Glencoe. Dalrymple was created Lords Newliston, Glenluce and Stranraer, Viscount Dalrymple and Earl of Stair on 8 April 1703. He succeeded his father, Sir James

Dalrymple, 1st Viscount Stair (born 1619), on 20 November 1695. The 1st Earl of Stair was married to Elizabeth (d. c. 1731), daughter and heiress of Sir John Dundas of Newliston, by whom he had three sons. John succeeded as 2nd Earl of Stair. The second son, William Dalrymple, was the owner of Glenmuir estate and married Penelope Crichton, Countess of Dumfries, in 1698, by whom he had various children, including the 3rd and 4th Earls of Stair. The third son was George Dalrymple of Dalmahoy, one of the Scottish Barons of the Exchequer, who died on 29 July 1745, leaving his eldest son, John, who became the 5th Earl of Stair. The 1st Earl was deeply keen on the Union of Parliaments in 1707, but died on 8 January that year.

JOHN DALRYMPLE, 2ND EARL OF STAIR (1673-1747)

John Dalrymple succeeded to the extensive estates of Stair. He was rarely in the district, for he was a Representative Peer, serving 1707-8, 1715-34, and 1744-47. He was a military officer of considerable standing. He was active at the victories of Marlborough, and fought at the battles of Ramilies, Outenarde and Malplaquet, from 1706-9, being the first to bring news of the victory back to Britain. He was raised through the ranks to Field Marshall, and was Commander of the forces which were fighting on the Rhine. He served as second in command at the Battle of Dettingen (under King George II). He latterly served as a diplomat in France. He was married to Eleanor, widow of James, Viscount Primrose, and daughter of the Earl of Loudoun. He died on 9 May 1747 with no children, whereupon the title passed to his nephew, James Dalrymple.

JAMES DALRYMPLE, 3RD EARL OF STAIR and 5TH EARL OF DUMFRIES (d. 1760)

James Dalrymple succeeded to the estate of Stair, but he retained them only for thirteen years, dying on 13 November 1760. He had no children, and the title passed to his brother, William. William Dalrymple had already inherited the title, Earl of Dumfries, on the death of his mother, Penelope, Countess of Dumfries, in 1742. The Dumfries and Stair titles remained together for this period, and on William's death in 1768 the Dumfries title passed to his sister's son and the Stair title to his cousin, John Dalrymple, who became 5th Earl of Stair. By this time Drongan estate had been deemed surplus to requirements, initially being leased by John Smith, who was to buy it. The remainder of the Stair estate around Stair House was also sold, being acquired by William Dick of Crombie.

DRONGAN HOUSE

Drongan Estate was placed on the market in 1747, as the advertisement in the Caledonian Mercury of 27 July indicates:

> To be sett by publick Roup at Lochmark, upon Tuesday the 25th Day of August next, Certain Parts of the Lands of DRONGAN and SHEILL, lying in the Shire of Air, which were in the natural possession of the late Earl of Stair; the Entry to commence at the Separation of Crop 1747 from the Ground. - The Articles of Roup to be seen any time after the 10th Day of August in the Hands of James Ferguson Writer in Air, or in the Hands of John Smith at Lochmark.

The estate was acquired by the tenant, John Smith. Smith appears to have died around 1763, and on 4 July 1765 another advertisement appeared in the *Glasgow Journal*:

> To sell, in the house of James Gibson, vintner, Ayr, on Tuesday 5th September. Lands of Drongan and Sheill, parish of Stair. There is a very genteel house, and very good office houses, a going coal and a fire machine for drawing the water. Also, a tenement of land in Ayr, the property of the late John Smith of Drongan.

The castle was by this time long abandoned. The ruins appear to have stood for many years afterwards, however, Rev William Rorison, in the Statistical Account of 1841 stating that, 'the walls of which were till lately almost entire'.

MUNGO SMITH (1738-1814)

John Smith was succeeded in Drongan by his son, Mungo Smith, who had been a surgeon in Greenock. Mungo Smith was a Commissioner of Supply for Ayrshire in 1758, and is listed as such at that time, even although he did not succeed to the estate until 1763. He was also a trustee of the Ayr Turnpike Roads. He served from 1767, when the trust was established by Act of Parliament, until 1805. He was also a Trustee of Ayr Harbour, being elected in 1784. He owned a coal yard at the South Quay at that time.

Smith built a new country house for himself, adjoining the old Lochmark House. In the sixteenth and seventeenth century true castles were abandoned in favour of fortified houses, though in many cases these were still named 'castle'. A few of these were erected in the parish, but only one survives today, though it too was virtually replaced by a Georgian country house, the old house retained as a minor part of the house. This house was Drongan House, the old part of the mansion being known originally as Lochmark. It is said that James Armour, the father-in-law of Robert Burns, the poet, was responsible for the construction work. The house must have been completed prior to 1775, for it appears on Armstrong's Map of Ayrshire.

As owner of Drongan estate, Mungo Smith transferred the Drongan name to his new mansion. This was designed in the typical classical style of the period, though not as grand as neighbouring examples at Auchinleck, Dumfries House, or Auchincruive. Drongan House comprises of a raised basement, over which are two floors, built of coursed stonework with quoins at the major corners, as well as on the projecting entrance front. Only three bays in length, on the front and rear facades are pediments, that to the front projecting slightly and adorned with an elliptical panel. On the north and south facades are tall pediments with chimney stacks surmounting, the frontages again of three bays.

During Mungo Smith's ownership, Drongan estate produced a rent of between £2,000 and £3,000 per annum. It comprised of around fourteen sizeable farms, plus some lesser cottages and other properties. He was one of Ayrshire's earliest improving lairds, commencing around 1770. The agricultural revolution took off in Ayrshire over the next ten years, with farm property being redefined, fields straightened and bounded with hedges and ditches, and many smaller properties abandoned.

4.10 Drongan House in 1920s *(Author's Collection)*

Mungo Smith was one of the subscribers to Robert Burns' Edinburgh edition of his *Poems, Chiefly in the Scottish Dialect*, printed by William Creech in 1787.

Mungo Smith was married to Marjory Brodie, daughter of Robert Brodie of Calderhaugh and Hessilhead and his wife, Marion Ewing. They had an only son, John, and two daughters, Isabella and Marion. Isabella Smith was married on 8 September 1806 to Mungo Gilmore of London. Marion Smith was married at Drongan on 20 October 1806 to David Limond of Dalblair, lately of India. She died on 6 September 1863, aged 80. Mungo Smith died on 4 February 1814, aged 76. By his will, the estate was to be sold, being described as being of 'not very great extent, and was largely encumbered'. The estate was worth around £50,000, from which his son, John Smith, was due £30,000 and the remainder was to provide an annuity for his wife and various amounts for his daughters.

JOHN SMITH (1786-1830)

The biggest portion of Drongan Estate was passed to Mungo Smith's son, John Smith, who had expressed a desire to take it on, paying off the debts over a period of time. This appears to have been agreed to by the trustees. John Smith was born in Ayrshire in 1786 and in 1805 went to Calcutta in India where he soon joined the merchant and banking firm of Fergusson & Company, working as a clerk. In 1807 he left and for the next seven years set up his own business as an indigo planter on various estates in Bengal, building for himself a house. In 1814 he returned to Calcutta where he was to become a partner in Fergusson & Company. He was married to Eleanor Gale (a daughter of Robert Brodie of Hazelhead and Ralston) in India in 1816, and had six children. Eleanor (6 November 1817-13 July 1818) and Mungo (23 August 1823-3 August 1824) both died in their infancy. The other four survived until at least 21 years of age. He returned to Scotland for a year, 1819-October 1820. Whilst in Scotland he decided to keep Drongan estate, arranging with his father's trustees to pay all of his father's legacies and liabilities. He also obtained plans for extensions and improvements to Drongan House, but this was never completed. Although he spent most of his time thereafter in India, he often spoke of returning to Drongan, an intention confirmed by his purchase of an adjoining property.

In 1825 John Smith's wife returned to Britain but died on the homeward voyage near Mauritius. Smith was to erect a monument to her memory in Calcutta. He sent his surviving children to England to be educated, but his eldest daughter died on her way back to India.

Marion Smith, the eldest daughter, was married in 1831 to William Fergusson, a member of the the family that owned Fergusson & Co. She returned to India. Margery Smith, second daughter of John Smith, was married on 7 September 1841 to John Jopp WS at Edinburgh. They lived at 30 Albany Street, Edinburgh, where Margery died in February 1893. The third daughter, Elizabeth Smith, was married on 18 July 1843 to Sir William Broun of Colstoun, 9th Baronet (1804-1882). Lady Broun died on 19 August 1899 aged 80 years.

In 1828 the situation regarding Smith's ownership of Drongan estate was challenged and it ended up in the Court of Chancery as Jopp versus Wood. The main question was whether Smith had adopted India as his main place of domicile, and given up his Scottish domicil. In evidence, a letter written by John Smith to his mother soon after his father's death (dated 16 November 1814) gives us some information about the estate:

> I hope at a period less distant than I ever dared flatter myself with before, once more to return to the bosom of my family, there to enjoy a felicity which so long an absence must tend to improve … Dr Clark is of opinion that ten or twelve years should be the utmost of my residence in India, perhaps even less if the coal could only do something to paying off the debt in England.

Further letters from Smith to the trustees indicated that he was keen on developing the property. He added additional lands and selected a 'proper site for the intended new house for the Drongan estate'. He wished the trustees to transfer some of the land to him, so that he could be placed on the roll of freeholders of Ayrshire. His letters make reference to the newly planted woodlands.

He wrote in another letter of 23 November 1830:

> I should be well pleased if no purchase should become nececessary until I have again the pleasure of seeing you, as I still hope I may be able to get away from this, at all events upon a furlough in another year or two, but I shall feel obliged by all the information you can supply me with on the subject in the mean time.

Unfortunately, he died of cholera at Calcutta on 3 December 1830. John Smith had been an active elder of the 'Scotch Church' in Calcutta. His will was written in Ayr. Drongan estate continued to be run by Smith's trustees until it was sold in December 1854 after some competition to Alexander Oswald of Auchincruive for £48,600. The estate had been offered for sale earlier, for in 1848 it was advertised in the *Ayr Advertiser*:

> The lands and estate of Drongan, containing 1,783 imperial acres or thereby, whereof about 180 acres are under thriving woods and plantations from 15 to 50 years growth, and the remainder is arable land, let in suitable farms and possessions to a respectable and industrious tenantry. The minerals are very valuable …

In 1841, Rev William Rorison, writing in the *New Statistical Account*, noted that the house 'is, at present, in a very dilapidated state. It is known that the late proprietor contemplated either the rebuilding or making great repairs and additions – all of which, as well as many other designs for the improvement of his estate generally, were frustrated by his much lamented death, which took place some years ago at Calcutta, where he had for many years resided as a merchant and banker, and when he was on the eve of returning home'.

ALEXANDER OSWALD OF AUCHINCRUIVE MP (1811-1868)
Alexander Haldane Oswald was basically an absentee landlord, living either locally at Auchincruive House or else on one of his many other properties. No doubt Drongan House would have been let to tenants for the fifteen years he owned it. Alexander had served as a Member of Parliament for Ayr from 1843-1852. He was married to Lady Louisa Elizabeth Frederica, daughter of the 1st Earl of Craven, by whom he had four children. The only son, James Haldane Oswald (1848-1866) died unmarried before his father and Auchincruive passed to Alexander's brother. In 1869, when Alexander Oswald's daughter, Edith May Haldane Oswald was married to the Hon. John Manners Yorke, he gave them Drongan estate.

JOHN YORKE, 7TH EARL OF HARDWICKE (1840-1909)
The Hon. John Manners Yorke was born on 30 October 1840, son of Charles Yorke, 4th Earl of Hardwicke. He was a captain and commander in the Royal Navy, serving in the Baltic Sea in 1854 and and the Black Sea in 1855. He became Inspector of the Coastguard at Folkestone (1870-74). He was a Justice of the Peace and Depute Lieutenant for Cambridgeshire. In 1904, on the death of his nephew, Albert Edward Philip Henry Yorke, 6th Earl of Hardwicke (1867-1904), he succeeded to the earldom as the 7th Earl of Hardwicke. He had four sons and one daughter by two wives – Charles Alexander Yorke, (11 November 1869-1 February 1936), who became the 8th Earl of Hardwicke; Albert Ernest Frederick Yorke (11 July 1871-24 August 1928); Claude John Yorke (17 October 1872-15 September 1940); Bernard Elliot Yorke (5 June 1874-23 December 1943); and Susan Yorke (7 May 1881-21 August 1865). Lord Hardwicke hardly visited Drongan, owning other houses at Sydney Lodge, Southampton and Rutlandgate, London. Lord Hardwicke died on 13 March 1909. He left an estate valued at £38,930 0s 2d. His widow, the Dowager Countess of Hardwicke, stayed for some time in Drongan House, but more often at her English homes in London and Southampton. She died on 27 July 1930.

CHARLES YORKE, 8TH EARL OF HARDWICKE (1869-1936)
The next owner of Drongan estate was Charles Alexander Yorke, 8th Earl of Hardwicke, who was born on 11 November 1869. He served as a Lieutenant in the Army Motor Reserve. He was married on 27 April 1911 to Ellen, or Nellie Russell, daughter of James Russell, of Auckland, New Zealand. She was awarded the CBE in 1918. Although he owned Drongan estate, Lord Hardwicke's usual residence was at 13 Queensberry Place in south-west London. The Earl and Countess did visit occasionally, such as in September 1912 when they entertained a family party at

Drongan House. They were to be divorced in 1927.

In 1919 Drongan estate was placed on the market. At the time it comprised of Drongan House and the farms of Craigbrae, Kerrston, Dickston, Mill of Shield, Hannahston, Shield, the Post Office, store and 67 houses at Taiglum. The estate extended to 1,766 acres. Many of the farms were sold off during the following years.

The lands of Drongan House, and the house itself, were purchased by David Downie JP, merchant of Coylton and Ayr, in 1919. He had been a grocer in Coylton and Drongan Store until he sold up in 1948. He died on 6 January 1949 aged 77. Henry and John Knox tenanted the farm in the 1920s, before it was taken over by Mrs Lena Downie or Lymburn, wife of James Lymburn.

Drongan House, by now the farmhouse of a large farm, was acquired by the Gemmell family, currently the property of David M. Gemmell.

POLQUHAIRN

The estate of Polquhairn was located on the southern extent of the parish, extending over the moorlands, plus three farms north-west of the village.

The estate was owned by the Cunninghames, a branch of the Cunninghames of Kilmaurs. A few names of owners can be found from old charters. On 4 July 1322 King Robert I issued a charter to 'the penny land of Polcairn' to Hugh De Cunningham. The family remained proprietors for many years, in 1400 a confirmation being issued for William de Cunningham.

In the Acts of Council reference is made to 'Marian Craufurd, the spouse of the umquhile [late] Robert Cunyngham of Polqharne', who pursued an action against Sir William Colville of Ochiltree on 21 June 1493.

In 1578 an 'Instrument of Seizin given by the hands of William Cuningham, younger, of Polquharne, as lord fiear and heritor, and James Cuningham of Polquharne, his father, as lord frank-tenementar, of the six shilling and eight penny lands of old extent of Burntoun, occupied by William Bell, lying within their lands of Easter Polquharne, King's Kyle and shire of Ayr, in favour of a prudent man, John Cuningham, sailor, lawful son of the said James, and brother-german of the said William, according to the tenor of the charter of blench-ferme made to him thereupon. Done on the ground of the said lands at eleven o'clock before noon of the 28th day of October 1578, before these witnesses, John Cuningham in Weleis, Gabriel Cuningham his son, and the said William Bell.'

On 10 March 1600 a charter was issued by the Cunninghams to the Fergushills:

> The quhilk day, etc., compeirt personally Robert Cuninghame, above the [Wallace] Tour, burgess of the burgh of Air, and brother germane to umquhile William Cuninghame of Polquharne, quha of his awin

frie motive, etc., gaif reall and actual possession to David Fergushill, Provost of Air, and Jonet Kennedy, his spous, being personalie present, of all the and haile the said Davidis croft land, callit Nolt Fauld, with housses, etc., occupyit of befoir be the said Robert.

The Cunninghams appear to have remained as owners until at least 1618.

In 1621 Wester Polquhairn (Bonnyton-Polquhairn) had been acquired by John Chalmers of Gadgirth, proprietor of extensive lands around Gadgirth Castle in the parish of Coylton. James Chalmers of Corraith (Dundonald parish) held Easter Polquhairn in 1623. By 1632 John Chalmers, second son of John Chalmers of Bonnyton, had become owner of both halves of Polquhairn estate. Only fleeting references to the family occur in the records: Reginald Chalmers, second son of James Chalmers of Gadgirth (c. 1595-1646), was given the estate of Polquhairn. Reference is found in 1675 of the baptism of Robert Chalmers, son of Ronald Chalmers of Polquhairn.

On 30 March 1689 Ronald Chalmers of Polquhairn turned out at Ochiltree Cross with fellow county lairds in support of the defence of the realm. 'A Proclamation for calling together the militia on this side of the Tay and the Fencible Men in some shires' looked for men who would rise in support of King William II and his wife, Queen Mary.

By 1696 Polquhairn had been acquired by John Dalrymple, 2nd Earl of Stair (1673-1747), adding it to Drongan estate and his caput at Stair House. He was succeeded by his son, James Dalrymple, 3rd Earl of Stair, who died in 1760. However, he probably sold Polquhairn in the early 1750s, at a similar period to the sale of Drongan estate. In 1704 Alexander Cuningham of Polquhairn is listed as a Commissioner of Supply. He had a daughter Marion Cunningham. She was married to Adam Craufurd Newall of Dalleagles (New Cumnock). There was also a second daughter, co-heiress to the estate, but her share was purchased by Adam Crawfurd Newall.

On 23 February 1756 Adam Craufurd of Dalleagles had sasine of the eight merk lands of Easter Polquhairn, with the manor place, and of the 33s 4d lands of Knockguldron, of old extent. He was one of the Commissioners of Supply for Ayrshire in 1755. He was the last representative of the Craufurds of Dalleagles. A relative, Mary Craufurd of Dalleagles, married Adam Newall, son of David Newall of Knockreoch. Their son, Adam Craufurd Newall succeeded James Cuthbert of Dalleagles, but sold Dalleagles in 1791 to Hugh Ross of Kerse, after which he was designated as Adam Craufurd Newall of Polquhairn.

In 1787 Polquhairn was the property of Adam Craufurd Newall or Newall Craufurd. He died of palsy on 21 June 1790. Apparently, he left his affairs 'in disorder', resulting in a case being brought to the Court of Session on 26 November 1796. His wife, Marion Cunningham, had died on 5 May 1768. He is known to have remarried, as he was survived by his second wife, who moved to Greenan House, south of Ayr. She died on 12 January 1800.

Adam Craufurd Newall had a son, Alexander Craufurd, who was friendly with James Boswell of Auchinleck. He dined with the diarist at Auchinleck House on many occasions, including 2 June 1779, when he is referred to as 'young Polquhairn' in Boswell's journal. He was in fact, one of the last house guests Boswell entertained at Auchinleck (on 8 January 1795) before the diarist died.

Polquhairn estate was acquired by Allan MacDougall, a Writer to the Signet, in early 1792. He commissioned Thomas Johnstone of Edinburgh, a land surveyor, to make a plan of the estate with the intention of laying it out in a more modern manner. By September he was offering leases for various farms on the estate on nineteen-year terms. In 1810 tenders were invited for alterations and extensions to the house. He died on 2 April 1814. He was succeeded by Lieutenant Colonel John MacDougall. His second daughter, Catherine Scott MacDougall, died soon after, on 25 June 1814. In 1815 the house was offered to let –it was described as having eight bedrooms, dining room, drawing room, kitchen and servants' quarters. Adjoining were newly built offices.

The estate was placed on the market again in August 1827. It was acquired by James Pettigrew Wilson (c.1790-28 March 1851). He married Isabella Mitchell (c.1799-21 February 1877). By her he had John Pettigrew Wilson, who succeeded; Sarah Pettigrew Wilson (d 27 December 1873 aged 37); Robert Pettigrew Wilson (died 26 March 1898 aged 59), James Pettigrew Wilson, who succeeded his brother, Thomas Pettigrew Wilson (d. 28 February 1905 aged 65) and Isabella Pettigrew Wilson (died 7 January 1905, aged 78).

The estate passed to their son, John Pettigrew Wilson. He served as an advocate in Edinburgh, living at 6 Dundas Street whilst working there. He lived in a large villa in Ayr, named Gargowan, which was named after one of the farms on the estate. Located in Racecourse Road, the house is now the Ayrshire Hospice. He was appointed Sheriff-Substitute of Inverness in 1871 and subsequently became Sheriff of Ross and Cromarty and Sutherland. He was a member of the Speculative Society of Edinburgh. Keen to support local organisations, he presented a cup to Ayr Rifle Volunteers in the 1870s. In 1883, when the new Road Act was introduced, he was elected as a road trustee for Ochiltree parish. He died on 4 March 1884, aged 60, and is interred in Ayr Cemetery. His estate was valued at £7,396.

Polquhairn passed to his brother, James Pettigrew Wilson JP. Born around 1829, he was noted for his considerable height, standing six feet four inches. He served as a county councillor for Ochiltree district, and a Justice of the Peace. He was noted for his entertaining skills and built up a considerable collection of violins, which he often played. He died on 20 January 1899 and was buried in Ayr Cemetery. His estate was valued at £6,400.

The estate of Polquhairn then became the property of Thomas Pettigrew

Wilson, brother to James and John Pettigrew Wilson. He died on 28 February 1905, aged 65, leaving a considerable estate – real estate valued at £25,000, an annual income from mineral rights of £540, mineral rights valued at £10,000 and a personal estate of £14,161. He was interred in Ayr Cemetery.

Much of the hill lands of the estate were acquired around this time by John Pettigrew Walker, their nephew (died 1929), who also tenanted the lands of Bellsbank at Dalmellington.

4.11 Polquhairn House *(Dane Love)*

Following the death of Thomas Pettigrew Wilson, Polquhairn estate was placed on the market. At that time, it comprised of five working farms - Polquhairn Home Farm, Elymains, Muirston, Piperhill and Steelpark, totalling around 1,600 acres. In addition, the lands of Hayhill and Laigh Elymains also formed part of the estate. Polquhairn House was described as having three public rooms, kitchen and domestic offices downstairs, plus six bedrooms upstairs.

The estate remained unsold, passing to John Walker of Polquhairn and Bellsbank. He was the son of William Walker of Bellsbank JP (c. 1819-1898) and Barbara Wilson, eldest daughter of James Pettigrew Wilson. The estate appears to have either been sold quite regularly around this period, or else failed to sell when placed on the market. It was offered for sale in 1930, when it comprised five farms and small properties extending over 1,600 acres (Home Farm, Piperhill, Elymains, Muirston, Steelpark, Hayhill and Laigh Elymains). In 1930 Polquhairn was sold to Archibald Pyper, leaving the farms of Steelpark, Elymains, Hayhill and Muirston as part of Bellsbank Estate, owned by the trustees of John Walker.

Again, Polquhairn was placed on the market in 1945, the Home Farm having 357 acres of improved ground, plus 500 acres of hill pasture, Piperhill having 166 acres, plus the lands of Heidmark and Knockguldron.

Through time, the estate of Polquhairn has been broken up, so that today it is more or less a farm of its own.

BONNYTON

Bonnyton was formed into a small estate in the fifteenth century or earlier. In 1523 there is reference to William Cunningham, depute to the Sheriff of Ayr.

In the late sixteenth and early seventeenth century the estate was the property of Josias Stewart, second son of Andrew, 3rd Lord Ochiltree. Stewart was able to build up a fair-sized estate during his lifetime, which included Blairquhan in the parish of Straiton. He was the executor of his sister, Jean Kennedy, Lady Bargany's will. This document is useful in describing the contents of a Scots country house of the period. The last reference to him dates from 1625 and he is known to have died without issue.

By 1704 the estate was the property of John Chalmers, who is noted that year as a Commissioner of Supply . In 1733 he erected a new double-storey house at the north end of the courtyard, with byres and barns. A datestone was included in the topmost quoin on the front façade, with a square stone bearing initials centrally placed on the wall. The western byre had a stone with the date 1741 and the initials JC and MS, probably indicating John Chalmers and his wife. Unfortunately, this latter stone was destroyed when the byres were developed for housing. In 1747, when General William Roy compiled his maps of the country, Bonnyton was depicted as having some improved estate policies around it. To the north of the house was a large enclosed field, whereas to the south an enclosure had two large circular woods, or 'mounts' at the southern end, probably forming a vista from the house itself.

The present Bonnyton House was erected in the mid nineteenth century as a sizeable residence for the owner. Built of coarsed rubble, it was enhanced by the presence of red sandstone quoins, window dressings and two double-height bay windows on the principal facade. Adjoining the house were stables and offices.

John Hunter W.S. owned Bonnyton in the late eighteenth century. He was born in 1746, the second son of Andrew Hunter, 8th laird of Abbotshill in Ayr, and his wife, Grace Maxwell, daughter of Colonel William Maxwell of Cardoness. He qualified as a Writer to the Signet in 1769. He married Jane Fergusson (1752-4 July 1838), second daughter and co-heiress of William Fergusson of Doonholm, Ayr, in 1773. By this marriage he acquired the estate of Bonnyton. They had seven children – Andrew, who succeeded; William (28 March 1778-25 March 1799); James (24 September 1783-30 April 1794); Christopher (4 October 1785-20 December 1790); John (17 April 1786-20 March 1803); Fergusson (14 January

1788-6 December 1800) and Alexander (9 January 1790-14 July 1862).

John Hunter W.S. was the owner of many other properties in the district, at times owning Greenfield (latterly called Cambusdoon House) and Alloway Croft, both Ayr, and Hollybush House (Dalrymple). He owned Doonholm House, Ayr, which became his principal home, and Bonnyton was often let to tenants. He died on 23 April 1823 and was buried in the Old Kirkyard, Ayr.

The next owner of Bonnyton was John Hunter's eldest son, Andrew Hunter. Born in Edinburgh on 7 August 1776, he married Helen Campbell (13 December 1788-24 February 1876), daughter of John Campbell of Ormadale in Argyll, on 21 April 1814. They had four sons and one daughter – John (19 September 1815-30 December 1846), Campbell (1818-1846), William Francis (who succeeded), Andrew (20 August 1821-20 September 1898) and Helen (27 January 1816-6 July 1888).

Andrew Hunter went to sea in 1791, much against the wishes of his family, sailing from Greenock in the *Countess of Haddington* for the West Indies and America. After an absence of seventeen months, he returned to Greenock. In September, 1793, he joined the *Royal William* at Spithead as a midshipman, and in October he was drafted to the *Resistance* and sailed in November for the Cape and East Indies. In June 1794, while sailing in the Straits of Malacca, they seized a French twenty-gun ship. Andrew Hunter was sent as one of the officers in charge. After arriving at Calcutta, he was recommended to the house of Messrs. Fairlie, Gilmore and Co., but he disliked working there, preferring the navy. However, he joined the firm at the request of his father. He does not appear to have remained long in the business, as in December, 1794, he went to sea on board the Dolphin as third officer, and sailed for the Malabar Coast, returning to Calcutta in May 1795, when he left the ship. This was lucky, for when it set off on her next voyage, it was never seen again. Hunter continued at sea, sailing to the Straits settlements, China, Ceylon, Burma, and other locations. In May 1803 his vessel was captured by a French privateer, and he was landed at Analaboo, in Malaya, where he remained for six weeks. In July an American vessel rescued him, leaving him at Muckee, where he heard of a Captain Petbury having been stabbed by the natives at Soosu, and his ship was in their possession. Hunter set off in an open boat to capture the ship, but was blown off course until he was picked up by another American vessel. The sailors managed to retake the ship, which they brought to Sappanooly. During Hunter's next voyage, in July 1806, his vessel was captured by the French frigate *La Simillliante*, and in September he was landed at the Isle of Bourbon. In November he was taken to the Mauritius. On 7 May 1807, he sailed from Mauritius in command of the Danish ship *Catharina* for Tranquebar, where he arrived on 29 May, and gave up the command. After staying in India for four months, he sailed for England, where he arrived in March, 1808.

Back on British soil, he joined the Ayrshire Regiment as a Captain at Gosport in July 1808. After some time spent in Scotland, he again joined the regiment in February 1809, at the Silver Hill Barracks in Sussex. In August he was back in Scotland, where he rejoined the regiment at Musselburgh, finally resigning in January, 1810.

Andrew Hunter also served as a Depute Lieutenant for the Ayrshire, and was gazetted Captain of the 2nd (or Cunningham and Cumnock) Ayrshire Yeomanry Cavalry on 28 June 1821. He was subsequently presented with a silver snuff-box bearing the inscription, 'Presented to Captain Hunter by the Cumnock Troop of Yeomanry Cavalry as a mark of esteem, February 8, 1828.'

Andrew Hunter died at Helensburgh on 30 December 1856 and was buried in Ayr's Old Kirkyard. He was succeeded to the lands by his son, Captain William Hunter.

Captain, or latterly, Lieutenant-Colonel, William Francis Hunter, was born at Hollybush House on 20 June 1820. He was married on 24 November 1859 to Eliza Burnley, daughter of William Frederick Burnley of Edinburgh. Hunter entered the Honourable East India Company's service by direct commission. He was quickly promoted, serving as Cornet in the Bombay Cavalry, from 16 April 1837. He was appointed to the 2nd Bombay Light Cavalry on 22 April 1838. He was raised to Lieutenant on 12 December 1840, then Captain on 8 May 1849. He was appointed Major on 6 February 1861 and Lieutenant-Colonel on 31 December 1861. During his war service, he was present at the capture of Bushire on 10 December 1856,

4.12 Bonnyton House, South front in 2020 *(Dane Love)*

during the Persian war. He was appointed Aide-de-Camp to Major-General Stalker, commanding the First Expeditionary Force to Persia, in January 1857, and was recommended for step in rank by Sir James Outram in June 1857. William Francis Hunter died at Bombay on 25 Fenruary 1862, however, by this time the lands of Bonnyton and others had been sold.

Bonnyton estate was purchased in 1859 by William Alison JP, of Coldwakening farm, near Strathaven, for £15,000. He also owned Dunavon, Strathaven. He emigrated to Sydney, New South Wales. He died in 1887. The Alisons are said to descend from the MacAllister family, but adopted the surname Alison to Anglify the surname. The family claim Archibald Alison, of Avondale, a Covenanter who was captured at the Battle of Airds Moss and subsequently executed in Edinburgh, as an ancestor. James Alison appears to have inherited Bonnyton. He was born in 1854 and served as a Commissioner of Supply for the county of Ayr.

In May 1879 the estate was offered for let. Included were the shootings over 1,500 acres and the mansion house, described as having a dining room, drawing room, nine bedrooms, bathroom, kitchen, servants' room and other conveniences. Adjoining were a coachhouse, three stalled stable and a harness room.

Bonnyton was subsequently acquired in 1888 by John Taylor Gordon of Nethermuir, Aberdeenshire. He was succeeded to the lands by his only son, Captain, subsequently Major John Maxwell Gordon.

By 1891-1909 the owner was Major John Maxwell Gordon of Bonnyton. Born on 8 July 1862, he served in the 12th Royal Lancers, being promoted to the rank of Major in May 1902. He was married on 29 September 1891 to Mary Dalglish, daughter of G. H. Dalglish of Rock Mount, Liverpool, at Tarporley Parish Church, Cheshire. He spent much of his time living in England, at Oaklands, a fine red brick mansion at Spurstow, near Bunbury, in Cheshire. At the time Bonnyton estate comprised of four farms – Drumbowie, Waterton, Ravenscroft and Bonnyton farm itself. Captain Gordon served in the Boer War, which he survived. He died on 17 January 1909, aged 46, as a result of an injury received in a riding accident. A substantial memorial window was erected to his memory by his wife in the south aisle of the church of St Boniface, Bunbury, depicting various saints.

From 1909-1936 Bonnyton House was leased, then owned, by Dr Alexander Macrae. Born in Ayr, the son of a hand-loom weaver, he qualified as a doctor in 1885 and found employment as medical officer to Merry & Cuninghame's coal pits at Rankinston. He originally did his rounds on horseback, latterly using a 'safety' bicycle, then motorbike and car. He also served for some time on the local school board and was regarded as a notable wit, entertaining folk with his anecdotes. He was a patron of the Scottish Opera and Celebrity Concerts held in Glasgow. A staunch radical, he acted as a steward at many of Gladstone's meetings. Dr Macrae's surgery was located in an outbuilding at Bonnyton House, which survives at Bonnyton House Cottage. Bonnyton House was often referred to as the Doctor's

House as a result of Macrae's ownership. He retired in 1935 and died in June 1936, aged 74. He never married.

Another doctor became the owner of the Victorian half of Bonnyton House – Dr George Bryden MBChB (by 1940). He had three sons, Robert, George and John. In Drongan, Bryden Way was named in his honour. In Dr Bryden's memory, items of furniture were gifted to various local churches in the area covered by his practice. These were a lectern and pulpit light for Coylton, where they were dedicated on 5 October 1969, a pulpit light for the Schaw Kirk, a chair for St Clare's R. C. Church, a pulpit light at Rankinston, table lectern at Ochiltree and a lectern at Dalrymple.

In 1971 Bonnyton House was bought by Dr Nicholas John Martin (1943-) and his wife, Alison. Dr Martin was a lecturer in biochemical sciences at Auchincruive College of Agriculture. In 2012 he was appointed as a director of the Dark Sky Observatory at Dalmellington.

Bonnyton House was divided into two halves – the Victorian wing and the 1733 original farmhouse. The latter was owned by the Jardine family until 2005, when it was sold to Andrew Kerr (1972-) and Laura Dunlop (1977-). Andrew Kerr restored the farmhouse part of the building, removing the rendering back to the orignal stonework. He added the new porch on the south front in a traditional style, matching the old farmhouse. A square stone with a carved thistle was added to the main façade, with the initials of the first names of the family – Andrew, Laura, Shauni and Kari. To the rear a stone lintel was inserted with the dates 1733 and 2007, the date of erection of the original farmhouse and date of renovations.

4.13 Bonnyton House, East front in 2020 *(Dane Love)*

Bonnyton farm was broken up and the steading was developed over a period of time into three cottages, built out of outbuildings and new build. Two bungalows were erected adjoining the road west of the steading in 2018-20.

DRUMJOAN

There were a few other landowners owning smaller properties in the parish. The Drumjoan estate was anciently owned by the Cathcart family, a branch of the Cathcarts of that Ilk, who became Lords Cathcart. In 1656 Cathcart of Drumjoan is claimed to owe David French, Writer in Edinburgh, 300 merks which his father had granted in his bond to William Mitchell. The case went to the Court of Session in 1696, where it was claimed this was a means of obtaining funds illegally. French apparently obtained the bond from James Cathcart of Carbieston, son to Francis Cathcart of Carbieston, no doubt close relatives.

The last Cathcart of Drumjoan was Robert Cathcart, who died unmarried on 19 February 1734. He had been noted as a Commissioner of Supply in 1704. The estate was in debt by bond during his ownership to MacRae of Ochiltree, and in 1727 he disponed the estate to Lord Cathcart, reserving a power to alter. Just before he died, he made a settlement of the whole estate to Abigail Rankin, second wife of Lieutenant John Campbell of Horsecleugh, Cumnock (died 28 July 1725). This was questioned by James Neil, merchant in Ayr, in the Court of Session in 1756, but Campbell won. Robert Cathcart was Abigail's mother's full cousin. John and Abigail's son, also John, adopted the older name of their family in lieu of that of Horsecleugh – Campbell of Skerrington, another property near Cumnock. He was an advocate, matriculating his arms around 1750 and making an entail of his estates in 1770. He moved to Little Cessnock, which he renamed Skerrington in 1763. He was married in 1758 to Wilhelmina Agnew (died 21 January 1800), daughter of Sir Andrew Agnew of Lochnaw, 5th Baronet. John Campbell died on 9 April 1781, being succeeded by his eldest son, also John.

John Campbell of Skerrington was a lieutenant in the Western Fencibles. He died unmarried on 28 May 1782. There being no other sons, he was succeeded in the estates by his sister, Eleanora, who was married to Charles Maxwell of Cowhill in Dumfriesshire. On her succession, Maxwell sold Cowhill to pay his debts. The family adopted the name Campbell thereafter. Eleanora Campbell died on 18 November 1788 and was succeeded to Skerrington by her son, Dougald John Campbell.

Dougald John Campbell was born on 17 February 1783 and succeeded officially at the age of seven. He was married on 25 August 1804 to Janet Baillie, fourth daughter of the Hon. William Baillie, Lord Polkemmet, one of the Senators of the College of Justice. He died at New Orleans, United States of America, on 25 October 1827. He left behind four sons and six daughters, the third surviving son, Robert Campbell, succeeding. One of his sons, William Campbell (1807-1825), attended Glasgow University. He was travelling on board the Christiana (launched 1818) heading for Trinidad from Greenock when it was wrecked at Patterson's Rock, Sanda, Argyll, on 2 December 1825. He was drowned with all others on board as a result of the terrible weather.

His brother, Robert Campbell was born on 19 December 1814 and succeeded as heir on 18 September 1829. He, too, attended Glasgow University. He was married on 25 January 1843 to Anne Carr (died 16 October 1886), daughter of John Carr of Dunston Hall, Durham. He served as a Justice of the Peace and an advocate. He died on 29 December 1868.

William Campbell succeeded, although he was regarded as a minor, being just thirteen years old. Born on 27 June 1855, he was educated at Edinburgh Academy followed by Edinburgh University. The estate factor was William Moncrieff, accountant in Edinburgh, and one of Campbell's tutors. At the time, the estate extended to 753 acres. He was married on 31 March 1880 to Alice Mary Fraser, second daughter of the Hon. Patrick, Lord Fraser.

Campbell was admitted to the Faculty of Advocates in 1878. He became a Queen's Counsel in 1898 and Dean of the Faculty of Advocates from 1905-8. In 1908 he was appointed as a judge of the Court of Session, entitling him to take a title. He adopted the name Lord Skerrington after his Cumnock estate, which at the time comprised of five farms – Bowes, Craigens, Horsecleugh, Netherthird and Skerrington. In Ochiltree parish he owned Drumjoan, Drumsmudden, Reidston and Whitehill. Lord Skerrington was to be the first Roman Catholic appointed as a judge in Scotland, resulting in some Protestant opposition. In 1919 he was given the honour of Knight Commander of St Gregory the Great by Pope Benedict XV.

4.14 Lord Skerrington in 1910
(Author's Collection)

Lord Skerrington retired from the judicial bench in December 1925. He died at his Edinburgh home after a long illness on 21 July 1927, his widow surviving until 21 January 1928. He was buried in the cemetery adjoining St John the Evangelist's Church in Edinburgh. They had three sons, Osmund William (11 February 1881-28 July 1907), who never married and who died in South Africa; Basil Patrick Campbell, who succeeded; Lieutenant-Colonel Frederick Robert Maxwell Campbell (born 27 January 1884); and a daughter, Gladys Anne Margaret (13 December 1886-17 March 1967), who died unmarried.

Drumjoan estate was broken up – Drumjoan farm itself being sold to the tenant, David Purdie. The other farms were gradually sold off in the years following, so that today the estate no longer exists.

SMALL ESTATES

Within Ochiltree parish there have been a few other landowners who owned lesser properties at different periods in history.

Barquharrie was classed as a small estate, though latterly became a farm on the Dumfries House Estate. In 1603 Barquharrie was the property of Hew Crawford. It is said that there had been a building of some considerable strength here, perhaps a small tower house.

David Crawford of Barquharrie was one of the local lairds who turned up at Ochiltree Cross for the defence of the realm, following the Royal Proclamation of 30 March 1689.

The lands became the property of Captain Hugh Campbell of Barquharrie, third son of Sir Hugh Campbell of Cessnock (1615-1686). He is thought to have been born around 1660. He was married on 5 June 1702 to Margaret Boswell (b. c. 1672), daughter of David Boswell of Auchinleck. In 1725 Hugh Campbell of Barquharrie is listed as one of the heritors of the parish.

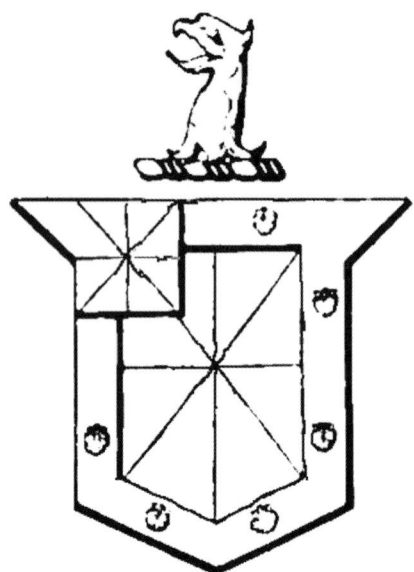

4.15 Campbell of Barquharrie and Sornbeg arms
(*Author's Collection*)

Captain Hugh Campbell and Margaret Boswell had at least one son, Hugh Campbell of Barquharrie, born at the farm around 1703. He later became the proprietor of Mayfield and was Comptroller of Customs. He married Margaret Henderson (b. c. 1706, daughter of David Henderson of Tinnochside) around 1725-27, by whom he had three children – Hugh Campbell, Claud Campbell and Bruce Campbell. The first two died without children, and Hugh was succeeded on his death in 1782 to Mayfield by Bruce Campbell (1735-February 1813). Bruce was married in February 1772 to Annabella Wilson, daughter of James Wilson of Kilmarnock. They had a son, Hugh Campbell of Barquharrie, a Justice of the Peace in Ayrshire and Captain in the 85th Regiment. Hugh Campbell was married on 18 December 1797 to Sophia, youngest daughter of Thomas Barber of Greasley, Nottinghamshire. He died at Bath, 5 January 1824. By this time, however, Barquharrie was no longer their property.

The representatives of the Campbells of Barquharrie retained the name in their surname. The eldest son of Hugh was Hugh Bruce, born 8 April 1803. He married Anne Hurd, but they had no issue. He married again, in October 1832, to Elizabeth, daughter of E. Werge of Hexgrave Park, Nottinghamshire. The second son was Thomas Alexander; the third, William; the fourth John. A daughter, Anne, was married to George Douglas of Rodinghead, Mauchline; another Annabella, married to William Comyn of County Clare; and a third, Sophia Elizabeth, who married Denis Browne of Brownestowne, Ireland.

In the 1770s the house was occupied by Rev George Reid, former minister of the parish. James Boswell often visited him, for example on 10 September 1780, when he walked from Auchinleck House to Barquharrie and back. It is worth quoting Boswell's Journal of that date, which gives a flavour of life at Barquharrie:

> … we walked on to Barquharrie. I had all my old ideas of Ochiltree as fresh as ever. One should in youth stock his mind with agreeable ideas, which, though they should die away for a time, will revive again. We found Mr George Reid quite hearty. He set before us a dram, white wine, strong ale, and bread. I drank a glass of ale. I then asked him to pray. He said he would sing a psalm and read also. He sung the 43rd Psalm, all but the last verse, to the French tune; and he read the 16 Psalm in prose, and in the old-fashioned way read the title, 'Michtam of David'. Then he prayed very well. The servants were in the room. It was truly comfortable and it was even wonderful to see my father's governor at the age of eighty-five, all but some days, quite entire in mind.

Bardarroch was a small property owned by the Colvilles, perhaps a younger branch of the Ochiltree family. In the late eighteenth century, a high square whinstone monument was erected near the house, in what became known as Monument Field. It is named on Thomson's *Atlas of Scotland* in 1832. This was supposedly erected by one John Donald, in memory of John, Earl of Cassillis. The memorial was subsequently destroyed, sometime around 1850, and the part bearing the inscription was built into the chimney head of the cottage at nearby Crawsland. The ornate copestone from the monument was used as a plinth at the front door of Bardarroch farmhouse. In 1894 Bardarroch, which extended to 335 acres, was described as an estate when it was sold for £9,600 to James Kenneth of Buckreddan House (Kilwinning). The estate rental was £405. The farm was subsequently offered to let.

James Kenneth (d. 23 May 1972) was the son of Captain Archibald Kenneth of Buckreddan House, Kilwinning, owner of A. Kenneth & Sons Ltd. This was an important firm of coalmasters and brickmakers. James Kenneth usually resided at Oakfield, Lochgilphead, Argyll, and with his brother, Robert (who lived at Bourtreehill House, Irvine) took over the business on their father's death. Kenneth's had five coal mines (in the Irvine area) in 1947 when the industry was nationalised, but latterly continued as brickmakers and suppliers of building materials. The business, which was latterly better known as Kenneth's Building Services Ltd., was sold on 31 December 1977 to the Glasgow Iron and Steel Company Ltd.

The lands of Burnockstone were owned by the Fergushill family for some years. Rev John Fergushill was the minister of Ayr from 1639 until 1642. He was born around 1590, the only son of David Fergushill (d. April 1613), Provost of Ayr, and Janet Kennedy. (He had a sister, Janet, who married John Cuninghame). He received his education at Ayr school, followed by the University of Edinburgh, Montauban (France), and the University of Glasgow. He was awarded the MA in 1612. He served as minister of Ochiltree from 1614-1639. Fergushill died on 11 June 1642. He was married twice, firstly to Agnes Eccles. By her he had Robert Fergushill of Burnockstone, who was apprenticed to Patrick Hepburn, apothecary, Edinburgh, on 23 February 1642; David, who became an apprentice to David Gray, merchant in Edinburgh, 7 September 1636; and William, who was apprenticed to Abraham Thomson, merchant in Edinburgh, 12 March 1646. Fergushill married for a second time, to Annabel Wallace, daughter of Matthew Wallace. By her he had three children, James, Isobel and Anne.

It was Robert Fergushill who was to receive the estate, being transferred to him by Lord Ochiltree in 1658. He is mentioned in the Presbytery Records of 2 May 1693. He received sasine of the lands of Auchinway, Corsehill and Clerkstoun on 15 December 1698. He was still alive in 1716. He was married to Jean MacDermeit.

Burnockstone passed to Rev John MacDermeit, who adopted the additional surname, Fergushill The estate was entailed in 1744. MacDermeit was a minister at Straiton, being born in 1724, the son of Rev John MacDermeit, minister of Ayr. He was educated at the University of Glasgow and and graduated Master of Arts in 1746. He was licensed to preach by the Presbytery of Ayr on 21 December 1748 and was ordained at Straiton on 3 August 1749. He assumed the additional surname Fergushill. He gave a band of relief to Charles Cochrane of Ochiltree from certain cautionary obligations entered into by his father, dated 1730. Rev John MacDermeit Fergushill was married on 11 January 1762 to Agnes MacJerrow, daughter of William MacJerrow of Altan Albany (Barr). By her he had - John (b. 24 April 1763); William (b. 12 December 1764); Giles (b. 25 December 1766); Janet (b. 27 February 1769), who married Andrew Wilson, merchant in Refrew; Agnes (b. 29 January 1771), married on 6 February 1792 Rev William Crawford DD, minister of Straiton, 1791-1816; Jean (b 12 January 1773); Robert (b. 17 September 1775) and Helen (23 May 1778-7 March 1828). Rev John's wife, Agnes, died at Largs on 20 June 1818, aged 81. Rev John MacDermeit Fergushill had sasine of the four merk land of old extent of Burnockstone, with the houses, biggings, yards, etc., dated 24 May 1763, according to a charter by the Rt. Hon. Elizabeth, Countess of Glencairn. Rev John MacDermeit Fergushill died on 13 September 1793. He was succeeded by his son, Robert MacDermeit Fergushill.

A James MacDermeit Fergushill was given sasine of the lands of South High Corton, High Broomberry-yards, High Carcluie and Aikers by the magistrates of

Ayr, 15 February 1755. He served as an Ayrshire Turnpike Road Trustee in the latter half of the nineteenth century.

Rev John MacDermeit Fergushill was succeeded by his youngest, and last surviving son, Robert MacDermeit Fergushill. Born on 17 September 1775, on 14 November 1802 he was commissioned as an Ensign in the Ayrshire Regiment of the North British Militia. He married Margaret Ramsay, daughter of Rev John Ramsay of Kirkmichael (1795-1861). Their only child, Margaret, died in Ayr in 1839, aged seven months. Captain Fergushill died in Ayr on 17 December 1862 aged 87 and was buried in the old churchyard there.

The lairdship passed to Andrew Fergushill-Crawford MD, eldest son of Rev William Crawford DD, minister of Straiton and Professor of Moral History in the University of St Andrews, and his wife Agnes Fergushill, sister of Captain Robert MacDermeit Fergushill. Andrew Fergushill-Crawford was born at Straiton on 29 May 1798 and was educated at St Andrews and Edinburgh universities. He graduated as a Doctor of Medicine at Edinburgh in 1815. He practised as a physician in Winchester for over forty years. He served as Physician to the County Hospital in Winchester from 1818-1831, when he retired due to illness. He married Emma (1806-5 August 1869), youngest daughter of Aaron Fernandex Nunez of Basing Park, Hampshire, by who he had four children. His poetry was published in 1868 as *Boyhood: and Other Poems*. Andrew Fergushill-Crawford died on 26 May 1867 at Winchester. He was succeeded by Rev William Andrew Fergushill-Crawford (b. 1831), who graduated as a Master of Arts from Exeter College, Oxford, and who became Rector of Shalden, Hampshire. However, during his lifetime Burnockstone was sold to the MacCosh ironmasters.

The lands of Knockguldron and Heidmark, located on the southern extremity of the parish, and comprising unimproved moorland and peat bogs, was in 1899 the property of Hon Augustus Murray Cathcart of Brockloch. He lived at Mowbray House, Ripon. The lands were leased to James Pettigrew Wilson of Polquhairn.

In 1837 a number of other owners of land are recorded for the parish. David Limond of Dalblair owned some property. In 1837 John Douglas Boswell of Garrallan owned a few farms – see the Farms and Small Lairdships appendix.

Historically, the lands of Waterton had a building of considerable strength, perhaps a small tower house, on it, indicating its age and importance.

CHAPTER FIVE

ECCLESIASTICAL

The original parish church of Ochiltree was located in the old kirkyard which is situated by the side of the Lugar Water. When this was established is not known, but it was probably in existence before the twelfth century. The church was historically dedicated to St Conal, who is thought to be buried on a hillside north of Kirkconnel. Within the church there was an altar dedicated to St Mary. King David I organised churches into parish areas in the twelfth century, setting up an organised church hierarchy that was to remain in use until the Reformation, and long after, though much altered.

One of the earliest references to a church in the parish dates from 1296, when Simon de Spalding, the parson of the church, swore fealty to King Edward I of England at Berwick upon Tweed. Simon's brother, John de Spalding, was reader in the church.

The patronage of Ochiltree church was granted to the monks of Melrose Abbey in 1316 by Lady Eustace de Colville. She was the Lady of Ochiltree and widow of Reginald le Chene. Ochiltree, Mauchline, and for a time, Tarbolton, were the three Ayrshire parishes that were linked with Melrose. The monks had their local control point at Mauchline Castle.

The grant of Ochiltree church to the Abbey of Melrose was reaffirmed in 1324 when Robert de Colville of Oxnam and Ochiltree made out a new grant of confirmation. During the period when the church was under the patronage of Melrose Abbey, the tithes, or tenth-part of the parish revenues, were sent to Melrose for the upkeep of the abbey. In return, the monks sent funds for the support of a vicar who carried out the day-to-day work of the church in the parish.

In 1527 Sir James Colville of Ochiltree granted an additional £10 per annum for the support of a chaplain to officiate at the altar of St Mary, within the kirk at Ochiltree. This grant was confirmed by King James V in 1528.

In 1530 David Colville is noted as being the parish clerk for Ochiltree. This position was basically an assistant priest for the chapel, often elected by the parishioners, as opposed to being presented by the bishop.

Andrew Stewart of Ochiltree was taken before the Bishop of Glasgow in 1533 for casting down images in Ochiltree Kirk.

In 1552 a 'Contract between the Commendator [of Kelso and Melrose] and the Bishop of Whithorn' was drawn up, in which mention is made of the church lands of Ochiltree:

> To all and sundry to whose notice these present letters may come, greeting in Lord …. Provided that in case the yearly pension or mails of the said lands of Kylesmuir, Barmuir, mills and profits thereof, excepting as aforesaid, shall extend to a greater sum than the foresaid sum of 400 merks yearly, in that event the said reverend father shall, by his letters made in due form under his seal and subscription, within three months after his return to Scotland renounce, quitclaim and discharge so much of the said rents or yearly mails of the said lands, profits and mills of Kylesmuir and Barmuir as shall be in excess of the said sum of 400 merks presently assigned, and thenceforward shall not intromit with a greater sum furth of the said yearly pensions, rents or mails, than the said sum of 400 merks, and his factors shall account to the Commendator and his factors for any such surplus year by year, his entry to the receipt of the said pension for the Michaelmas term 1552 to be at Martinmas next, and his entry to the fruits of the kirk of Ochiltree to be at Allhallowmas 1553, and thereafter the same to be payable year by year at the terms used and wont. It is also provided that notwithstanding this assignation it shall be lawful to the said Commendator to grant feu charters, tacks, and rentals, and input and output tenants and farmers of the said lands, mills and churches, as freely as he was able to do before the making of this assignation, and to uplift and receive from the said subjects all and sundry profits, tack duties, grassum, entry silver, poultry, kain fowls, arreage and carriage, etc., which pertain and belong to him, so that the said reverend father shall have no right to intromit with the said subjects further than for payment of his yearly pension foresaid; and in the event of the subjects being leased for greater sums than they now pay, the increase and augmentation shall pertain to the said Commendator and his successors…. Further, the said pensioner shall be held to resign his right of 300 merks furth of the fruits of the kirk of Ochiltree at such time as the Commendator shall make to him a sufficient and similar assignation to some other place or shall find sufficient caution in the books of Council for yearly payment of the said sum of 300 merks. If at any time the Commendator make obstruction to the fulfilling of all the premises, the pensioner

may take legal proceedings against him for performance thereof according to his bull of provision, but a year must elapse as to the 300 merks payable from the kirk of Ochiltree and fruits thereof, which have been otherwise farmed out by the said Commendator. Moreover, notwithstanding this assignation, the said reverend father shall pay his proportion, effeiring to his pension, of all taxes, contributions, levies and burdens imposed upon the said monastery of Melrose in time coming after the date of the said assignation for whatsoever cause or fact that shall arise; provided however, that he shall not be liable for any contribution towards repair of the ruined and burned edifice, or for any actions or causes prior to the date of this assignation. This assignation, moreover, shall not confer or imply any further title or strengthening of the right of the said reverend father beyond what is contained in his bull of provision, nor shall it militate against or prejudge the right of the said Commendator to pursue for reduction and cancelling of the said pension, further than if this present assignation and agreement had not been made. Also the Commendator shall enact himself between this date and 8th September next by his commissary or procurator to deliver to the said reverend father the sum of 300 merks for satisfaction of the first year's pension assigned furth of the kirk of Ochiltree, viz. 150 merks on 1st November next (1552) and 150 merks between then and 1st May 1553; which sums, however, shall not be so paid if the Commendator have made satisfaction of the full sum of 500 merks at either of the terms of Michaelmas or Easter as before arranged, or within thirty days thereafter. The payment of 3000 merks due to the said reverend father for bygone terms of his pension, and the payment of the foresaid 300 merks for the fruits of the kirk of Ochiltree, shall likewise not import a further title or strengthening of the pensioner's right beyond what is contained in his bull of provision, or prejudge the Commendator of his right to pursue as above for reduction of the said papal bull. And this assignation shall only extend and be limited, restricted, and understood in terms of the foresaid contract made at Paris between the said Commendator and Bishop, and shall have as great faith and strength as if the said contract were word for word recited in the same.

In witness whereof to these presents, subscribed with the hand of my Commissary foresaid and the hands of the said convent, the common seal of the said monastery of Melrose is appended at, etc. Sir John Dury, with my hand.

In 1556 Rev John Knox came to Ochiltree and is known to have preached in the church. Knox was instrumental in bringing about the Reformation, when the Scots abandoned the Church of Rome and adopted the Protestant Presbyterian form of church government. The Reformation was virtually completed by 1560, when many folk went into the parish churches and cast down and destroyed anything that was regarded as being associated with the Romish church. No doubt, this took place in Ochiltree too, especially as the local laird was of the Protestant persuasion, and the ancient altar and other relics would have been destroyed.

Around 1564 the Commendator of Melrose, Michael Balfour, prepared a Rental of the Abbeylands of Melrose. In it, the lands of Ochiltree are referred to as follows:

> Item, the teynds of the kirk of Uchiltrie extendsin the yeir to xxxiiij ch.
> Togidder with the teynd meill of the kirks of Mauchling and Ouchiltrie, extending to lxviij ch. Meill, and that in contentatioun of ane pensioun grantit to the Lord Seytoun and his barnes of xvjc merks.

Robert Campbell of Kingencleugh's support for the church is seen in his decision to give up half the teinds that he was due from the parish of Ochiltree to support the protestant minister there.

The first post-Reformation minister was Rev Robert Hamilton, who also ministered at Mauchline. He seems to have been a student at St Andrews in the 1550s. He had been appointed by the General Assembly to preach in the unplanted kirks of Carrick on 2 July 1562 and to serve until the following assembly. However, he was appointed to the charge at Ochiltree later the same year. On 29 December 1562 Rev Hamilton was appointed to a small committee that was to preside over the Act of Admission of Superintendents, a short-lived group that temporarily replaced the bishops. That he was held in high regard is obvious from the reference to this committee, which notes that it comprised, 'The Superintendent of Glasgow, Mr Knox, minister of Edinburgh, Mr Robert Hamilton, Minister of Uchiltree and Mauchline, and other learned men.' Similarly, in 1567, he was one of seven men who made up a committee appointed by the General Assembly of Scotland 'to decide questions'. Around the year 1566, Rev Hamilton was translated to the church of Irvine where he remained until 1568.

In 1567 Adam Landells was given the position of exhorter in Ochiltree kirk, in addition to Cumnock and Auchinleck. Landells was actually born in Ochiltree in 1507 and had been involved in many transactions with Lord Ochiltree, to whom he was chaplain. It is known that he married Helen Wilson.

The next minister at Ochiltree was Rev John Inglis, appointed in 1567. He was given the job of ministering to three parishes – Ochiltree, Auchinleck and Cumnock (which at that time had still to be separated into Old and New Cumnock parishes - this took place in 1650). Inglis was a member of the Convention held at Leith in 1571 and of the Assembly in 1572. Inglis appears to have moved to Auchinleck in 1574, but had returned to Ochiltree in 1580. On 6 March 1589 Inglis was named as one of the commissioners by the Privy Council to the preservation of true religion in the bailiary of Kyle. In 1606 he was nominated as the constant moderator of the Presbytery by the General Assembly. He continued as minister until at least 1608.

Inglis studied at St Andrews University, where reference to him is found between 1540 and 1557. He was married to Agnes Grosar, by whom he had five sons. These were John, who was apprenticed to Robert Skinner, flesher, on 20 January 1587; Joseph, apprenticed to Robert Graham, tailor on 25 February 1590; Daniel, apprenticed to John Skinner, 1 April 1607; Samuel, apprenticed to Patrick Hepburn, apothecary, 26 December 1610; and William, apprenticed to Thomas Finnie, tailor, 8 September 1613. These apprenticeships took place in Edinburgh.

On 2 March 1570 a complaint against the minister of Ochiltree, Rev John Smyth, was made to the General Assembly of the Church of Scotland. This reads:

> Anent the complaint give in be Thomas Smith in Ochiltrie, against Mr John Smyth, minister in Ochiltrie, for debarring the said Thomas from the Lord's Table because he removit ane shae off ane horse upon ane Sunday afternoon in Ochiltrie, where neither preaching nor publick prayers was. After long reasoning, the said Thomas was ordainit to be receivit to the participation of the Lord's Table and other benefits of the Kirk, heareafter, notwithstanding of the alleadgit fault aforementioned.

In 1614 Rev John Fergushill MA was appointed as the parish minister. He was the son of David Fergushill, merchant and Provost of Ayr, where he was born. His mother was Janet Kennedy, a sister or near relation of Hugh Kennedy, another provost in the county town. John Fergushill was educated at the University of Edinburgh, where he studied for three years. Whilst studying, an outbreak of plague occurred, resulting in the course being halted. Fergushill was sent to France, where he continued under Robert Boyd of Trochrague at the Protestant Academy of Montauban. The plague reached Montauban in 1605, whereupon Fergushill returned home. He was unsure whether to become a minister or else join his father in business, and he wrote to Boyd in December 1608 for advice. He appears to have resumed his studies at the University of Glasgow, where he matriculated in 1611.

On 31 July 1616 the Presbytery of Glasgow 'ordanit that Messrs John Haye, Thomas Boyde, Jhone Fergushill, for their farther qualificatioune befoir admissioune to ye holie ministrie suld mak ane lang lessoune upone some place of Scripture, and sustain the disput upon some controvert heid.'

Fergushill was a supporter of the Covenant, and suffered imprisonment for a period for his opposition to the policy of the bishops. On 28 March 1620, Fergushill was deprived of his charge by the Court of High Commission for his non-conformity to the Perth articles. He declined the jurisdiction of the court, whereupon he was suspended from his charge and sentenced to be warded at Perth. However, Boyd of Trochrague and John Chalmers intervened and had the last part of his sentence modified, allowing him to return to Ochiltree under certain restrictions.

In 1638 Fergushill was a member of the Assembly. On 14 November 1639 he was called to Ayr, where he became minister of the First Charge on a stipend of £500 plus glebe per annum. No major event associated with Fergushill in Ayr is noted other than his solemn administration of the Solemn League and Covenant to his congregation in November 1643. He died on 11 June 1644.

A couple of years passed before the pulpit was filled again. Rev John Blyth was admitted as minister on 27 May 1641. He was born in 1604, the son of Rev Henry Blyth, minister of Eccles in Berwickshire. He was trained at the University of Edinburgh, from where he graduated with a Master of Arts degree on 24 July 1630. He was on the Exercise at Kirkcaldy in Fife on 7 January 1636. In 1642 he held a communion service at which 1,200 members attended. He was collated on 29 November 1643. Rev John Blyth died in April 1665.

The next minister was Rev Robert Miller, son of Rev Andrew Miller, minister of Girvan Parish Church. He was educated at the University of Glasgow, where he distinguished himself. He was admitted to Ochiltree sometime between 24 November and 15 December 1661, most likely as a colleague and successor to Rev Blyth. His daughter was Euphame Miller.

Robert Miller was a supporter of the Covenanters and was removed from the charge on 1 October 1662 for failing to swear allegiance to the king as head of the church. He fled to Holland and France. In 1668 he obtained the degree of M.D. On 27 July 1669 he was able to return to Ochiltree as minister under an Indulgence of the Privy Council. The act reads as follows:

> Forasmeikle as the kirk of Ochiltree is vacant, the lords of his majesty's privy council, in pursuance of his majesty's command signified by his letter of the 7th of June last, and in regard of the consent of the patron, do appoint Mr Robert Miller, late minister there, to teach and exercise the other functions of the ministry at the said kirk of Ochiltree.

On 8 July 1673 the Privy Council fined him for not celebrating the Restoration of the monarchy. Again his Covenanting adherences caused him trouble, for on 22 October 1674 he was accused by the synod of not observing the instructions prescribed by the Privy Council. He was libelled twice, on 3 November 1681 and 17 December 1683. However, the Lord Advocate was to state that Miller 'had behaved himself loyally and dutifully in reading the proclamation and declaration against the Rye House Plot, and preaching against it.' Miller was ordered to find caution to the value of 3,000 merks (around £166) and to appear before the court whenever he was called.

Rev Robert Wodrow, in his *Analecta*, makes reference to Miller:

> Mr Robert Miller was ordained Minister of Ochiltrea. He was a very great schollar when he was at the University. He was one of the best in all his class. His Regent, I heard, said this of him, 'I never heard argument proposed but thou, Robert Miller, was ever ready to give it an answer'.
>
> He was a most eloquent man as ever I heard preach, a great orator, and most plain, but he spoke too fast … I never heard a man preach like ane great orator than Mr Miller … I have often wished he had been one of the ministers of the New Kirk of Edinburgh; he had such ravishing eloquence and oratory.

Rev Miller was married to Margaret Kennedy, daughter of Gilbert Kennedy of Girvanmains. He was to marry for a second time, to Grizel Cochrane, daughter of Colonel Hugh Cochrane, brother of William Cochrane, Earl of Dundonald. He had eight children – Rev Robert Miller, who was to become the minister of St Quivox Church, near Ayr; Dr William Miller M.D.; Rev John Miller, minister of Neilston Parish Church in Renfrewshire; Hugh; Margaret; Katherine; Mary and Jean. Rev Robert Miller died in 1685.

COVENANTERS

The seventeenth century was a time of immense strife within the church. The king, Charles I, wished to impose Episcopacy on the Scots, bringing the country's church into line with that of England. The Scots were for none of it, however, seeing Episcopacy as bad as Roman Catholicism. They campaigned against the king with such vigour that he had to send soldiers around the country killing or imprisoning those who refused to swear to him as head of the church. A Covenant was signed in 1638, and the 'Covenanters' were soon wanted men. Thousands were banished to America, hundreds were executed throughout the country, and hundreds more killed on the moorlands of Ayrshire where they were forced to hide.

In the years 1663-64 the church at Ochiltree appears to have been regularly visited by government soldiers. They surrounded the building whilst worshippers were inside, barred the doors and arranged for those within to leave one-by-one. They were interrogated as to their origins and beliefs, and those who did not belong to the parish were often fined or imprisoned.

The village was to witness one of the greatest risings that took place during the time of the Covenant. On 13 November 1666 the Covenanters in St John's Town of Dalry, in the Stewartry of Kirkcudbright, rose up in arms against the persecuting soldiers who were bent on harming an old farmer named Grier. As soon as the soldiers had been forced from the village, the Covenanter support grew in number, and it was decided to march on Dumfries and take Sir James Turner as hostage, to use as a bargaining tool in proposed discussions with the authorities in Edinburgh. The Covenanters, with their prize, marched back through Galloway from Dumfries and settled at Ayr for a short time. There they were drilled in military action by Captain James Wallace of Auchans, before the march for Edinburgh.

The Covenanters left Ayr on the 21 November 1666 and made their way to Coylton, where they rested for the night. The next morning, after breakfasting and organising themselves, the Covenanters assembled to hear a sermon from Rev Gabriel Semple. The infantry made their way eastward. It was the evening of 22 November 1666 when they arrived in Ochiltree, probably around 700 strong. The infantry camped around the village, the horsemen to the east of the village.

Some of the horsemen were sent to Barskimming Bridge, where they were to guard the crossing. The bridge, which lies to the south of Mauchline, on a minor road to Ochiltree, spans the River Ayr, and was thought to be 'the only passage of the water [of Ayr] at the time', perhaps due to the floods in the river making many of the other fords impassable.

James Wallace and his officers made their way to Ochiltree House, or Castle, which stood at the east end of the village, on a low eminence above the Lugar Water, at the mouth of the Burnock Water. An old tower house, this was the property of Sir John Cochrane. Wallace was later to complain of the 'very cold welcome' he received there. Lady Cochrane was not impressed at her guests and appears to have treated them with disdain. Wallace was to comment, 'I hope whatever incivilities we had from the lady, she had none from us'. Lady Cochrane was a Yorkshire lass, born Margaret Strickland, daughter of Sir William Strickland of Boynton, Yorkshire. She married Sir John, who was the second son of the 1st Earl of Dundonald.

Turner was taken to the main inn in the village and held there. He recalled that he was lodged 'at the principall alehouse of the toune, where I was indifferentlie well used.' What inn this was is unconfirmed, but may have been the Heid Inn, or its predecessor.

It was with some rejoicing that the Covenanters were joined with other reinforcements at Ochiltree. Rev John Welch had travelled through Galloway looking for support. Leaving the rising as it made its way through Dalmellington, he scouted for known Covenanters to join him. He arrived with around 100 men on foot, poorly armed, and about fifteen or sixteen men on horseback. They were called an army by the rebels.

The scouts at Barskimming Bridge sent word to Ochiltree that Dalziel's men had reached Mauchline, and therefore there was a danger of being caught by him. Wallace sent reinforcements to the bridge, but it was discovered that Dalziel was still some miles off, not leaving Glasgow until the following day.

John Ross and a few companions were selected to make their way to Mauchline to find out where Dalziel actually was. Arriving in Mauchline, they found nothing. However, there were rumours that the troops were in Kilmarnock. Accordingly they made their way to the town. Near to Kilmarnock the party was arrested and taken to prison. Ross was subsequently executed in Edinburgh on 7 December 1666. His head was severed from his body and sent back to Kilmarnock for public display. It was later taken from the tolbooth and buried in the Laigh Kirkyard where a headstone marks its resting place.

During the evening of 22 November, the Covenanters prayed for advice. Wallace recalled, 'That night, after prayer to God for direction what to do next, it was concluded that we should march eastward. For there was no staying where we were, and there was no expectation of any farther help from the south and south-west hand.'

With threat of an advancing army, the Covenanters moved on to Cumnock the next day, and then Muirkirk, Lanark and onwards to Edinburgh. On 28 November they had reached the outskirts of Edinburgh, but they were caught up by the soldiers of General Tam Dalyell of the Binns. A battle ensued at Rullion Green, where the Pentland Rising was soundly defeated.

Whether any locals joined the Covenanters as they made their way through the village is unknown, but certainly the village was very supportive of them.

As part of the authorities' attempts at quelling the rise of the Covenanters in the south-west of Scotland, parties of Highland troops were quartered on many suspected Covenanters in the area. Known as the 'Highland Host' these ill-trained soldiers were wont to steal and rob items of furnitures and domestic goods from their hosts. Much of this was taken back to the Highlands. The damage done to the cause of the authorities was considerable, and the soldiers were withdrawn. From then on, Highlanders were ill-regarded in the south, the memory of their actions lingering long in local memory. An account of the losses sustained in many parishes across the area was compiled, it being reckoned that £137,499 6s 0d Scots worth of damage was done in the county of Ayr. The losses in the parishes of Ochiltree and Auchinleck were linked:

The parishes of Ochiltree and Auchinleck sustained of loss, by quartering two hundred and forty of Perth's foot, from February 5th to February 24th, nineteen days, besides officers, £1,368. By quartering eighty Perthshire gentlemen, allowing but one servant to each, and reckoning both at 24s each day, from February 5th to February 25th, is £1,920. By quartering sixty foot from February 25th to March 5th, eight days, is £144. Exacted of money and plunder by these former, £1,170 14s 4d. Plundered in money and goods by soldiers in passing through, or by those quartered in adjacent places, £432 6s 8d. By quartering two hundred and forty Caithness men one night, £72. Exacted by them of money £68 6s 8d. Three horses taken by Strathmore's men, for recovering of which was expended, £36. Which, besides baggage horses and other horses ridden down by them, extends to £5,211 7s 8d.

Sir John Cochrane of Ochiltree and his son, John Cochrane of Waterside, were both notable Covenanters. Accounts of their Covenanting activities have been related in the chapter on Estate and Landowners.

In 1684 the authorities drew up a list of Covenanting rebels wanted by the state for their uprising. The list includes five men from Ochiltree parish, namely, Charles Colvil, younger, in Townhead; James Johnston, son to John Johnston in Townhead; David Dun in Closs; William Symonton in Butts; and Mr William Gilchrist, son of the schoolmaster in Ochiltree.

David Dun in Closs (an old farm which was located to the east of Auchlin farm) had attended a conventicle at Kilmein Hill, north of Dalmellington, when the party were overtaken by a group of soldiers. It is said that Dun would have escaped, apart from the fact that his horse became bogged down in the peat, allowing the dragoons to catch up with him. Some of the Covenanters were shot on the spot, near the summit of Carsgailoch Hill, south of Cumnock, where a memorial stone marks their graves. David Dun and one other Covenanter, Simon Paterson, were arrested and taken to Cumnock. The two were shot dead on the same day. Tradition has it that this took place in the Square, which at the time was still the parish burial ground around the old church. Rev Robert Wodrow, who gathered the accounts of the sufferings during the Covenanting period, states that they were hanged. Their bodies were taken to the site of the gallows tree on Barr Hill in Cumnock, where they were buried at the foot of the tree, a spot reserved for criminals. In later years, this site was selected by the people of Cumnock to become their parish burying ground.

David Dun's sister, Margaret, went to Cumnock to ask what was to be his fate but was shot by the dragoons on the way.

An old story tells of an earlier time when Dun and his companion was arrested. It is said that they were in the Wanlockhead area, along with four other Covenanters. They were hiding from the soldiers who were searching the district for them. The hideout used by the Covenanters was discovered by the soldiers, and Dun, Paterson, and one other were captured. However, a severe thunderstorm erupted, the lightning and thunder scaring the soldiers. The horses were so frightened by the banging and lightning that they bolted, taking their riders with them. The Covenanters were left unguarded and they were soon to escape once more.

Whilst a young man, David Dun is thought to have lived in Selkirkshire, perhaps trying to escape the attention of Graham of Claverhouse. It was there that he became friendly with Halbert Dobson, known locally as 'Hab Dob'. The two were involved in a number of exploits in the hills between Moffat and Selkirk, and Dobb's Linn, a waterfall at the head of Moffat Dale, is said to have been named after Dobson. Their story is related in James Hogg's poem 'Mess John', in which it is related:

> Hab Dob and Davie Din,
> Dang the Deevil ower Dobb's Linn.

Around 1710, a small headstone was erected over the grave of David Dun and Simon Paterson. The simple blonde sandstone memorial reads:

> HERE LYES DAVID DUN
> AND SIMON PATERS
> ON, WHO WAS SHOT
> IN THIS PLACE BY
> A PARTY OF HIGHL
> ANDERS FOR THER
> ADHERANCE TO THE
> WORD OF GOD AND
> THE COVENANTED
> WORK OF REFORMA
> TION. 1685.

It is reckoned that Robert Paterson, the 'Old Mortality' of Sir Walter Scott's novel of that name, came to Cumnock and recut the inscription on the stone. In the twentieth century, the soft sandstone gravestone became eroded, so much so that the inscription became difficult to read. In June 2002 a new pink granite headstone was erected alongside by the Scottish Covenanter Memorials Association, copying the original inscription and style.

Andrew Welch, a Covenanter from Ochiltree parish, was captured after the

Battle of Bothwell Bridge in 1679 and held prisoner in Edinburgh. He was placed on board the *Crown of London* which was taking captive Covenanters to America when it was shipwrecked off the coast of the Orkney islands on 10 December. Welch was one of 209 drowned in the wreck. A monument at Deerness in Orkney commemorates the incident.

There were many Ochiltree parish residents who were to suffer imprisonment, banishment, or fines for their support of the Covenant. In 1687 Rev David Houston conducted a conventicle at Polbaith Burn, north of Galston, to which around 300 Covenanters attended. Many were women, and it is known that Houston conducted a number of baptisms. Nineteen Covenanters were captured after the meeting, four of whom are known to belong to Ochiltree. These were Patrick Harvie, James Thomson, William Murray and Bessie Strathearn.

Patrick Harvie, or Harvey, was taken before Captain Thomas Douglas at Ayr on 21 January 1687. The Privy Council records note that he was 'aged tuentie or thereabouts, declairs that upon Sunday last being the 16th instant he was present at ane conventicle, and that one James Thomsone in Burnock Mill in Ochiltree parish conducted him thither; he thinks the number of these persons consisted of three or four hundred, he thinks there were about three score in armes; he declairs that Thomson had a carabine; he declairs that he neither knows the minister nor the place wher the meeting was but he thinks it was some six myles eastward from Mauchline.' Harvie appears to have been sent on to Edinburgh, where he was tried by Lt. Gen. William Drummond, Viscount Strathallan. The records note that 'Patrick Harvy in Ochiltree paroch confesses he was at a conventicle where one Howstoune preached; sayes he only went out of curiosity, and promises never to goe to any such meeting hereafter; acknowledges the King to be his lawful soveraigne, and never to ryse in arms against him or his authority; and declares he cannot wreate.' No further note is found about Harvie, and it is assumed that he was released, perhaps on his accepting the test.

James Thomson was the tenant in Burnock Mill. He may have been responsible for taking Harvie, Murray and Strathearn to the conventicle, but appears to have escaped capture.

William Murray belonged to Hillhead farm, Ochiltree. He went to the conventicle armed with a sword. After being captured he was interviewed by Captain Douglas at Ayr on the same day as Harvie. The Privy Council records give some details: 'William Murray, aged tuentie years or therby, duelling in Hillheade in Ochiltree parish, declairs that upon Sunday last he was at ane conventicle, where there were mett about four or fywe hundred persons, wherof one hundred or therby in armes; he declaires that [Patrick] Harvie carried him thither and that himselfe hade ane suorde which another gave him whom he knows not; he declairs that he knows neither the minister or ministers name nor the place of the meiting, but judges the meiting was northeastward from Ochiltree about nine milles.'

Like Harvie, Thomson was sent to Edinburgh, where he was tried before Lord Strathallan. It is recorded that 'William Murray in Ochiltree paroch confesses [to being at conventicle], promises [not to attend conventicles] and acknowledges [the King's authority] ut supra; cannot wreate.' Like Harvie, he was probably released.

Bessie Strathearn lived at Boghead, which was a small farm which used to exist midway between Crofthead and Knockshiffnock farms. She, too, was brought before Captain Douglas in Ayr. The Privy Council records the facts: 'Bessie Streahearn, about tuentie or therabouts, duelling in Bogheade in Ochiltree parish, declairs that upon Sunday last she was at ane conventicle, and that [Patrick] Harvie and [William] Murray carried her thither; declairs she knows not what number they were; declairs she knows neither the ministers name nor the place of the meeting.' No reference is made to Strathearn being sent on to Edinburgh, perhaps as she was a woman she was released at Ayr.

Other suspect Covenanters succumbed to the authorities to save their lives. James Napier, a mason in Ochiltree, was captured and held in prison on threat of death. He had been sentenced by Commissioner James Douglas to die on 20 April 1685 but, with two Cumnock men, sent a petition to the Privy Council, accepted the Oath of Abjuration, and were reprieved. Although they remained in jail for a time, they were set free in July.

The famous Covenanting minister, Rev Alexander Peden, has a connection with the parish of Ochiltree. He was born around 1626 at Auchencloigh in the parish of Sorn and initially trained to be a minister. Not finding a charge, he served as a schoolmaster at Tarbolton, before being ordained as minister at New Luce, in Wigtownshire, in 1659. When the ministers were outed in 1662, he left New Luce and threw his lot in with the Covenanters. He is known to have preached across most of southern Scotland, often in hiding in the Southern Uplands, but also into northern England and over to Northern Ireland. He was a keen prize for the dragoons who were searching for him, and on more than one occasion he was captured, only to find himself 'miraculously' released later. Near the end of his life, he wished to return to see his brother, who tenanted Tenshillingside farm on Auchinleck estate, within that part of the estate which extended into Mauchline parish. He may have hidden in a hollow in a remote rock in the gorge of the Lugar Water, below Auchinleck House, but on the Ochiltree side of the river. There, at Peden's Cave, is a depression in a large rock boss, high above the river, access to which can only be made by descending a steep couple of steps carved into the sandstone. Within the depression is a stone bench, cut from the natural rock, where the Covenanting minister could rest. Peden actually died at his brother's house on 26 January 1686, and the family buried him in secret in the Peden burial plot at Auchinleck kirkyard. The soldiers, incensed at not capturing him, dug up his body three weeks after its burial, and carried it to Cumnock, with the intention of hanging the lifeless corpse from the gallows tree on what became the Barrhill. The local landowner's wife, the lady of Leifnoreis, refused to allow this to happen, and so the soldiers just buried it at the foot of the gallows, 'out of contempt', according to the older gravestone.

On 30 March 1689 a proclamation was issued which called together the militia across southern Scotland and the fencible men to turn out in support of King William, defending any attempt by James VII and II at reclaiming the throne. Sir John Cochrane of Ochiltree met at the Cross of Ochiltree, along with some other landowners, and their retainers. Cochrane had a special flag made for the occasion.

The Covenanters' Flag carried by the adherents in the parish was brought back to Ochiltree following the Battle of the Boyne. It hung on the walls of Ochiltree House for many years, but it is said that a cook in the house stole it. She gave it to a friend in the village, and on one occasion it was in danger of being used as a winding-sheet. It was rescued in time and was held by Patrick Simson, schoolmaster. In 1818 he handed it back to Alexander Boswell, superior of the village, and thus it returned to Ochiltree House. In 1832 a number of political reformers borrowed the flag for some demonstrations, and it disappeared for some time thereafter, presumed lost. However, it was acquired by Rev John Warrick of Old Cumnock and presented to the National Museum of Antiquities in Edinburgh, where it remains. The flag bears the motto: *DEUS EST SEMPER IDEM. Ochiltree for God The Covenanted Presbyterian Reformation Croun and Countrie 1689.*

Local traditions concerning the Covenanters have been handed down by word of mouth over the centuries. One account claims that on Barlosh farm there is a straight dike that makes its way from the farm towards the direction of Bardarroch. At one point the dike makes a short bend around an area for no apparent reason then continues on its straight way. The farmers at Barlosh were always told that this had something to do with the Covenanters, whether or not some were buried there is no longer known.

PARISH CHURCH POST COVENANTER

During the years of Covenanting struggle, Ochiltree does not appear to have had much supply in the pulpit. After Rev Miller's ejection in 1662 there were few serving in the parish. On 3 September 1672 Rev Patrick Peacock MA, the outed minister of Kirkmabreck in the Stewartry of Kirkcudbright, was appointed as the indulged minister of Ochiltree, to serve alongside Rev Robert Miller. However he does not appear to have accepted this, or if he did then he did not remain for very long, for he is known to have moved to Ireland where he became chaplain at Killyleagh Castle.

Ochiltree's first proper minister appointed after the Glorious Revolution was also to be short lived – in fact, so short-lived that his ministry is often referred to as the shortest in the church nationally. Rev John Mitchell was called to the charge in February 1690. He was admitted on 29 April that year, but died on the following day, 30 April 1690. He had been married and on his death left a widow.

The Rev William Dunlop was approached to be the next minister of the parish and appears to have accepted. He was the son of Alexander Dunlop, minister of Paisley, and a descendant, through his mother, of the Mures of Caldwell. He studied at Glasgow College and was licensed to preach around 1679. Due to the Covenanting struggles, he emigrated to Carolina, where he remained until 1689. He was presented to Ochiltree parish in 1690, however, before he was ordained, he was promoted to the Principal of the University of Glasgow. He was instrumental in getting funding from the bishops' rents to the universities of Scotland. He died in March 1700, aged 47.

Five years passed before the parish was able to find another minister. On 21 August 1695 Rev Mathew Couper was admitted as minister. He had previously served at Lilliesleaf Parish Church, Roxburghshire. Couper remained at Ochiltree for five years before accepting a call to Kinfauns Parish Church, Perthshire, on 12 September 1700.

Another five year vacancy ensued before Rev Samuel Lockhart was appointed as minister on 12 September 1705. Educated at the University of Glasgow, he was

5.3 Manse 2019 *(Author's Collection)*

licensed by the Presbytery of Ayr on 7 February 1705 and called to Ochiltree on 3 May 1705. There is a curious reference to Lockhart in 1713, recorded by Wodrow: 'They say that Sir William Cochrane of Ochiltree will suspend Mr Samuel Lockhart's stipend at Ochiltree, because of some gum there is between them'. Lockhart was married on 16 March 1709 to Ann Orr, daughter of Rev Alexander Orr, minister of St Quivox, near Ayr. They had seven children - the eldest, Alexander, dying young; Mary was probably married on 18 January 1736 to Baillie William Adie, merchant in Dunfermline; a second Alexander followed, with Margaret, James, Samuel and Janet. His son, Alexander, was apprenticed to George Cowan, wright, in Edinburgh on 10 September 1729. Rev Lockhart died on 8 March 1724 at the age of 48.

Rev George Reid was ordained as minister of Ochiltree on 16 June 1725. A native of Kirkliston, West Lothian, he had been chaplain to James Boswell, father of Lord Auchinleck, and served as tutor to Lord Auchinleck himself. Reid was married on 24 November 1746 to Jane or Jean Campbell, Barquharrie, daughter of George Campbell of Treesbank. The manse at Ochiltree was in a very poor condition, and from 1746 until he retired, Barquharrie served as the residence of the minister. James Boswell, the noted diarist, often visited him at Barquharrie. In Wodrow's *Analecta* there is a reference to Reid:

> Synods now are but melancholy times by what I have seen them. There is a lightness and vanity among too many ministers. They have their clubs, and meetings, wherein great freedoms are used, as I am told, against Confessions, for liberty of thinking [by] Mr George Reid, Minister of Ochiltree … and some others. I hear in the Privy Censures in the Presbytery of Air, they had some expressions of Mr George Reid of Ochiltree, not very favourable to Confessions, before them, and he declared he had signed; but did not think himself bound up by his signing to receive new light, and to alter his sentiments. The matter was not further discussed.

Reid was well respected in the parish. When he was young his regular visits and sermons were his strong points – as he aged he was more noted for his kindliness and willingness to help. George Reid died on 6 April 1786 and was buried in the old kirkyard on 11 April, near to where the old kirk stood, but no memorial marks his grave. At the time he was the Father of the Church of Scotland. He was buried

5.2 Ochiltree Communion Token

From 1776 until 1780 Rev Stephen Young served as an assistant to the minister. Rev Young was born in 1745 and was licensed to preach by the Presbytery of Lanark in 1776. He appears to have come to Ochiltree soon after. He was ordained as the full-time minister at Barr Parish Church on 8 March 1780. In the same year he was married to Elizabeth Patterson (died 1781). He was married for a second time, in 1784, to Mary MacWilliam. Young had a son, Rev Archibald Young, minister at Hyndford Parish Church in Lanarkshire. Rev Stephen Young remained as minister at Barr, dying in the manse there on 21 February 1819, at the age of 74.

A second assistant to Rev Reid was Rev John Kennedy, who appears to have served for around one year. He was appointed as minister of Terregles in Kirkcudbrightshire in 1781. He became known to Robert Burns, who immortalised him as 'Wee Johnnie' in one of his rhyming epitaphs.

In 1786 Rev David Grant was appointed the next minister of Ochiltree. The Kirk Session records state: 'Decr 14th 1786 – Rev David Grant, from Ettrick, was this day admitted to the pastoral charge of this congregation, the Rev Mr Peebles, Newton-of-Ayr, presiding at the occasion, accompanied with a competent number of other ministers of this Presbytery.' He was presented to the charge by the Dowager Lady Glencairn. He was to remain for four and a half years, but during his term of ministry the church in the village made considerable strides forward. The Dowager Countess of Glencairn appears to have been friendly with Rev Grant, and a number of letters from the Countess to him survive. Lady Glencairn was instrumental in establishing a Bible Class at the church during this time, one of the earliest in Scotland. The first mistress of the class was Jean MacLatchie, who was later to become the wife of James Tennant.

The old church of Ochiltree was starting to show its age, and it was decided that it would be better to erect a new church to replace it. It was determined that this should be located more central in the village, and a site was selected on the Main Street. The new parish church was erected in 1789-90. The foundation stone was laid on 16 May 1789 by James Boswell, Laird of Auchinleck (1740-1795), and the Rt. Hon. Elizabeth Cunninghame, Dowager Countess of Glencairn (1725-1801). The builder-architect responsible for the design was Hugh Morton, Williamsfield. The new church could seat 900. For many years the church was divided internally with seats for the heritors and their tenants, the space allocated according to the valuation of their properties. However, this left many village residents with little space, and they often complained of the matter.

Rev David Grant was involved in a bit of controversy in the county during his term as minister of Ochiltree. He was the convenor of the Presbytery's Committee on the Publications of Rev Dr MacGill of Ayr. MacGill's works were regarded as being heretic, and the Presbytery had to investigate the matter. Robert Burns was aware of the controversy, resulting in him writing his poem, 'The Kirk's Alarm'. In the verses he makes reference to Grant:

> Davie Bluster, Davie Bluster,
> If for a saint ye do muster,
> > The corps is no nice of recruits;
> Yet to worth let's be just,
> Royal blood ye might boast
> > If the ass was the king of the brutes.

Burns did not think much of Rev Grant, as revealed in one of his letters to Lady Elizabeth Cunningham (sister of the Earl of Glencairn), dated 23 December 1789, written at Ellisland. In it he says, 'I ought to apologise to your ladyship for sending you some of the enclosed rhymes, thay are so silly. Everybody knows of poor Dr M'Gill. He is my particular friend, and my ballad on his prosecution has virulence enough if it has or wit. You must not read Lady Glencairn the stanza about the Priest of Ochiltree. Though I know him to be a designing, rotten-hearted Puritan, yet perhaps her ladyship has a different idea of him.'

John Tennant of the Glen told Burns that he had got the wrong end of the stick with Rev Grant, and it is said that he took the bard to meet the minister at his manse. The two got on well-enough and were to be friendly thereafter.

Soon after his death a book of Rev Grant's sermons was published, appearing in 1793: *Sermons, Doctrinal and Practical, to which are Prefixed a Recommendation, by the Rev. Andrew Hunter, D.D. Professor of Divinity in the University, and One of the Ministers of Edinburgh, and a Short Account of the Author: at the End of the Volume is Added, a Sermon, Preached on the Occasion of His Death, by The Rev. William Peebles, Minister at Newton Upon Air.*

Rev Grant gained some respect from the evangelical group within the church, as Hew Scott said of him in his *Ecclesiastical History of Scotland*:

> He was singularly upright in his intention, animated in his address, and cheerful in his conversation…. An enlarged knowledge of mankind was improved by him for the great purpose of rendering his ministerial labours more useful. His piety was unaffected, and his mind strongly impressed with a habitual sense of Divine Providence in every occurrence of life.

Rev Grant was married in 1783 to Miss Mills, sister of Sir Thomas Mills (d. 1793), governor of Quebec. They had one son, James, born 3 April 1784. Rev Grant's wife died in April 1785. Rev David Grant died of an asthmatical and dropsical complaint on 16 July 1791, in his 42nd year. He had been a minister for ten years in total. He was buried in the old kirkyard, at his request as close to the site of the communion table in the now-demolished kirk as possible. His funeral service was taken by Rev Dr William Peebles of Newton-upon-Ayr.

Rev William Thomson was presented as the assistant minister of the parish by the Countess-Dowager of Glencairn in October 1789 and ordained as minister on 12 April 1792. Thomson had trained as a schoolmaster, and taught at Kirkpatrick-Fleming in Dumfriesshire, and from 8 October 1787 at George Heriot's Hospital in Edinburgh. He graduated with a Master of Arts degree and was licensed by the Presbytery of Edinburgh on 22 April 1789. On arrival at Ochiltree his stipend was around £95 per annum. Lady Glencairn wrote to him the same year, stating that, 'I hope you like your situation, and find the charge of your parish as easy and pleasant as you could expect'. Within a few month Rev Thomson was negotiating with the Countess of Glencairn over the glebe, which she appears to have been agreeble to – 'With regard to the Glebe, I have written about that too, if you can feu'. In January 1793 Lady Glencairn sent the minister books for the Sunday school, apologised about the delay regarding the glebe, and hoped that, 'everything is going on to your satisfaction in your parish with regards to the morals of the inhabitants; thair instructions will be sound and orthodox, and I sincerely wish them success.'

During Thomson's ministry the manse and office-houses were rebuilt between 1798-1800. The old manse was in a poor condition, and Lady Glencairn wrote to him regarding the situation in 1792 - 'I desired your house should be repaired without delay'. Whether work took place at the time or not isn't known, but within a few years a new building was erected. This was a far superior building to the old manse, being a double-storey house, of three bays, erected in its own grounds off Mauchline Road. The design of the manse was a copy of that erected at Straiton in

5.3 Ochiltree Parish Church *(Author's Collection)*

1794-96. The work was carried out by John Murdoch and John Kay, both Ochiltree, as an estimated cost of £498. A porch at the rear door was added in 1819.

Thomson was a literary person, and contributed a short account of the parish for Sir John Sinclair's *Statistical Account of Scotland*. In 1793 he published two volumes in defence of the orthodox faith, entitled *The Divinity of Christ* and *The Atonement*. In 1816 he published a three-volume modern translation of the New Testament

Thomson was married to Elizabeth Johnston on 13 September 1792. She died at Newton-upon-Ayr on 31 August 1801. They had four daughters, Elizabeth (26 December 1797-1876) and Mary (24 June 1800-1872), who were to have their father's manuscripts bound and presented to the Free Church College in Glasgow. The other two daughters were Margaret (10 July 1793-24 May 1823) and Jean (15 September 1795-16 June 1822). Rev Thomson himself died on 26 August 1817, aged 55, and was laid to rest in the auld kirkyard.

The next minister appointed to the parish was Rev John Lindsay, who was translated from Auchinleck parish on 5 June 1818, being presented by James Boswell of Auchinleck on 20 January. Believed to have been a native of Dunoon, he had served at Auchinleck, his first charge, where he was ordained on 29 August 1793. He was a graduate of Edinburgh University and was licensed by Edinburgh Presbytery on 28 April 1790. Rev John Lindsay died on 6 July 1832. He was buried at Auchinleck, where a memorial stone on the old church wall states that he 'was instrumental in gathering many souls into the fold of the Redeemer.' At Ochiltree, the parishioners wished to commemorate him also, and thus erected a memorial on the west wall of the kirkyard. This bears the inscription: 'Sacred to the memory of the Reverend John Lindsay, minister of Ochiltree, who died at Ochiltree on 6th July, 1832. His early distinction as an accomplished scholar and a learned divine, his talents and erudition, cultivated with ardour to the very close of life and consecrated to the service of his Heavenly Master, his pastoral ministrations, affectionate and faithful, his intercourse with his friends, cheerful and exemplary, his zeal against error, his rich discoursing on Divine Truth, his holy life and peaceful death, will long render his name dear and venerable.' Lindsay had married Janet Blackstock on 28 April 1802. They never had any children, and she died on 16 November 1842.

The successor to Lindsay was also translated from Auchinleck. Rev James Boyd, born in Dunkeld in 1785, licensed by the Presbytery of Edinburgh on 28 June 1815 and ordained on 11 February 1818 as chaplain to the Caledonian Asylum, Hatton Garden, London. Whilst there he had the honour of baptising John Ruskin (1819-1900), the famous English art critic, watercolourist and philanthropist. Boyd was presented to Auchinleck in November 1818 and admitted on 6 May 1819. He was translated to Ochiltree on 18 April 1833, but he had been presented by the Presbytery *jure devoluto* on 30 January.

Rev Boyd's son, Andrew (who wrote with the pseudonym 'A. K. H. B.') was born in the manse at Auchinleck on 3 November 1825. James Boyd was At the time of his arrival the manse was totally repaired and an extension added. The glebe extended to nine acres. Boyd's stipend, agreed by the Court of Teinds in January 1835, was sixteen chalders of victual, half meal and half barley, with £10 for communion elements.

According to the *New Statistical Account*, the Ochiltree part which Boyd compiled in association with Robert Pettigrew of Polquhairn, almost everyone in the parish was a member of the established church, only five or six families not being. Each Sunday the congregation numbered from 800-900. There were 764 communicants. The regular collections for the poor amounted to £62 per annum.

Rev Boyd was translated to St Mary's Tron Kirk, Glasgow, on 18 April 1843. On 14 May 1844 a deputation of residents of Ochiltree visited him at the manse and presented him with a silver salver. This was inscribed, 'Presented to the Rev James Boyd, by the inhabitants of Ochiltree, on his removal to the church and parish of St Mary's, Glasgow, in testimony of their respect and gratitude for the zealous and faithful manner in which he has uniformly discharged the duties of the pastoral office in this place. – Ochiltree, April 1844.' He was granted a Divinity Doctorate by the Senatus of the University of Glasgow, and served as a minister for a total of 48 years. He died on 27 March 1865 and was buried in Glasgow's Necropolis.

On 15 August 1844 Rev William Montgomery Walker was appointed minister. He was born in Irvine on 18 February 1805, the fourth son of Dr Thomas Walker and Mary Fleeming (daughter of Charles Fleeming MD, RN), and grandson of Rev Thomas Walker (1704-1780), minister of Dundonald. His uncle Josias Walker was Professor of Humanity at the University of Glasgow. He was educated at Irvine Grammar School, followed by the University of Glasgow. He worked in London, before returning to Scotland and being licensed by the Presbytery of Irvine in 1829. He served as an assistant minister at St George's Church in Glasgow. He was ordained on 5 November 1834, his first charge being in Canada, in the newly-founded township of Huntingdon, in Quebec, where he remained for around ten years. So well liked was he in that dominion that he earned the sobriquet, 'the Chalmers of America'. He was presented to the charge at Ochiltree by the 2nd Marquis of Bute on the recommendations of Mr Stewart of Liberton. When he first arrived, his 'American' style of dress and other eccentricities amused the parishioners, but they soon recognised his skill in preaching. He did not write out copious notes, instead just used skeletal jottings, to which he added meat in an extempore fashion. He became a noted public speaker but was retiring in character, resulting in his preference to the rural charge of Ochiltree as opposed to a more populous urban charge. He was a regular correspondent to the *Ayr Advertiser*.

Walker's preaching was held in regard. 'A. K. H. B.' wrote that:

> I have heard many great preachers hold forth from the pulpit, and I have seen less or more of various human beings who are supposed as distinguished men. But the best preacher I ever heard, and the truest genius I ever knew, was a minister of the Scottish Church whose name will be quite unfamiliar to most readers of this page, and who died within the last few years as indumbent of a quiet rural parish in Kyle.
>
> Mr Walker of Ochiltree … could preach better than Henry Melville, than Bishop Wilberforce, than Dean Stanley, than Dr Vaughan, than Dr Liddon; incomparably better than Hugh MacNeile, or Dr Farrar, or Bishop Boyd Carpenter. I have heard him preach better than ever I heard Caird, Guthrie, Norman MacLeod, or Dr MacGregor … If ever there was real genius in any preacher, a springing fountain of eloquence and light and pathetic in beauty, it was in him.

Rev Walker had a number of children – Margaret Laird Walker died unmarried on 1 February 1912; Jane Walker (21 September 1844-19 April 1930); William Hugh Walker (25 July 1847-25 June 1913); Josiah Charles Walker (6 May 1851-28 April 1882); Frances Hunter Walker (21 October 1854-17 June 1933); Dr Patrick Hunter Walker M.B., C.M. (15 April 1858-14 September 1939) became a district surgeon in Tembuland, South Africa. Rev Walker's eldest daughter, Mary Fleeming Walker (b. 1 January 1838) married Rev James Wilson, minister of St Quivox, Ayr. His eldest son, Rev Thomas Walker (b. 23 September 1841) became the minister of St John's Town of Dalry in Kirkcudbrightshire.

Frances Hunter Walker, daughter of Rev William Walker, was a writer of poems and prose sketches. Amongst her works was About *'The Old Place'*, sketches of life in Ochiltree, published, in 1927. On 15 May 1880, Frances Walker was presented with a walnut writing desk by the children in Ochiltree Sabbath School.

Another child of Rev Walker's, William Hugh Walker, became M.P.P. for Huntingdon County, Canada, and was a member of the Legislative Assembly, Quebec. He died on 25 June 1913 at Hillside, Huntingdon, Quebec, Canada.

During Walker's ministry, the church underwent some alterations. Internally, the galleries and wooden stairs were built in 1854, the old stone staircases being removed. The table seats were removed and part of the nave was reseated. The roof was reslated, the work all completed by A. & A. Murdoch of Ochiltree. The new porches were added in 1862, to plans by William MacLetchie & Son. At the same time the southern doorway was blocked up. The cost of works was £383 18s. In December 1864 Rev William Walker was presented with a new pulpit gown and cassock, on the occasion of the reopening of the church following the alterations to the church building.

5.4 Ochiltree Church hall architect drawing

Rev Walker died at Ochiltree manse on 24 April 1880 and was interred in the old churchyard by the side of the Lugar Water.

Rev Niel Mackay BD was ordained as minister on 15 September 1880. Born at Southend in Argyll, on 14 October 1851, the son of Peter Mackay and Janet MacKerrell, he was educated at Southend Public School, followed by the University of Glasgow. Mackay graduated as a Master of Arts in 1875 and with a Bachelor of Divinity in 1878. He was licensed by the Presbytery of Kintyre on 8 September 1878. Prior to arriving in Ochiltree he served as the assistant to Rev David Strong at Hillhead Church in Glasgow. He was married on 10 August 1882 to Teresa Kossuth Forbes, daughter of Duncan Forbes. She died on 29 June 1935. Rev Mackay retired as minister on 1 July 1923. He died on 19 July 1930. During his term of ministry, the Women's Guild was established in 1887.

By 1897 it was felt that Ochiltree Church was past its best, and various options were considered for a replacement. It was noted that the galleries were in a dangerous condition and that the ceiling had sunk. The architect, J. B. Wilson of Glasgow, visited the building and reported that its condition was not only unsuitable for public worship, it was dangerous. He reckoned that the cost of repairs was about three quarters of the price of demolishing the building to the foundations and rebuilding. In February 1897 David Dunlop informed the Sheriff Court that he had been authorised by Rev Mackay to make an offer to the heritors. This was that, 'if the heritors paid £1,250, Mr Mackay would undertake to hand over to them a new church for £2,000. They were advised it would be a very substantial building.' As a result, in 1897 the church building was altered. The Edinburgh architects, Peddie and Washington Browne, were consulted and the new round-headed windows were added. New floors were laid, new seats installed, the galleries and ceiling were repaired, costing £1,186. After being closed for a few months, the rebuilt church opened for worship once more on 11 December 1898. The official opening was carried out by Rev Thomas Walker B.A. of Dalry, son of the previous minister, Rev William Walker.

Around 1895 a bell was ordered for the western belfry from John C. Wilson & Co. Ltd. of the Gorbals Bell Foundry in Glasgow. This measures about thirty inches in diameter and bears, in addition to other words that cannot be made out from the ground:

……BELL ERECTED BY THE CHURCH…….
JOHN C. WILSON & CO LTD FOUNDERS GLASGOW…….

In May 1908 plans for a new church hall that could seat 300 were proposed. The cost of the building was to be underwritten by Mr and Mrs James Angus of Ladykirk in memory of their son, James Angus (d. 1902). Work on the hall commenced soon after, the mason work being undertaken by the former provost of Cumnock, James Richmond. Messrs MacLeod were the joiners, Mr M. Taylor the plasterer, Messrs H. & T. Morrison, plumbers – all tradesmen from Cumnock. The architect

5.5 Ochiltree Parish Church

was Robert Ingram. The stone was quarried at Skares, but it was coated with roughcast. The new hall was opened on 14 January 1909, Mrs Ingram handing Mrs Angus a golden key with which to open the door. Within the hall a tablet bears the inscription – *In loving memory of James Angus, who died at Ochiltree House, 17th December 1902. This hall was erected by his parents in 1908.* At the same time the piano from Ochiltree House was presented to the hall by Mrs Angus. Present at the event was Rev Dr Theodore Marshall, the Moderator of the Church of Scotland, reckoned to be the first time a moderator had visited Ochiltree. The main hall in the new building measured forty feet by twenty feet, with a boarded wagon roof; the Lesser Hall, twenty feet six inches by twenty feet. A folding partition between the two opened to allow the accommodation to reach 300, or else two hundred in the large hall and 100 in the lesser hall. In addition, there was also a retiring room, kitchen and lavatory. A moveable platform was presented for use in the hall by the Women's Guild, subsequently replaced by a fixed stage.

5.6 Ochiltree Communion Token

Rev David Sinclair Rutherford MA was ordained at Ochiltree on Thursday 3 May 1923 as assistant and successor to Rev Niel Mackay. After the service the congregation retired to the Heid Inn where lunch was served. Rev Rutherford had previously served for six months as an assistant at St Mary's Church in Edinburgh, under Rev A. T. Laurence. He was elected as successor on 28 March 1923. His father was the Rev Robert W. Rutherford, minister of Gartsherrie Parish Church, Coatbridge. He received his education at Fettes School (1909-14), Edinburgh University (1914-15) and Glasgow University (1918), graduating with a Master of Arts degree with honours. He served in the army from 1915-18. Rev Rutherford was translated to Biggar on 20 June 1928.

During the ministry of Rev Rutherford, the Men's Club had a major disagreement with the church, and moved out into the Crown Inn. They held a meeting in February 1925 to decide what to do, agreeing to form a new recreation club independent of the church, named the Burnock Recreation Club.

At the time Rev Rutherford left the parish church, the Free Church also had a vacancy, and many locals felt it was time for the two churches to unite. However, both were still independent of each other, and the national churches had not started the formal process of uniting. As a result, each church was left to call their own minister and the churches remained separate for another seven years.

The pulpit was filled by Rev Angus MacLeod MA, who was translated to Ochiltree on 30 November 1928. Rev MacLeod was born on 6 July 1893, the son of Angus MacLeod, a slate quarryman, and Annabella Gillies. He was educated at the University of Glasgow where he graduated Master of Arts in 1919. He was licensed by the Presbytery of Glasgow in December 1923. He worked as assistant minister at the Martyrs' Church, Glasgow, from 1923 until 1924, when he was ordained to Salen in Argyll, followed by Kilcalmonell, also Argyll, in 1925. Having served as minister of Ochiltree parish for sixteen and a half years, he died on 3 March 1945. He was buried in Ochiltree New Cemetery. Rev MacLeod was married on 28 December 1923 to Helen Cowan MacIntyre, daughter of John Ranken MacIntyre and Margaret Cowan Wilkinson. They had two sons, Angus Ian MacLeod, born 8 December 1924, and Kenneth Gillies MacLeod, born 11 September 1928. Helen MacLeod died on 15 February 1980.

During the ministry of Rev MacLeod, the Church of Scotland and the United Free Church united nationally in 1929. This created two parish churches in Ochiltree, and it was decided to name them simply as Ochiltree North Parish Church (the original and present parish church), and Ochiltree South Parish Church (the former Free Church). In many smaller parishes across the country it was not sensible to keep two distinct congregations, and so many parishes had their congregations reunited. Thus, in Ochiltree, the North and South parish church congregations were reunited on 6 March 1935. The former parish church was retained as the place of worship.

5.7 Ochiltree Free Church

Also occurring in 1929 was the termination of the responsibility of the parish heritors for the upkeep of the church building and other costs. To replace this, seat rents were introduced, each parishioner paying a sum agreed annually for the right to their own seat in a specific pew.

Rev David Priestly Leishman BD MA was the next minister at Ochiltree. He was born at Dalserf in Lanarkshire and educated at Larkhall Academy. He worked as a mining engineer but received a calling to the ministry. He trained at Glasgow University, graduating in 1933 with a Master of Arts degree. In 1936 he obtained a Bachelor of Divinity degree and was licensed by the Presbytery of Hamilton. His first charge was at Galashiels, where he remained until 1939. He then moved to Bargrennan Church, near Newton Stewart, remaining for the duration of the Second World War. He was translated from Bargrennan to Ochiltree on 10 October 1945. He served at Ochiltree for just over six years, being translated to St Boswells in Roxburghshire on 20 March 1952. He was to remain at St Boswells until he retired in 1973. He died at Durisdeer, Dumfriesshire, in 1989, aged 84.

Two stained glass windows were installed in the parish church in 1947. These were the work of the stained glass artist, Stephen Adam. They had originally been inserted in the Free Church, but were removed to the parish church when it closed.

Rev William James Hutton was appointed as the next minister to the church in Ochiltree, on 24 September 1952. He was born on 10 June 1919 at Borthwick schoolhouse, Midlothian, the son of William Hutton and Roberta Christina Dickson. He received his education at Borthwick Primary School, followed by Dalkeith High School and then the University of Edinburgh. His time at university was broken by the outbreak of war, for he studied from 1938-9, and then from 1946 until 1948, serving in the forces during the war. He graduated as a Master of Arts. He worked as a student assistant at Granton Parish Church in Edinburgh from 1947-48 and was licensed by the Presbytery of Dalkeith on 1 July 1948. From 1948 until February 1952 Rev Hutton served as a missionary in Jamaica, having been ordained by the Presbytery of Dalkeith on 18 July 1948 for that purpose.

In 1950 the parish church had a membership of 412, comprising 250 women and 160 men, with an average Sunday morning attendance of 100. The Women's Guild had 40 members. Around 130 children attended Sunday School.

Rev Hutton remained in Ochiltree for six years, being translated to Glasgow Trinity Duke Street Church on 13 August 1958. Rev Hutton was married on 30 June 1943 to Mary Wishart (b. 2 May 1920), daughter of William Brazenall and Mary Wishart Adams Revie. They had two children, David Hutton (born 15 May 1947), and Elizabeth Hutton (born 28 June 1950).

The church hall was extended in 1958, during Rev Hutton's ministry, at a cost of £2,300. The boundary wall of the church grounds adjoining Main Street was partially removed to allow vehicular access to the church hall. In 1947 there was a proposal to do away with seat rents in the kirk and replace them with the introduction of a 'free-will' offering. This was not passed at the time. In 1951 this issue came up again, and by 41 votes to 21 it was passed.

The next minister was appointed in 1959. Rev Duncan Stewart MacAlpine was translated from Macduff Doune Parish Church, in Banffshire, and he was inducted on 4 March 1959. He was born on 23 October 1912 at Thornton, Fife, the son of Archibald MacDonald MacAlpine and Catherine Nesi Spittal. He received his education at Thornton Public School (1917-22), Burntisland High School (1922-27) and Airdrie Academy (1927-30). He then studied at the University of Edinburgh and New College, Edinburgh (1938-42), from where he graduated as a minister. He served as a student assistant at Edinburgh Tolbooth – St John's church in 1942, and then was licensed by the Presbytery of Dunfermline and Kinross on 26 September 1943. He served as a temporary locum at Insch (Aberdeenshire) in 1943. He then moved to Rosyth, Fife, where he was responsible for a church extension charge (1943-44). On 25 August 1944 he was married to Helen Manuel

Ritchie Wilson (b. 21 November 1917), daughter of Henry Wilson (an architect and Lieutenant Colonel in the Royal Army Service Corps) and Janet Ritchie. They had two sons, Archibald MacDonald (b. 11 December 1945) and Rognvald Henry (b. 18 October 1949). Rev MacAlpine was ordained and inducted as minister at North Ronaldshay Parish Church in Orkney on 13 September 1944. He was translated to South Ronaldshay St Mary's church on 10 December 1947. After three years, on 5 April 1950, he was translated and inducted as minister at Doune Parish Church, Macduff, Banffshire. Rev MacAlpine did not hold the position of minister at Ochiltree for very long, around two and a half years, as he died on 3 October 1961.

Rev Iain Lachlan Gillies was next to serve in Ochiltree. Born in Glasgow on 20 February 1917, he was the son of Neil Gillies and Euphemia MacVicar MacDonald. He received his education at Hillhead High School (1923-34), followed by Skerry's College (1935-37), the Bible Training Institute, Glasgow (1945-47), and then Glasgow University (1948-56). During the war he served with the Royal Air Force (1942-44). Rev Gillies served as assistant minister at Barmulloch (Glasgow) from 1954-55, then Provanmill, also Glasgow, 1955-56. He was licensed to preach by Glasgow Presbytery on 12 June 1956. His first charge was at Kildalton Parish Church, Island of Islay, where he was ordained and inducted on 25 October 1956. He was married on 25 September 1952 to Mary Findlay Murray (b. 12 February 1922), daughter of David Murray and Jeannie Balfour. They had a son and daughter, Neil Macdonald Gillies (b. 30 October 1958) and Joyce Mary Murray Gillies (b. 7 March 1960). He was translated from Kildalton and inducted at Ochiltree on 12 April 1962. He was appointed as a Lieutenant in the Army Cadet Force at Ayr on 29 October 1963. He transferred to Glasgow Bluevale and Whitevale church on 19 October 1966. He retired as minister from there on 24 January 1975.

Rev James Currie was translated to Ochiltree parish church on Wednesday 19 July 1967 from Galashiels St John's Church, where he had been ordained and inducted on 22 October 1964. James Currie was born on 5 April 1918 in Glasgow, the son of John Kennedy Currie and Matilda Spence MacFarlane. He received his education at Lorne Street School from 1923 until 1929, followed by Bellahouston Secondary School from 1929-33. He carried out his war service with the Cameronian Regiment (Scottish Rifles) from 1940-6. He studied at Trinity College, Glasgow University, from 1960-4. Currie was assistant minister at Glasgow St Andrew's East Church from 1961-4, and he was licensed by the Presbytery of Hamilton on 15 April 1964. He was married on 31 March 1954 to Elizabeth Hannah Elliot Cook (b. 23 July 1927), daughter to John Porter Cook and Annie Elliot, whom he met whilst he was a patient at Ballochmyle Hospital and she was a nurse. They had two daughters, Anne (b. 9 May 1957) and Susan (b. 14 July 1966). Rev Currie remained as minister at Ochiltree until he retired on 31 October 1970. He died on 1 October 1986.

The next man of the cloth to fill the pulpit at Ochiltree was Rev John Heron, who was translated from Mochrum Parish Church, Wigtownshire, and inducted to Ochiltree on 22 April 1971. He was born on 9 January 1915 in Kilmarnock, the son of William and Margaret Heron. He received his education at Prestwick High School followed by Kilmarnock Academy. On leaving school he found employment with Glasgow Rate and Salvage Association, working with them for eight years from 1932. During the Second World War he served with the Royal Air Force (1940-46). When he was demobbed, Heron studied at Glasgow University from 1947-51 to become a minister. He was married on 27 August 1946 to Elizabeth, daughter of Robert and Margaret Kennedy. He was a student assistant at Troon Old Church from 1949-51, and was licensed by the Presbytery of Ayr on 15 April 1951. Rev Heron's first charge as a minister was at Sorn, where he was ordained and inducted on 5 September 1951 at the age of 36. He remained in the pulpit there for six years, being translated to Strathaven Rankin Parish Church on 18 October 1957. He was translated from Strathaven to Mochrum Parish Church, Wigtownshire, on 29 August 1968. Rev Heron retired from the pulpit in 1979 and died in 2002.

The Church of Scotland nationally had difficulty in finding enough ministers for all of its churches, and with a falling roll in many rural parishes, linking churches was one solution. Ochiltree Parish Church was linked with Stair Parish Church on 6 January 1979, sharing the same minister, but retaining their independence.

The first minister of the new linked charge of Ochiltree and Stair was Rev Raymond David Mackenzie BD. He had been ordained and inducted to Stair Parish Church on 9 May 1978. Mackenzie was born on 6 December 1947 in Glasgow, the son of David Murdoch Mackenzie and Margaret Queen. He was educated at Knightswood Secondary School in Glasgow and then attended the College of Commerce from 1964-68 (attaining an SNC in Business). From 1970-72 he attended the Bible Training Institute, graduating with a DTh. From 1972-77 he attended the University of Glasgow, gaining a Bachelor of Divinity degree. From 1964-67 Mackenzie worked with the City Line Shipping Co. Ltd. He then worked for Albion Motors from 1967-79. Mackenzie was licensed by the Presbytery of Glasgow on 30 June 1977. He worked as assistant minister at Bearsden Killermont Parish Church from 1973-75, followed by Glasgow Scotstoun West (1975-76), Milngavie St Paul's Parish Church (1976-77) and Bathgate High Parish Church (1977-78). He was married on 23 August 1973 to Susan Mary Hallett (b. 23 April 1946), daughter of Norman Frank Hallett and Doris Ethel Luck. They had three children – Gregor Raymond (b. 14 April 1976); Ross Norman (b. 14 April 1976) and Morven Ann (b. 17 December 1981). He remained in Ochiltree for nine years until 1987. On 13 March 1987 he accepted a call to Hamilton Burnbank linked with Hamilton North parish churches.

The Rev Kenneth Burgoyne Yorke BD was translated to Ochiltree with Stair parish churches on 25 August 1987. He had previously served as the minister of Kirn Parish Church in Argyll, where he was ordained and inducted on 5 May 1982. Kenneth Yorke was born on 13 June 1939 in Aberdeen, the son of James Burgoyne Yorke and Elizabeth MacCallum. He received his education at Prestwick High School from 1951-55. He was married on 13 August 1966 to Ann Ironside Brown (b. 7 July 1941), daughter of James Brown and Charlotte Caldwell. They have two sons – Kenneth James Yorke (b. 31 January 1968) and Callum Peter (b. 16 August 1969). On 15 May 1991 Rev Yorke was married for a second time, to Margaret MacIntyre (b. 5 April 1948), daughter of Harold Raymond Beggs and Margaret Sands. They had a daughter, Eiley, born on 22 September 1990. Kenneth Yorke worked as a motor engineer from 1955 until 1977. He then studied at the University of Glasgow from 1977-81, graduating with a Bachelor of Divinity degree. He was licensed to preach by the Presbytery of Ayr on 28 June 1981. He served as assistant minister at Alloway Parish Church from 1981-82. From 1992-93 he studied at the University of Strathclyde, becoming a Bachelor of Education. Rev Yorke left the church in Ochiltree to pursue a career as a teacher of Religious and Moral Education on 16 August 1993. He continued this career until 1999 when he accepted a call to become minister of Dalmellington Parish Church, being inducted on 9 March 1999. He retired in 2009.

Rev Kevin MacKenzie was translated to Ochiltree Parish Church on 30 March 1993. He was born on 30 August 1962 at Aberdeen, the son of Roy MacKenzie and Henrietta Mary Strachan Craig. He received his education at the Gordon Schools in Huntly from 1974-79, followed by the University of Aberdeen from 1982-88. He graduated with a Bachelor of Divinity degree and a DPS. He was licensed by the Presbytery of Aberdeen on 27 June 1988. At first he served as an assistant minister at Edinburgh Murrayfield Parish Church from 1988-89. He was ordained and inducted to Wemyss Parish Church on 16 May 1989. He was married on 16 August 1985 to Linda Anne Wylie (b. 19 May 1962), daughter of Alexander Wylie and Anne Gillespie. They had three children – Hollie (b. 7 October 1986); Katie (b. 18 April 1989) and Christopher (b. 29 December 1990). On 12 December 1996 Rev MacKenzie accepted a call to East Kilbride Westwood Parish Church.

On 16 September 1997 Rev Carolyn Mai Baker was ordained and inducted to Ochiltree Parish Church. She had been born on 1 August 1943 at Colchester, daughter of John Emrys Jones and Christina Nicol Stott. She was educated at Colchester County High School, followed by Gairloch High School. From 1972-89 she worked as a social worker. Carolyn Baker then studied at the University of Aberdeen (1991-95) from where she graduated with a Bachelor of Divinity degree. She was licensed by the Presbytery of Aberdeen on 14 November 1995. She was married on 31 August 1963 to Colin Ernest Baker (b. 22 February 1941), son of Ernest and Violet Baker. Colin and Carolyn Baker had one son, David Emrys Baker (b. 26 March 1967), who was married to Sheila.

The Rev William Roger Johnston became the next minister, being inducted to Ochiltree linked with Stair on 28 April 2009. He was born on 1 May 1948 in Irvine, the son of Hendry MacLean Curdy Johnston and Letitia Coulter Ross. He was educated at Belmont Academy in Ayr, followed by Ayr College. He worked as a butcher from 1964-91. From 1992-96 he attended the University of Glasgow, graduating with a Bachelor of Divinity degree. He was licensed to preach by the Presbytery of Ayr on 21 July 1996. At first, he served as assistant minister at St Leonard's Church in Ayr (1996-98). He was ordained and inducted to Ardrossan Park Parish Church on 28 January 1998. Rev Johnston was married on 30 March 1968 to Anne Murphy Bone (b. 18 May 1947), daughter of James Bone and Agnes Johnstone. They had two children – Shona (b. 28 November 1973), who married Shaun Lidbury, and Graeme (b. 9 August 1975). Rev Johnston retired from Ochiltree and Stair on 31 January 2016. He died on 4 March 2019.

The next minister was Rev Morag Garrett BD, translated on 1 November 2017. Born in Ayrshire, Morag Violet Garrett grew up in Kilmarnock and Dundonald. She was educated at Onthank and Dundonald Primary Schools followed by Marr College. On leaving school she emigrated to South Africa, followed by Australia, and then back to South Africa. She returned to Scotland, settling in Troon. She then studied Ministry of Word and Sacrament at Glasgow University, graduating with a Bachelor of Divinity in Ministry. She was ordained by the Presbytery of Ardrossan and inducted to Kilwinning: Mansefield Parish Church on 23 November 2011. She translated to Ayr: St Andrew's Parish Church on 28 February 2013.

FREE CHURCH/SOUTH CHURCH

In 1843 the Church of Scotland nationally split into two, creating the Established Church and the new Free Church. This came about as a result over a dispute concerning the Act of Patronage, whereby the local landowner appointed the minister, whether the parishioners wished him or not. Free Church congregations could call whichever minister they liked. In Ochiltree the Free Church congregation was formed in 1843 when seven elders came out of the parish church. For a time they were under the charge of a probationer. The first meeting place of the new congregation was in a cheese-house below Burnockholm House, but they were a keen group.

In June 1843, 300 people were addressed by Rev Ninian Bannatyne of Cumnock. The meeting took place at Burnockholm, belonging to Thomas Cuthbert, merchant. Cuthbert offered the fledgling congregation the use of his house until a more appropriate place for a church could be found.

In February 1844 a prayer meeting under the auspices of the Free Church was held in the village, where Rev Joseph Patrick preached to a large congregation. Rev Patrick was touted as a possible minister for the new church.

Collections began in September 1845 by the members towards the cost of a church building. Work on this commenced soon after. Almost simultaneously a Free Church School was established and a manse erected for the minister. The ground for the Free Church Manse was donated to the congregation by Alexander Ross of Lessnessock, his act being unsolicited. The title to the ground included the nominal feu of one shilling per annum, if demanded. Ross also contributed a large sum towards the manse building fund. The building was constructed by A. & A. Murdoch.

The site chosen for the new Free Church was a triangular piece of ground, bordered to the east by Ayr Road and to the west by the Doctor's Road. The foundation stone was laid on 25 June 1845 and two months later the mason work was complete. The building constructed was a fairly significant one for the size of the congregation, being rectangular in plan, with a simple slate-covered roof. Along each long side were three arched windows. The gable facing to Ayr Road was the most elaborate, having Tudoresque corner pillars and a projecting doorway. This projection continued up to the top of the gable end, where it was

5.8 Rev A. Gordon MacLeod *(Author's Collection)*

surmounted by a pediment, over which was an octagonal belfry, with a lead cap-piece. The open belfry had a bell within it,. To ether side of the arched front door were lancet windows, and a third lancet on the gable was positioned above the door. The architect was John Baird, Cumnock.

The new church building was opened on Sunday 8 March 1846, the officiating minister on that occasion being Rev Thomas Guthrie, afterwards Rev Dr Guthrie (1803-1873). He was a significant figure in the Free Church, being leader at the time, and he was later to be the subject of a statue in Edinburgh's Princes Street in 1910. The collection on the day of opening was £125 3s 1¾d. The bell in the belfry had been manufactured by the Gorbals Bell Foundry in Glasgow. It weighed five hundredweight and measured thirty inches at the mouth. The bell was donated to the church by John Bryden, who had died in March 1845, aged 93, and the bell was bought in August 1845.

Although Ochiltree Free Church had a capacity for a congregation of 500, it was rarely filled. In 1848 membership of the church was 184, but by 1900 it had fallen to 123.

The first minister was Rev Joseph Patrick MA, who served at the church from 1844 until his death in 1871. Born in 1814, he was married to Mary Barbour (12 December 1824-3 March 1897), daughter of John Barbour of Macdonallie, Lochwinnoch. Mary Patrick was buried in Lochwinnoch. They had two sons, the eldest, Dr David Patrick, the other, Joseph Patrick CA, working in Glasgow.

Dr David Patrick MA (1849-1914) graduated with a Bachelor of Divinity degree from the University of Edinburgh in 1872. He held the Cunninghame Fellowship in the New College in 1872. He became the head of the literary staff of Edinburgh publishing firm of W. & R. Chambers, and was responsible for the firm's *Biographical Dictionary*. He was also the editor of *Chambers' Encyclopaedia*, and other works. In 1894 he had the honour of Doctor of Laws conferred on him by the University of Edinburgh. He died in 1914 and left £17,233 in his will. He was buried in Lochwinnoch.

Rev Patrick was followed by Rev (Alexander) J. S. Macdonald who served at Ochiltree from June 1872 until 1881. Born at Kirkmichael, Banffshire, in 1842, he studied for the ministry at the University of Edinburgh and New College. He was introduced to the church at Ochiltree by Rev Dr Julius Wood of Dumfries. In 1873 he was married to Janet Thomson. He was married for a second time in 1884 to Alice Warrick. He was translated to South Leith Free Church in 1881. He died in 1898.

The third minister was Rev Adam Andrew Gordon MacLeod, who served from 1881 until 1928, although from 1923 he was senior minister. He was born at Inverness in 1856. He studied at the University of Edinburgh and New College. At the same time as arriving in Ochiltree, he was married to Jessie R. Inglis. He was married for a second time, in Cumnock, on 10 October 1916 to Margaret Johnston Dow. During his period as minister, the Free Church of Scotland merged with the United Presbyterian Church of Scotland to form the United Free Church of Scotland. Thus, Ochiltree's Free Church became a United Free congregation.

Gordon MacLeod was a keen writer and wrote a number of novels. Satan's Fool, set in a highland parish, was published in 1909 by Alexander Gardner of Paisley. Rev MacLeod died at Gordon Cottage in Ochiltree on 10 May 1928 at the age of 78.

5.9 Rev Angus MacLeod's gravestone *(Dane Love)*

Two new stained glass windows were unveiled in the U. F. Church in March 1905, the work of Stephen Adam (1848-1910) of Glasgow. The windows represent 'He is not here but risen' and 'Why seek to the living among the dead?' One was dedicated to the memory of John Lammie (1785-1875) and Jean Mearns (1789-1868), the other to Alexander Gregg (1791-1882) and Agnes Gregg (1795-1864). The windows were donated by George Lammie of the British Linen Bank and his wife, Jean Gregg, in memory of their parents. George Lammie was to be a speaker at the Glasgow Ochiltree Society in 1875.

On Wednesday 14 November 1923 Rev Andrew Drummond Baird MA was ordained and inducted as Colleague and Minister of Ochiltree United Free Church, assisting Rev MacLeod. Born in Paisley, he was the only son of Andrew Baird. Educated at Paisley Grammar School, he studied at Glasgow University, from where he graduated as a Master of Arts with honours. He continued his studies at the United Free Church College. During the war he served with the Argyll and Sutherland Highlanders. From 1920 until 1923 he acted as assistant to Rev C. MacIan Jack at Martyrs United Free Church in Paisley.

The church building suffered a fire during the morning service on 20 January 1924. A faulty vent caused part of the roof over the boiler to catch alight and Rev Baird had to request that the congregation leave the building. The fire was soon extinguished, a tarpaulin placed over the hole, and the evening service was able to take pace as normal. Rev Baird was transferred to the Guthrie U. F. Church In Cowdenbeath in 1927.

Rev George Riddell Aitken MA was inducted to the United Free Church on Thursday 2 June 1927, moving from Kirkintilloch South U. F. Church. He was born on 14 May 1866 at the Original Secession Manse, Midlem, Selkirkshire. He was the son of Rev William Ferguson Aitken and Hannah Riddell. He received his early education at Lilliesleaf and Midlem public schools, followed by Hampton Court Academy and the High School of Glasgow. He attended Glasgow University where he obtained a Master of Arts degree in 1894. Aitken then attended the Original Secession Divinity Hall, then Glasgow Free Church College. He was licensed to preach by the United Original Secession Church, Presbytery of Glasgow, in autumn 1895. He was ordained and inducted to Kirkintilloch Original Secession Church on 2 July 1896. He was inducted to the same congregation by the Presbytery of Glasgow in June 1902. He resigned his position in Kirkintilloch in 1927. Rev Aitken did not remain at Ochiltree for very long, and on 27 September 1928 was transferred to Kirkpatrick Durham Craig U. F. Church in Kirkcudbrightshire. He demitted the post in 1937 and died on 19 September 1938.

Rev Aitken was married on 12 April 1906 to Annie Clark MacArthur. She was a writer, who wrote with the pseudonym 'Jean Oliver Riddell'. She had a number of books published, such as *Windyridge, There's Wind on the Heath* (1924) and *Netherleigh*, which proved to be popular at the time.

5.10 Ochiltree Free Church *(James Brown)*

New Cumnock United Free Church was being rebuilt in 1928 and the pipe organ became surplus. It was gifted to the United Free Church in Ochiltree and installed there. On 4 March 1928 it was up and running, when a recital was played.

The last minister of the United Free Church was Rev Gustavius Aird Sim. He was inducted at Ochiltree on 7 February 1929, moving from Kirkurd in Peeblesshire. Born on 9 June 1866 at Ardullie, Kiltearn, Ross-shire, he was the son of Henry Sim and Helen Montgomery Ross. He was named after his uncle, Rev Gustavius Sim, a Highland minister, who served as Moderator of the Free Church Assembly in 1888. Sim was educated at Inverness Royal Academy, followed by Aberdeen University and then New College, Edinburgh. He was licensed by the Free Church Presbytery of Dornoch on 30 April 1890. His first position was as assistant minister at Dysart, Fife, followed by similar positions at Forres (Moray) and Malta. He was ordained at Genoa by the Presbytery of Italy and inducted at Malta on 28 January 1896. Rev Sim was appointed as Chaplain to H. M. Fleet in Malta, where he served until his retiral in 1920. He was inducted as the minister at Kirkurd United Free Church in Peeblesshire in 1921. He remained at Kirkurd until moving to Ochiltree.

Gustavius Sim was a keen historian, being elected a Fellow of the Society of Antiquaries of Scotland. He had a number of articles published in various periodicals. He died on 5 July 1934.

In 1929 the United Free Church of Scotland rejoined the Church of Scotland nationally. This resulted in Ochiltree having two Church of Scotland congregations. The former United Free Church was renamed Ochiltree South Church of Scotland. It was decided that the South Church would be closed, and the congregation merged with the parish church, which took place on 6 March 1935. The former United Free manse was accordingly sold in August 1935 for £565.

The church building itself was also sold, and it was used for a time as a hosiery factory. In 1947 the two stained glass windows by Stephen Adam were transferred to the Parish Church, where they were inserted in the window openings to either side of the pulpit. The old Free Church was demolished in 1967. The site of the kirk is now occupied by the war memorial, moved to this location in 1973.

DRONGAN SCHAW KIRK

With the new community at Drongan growing in size, and with a projected population in excess of 30,000, the Church of Scotland felt that it was time to erect a new place of worship in the village. In Lane Crescent a church building was erected in a loop formed by Cairnston Avenue. The foundation stone was laid by Captain Oliver Hughes-Onslow on 6 July 1955. The brick-built church was opened on 14 September 1956 by the Very Rev E. D. Jarvis DD, who had been Moderator of the General Assembly of the Church of Scotland in 1954. The church was named Drongan: The Schaw Kirk, for it had been agreed that the old Schaw Kirk should be closed and the minister and congregation be rehoused in Drongan. Thus, the first minister in the church was Rev G. L. Hunter, who had been inducted to the Schaw Kirk in 1949. On 4 November 1956 the church received its largest number of new communicants, when 63 joined.

The history of the Schaw Kirk prior to its move to Drongan dates back to 1843, when the Church of Scotland nationally was split in two over the subject of patronage, or the right of the local landowners to appoint the minister. Many ministers and congregations argued that it should be the congregation itself who should call the minister. In Stair, meetings regarding the matter of patronage had taken place during the summer of 1842, when the congregation was addressed by Rev John Allan (1798-1885) of Aberdeen. In the spring of 1843, a further meeting was addressed by Rev Dr Nathaniel Paterson (1787-1871) of Glasgow and Rev William Buchan (1806-1869) of Hamilton. At the General Assembly of the Church of Scotland, held on 18 May 1843, 450 ministers refused to accept the decision of the assembly regarding patronage and walked out. Within a short period of time the Free Church of Scotland was established. In many parishes this resulted in what became known as the Disruption, when the ministers who walked out of the parish church set up their own congregations and met elsewhere. In Stair parish, the minister, Rev William Rorison, remained in the parish church, so the new congregation had to start from scratch.

The new Free Church congregation of Stair parish met in the open air at Burn farm for their first service on 21 May 1843. The congregation continued to meet there for the following three months, including a communion service held on 16 July 1843, officiated by Rev Thomas Burns of Monkton (nephew of Robert Burns), but soon three farmers agreed that they could meet in their barns, and also in a workshop at Boghead. Thus, the meetings alternated between them whilst plans for a new church building were made. The congregation was served for the first few months by Rev John MacFarlan, probationer minister, who was to accept the call to Monkton.

A committee within the congregation was formed to organise the erection of a place of worship. However, they could not agree a site, and the committee was disbanded, having argued over sites at Burn and Schaw. A new committee was formed and a site at Schaw, near to Windmillhall, was obtained and the foundation stone of the new church building was laid on 3 October 1843 by Miss Isabella Christina Burnett, daughter Lt. Col. Joseph Burnett of Gadgirth. The plan was a copy of the Free Church of Newton-upon-Ayr. The mason work was completed by James Duncan and the woodwork by Mr MacNab, Old Toll. It was estimated that the church cost £320 to build, local subscriptions contributing £148 14s 6d. A further £112 14s 4d was obtained from the building fund and it was reckoned that the remainder of the cost was covered by donations of stone and free labour. The church was opened for worship on 24 March 1844, the opening service conducted by Rev Dr Patrick MacFarlan DD (1781-1849) of Greenock. On the following Sunday, the service was conducted by Rev David Wilson of Irvine. When opened, the church was free of debt. The church was run by four elders and eleven deacons.

In 1846 a stable for six horses was erected at the church and this remained until 1930 when it was converted into a waiting room. In 1945 it was demolished to leave room for parking of cars. In 1859 a Session House was added to the rear of the church to allow the office bearers to hold meetings. Whilst this was being erected the church was closed for three Sundays, the congregation advised to worship at either Tarbolton or Ochiltree Free Churches. Work took longer than anticipated due to the weather so services resumed in Mr MacIntyre's workshop, followed by a large room in Drongan House. In 1861 Tarbolton Church was lit by gas, so the congregation there offered their candlesticks to Stair.

5.11 Schaw Kirk *(Author's Collection)*

The first minister at the Free Church at Schaw was Rev Dr Neil Livingston DD. In the meantime, the Free Church Presbytery had arranged the union of Stair and Tarbolton Free Churches. Rev Livingston was born at Johnstone in Renfrewshire in 1811. He studied at the University of Glasgow and was ordained and inducted to Stair and Tarbolton on 4 April 1844. He was married in 1856 to Jane Thomson Geddes. In 1849 a new manse was erected for the minister, but this did not have the luxury of running water, the minister relying on rainwater or supplies from neighbours. The titles to the manse were signed by the trustees on 12 December 1849. Rev Livingston was to receive an honorary Doctorate of Divinity from the University of Glasgow in 1882. Livingston became the Senior Minister in 1886, having an assistant in Rev John Ewing Thomson. Rev Dr Livingston was a keen church historian, with a strong fascination for Scottish Church Music. He wrote extensively on the subject, among his works being a facsimile reprint of the Scottish Metrical Psalter of 1635. He also compiled *A Complete Vocabulary of the English Language, Infantia Mundi*. Dr Livingston was convenor of the church's psalmody committee. He died peacefully at home on Friday 7 July 1899.

In February 1844 a plot of land at Schaw farm was obtained on a 99-year lease at one shilling per Scotch fall. John Baird of Glasgow provided plans for a manse for the minister that was erected by Mr MacGeachan (mason) and Mr MacIntyre (joinery).

5.12 Schaw Kirk in 2020 *(Dane Love)*

The church was originally known as the Free Church at Shaw (or Schaw), but in April 1858 onward it was referred to as the Free Church Stair. However, it hadn't occurred to the congregation that the church had actually been built within the parish of Ochiltree! Early services were held in the afternoon, on account of the union with Tarbolton. These originally lasted 2¼ hours, but in November 1858 it was decided to reduce the length to two hours, starting at 2 o'clock in the afternoon. In 1861, when Tarbolton church was separated from Schaw, the service was moved to half past eleven.

Dr Livingston's assistant, Rev John Ewing Thomson MA, was ordained and inducted as minister of the Free Church on 18 November 1886. He had been born on 2 January 1859 at Dumbarton and was educated at Dumbarton Old Free Church School, followed by the Burgh Academy. He served as a pupil teacher there from 1874-77. Thomson studied at the University of Glasgow from 1877-81, graduating as a Master of Arts. He then studied for the ministry at the Glasgow Free Church College and was licensed by the Free Church Presbytery of Dumbarton on 4 November 1885. He was married to Jane Maitland Campbell Dodds on 4 December 1900. During his time at Stair, Rev Thomson served on the

School Board from 1909-1919 and on Stair Parish Council from 1910 onwards. He was the chairman of the Parish Council from 1919. Despite proposing to retire in 1930 due to ill-health, he remained in post until he demitted his position on 31 March 1939, retiring to Cuilaven, Balmaha, Stirlingshire. The church celebrated his Jubilee as minister on 27 June 1935. He died very soon after, on 6 January 1940. He left £11,917 in his will. A memorial was erected within the church in his memory, later relocated to Drongan.

In the late nineteenth century, evening church services were held in an empty house at Drongan's Old White Row. When the Public Hall was opened in 1903, evening services were held there, ministered in turn by the ministers from Stair Parish Church and the Schaw Kirk.

On 19 December 1920 the war memorial at Coylton was unveiled, to which Rev and Mrs Thomson attended. On their return, the driver of their car swerved to avoid some dogs which had ran onto the road. Unfortunately, he hit some pedestrians who were walking back from the ceremony. Five or six of them were injured, and a Mrs Jane Peebles was killed. The car overturned, causing injuries to the minister and his wife. She was never to fully recover and died at a nursing home in Glasgow on 23 October 1923. In her memory a memorial tablet was unveiled in the church by Hugh MacQueen in Quilkieston on 25 March 1925. Presiding over the service was Rev John Warrick of Cumnock.

In 1849 proposals had been made to disjoin Tarbolton Church from the shared ministry with Stair, but this failed to materialise. Eventually, in July 1861, Tarbolton was disjoined and erected into a Church Extension Charge. Tarbolton was to call its first minister, Rev Robert Campbell Lindsay, on 13 March 1862.

A Sunday School was established in 1861 and soon trips were offered to the children, to the likes of Montgomerie Castle, near Tarbolton. A second Sunday School was held at Coalhall Pottery and also at Taiglum, where three teachers taught up to forty pupils. From 1906 Drongan Public Hall was used as a Sunday School for residents in that district.

The work of the Deacons Court included giving grants to the poor of the parish. Originally, these were in the form of cash, but from 1866 it was often made in coal. By 1908 cash was again the preferred means of assisting the poor.

In September 1882 suggestions that the church should add a porch with belfry were made, and these were pursued. In January 1884, a new belfry was added to the church and a bell weighing 322 pounds that had been purchased from a Free Church in West Kilbride was added to it. This bell measured two feet across and cost £11 to purchase and remove. The ringing of the bell was placed in the hands of Mr Graham.

In 1890 a beadle was appointed to the church on a salary of £2 per annum. The first beadle was John McGinn, who was to carry the Bible, light the lamps and general duties. In 1890 there were 117 members of the church, thought to be the lowest in its history. In September 1891 hot water pipe heating was introduced to the church, replacing the old paraffin stoves. The first wedding took place in the church in 1898 when Miss Cameron, housekeeper at the manse, was married to John Kerr in Drumdow.

Evangelistic meetings were held in Drongan from 1896 onwards, increasing attendance and affiliation to the church. By 1921 the minister was conducting open-air services at Drongan and Trabboch. A Men's Club was established in 1908.

In 1897 a new church hall was built alongside the church. This was a corrugated iron building, with timber lining. It was opened by a soiree on 11 June. Other improvements included an organ being installed in the church for the first time in October 1903, and an organist was employed.

By 1923 the older name of the Schaw Kirk became common once more and, in 1929, when the Free Church nationally was reunited with the Church of Scotland, the parish of Stair had two Churches of Scotland. The congregation of the Schaw Kirk had voted in favour of the union, despite having been against it in 1925. The former Free Church became known as the Schaw Kirk officially. It served the community that had been created at Trabboch, as well as many of the miners who lived in the rows at Taiglum and other places in the locality.

In 1930 the Sunday School at Drongan Public Hall was moved to the Infant School, the hall deteriorating and not fit for purpose. In 1931 a redrawing of church parishes added Rankinston to that of the Schaw Kirk.

Communion was dispensed by a common cup from the formation of the congregation, but in 1937 there were moves to replace it with individual cups. At the time no change was agreed, but in 1945 the session purchased individual cups. In February 1946 a branch of the Women's Guild was formed, with over 100 members joining within a few weeks. The minister established a Men's Guild in 1951. However, it stopped around 1964.

In 1955 the church was lit with electricity for the first time, but its future was already one of planned closure. The manse was lit with electric light from July 1954. In 1956 the boundary of the church parish was redrawn to include Sinclairston and district.

Rev Andrew MacBride MacKirdie was inducted as minister of the Schaw Kirk in July 1940. Born on 26 June 1877 at Renton in Dunbartonshire, he was educated at Renton Public School and the Vale of Leven Academy. He then attended the University of Glasgow and Glasgow Free Church College. He was appointed as Student Assistant at Ardlui Parish Church, Dunbartonshire, in 1906, remaining for a year. He then served at Glasgow Oatlands Parish Church from 1908-1910, then Glasgow Warrick Street Church from 1910-1912, followed by Broomielaw Parish Church from 1912-1913. He was licensed by the Presbytery of Dumbarton on 25 April 1913. His first charge was at Ellsridgehill (Elsrickle), Lanarkshire, where he was ordained and inducted on 3 August 1913. Rev MacKirdie served with the

Y.M.C.A. during the First World War. He was inducted as minister at Clydebank West Parish Church on 8 June 1920, remaining there for ten years. He then was translated to Glasgow Union Church on 28 October 1930. Rev MacKirdie demitted his charge on 11 January 1938. In 1940 he was inducted as minister at Drongan. He remained for four years, before accepting a call to Lugar Parish Church, parish of Auchinleck, on 10 May 1944. He remained eight years, before demitting the charge on 31 March 1952. He died soon after, on 8 March 1953. Prior to the arrival of a new minister, Rev J. Campbell Rae was appointed as Interim Moderator.

Rev Hugh Blackadder was ordained to the Schaw Kirk on 2 May 1945. He was born in Harthill, West Lothian, and initially worked in the coal-mines there. After study at New College, Edinburgh University, he was licensed by the Presbytery of Edinburgh on 5 April 1935. He was appointed as assistant minister at Edinburgh Barony Church, and also at Longniddry and in Orkney. He was ordained and inducted as minister to Bruan Thrumster Parish Church (Caithness) on 18 June 1935. He was translated to Savoch Parish Church (Aberdeenshire) on 8 June 1938. On 13 September 1948 he accepted a call to Hownam (Roxburghshire). He then moved to Alves in Moray. He retired in 1963 and returned to Whitburn, where he often preached in vacant pulpits. He was married to Janet Russell Taylor. He died on Tuesday 26 June 1973, aged 80, and was buried at Shottskirk Cemetery.

Rev George Lindsay Hunter was ordained and inducted to the Schaw Kirk on 29 June 1949. He was born at Prestonpans in East Lothian on 27 June 1917. From 1928 until 1935 he was a pupil at George Watson's College in Edinburgh, followed by study at the University of London, from where he graduated with a Bachelor of Arts degree. He studied at the New College in Edinburgh, and served for a time as a student assistant at Edinburgh St Christopher's Parish Church. He was licensed by the Presbytery of Haddington and Dunbar in April 1949. He served as a minister for around ten years, demitting office on 29 September 1960 to follow a career as a teacher of Religious Education. He retired on 27 June 1982. He was married to Elizabeth Downie Clarke of Glasgow on 3 April 1948, and had a daughter, Margaret (b. 5 November 1959), the first child ever to be born in the manse. He studied for a PhD and wrote a thesis entitled *The Life and work of Gaston Frommel*. This has been lodged with the University of Edinburgh.

With a growing community at Drongan, the opportunity to build a new place of worship was seized. William Cowie & Torry, architects, were commissioned to design a new building, the foundation stone of which was laid on 6 July 1955. The church was dedicated on 14 September 1956. The new church in Drongan allowed the congregation and minister to extend their reach into the community. Services were held every Sunday morning and an evening service once a month during the winter. The cost of the new church totalled £20,564 16s 4d, most of it paid from Church Extension funds, but the congregation had to contribute £4,112 19s 3d to this. To help offset this, the old bell, which was unsuitable for the new building, was sold for £15. The old church building itself was sold for £400 and the old hall for £32. In 1961 the old manse was sold for £2,650 and the funds put towards building a new manse in Watson Terrace, Drongan. This was completed on 5 March 1964, when the minister and his family moved in from their temporary council house into a new manse at 73 Watson Terrace.

The next minister at the Schaw Kirk was Rev Edward Mackay. He was born on 29 March 1907 in Glasgow. He received his education at Colston Public School in Glasgow from 1912-21. He then studied at Bennet College from 1938-41. He was married on 15 April 1943 to Agnes Littlejohn. From 1943-46 he served in the armed forces. In 1946 he enrolled at the University of Glasgow and graduated in 1950. He was licensed by the Presbytery of Glasgow in April 1950. His first church was at Westruther in Berwickshire, where he was ordained and inducted on 22 March 1951. On 29 February 1956, he was translated to Bargeddie Parish Church in Lanarkshire. He was translated to the Schaw Kirk on 28 June 1961. In 1965 the church roll was reckoned to be 738, thought to be the highest it ever reached. Rev Mackay remained at Drongan for just over five years. He was translated on 15 September 1966 to Selkirk Heatherlie Parish Church. He retired as minister there on 31 March 1977. He died on 26 May 1993.

Rev William Muir MacPherson was ordained and inducted to the Schaw Kirk on 23 February 1967. He served at Drongan for five years before accepting a call to Glasgow Gorbals Parish Church on 22 November 1973. William MacPherson was born on 12 August 1920 at Greenock. He was educated in the town from 1925-1936. During the war he served in the Royal Engineers. He was captured and held as a prisoner of war in the far east for a time. He was married on 18 September 1948 to Sheena MacKean Campbell. He studied at Edinburgh University from 1948-1950. From 1950-52 he studied for the ministry at the Scottish Congregational College. Following his ordination on 5 July 1952, he served as a minister in the Congregational Church from 1952 until 1965. He served as minister at Innerleithen Congregational Church (Peeblesshire) from 5 July 1952 until 1954. He then moved on to Lanark Evangelical Union Church, serving from 2 July 1954 until 1958. He accepted a call to Stewarton Congregational Church on 7 December 1958, and served there until 1965. He changed denominations around this time, and returned to university (Glasgow) from 1965-66. At this time, he served as an assistant minister at Glasgow St James Church in Pollok, until he was licensed by the Presbytery of Glasgow on 25 June 1966. His first charge as a minister of the Church of Scotland was at Renfrew Trinity Parish Church, where he served from 1966-67. After leaving Drongan on 22 November 1973, Rev MacPherson remained at the Gorbals church for just over five years before accepting a call to Auchencairn with Rerrick Parish (Kirkcudbrightshire) on 16 March 1979. He retired as minister on 31 December 1986. He died on 10 February 1991.

On 4 May 1974 Rev Gordon David Jamieson was ordained and inducted to the Schaw Kirk. He was born in Glasgow on 1 March 1949 and was educated at Cambuslang from 1954-61, followed by Hamilton Academy, until 1967. He studied at Edinburgh University from 1967-73, from where he graduated with a Master of Arts degree and Bachelor of Divinity. He served as an Assistant Minister at Edinburgh Tron Moredun Parish Church from 1973-74. He was licensed by the Presbytery of Edinburgh on 20 June 1973. Like Rev MacPherson, Jamieson remained for five years before accepting a call to Fife, where he became minister of Elie with Kilconquhar and Colinsburgh parish churches. He was translated on 25 July 1979. Rev Jamieson then moved on to Dundee Barnhill St Margaret's Church on 12 June 1986. He was married on 28 March 1969 to Annette Sutherland. They had a daughter, Elspeth, who was married to Murray MacKenzie, and a son, Andrew David, born on 19 February 1975.

In November 1976 there was a proposal that the church be renamed 'The Schaw Kirk Drongan'. This was agreed to at a meeting of the congregation on 30 January 1977. In 1977 the heating of the church was converted from coal to gas, and again in 1992 it was converted to mains gas.

On 30 April 1980 Rev James Sidney Allison Smith accepted a call to the Schaw Kirk. Smith was born at Kelty in Fife on 26 December 1925. He received his education at Coatbridge in Lanarkshire from 1931 until 1944. During the Second World War he served with the Royal Navy as a radar mechanic, continuing from 1944 until 1947. In 1947 he matriculated at Glasgow University, where he studied until 1949. From 1951 until 1956 he studied at the University of Edinburgh. During that time, he served as Student Assistant at Edinburgh North Leith Parish Church (1954-56). He was married to Jean Shields Hendrie Jamieson on 14 August 1954. He was ordained and inducted to Yoker St Matthew's Parish Church, Clydebank, on 21 November 1956. He was translated to be the minister of Stromness St Peter's and Victoria Street Church (Orkney) from 13 June 1963 until 28 September 1966 when he accepted a call to Alford with Tullynessle and Forbes in Aberdeenshire. Alford church was linked with Keig Parish Church on 1 February 1977, Rev Smith taking over that congregation also. Rev James Smith remained at Drongan until his retirement on 30 September 1991. During his final year he served as Moderator of Ayr Presbytery. He had three children. He died on 28 August 2016.

The Schaw Kirk was linked with Coylton Parish Church on 8 October 1991 and the two congregations shared a minister thereafter. The first shared minister was Rev Paul R. Russell, who was inducted on 9 January 1992. Paul Russell was born on 26 July 1955 in Glasgow, the son of Robert Andrew Russell and Frances Margaret Watson. He received his education at Heathfield Secondary School and then Ayr Academy from 1967-73. He then studied at the University of Glasgow from 1973-78, graduating with a Master of Arts degree. Further studies at the university from 1978-82 resulted in a Bachelor of Divinity degree. He was licensed to preach by the Presbytery of Ayr on 5 July 1983. As a student, he served as assistant minister at Montrose Old Parish Church (1982-83). He was ordained and inducted to Clydebank Radnor Park Parish Church on 17 February 1984. Rev Russell was married on 10 October 1986 to Shirley Anne Walker (b. 20 March 1961), daughter of James Walker and Evelyn Speirs. They had three children – Kirsten Iona Megan (b. 5 June 1991); Caitlin Ilona Mhairi (b. 8 October 1993) and Matthew Michael Stewart (b. 16 August 1995). Rev Russell left the churches at Drongan and Coylton to take up a position as hospital chaplain at Crosshouse Hospital on 2 April 2006. On 5 September 2019 he accepted a call to Castlehill Parish Church in Ayr.

In 1992 the manse in Drongan was sold, the minister moving to the manse in Coylton. In 1993 the church roll was 333. In that year a memorial plaque commemorating those who had served and died in the war was unveiled in the church. It had been promoted by Drongan Community Council.

On 22 April 2008 Rev David Whiteman BD was inducted to Drongan Schaw Kirk at a service held in Coylton Parish Church. Whiteman was born on 22 February 1960 at Blyth in Northumberland, the son of Henry Whiteman and Joy I'Anson. He received his education at Manor Park School in Newcastle-on-Tyne from 1971-77, followed by the University of Edinburgh, from 1992-96. Previously he worked as a buyer from 1978-92. He was licensed by the Presbytery of Falkirk in 1996. Rev Whiteman was married on 14 July 1990 to Susan Farmer (b. 5 June 1967), daughter of Douglas Farmer and Heather Farmer. They have two children – Rachel Susan (b.

5.13 Hardwicke Hall in 2020 *(Dane Love)*

28 May 1996) and Rebecca Joy (b. 19 December 1997). Rev Whiteman received his first calling to Maybole Old Parish Church, where he was ordained and inducted on 10 February 1998. On 28 January 2015 Rev Whiteman was translated from Drongan to Kilbirnie Auld Kirk in the northern part of the county. He demitted that position on 6 September 2017.

On 1 May 2015 Rev Douglas Moore was appointed as the auxiliary/ordained local minister for Drongan Parish Church.

After a long vacancy, the pulpits at Coylton and Drongan was filled by Rev Dr Alwyn Landman on 25 June 2019. Rev Landman was born in 1962 in the Free State province, South Africa. He was educated at Adamantia High School, Kimberley, followed by the University of the Free State (2000-2008), where he graduated as a Bachelor of Theology, and Master of Theology. He served as a policeman in South Africa, gaining the rank of Lieutenant Colonel. He retired from the police force in 1996 and set up in business, but soon turned to the ministry, selling the company in 2000. In 2005 he became the minister in a town called Theunissen, Free State. In August 2011 he moved to Durban where he was minister in the Dutch Reformed Church, before leaving South Africa in 2018. He studied at Fuller Theological Seminary in Pasadena, United States (2011-2015) where he completed his doctorate. In 2018-19 he served as minister at Mearnskirk, Renfrewshire. He is married to Hennelien and they have two children, Wynand and Werner.

BRETHREN

Across many mining communities in Ayrshire and beyond, assemblies of Christian Brethren, or Brethren were formed in the late nineteenth century. A gospel hall assembly of Brethren was formed in Drongan sometime before 1884, meeting in a 'tin kirk' or corrugated-iron building. Prominent in the group was David Good, some of whose family became significant members of the Brethren in Ayr in the 1920s. James Haswell (1880-1966), blacksmith in Drongan, and noted beekeeper, was a n significant member at Drongan, and he donated the ground on which a new hall was erected. This was named the Hardwicke Hall, after the Earl of Hardwicke, owner of Drongan estate. Due to a fall in numbers, the brethren appear to have disbanded around 2013.

Sometime between 1891 and 1904 an assembly of Brethren was established in Ochiltree. This group appears to have disbanded within a few years. Brethren from the assembly in Auchinleck regularly came to the village and were influential in reforming the assembly in 1915, aided by Adam Hannah and his family, who had moved to Ochiltree from Dreghorn. The Open Brethren met in the Hannah's house to start with, three doors up from the House with the Green Shutters. Adam Hannah was a prominent preacher, and would often head to the north-east of Scotland for weeks on end to preach to brethren and any other church congregation that would allow him. He moved to a smallholding at Springs, near Stair, around 1935, after which he attended the gospel hall in Tarbolton. The assembly in Ochiltree continued to meet until 1945.

ST CLARE'S R. C. CHURCH

Before the establishment of St Clare's Roman Catholic Church in Drongan, adherents of the Roman Catholic faith had to worship at either St John's in Cumnock or St Patrick's in Auchinleck. The former church had a short connection with Ochiltree, for in 1899 Rev Daniel Keogh lived in Burnock Street. He was born and educated in Ireland and ordained at Maynooth in 1893. He was lent to the Diocese of Galloway, serving firstly at Annan (1895-1898) after which he moved to

St John's in Cumnock, where he remained until 1903. He then returned to Ireland and died in Dublin on 22 September 1922.

With a growing population of Roman Catholics moving to the new community of Drongan it was decided to establish a place of worship. A plot in Watson Terrace, Drongan, was acquired by the Roman Catholic Diocese of Galloway and a timber chapel was erected there. However, plans were made for a new place of worship for the growing community, to be erected on the same site. In 1967 the new chapel was opened, named St Clare's, designed by Douglas Hay, Ayr. The church is a simple rectangular building, a rooflight allowing sunlight to light up the altar. The church is linked with St Paul's Church in Ayr, as well as St Francis Xavier's Church at Waterside.

The church of St Clare has been served by a number of priests over the years, mostly in conjunction with other churches. When it opened, the first priest was Father Frank McHugh, who had a house in Hannahston Avenue. Francis Patrick McHugh was born in Glasgow in 1931 and was educated for the priesthood at Blairs and St Joseph's College, Upholland. He was ordained at Kilmarnock in 1956 and served at St Margaret's Cathedral in Ayr as an assistant from 1956-61. He then spent time at the Catholic Workers' College in Oxford (1961-3), before returning to Scotland, to become assistant priest at St Joseph's in Kilmarnock, 1963-7. He then served at St Clare's. Father McHugh was noted for his singing, and he released a number of records throughout this life. He retired from the church in 2004, settling in Ireland, dying in Letterkenny, County Donegal, on 6 December 2019.

After Father McHugh, priests from surrounding parishes assisted at Drongan. These include Monsignor Francis Owen Duffy (b. 1914), Father Francis Aloysius

5.14 St. Clare's R.C. Church *(Dane Love)*

Kiernan, Father Thomas Leverage (1934-1996), Canon John Donnelly (b. 1921), Father Martin Dominic Poland (b. 1955), Father John Anthony McGee (b. 1947), Father Alexander McGarry (1934-), Father Neil O'Donnell, Father Alan John Wilson (1953-2012), Monsignor William Raymond McFadden (b. 1961), Father John Walsh, Father Michael Farrington (1944-2009), and Canon Gerald Donnelly. Father Gerald Donnelly served as priest to St Paul's (Ayr), St Francis Xavier's (Waterside) and St Clare's until 2016. He then moved to Dumfries, and was replaced by Father David Borland, who also served as Administrator of St Margaret's Cathedral in Ayr and as a chaplain to Ayr Hospital. Since around 2010, retired priest, Rt Rev Monsignor Joseph Boyd, has looked after the congregation.

MINISTERS

A number of Ochiltree sons became ministers elsewhere. Rev John Andrew (1826-1898) was a minister with the E. U. church congregations in Glasgow, Tillicoultry, Barrhead and Dundee. He later joined the Apostolic Church in Dundee and Belfast.

Rev Edward Miller (1863-1929) was born in Ochiltree and wrote a novel about the life of George Douglas Brown with the pseudonym 'John Innes'. This was entitled *Till a' the Seas Gang Dry*, and was published in London and New York in 1924. Miller was the son of a shoemaker, John Miller. He became a minister of the United Free Church but left to pursue a career in writing. He died in Madeira. On 6 April 1958 a plaque in his memory, that formerly adorned the walls of the Scots Church in Cannes, was relocated to the church in Ochiltree.

CHAPTER SIX

EDUCATION

When schools were first established, they were under the control of the church. At the Reformation in 1560, one of the principle aims of the Church of Scotland was the establishment of a school in every parish. This took a number of years to execute, and some parishes had to wait decades before they could find a suitable building and teacher. Having been established by the church, the presbytery was very influential in their operation, being involved in inspecting the schools and appointing schoolmasters. From the old presbytery minute books, we can find some early references to the parish school.

One of the first instances of a school being mentioned in Ochiltree dates from 17 May 1642, when it is noted that, 'The said Mr Johne [Blyth] declared that William Gillchryst was their Reader and schoolmaster. And that thair wes no exercise of prayers or reading on the weik dayes, becaus thair culd not ane auditorie be had in the clawchen, bot only on the Sabbath day befor preaching; and that his maintenance wes onlie Thrie score punds money peyed by the Laird of Capringtoun, patron.' William Gilchrist had a son, also William, who was listed in 1684 as a Covenanting fugitive.

On 5 February 1695 it was announced that the school was to be visited by John Hunter, John Laurie, Mr Roger and Mr Lindsay, along with the Laird of Logan, the ruling elder, on 5 March. A report was issued on 6 March that the visit had taken place, and that the schoolmaster was to attend the next meeting of the presbytery.

The schoolmaster in 1695 was William Stewart, and on 23 July he declared that 'he owns the confession of faith to be agreeable to the word of God, & that they are the principles of his faith; he is exhorted & required to attend ordinances & teach his schollars diligently in learning & instruct th[e]m in the principles of religion, & to convene & dismiss th[e]m w[i]t[h] prayer, evening & morning, all q[uhi]ch he says he endeavours to doe & engadges to doe it furder. The presbyterie are to enquir further anent him at their next meeting at Ochiltree.' William Stewart's religious principles appear to have been of some concern, for he had been cited to attend a number of presbytery meetings before this time, on 10 April being excused for 'being valetudinary'.

By August 1695 William Stewart was met by Matthew Baird and Mr Gilchrist Jr., who had been sent to find out Stewart's sentiments regarding the Presbyterian government. According to the minute book, they conferred with him, 'to know q[uha]t are his sentiments of Presbyterian Goverment who report it will be fitt th[a]t he give it judicially who being called thus declares it. That presbyterian goverment is lawfull & agreeable to the generall rules of the word of God for decency & order in a christian form; he is exhorted to diligence in teaching his school.'

This rumbled on, for on 26 September 1695 it is noted that 'Mr Wm Stewart, Schoolm[aste]r at Ochiltree his opinion concerning church goverment by presbyterie is to be advised with some judicious members at the ensueing Synod.'

Within a couple of years Ochiltree had a new schoolmaster. He was Thomas Fleming, who had previously worked as schoolmaster at Biggar in Lanarkshire. He was invited to the position in Ochiltree by the heritors and others in the parish. His testimonials from Biggar were approved and John Laurie and James Gilchrist were given the task of determining his fitness for the job. Accordingly, they reported that 'he is fitt to teach humanity, & may improve if he be diligent; He is enjoyned to shew a good example to the children, & instruct them in the principles of Christian religion, & pray at th[ei]r conveening & dismissing; & that he sign the confession of faith q[uhe]n required; all q[uhi]ch he undertakes to doe, the Presbyterie allow him to teach in the fors[ai]d place.'

Thomas Fleming appears to have acted inappropriately as schoolmaster, or at least according to Rev Matthew Couper, the minister. In August 1699 we find that Sir John Cochrane, the laird of the parish, 'gave an accompt that Mr Cowper had receaved letters one or moe from some private hand q[uhi]ch accuses Mr Tho. Ffleeming ... of some grosse villanies the subscriptions of q[uhi]ch ... & some materiall purposes th[e]r[e]in were dilated; q[uhi]ch letters he desyres the preb[ytrie] to order Mr Cowper to give up & ane accompt of the mater obliterate with the persons names of these aledged villanies. The preb[yteri] appoint M[ess]rs Hugh Campbell, Jon Laurie, Wm Maitland, Mo Lindsay & Jon Hunter to meet ... & to doe th-[e]r[e]in as they see cause .... Also, they are appointed to visit the school, & the schoolm[aste]r is not to gett testimonialls till th[i]s busines be at an end.'

It was noted on 20 September 1699 that the presbytery could not do anything about the situation in Ochiltree school due to the absence of the laird, Sir John Cochrane. The education board paid a visit to the school, 'q[uhe]rin they found very few schollers.' Sir John Cochrane was later able to supply testimonials on Mr Fleming's behalf, and it was agreed that the presbytery should call both Fleming and Cowper and inform them that they had to 'lay aside all grudge', and that Mr Fleming should be respectful to the minister. This was to be publicly announced in the kirk, stating that 'Mr fleeming is free of all publick scandall during his abode in these parts & that it doth not appear to us that there is any truth in these reports.'

Mr Fleming signed the confession of faith on 13 February 1700. The dispute between him and Rev Cowper does not seem to have been settled, for on 13 March 1700 Fleming passed a petition to the presbytery in which he complained that Mr Cowper 'had lately published a letter to his defamation; & desyres the presbyterie would interpose their interest to bring matters … to a further ishue.' An investigation ensued, with further contact made with the presbytery of Chirnside, Berwickshire. Accusations were made that Rev Couper had forged the letters which defamed Fleming. However, word came back from Chirnside to state that Fleming had 'made ane attempt on another man's wife, & that he had enticed young Ninewells to steal his father's books to him, & th[e]n threatened and made him swear he should never reveal it, q[uhi]ch the boy confessed to his great grief & sorrow on his death bed.'

Fleming made defamatory claims against the minister, too. He stated that the minister was 'wallowing in the mire of fame polluting calumnies', 'guilty of the reigning gangrene of evil speaking' and 'publishing notoriously grosse and groundleess lies'. Eventually, the Presbytery of Ayr decided that Fleming was a 'gross slanderer' of Rev Cowper and appointed him to appear before the congregation in the kirk on two Lord's days at the ordinary place of public repentance during the time of the forenoon sermon. Eventually, by the first years of the 1700s, the church as able to dismiss Fleming as schoolmaster.

On 16 August 1704 Ayr Presbytery sent a letter to Sir John Cochrane regarding the planting of Ochiltree and the application of vacant teind for pious uses. It was agreed to mortify eight merks Scots of the vacant stipend to be paid yearly for the maintenance of four English schools in the several corners of Ochiltree parish, 'q[uhi]ch with some addition he had made to the sallary for a schoolmaster that teaches the grammar, doth exhaust the whole th[e]r[e]of'.

By 1709 the schoolmaster was a William Mitchell. However, his tenure as headmaster doesn't appear to have been particularly successful, for on 2 September 1713 it is noted that 'M[ess]rs Andrew Rogers & Henry Osburn were appointed to speak to the Lairds of Ochiltree elder and younger (being both in town at the time), anent the present circumstances of the grammar school of Ochiltree, which used to be very flourishing, & now there is not one scholar there & its imputed to the person who was installed, his being imployed about other business of their concern & report.'

The headship of the school appears to be vacant once more in 1720 and an inquiry was carried out as to why there was not a grammar school in the village despite there being a salary available. William Mitchell apparently continued as the basic schoolmaster for a few years more, despite causing some issues in the parish. He appears to have been regarded as unfit to be the schoolmaster, and in 1728 was accused of offensive conversation. However, the session had little choice but to keep him on as teacher in the school. On 3 September 1728 the session made reference to Mitchell's neglect of his office and lack of work for ten years, despite lifting the salary. They wrote to John Cochrane of Ochiltree to request that he be dismissed. However, Mitchell appears to have requested that he be given a second chance, 'desyring he might be allowed to make new tryall of keeping school there'.

Mitchell must have given up or been fired, for by 1733 reference is found of the death of Mr Beattie, schoolmaster, and of the vacancy at Ochiltree school. The next schoolmaster of which there is reference is James Todd, referred to in 1742 as having 'taught the school of Ochiltree for a considerable time'.

Ochiltree Parish School was originally located in Mill Street, on the south side. Built by the heritors, it served the village for many years. The schoolmaster here was a Mr Manson, a strict disciplinarian. He was later to become the schoolmaster at Kilbarchan in Renfrewshire.

William Simson was one of the schoolmasters in Ochiltree. He was born in 1758 at Tenpoundland, which was a smallholding attached to Creoch farm. The family had been tenants of Tenpoundland for many generations. William was the eldest son of John Simson. Two of his brothers were also to become teachers – Patrick Simson taught at Straiton and then came to Ochiltree to succeed his elder brother in the parish school; and Andrew Simson (1770-1832) became a teacher at Strathaven in Lanarkshire. At the age of fourteen Simson moved with his family to New Cumnock, where he continued his education in classics under a Mr Ferguson. Simson was lame in one foot, which prevented him from taking on more strenuous tasks, and as such decided to train for the ministry. Simson was educated at the University of Glasgow, but did not enter the ministry, for when the vacancy for a schoolmaster at Ochiltree occurred he applied for the job. He was appointed to the position in 1780, and served for eight years. He had also been appointed as Session Clerk of Ochiltree church on 26 July 1779.

William Simson became a friend of Robert Burns, and the poet refers to him as 'Winsome Willie'. The earliest known connection between the two appears to date from 1783. In that year the poet had published anonymously a poem at Kilmarnock, entitled 'The Twa Herds'. Patrick Simson, his brother, bought a copy, and he was the first to return to Ochiltree with a copy of the bard's works, showing it to William, who recognised Burns' style. It is thought that William Simson and Burns knew each other before this, however, and on reading 'The Twa Herds' Simson was induced to write an epistle to Burns. This poem does not appear to have survived. Burns' reply of May 1785, however, does, and in his 'Epistle to William Simson', he wrote:

> I gat your letter, Winsome Willie;
> Wi' grateful heart I thank you brawlie;
> Tho' I may say't, I wad be silly,
>   And unco vain,

> Should I believe, my coaxin billie,
>   Your flatterin' strain.
>
> ----
>
> Ev'n winter bleak has charms to me
> When winds rave thro' the naked tree;
> Or frosts on hills of Ochiltree,
>   Are hoary grey;
> Or blinding drifts wild-furious flee;
>   Dark'ning the day!

The poem runs to eighteen verses, with an additional thirteen in a 'Postscript'.

Simson was keen on poetry, and wrote a number of other verses. Few of these survive, but one, 'The Harvest Kirk' (written in 1783) was discovered and published in a collection of Ayrshire tales and verses entitled *The Ayrshire Wreath* in 1844:

> When shearing's dune, that weary dark,
>   And corn's in ilka threave;
> Before the shearers, young and stark,
>   Get baith their fee and leave.
> The farmer, a gae jolly spark,
>   In cash and credit steeve –
> Gies them a kirn to end the wark,
>   Whilk maks their hearts to heave
>   Wi' joy that day.

Another poem was written as an acrostic:

> Read, spectator, ere you go,
> O'er my life as penned below,
> Born in Kyle, a ploughman long,
> Eminent in Scottish Song:
> Rhyming got me the Excise,
> There in death I closed my eyes.
>
> Born a Bard, the Muse obeyed me,
> Unimplored, as nature swayed me,
> Round on Fancy's fairy wings,
> Nature's pure poetic springs;
> Satire lent me all her strings.

It is said that Burns urged Simson to publish his poems at the same time as him, but that Simson refused, not wishing for them to appear in print. He said, 'I write for amusement, and will never consent to publish for profit.'

In 1788 Simson moved to become the schoolmaster at Cumnock, where he remained until his death. He left a manuscript collection of poems with his brother, Patrick, who succeeded him as schoolmaster in Ochiltree.

Simson died at Cumnock on 4 July 1815, aged 57. His wife, Sarah Howatson, survived until 10 June 1834. He was buried in the Old Cemetery on Barrhill Road in Cumnock. A headstone was later erected over his grave, bearing an epitaph:

> Here 'Winsome Willie' lies, who's worth
> In Burns woke equal love,
> But death, which wrenched the ties on earth,
> Hath knit them now above.

The epitaph was composed by a local poet, Adam Brown Todd (1822-1915). A second stone was erected in Simson's memory in the kirkyard at Ochiltree. This bears the inscription:

> William Simson, sometime schoolmaster of Ochiltree, afterwards of Cumnock, the 'Winsome Willie' of Burns. Himself a poet, a wit, a scholar, and a gentleman. Born 1758, died 1815. Semper honos monenque tuum laudesque manebunt.

Simson's school is known to have been located at the foot of Mill Street, almost the last building on the right before Ochiltree House stables. In the grounds there was at one time a stone inscribed to mark the site of the school, erected by James Tennant, who latterly owned the cottage. The inscription read: 'Winsome Willie's School stood in the centre of this garden, and this stone was part of the building'. The stone was latterly built into the rear walls of the cottage that stood here.

The next schoolmaster, Patrick Simson, was born in 1765 and appears to have been an intelligent child. He started working as a teacher to a private family at the age of twelve years. In 1783 he obtained the charge of the public school at Straiton. In 1788 he took over Ochiltree Public School, serving as its headmaster for the following 64 years. The salary in 1792 was only £8 per annum. At the time there was also one other private school in the area.

To celebrate the golden jubilee of his time as a teacher, in 1833, a special dinner was held in the village, attended by many of his former colleagues and pupils. Patrick Simson was much admired, James Paterson, the Ayrshire historian, commenting that, 'Seldom have I been more gratified than in the enjoyment of his company.' Simson had a good memory and was able to recount tales of incidents that happened in his youth. He was a good singer, as well as being a competent reciter of poetry, including that composed by his elder brother. He was an excellent Latin scholar, and his knowledge of the English language was good. When Sir Alexander Boswell was away from the district, it was Simson who did the proof reading of the first draughts used in the Auchinleck press.

Patrick Simson also transcribed the old registers of Ochiltree, the originals being handwritten in the old style. The register of births and marriages book dated from as early as 1641, but had become disused for many years. Rev William Thomson asked Simson to transcribe the records, and he attested these as being the same as the original records on 3 November 1803.

6.1 William Simson's Monument in the old kirkyard *(Dane Love)*

In 1833 Patrick Simson was honoured with a jubilee dinner and presentation to mark fifty years as teacher at the school. Many former pupils attended, including some who had achieved high levels in their careers.

An unconfirmed story claims that Sir Walter Scott, when in the district, wished to meet Patrick Simson. He apparently arrived at the Head Inn and asked of the landlord if someone could direct him to Mr Simson's home. The landlord, recognising Scott, decided to do it himself, and accompanied the 'Wizard of the North' to the schoolhouse. Soon after, when Scott published *The Antiquary*, one of the main characters was 'Edie Ochiltree', which is claimed to be derived from Andrew Edgar, the Head Inn landlord, and the village name.

In 1795 Lady Glencairn sent funds to the minister to allow the purchase of various books which were to be distributed amongst the scholars at the school. These were in memory of her two granddaughters who had drowned in the River Eden.

In 1837 the school had an average attendance of 100 pupils, who were taught English reading, grammar, writing, arithmetic, Latin, Greek and geography. Simson received the maximum salary, and he also received the produce of a mortification, or legal bequest, on the lands of Shield, which was left by Patrick Davidson. This later brought an income of £6 3s 4d yearly. Pupils paid the teacher two shillings per quarter for English and grammar. Writing cost a further sixpence, and arithmetic and writing three shillings. Those who wished to study Latin and Greek had to pay five shillings per quarter, and Geography was free. The total income for the teacher was £30 per annum. He also earned £6 for being the Session Clerk.

Patrick Simson died in 1851, at the age of 85. He was interred in Ochiltree kirkyard. He was married to Helen Howatson (1765-1833). She died at Strathaven. Patrick Simson was commemorated on the same memorial in old kirkyard, where the inscription reads:

> PATRICK SIMSON
> FOR SIXTY FOUR YEARS
> SCHOOLMASTER
> OF OCHILTREE
> AN EXCELLENT LINGUIST
> A KIND FRIEND
> AND
> AN HONEST MAN
> BORN 1765 – DIED 1851

6.2 Ochiltree School architect drawing *(Author's Collection)*

The old school was replaced in 1852 and the former parish school was converted into a house for the schoolmaster. The cost of building works was £297 3s 5d, the architect being Robert Pettigrew of Tarshaw, the mason work being erected by A. & A. Murdoch of Ochiltree; James Johnston, joiner.

For the support of poor children, in the early nineteenth century the Marquis of Bute presented the schoolmaster with funds which allowed ten children to be educated.

The next headmaster was Quintin Stewart, who was well-respected for his knowledge of the Classics. Born on 6 January 1806, Stewart was appointed as a teacher at Ochiltree in 1845. He was married to Margaret MacCrindle (16 October 1817-7 February 1886) and had four sons and four daughters. John, the eldest son, emigrated to America; Andrew became a schoolmaster and was headmaster at Tarbolton followed by Kirkintilloch; David Caldwell (25 September 1860-11 February 1950) became minister of Currie Parish Church, near Edinburgh; and Kennedy became a chemist and druggist in Edinburgh. On 27 June 1868 he was presented with a watch, fishing rod and £40 by a group of former pupils. In 1872 the Education (Scotland) Act brought about the formation of school boards in every parish, responsible for educating children between the ages of five and thirteen. Quintin Stewart resigned as schoolmaster in that year, not wishing to accept the outcomes of the act. He died on 17 February 1888.

6.3 Quintin Stewart's gravestone, old kirkyard *(Dane Love)*

David Caldwell Stewart was originally going to be a teacher, like his father, but changed his mind and studied for the ministry at the University of Edinburgh. Perhaps trying to teach a 'group of unruly boys' in Mathieson Street School in the Gorbals was influential in his decision. He served as an Assistant Minister at St Cuthbert's Parish Church, Edinburgh, followed by Lady Glenorchy's and Roseneath churches. In 1899 he was appointed as minister at Currie in Midlothian, where he remained for just over fifty years. He was presented with £1,000 from his parish when he reached his half century. In 1899 he had married Annie Morton (d. 1902), a native of Ochiltree, by whom he had two children, Quintin and Annie. In February 1943, the BBC made a documentary on Rev Stewart's life, entitled, 'Professional Portrait: a Scottish Country Minister'. At Currie Church, the session house was named in his honour, and five streets in Currie were named after him.

The first teacher employed at Ochiltree under the new Education Act of 1872 was James Aird, a native of Sorn. His parents were Robert Aird, contractor, and Margaret Thomson. He was born on 20 March 1850 and attended Sorn school. He studied to become a teacher and taught for a while in Glasgow before taking up the post in Ochiltree. He then went to the University of Glasgow, graduating as a Master of Arts in 1882. He won the Ettles Bursary in the same year. He then studied at Edinburgh, becoming a Bachelor of Divinity in 1885. He was licensed by the Presbytery of Edinburgh on 10 June 1885. At first, he served as assistant minister at St Mary's Church, Edinburgh. He was ordained on 7 June 1888 at Peterculter Parish Church, Aberdeenshire. On 24 February 1899 he was presented with a gold watch and chain by his congregation to mark ten years of his ministry. He died on 18 May 1905 and was buried at Peterculter. He was married on 8 April 1874 to Margaret Clark. They had Robert Aird, born 16 October 1876 and who became a doctor; Marion Lindsay, born at the schoolhouse in Ochiltree on 1 August 1879, married John Robertson, Ashby-de-la-Zouche, and died on 11 August 1917.

Archibald Andrew BA was appointed headmaster in 1880, at which time there were 153 pupils on the roll. He was a native of Tarbolton, where he had been a pupil teacher, followed by training at the Normal Training College. He worked at St Rollox School, Glasgow, and was headmaster at Kirkmichael Public school for six years before coming to Ochiltree. He was awarded his BA from the University of London in 1891. He was appointed as a Justice of the Peace in 1914. His brother Thomas was a solicitor and another, John Andrew, served as Provost of Cumnock from 1899-1902. Andrew was the chairman of Ochiltree Parish Council for a time. He taught until July 1915, when he retired, moving to live at Maybole Road, Ayr. In that year there were 200 pupils at the school. He died in 1932 at the age of 81.

The roll at the public school in February 1903 was 148. In 1908 the average attendance was 158. In 1909 the roll was 199, the average attendance being 180. With a growing roll, the school board needed to make plans for additional classrooms.

In 1908-9 a new extension to the school building in Main Street was erected by the Ochiltree Parish School Board to the plans of Alexander C. Thomson (1873-1925) of Ayr. The extension was expected to cost £1,650 and was in fact larger than the original school to which it was attached. The building was designed with two halves, the boys' entrance to the left, or lower end, the girls to the right. In the middle was a large hall, and there were two classrooms to either side of it. Built of red Ballochmyle sandstone, the roof was slated. At one corner was a small open belfry, containing a bell. Tenders accepted were digger, mason and brickwork – Messrs Morton & Kerr, Ochiltree, £982 1s 8d; carpenter and joiner – John Dalziel, Auchinleck, £530 5s 0d; slater, plumber and gas-fitter – James C. Highet, Alloway Street, Ayr, £255 2s 2d; plasterer, cement and tile work, William Miller, Kyle Street, Ayr, £238 17s 3d. In May 1909 the parish council agreed to hand over the old village clock to the School Board for inclusion on the new school extension. The extended school was reopened on Monday 23 August 1909 by Mrs David W. Shaw, wife of the chairman of the School Board. The architect presented Mrs Shaw with a gold key with which to open the lock on the door. The final cost of the extension was £3,055 5s 11d. When it opened, 190 pupils enrolled.

Accounts for Ochiltree School Board for the year ending 15 May 1912 showed that it received grants from the Scotch Education Department of £769. The board also received £1200 from the rates in the parish.

On Archibald Andrew's retiral, the headmaster's post was filled by Alexander Jamieson Ross MA BSc, who served from 26 June 1915 until 30 October 1916, when he moved to Eastriggs in Dumfriesshire, becoming headmaster at His Majesty's School under the Ministry of Munitions. Ross moved to Ochiltree from Killin Public school in Perthshire. He had previously been pupil teacher for four years at Moray House Practising School, Edinburgh. He graduated from Edinburgh University in 1903 with MA and BSc. He then taught at James Gillespie's Higher

6.4 Ochiltree Public School *(Author's Collection)*

Grade School, Edinburgh, and then served for two years in India before returning to Scotland, serving at Killin for six years.

Ross was replaced by John Thomson Davidson MA. He was a native of Perth and was educated at Edinburgh University, gaining a Master of Arts degree. He worked at Dunoon Grammar School, followed by Strone Public School, both Argyll. He was appointed to Ochiltree in 1916, and remained until his death on 6 April 1929, at the comparatively young age of 46 years. Davidson suffered illness, and in September 1928 James S. Henderson of Cumnock was appointed as temporary headmaster due to Davidson's extended leave of absence. Davidson was a keen golfer and served as an elder and treasurer at the parish church. During Davidson's period as headmaster, Miss Ellen Stewart retired in 1920 after forty years of teaching at the school.

In 1921 an additional hut was added to the school. This contained a new cookery room, classroom and a lavatory. Again, in 1925, a new annexe was added, at a cost of £2,500. This contained a workshop, laboratory, domestic science room and a classroom. In addition, new latrines and shelter sheds were added.

In 1929 James S. Henderson was appointed as headmaster. Henderson had previously taught at Kilmarnock and Cumnock Academy. He was the son of James Henderson, of Cloverlea, The Holm, Cumnock, and was educated at Cumnock Public School, Kilmarnock Academy and Glasgow Provincial Training College. On qualifying as a teacher he worked at Bentinck Public School in Kilmarnock, followed by Cumnock Public School. He retired in 1950 and on Monday 14 August a presentation was made in the Bowlers' Hall. Among some of the highlights of the pupils' time at Ochiltree was the occasion on 20 March 1929 when they were given a half-hour holiday to allow them to watch the Eglinton Hunt leaving from Ochiltree Cross.

In 1946 the senior school was closed, the pupils transferring to the High School in Cumnock. By 1950 Ochiltree Junior Secondary School had 194 pupils on the roll.

Once more the old school became too small and inconvenient for the number of pupils enrolled at it. A replacement school was proposed, designed by Ayr County Council Architects' Department. An initial proposal to erect the school at Broom Crescent failed due to the landowner not willing to sell. Instead, a site at 55-61 Main Street was acquired. Work began in 1974 and the new Ochiltree Primary School was opened to its first pupils in July 1976. This has five main classrooms arranged around a central multi-purpose hall and gymnasium. Additional facilities include a teachers' resource area, activity area and kitchen, plus offices. The old school was retained by the council, who used it as a store. The old school building was converted into residential dwellings in 2007-8, with additional housing erected in the former playground to the rear.

John Reid was appointed as headmaster in 1951. He was born on 9 October

6.5 Ochiltree Primary School *(Dane Love)*

1913 and educated at Dalry Higher Grade School then graduated from Glasgow University with a Master of Arts degree in 1934. Following teacher training at Jordanhill College, he taught at Cumnock Academy, broken by a period of war service as a flight-lieutenant with the Royal Air Force. He married Isabel Gray (d. 2003) in 1940, by whom he had a daughter, Helen, and a son, John, who also became a headteacher. John's teaching career began at St Rollox School in Glasgow. He then worked at Cumnock Academy then Auchinleck Academy, becoming headmaster at Ochiltree in 1951. He moved from Ochiltree to be headmaster at Eglinton-Winton Junior Secondary School in Ardrossan in 1960, a school that became Stanley Junior Secondary School, until he retired in 1978. John Reid was a keen angler and was the first President of the Scottish Anglers National Association, a member of the Ayrshire and Clyde River Purification boards, secretary/treasurer of Ayrshire Anglers Association for 36 years and contributed droll articles on a regular basis to the Glasgow Herald in the 1960s and 1970s. He was the co-author, with Dr James Andrew Begg, of The Dipper an the Three Wee Deils, a collection of poems in Ayrshire Scots, published in 1991. John Reid was awarded the MBE in 1975 for his contribution to angling in Scotland. He retired to Lockerbie where he died on 5 June 2010.

Alan Davidson was appointed as the next head teacher. He retired in 1977.

Dorothy K. Houston was appointed as the next headteacher. She moved to take up the post of head teacher at Coylton Primary School in 1982, where she remained until 1990. She was awarded the MBE and DCE.

Terri Porter was headteacher from 1982 until 1986.

In 1986 W. Allan McWilliam was appointed as head teacher of the school. He was born in 1953 in Craigie, Ayr, and was educated at Prestwick Public School, Prestwick High School, and Ayr Academy. He then attended Dundee University from 1970. He worked at BMK in Kilmarnock before matriculating at Hamilton College of Education. After graduating in 1975 he took up a teaching post at Dalmilling Primary School, Ayr. He was appointed headmaster at Littlemill Primary School in 1981. He moved to Ochiltree where he remained until July 1992, moving to take up the post as headmaster at Dundonald Primary School, where he continued until 2004. He is married to Lynn McWilliam, also a teacher. In 1991 the school had to close for six months to allow structural repairs to be carried out. During this time, pupils were bused to Drongan Primary School.

The next head teacher was Janet Ure, appointed in 1992. She retired in 2003. Her brother, Ian Ure (b. 1939), was a professional footballer, playing for Dundee, Arsenal, Manchester United and Scotland.

In 2003 Fiona J. M. Black was appointed head teacher. In 2011 the school roll was 112, rising to 122 in session 2014-15, with a quota of 6.8 teaching staff. By 2019 the roll had fallen to 105.

GIRLS' SCHOOL

In 1789 a Girls' School was established in Ochiltree, funded by Elizabeth, Dowager Countess of Glencairn (1725-1801). The school was located at the bottom end of Mill Street, in a single-storey thatched building opposite the stables of Ochiltree House, rented from John Samson. One of the teachers was Agnes Smith. Here girls were taught the skills of spinning, knitting, and weaving. As the Countess lived in Edinburgh, the management of the school was entrusted to the local minister, Rev David Grant. In one of her letters to the minister, she wrote:

> I am now told that there is a wheel made that can admit twelve children working from five years old and upwards. This with proper attention shown to the other branches such as knitting and sewing by a woman of pious principles, of good life and conversation, I think may be useful to your town, assisted by the schoolmaster in reading and writing.

OCHILTREE FREE CHURCH SCHOOL

When the Free Church was established in 1843 one of the first things the new denomination undertook was to mirror the parish schools in each parish. At Ochiltree the church acquired the upper floors of a building on Weir's Brae, Main Street. The school was run on what was at the time termed modern lines, that is following the training system devised by David Stow, which had object lessons, breaks for songs or other diversion, and physical activity. The first teacher in the Free Church School was Mr John Stark. He was later to train for the ministry and became the minister of the United Presbyterian Church at Gordon Street, Glasgow. He moved to Duntocher, near Clydebank, in Dunbartonshire, where he was ordained on 17 March 1860. He was noted for his part in national debates on education.

Mr Stark was succeeded by William Young around 1851, described as being a very painstaking teacher, thorough in the education of his charges. It has been noted that many of Young's former pupils went on to train as teachers themselves. One of these, John Boyd, was eventually promoted to become H. M. Inspector of Schools, firstly for the counties of Renfrew and Argyll. He was then promoted to Senior Inspector, covering the northern district of Scotland. William Young was presented with a watch by former pupils, to mark ten years as teacher. It was inscribed, 'To Mr William Young, teacher, Ochiltree, as a token of affection and esteem, from a few of his old pupils, Dec. 30th 1861.' Other teachers at the school included Miss Syme (in the 1860s), Mr Colville (also in the 1860s) and Mr MacKechnie. The school was closed when the Education Act took schools into school board control.

SINCLAIRSTON PUBLIC SCHOOL

There was a private school at Sinclairston as early as 1809, when the heritors agreed to establish a school there, 'where a commodious schoolhouse is intended to be built as soon as possible'. The schoolmaster did not receive a salary, but the forty

6.6 Sinclairston Public School *(Author's Collection)*

pupils who attended paid a fee for their education. In 1840 the Ayrshire Educational Association made a grant of £5 to the school. The *Ayr Advertiser* of 22 April 1842 noted that, 'the proficiency and activity displayed by the pupils in their various lessons, bore testimony to the diligence of Mr Wood, their teacher, and called forth the approbation of all present'. Mr Wood followed 'the intellectual system of teaching, and the utmost attention is paid to their religious as welll as moral training'. This school was located in a small building on the south-east side of the street. It had stone walls and a thatched roof. Up until 1845 the schoolmaster was Alexander Greig (1819-1871). He was the son of the parochial teacher at Aberdour in Fife. On leaving Sinclairston to return to Fife, he became teacher at Anstruther, and served there as a town councillor, inspector of poor, registrar of the burgh and session clerk of the parish.

In 1855, the Ordnance Survey map-makers visited Sinclairston and noted 'at this place there is a school in which the following branches are taught: writing, arithmetic, composition, grammar and geography. Average attendance: fifty. Partly endowed.'

This 'adventure' school was to be replaced with a new building on the opposite side of the street, where the later school was to be built. The new school was little more than a large timber hut, containing two rooms. Around 1870 the teacher was Mr Campbell. In that year a series of 'Readings' or social evenings with talks, music and singing, was held in the schoolroom, often to crowded audiences. In 1874 a talk was given by Professor Allan.

When the Education (Scotland) Act was passed in 1872, the hut at Sinclairston was retained by the newly-formed School Board to serve the residents at the west end of the parish. The building remained unchanged, however, for some time. In 1875 a new school building was erected, the work by John Murdoch of Ochiltree.

Eventually a new sandstone-built Sinclairston Public School was erected by the School Board. Initially, the school comprised of a single block, in which were two classrooms. These were divided by a partition which could be opened to create a larger function hall. This soon proved to be too small, and a second pair of classrooms were added on to the rear, with a hall between. The roll in 1903 was 187, but it was noted that many of the pupils from the Drongan area were more inclined to attend other local schools, outwith the parish. At the time 25 attended Coylton Public School, 10 attended Stair Public School and 8 attended Littlemill Public School.

With the raising of the school leaving age and an increasing population hereabouts, in 1909-10 the final additions were made to the building, designed by A. C. Thomson. These cost around £3,000, with the bonus of a heating system and lighting from acetylene gas. The extended school allowed for the teaching of 'special subjects' such as woodwork for the boys and domestic science and laundry for the girls. In 1909 the roll was 142 with an average attendance of 129. The extended school was officially opened in August 1910 by James Pettigrew Wilson of Polquhairn.

6.7 Sinclairston School football team, 1922 *(Jo Stewart)*

The first schoolmaster at Sinclairston after the Education Act of 1872 was a Mr Moore, who remained only for a short time. He was replaced by William Smith (served in the 1880s), who sufered from poor health. The next schoolmaster was Alexander Green (who served from the 1890s until the 1920s). He was appointed as a Justice of the Peace in 1920. In 1915 a fourth teacher was appointed due to the increasing roll. Headmasters in the twentieth century included John W. C. Drever (from the 1940s-1948) (1892-20 December 1948) and James Gold (1949-1950s).

In 1912, during a miners' strike, the children at the school appeared destitute to Mr Green, and he appealed to the school board to allow them to be given a midday meal. This comprised of soup and bread. Again, during the First World War, the children were to be fed at the school.

In 1950 Sinclairston school had 195 pupils on the roll, of which those up to the age of nine were educated in the wooden hut in Drongan. In 1956 the roll was such that the building could not accommodate all the pupils, so temporary huts were erected in the playground.

Sinclairston Public School closed in 1959 when Drongan School was opened. However, the school building remained in use, for it was renamed St Clare's Roman Catholic School, and replaced the R. C. school which was located in Drongan and which was too small to cope with the number of pupils.

DRONGAN SCHOOL

The children from Drongan originally had to attend the school at Sinclairston, resulting in them requiring to walk there and back each day, a distance of five miles round trip. As Drongan grew, the locals sent petitions to the school board, requesting that it established a school at Taiglum for the benefit of the children there. The first petition was received by Ochiltree School Board on 6 August 1904, but it was decided not to act upon it. A second petition was received and debated on 10 June 1908. The Drongan residents even suggested that if a school for all children could not be built, then at least a small temporary building should be erected to allow the infants to attend. In 1911 it was agreed that the children aged from five to seven years should be provided with transport to get them to Sinclairston and back. William Drain of Kayshill was paid thirty shillings per week to provide it. During the First World War there was little money for anything in the parish and demands for a school at Taiglum waned. Petitions to the school board were sent again in 1918, but the board was still in financial difficulty, so no action was again taken.

Eventually, in 1922 Ochiltree School Board agreed to the construction of a school in Taiglum. This was erected by William Paton & Sons, Ayr, with other work by Hart & Cumming, Ayr; Alexander Dalrymple, Ayr; J. Brown & Sons, Muirkirk; and D. Mackintosh, Ayr. The cost of the new school was £3,580. Designed to accommodate around 50 pupils, the building was originally a hostel that had been relocated from the munitions work at Gretna.

At Easter 1923 the new Drongan Public School was opened. This was a rather grandiose name for a wooden hut that was painted green, hence its local nick-name – 'The Wee Green Hut'. Built at the corner of the Toll Road and the Main Road, the school had three classrooms within it. The school only provided education for the younger children, the older ones still having to attend at Sinclairston, but by this time transport there and back had improved.

Originally, headmasters were linked with Sinclairston School and included John W. C. Drever (1892-1948). From 1949 Drongan and Sinclairston had separate head teachers, the first appointed being Margaret Thom.

With plans for a large new town at Drongan, a new school was required and work commenced on a new building in the field bounded by Coronation Road and Millmannoch Road. Known as Drongan Junior Secondary School, the primary department opened in 1959 and in 1960 the secondary department followed. The buildings were designed by Robert G. Lindsay, Ayr County Council architect. In 1960 a new schoolhouse for Drongan was erected at 23 Garronhill Drive. The secondary department was closed in 1971 when Auchinleck Academy opened, pupils from Drongan being transferred there for secondary education. The school was then renamed Drongan Primary School.

Headteachers at the new school have been William Gold (from 1959 until 1975), followed by Samuel Johnstone (1975 until 1992). He died in 1994.

The next headmaster at Drongan Primary School was John Stuart Crawford (born in Thorneyflat Maternity Home, Ayr, 1953). He was educated at Ayr Grammar School followed by Ayr Academy, including one year of secondary education at Takapuna Grammar School in Auckland, New Zealand, before returning to Ayr Academy in 1967. He then studied at Craigie College of Education in Ayr, graduating in June 1976. He worked at Netherthird Primary School in Cumnock, and was promoted to Assistant Head Teacher at Annick Primary School, Irvine, before becoming head teacher at Littlemill Primary School in 1989. He was appointed Head Teacher of Drongan Primary School in June 1992, taking up the post in August. He retired in June 2013. During this time the school celebrated 25 years as a primary school in 1995, the school sports facilities were enhanced by the official opening of the Astroturf in March 2006, and in 2009 the school celebrated fifty years of existence.

6.8 Drongan Primary School *(Dane Love)*

The next headteacher was Margaret Newall, appointed to the post in August 2014. The roll of Drongan Primary School then was 295 pupils. In 2019 Sean Maddocks was appointed as headteacher. The son of Brian Maddocks, he was born on 18 April 1982 and is married to Emma, by whom he has two children. The roll in 2019 was 270.

ST CLARE'S R. C. SCHOOL

Provision of schooling for Roman Catholic Children in the parish has only really existed since the Second World War. A primary school was held in the hall at Drongan, but as the village grew, the number of pupils on the roll meant that it was overcrowded. When the new Drongan Junior Secondary School opened, the pupils at Sinclairston Primary School were transferred there, leaving a suitable school building at Sinclairston for the Roman Catholic children to occupy. Accordingly, St Clare's was opened on 3 January 1960.

A small, but friendly, school, St Clare's has had a number of head teachers in charge over its lifetime. The first one was Patrick, or 'Paddy', Diamond. Others were Mr McCardle, Mr O'Hare, Mrs Catherine McGhee, Mrs Jean Bradley and Miss Bernadette McCrorie. Mrs Helen Rorison was an acting head for a time.

St Clare's Primary School was closed in July 1996 and if they wished to continue being educated at a Roman Catholic school, then they were transferred to St Patrick's Primary School in Auchinleck. Due to the distance to Auchinleck, many of the pupils enrolled at Drongan Primary School. The building was later sold and converted into housing.

COYLE SCHOOL

The former 'Green Hut' school building was used for a number of years to house the Coyle School, a place where children with disabilities could be educated. The school was opened in 1962. This closed prior to 1978.

CHAPTER SEVEN

HEALTH

Dr John Nathan (or Johnathan) Campaign was a surgeon in the parish. He appears to have moved to Strathaven around 1839, his house being placed on the market at that time. It was a double-storey building, roofed with slates, with kitchen, parlour, dining room, four bedrooms, garden, stable, boiler house, milk house and well. Dr Campaign died on 13 April 1846 aged 48. He was married to Helen Dalziel on 10 January 1809 and had various children, including Helen, born 4 November 1810; John Nathan, born 1812; Hannah Campaign, died on 3 October 1837 aged 22; Marianne, born 8 December 1816; William Campaign died on 29 December 1828, aged 7; Margaret, born 1824, died 23 February 1844 and buried in Strathaven; James Campaign, died on 9 August 1828, aged ten months; and Wilhelmina, born 6 September 1829.

In 1837 the *New Statistical Account* gives a fairly positive account of the health and appearance of the parishioners. The minister and the editor note that 'the inhabitants of this parish are very cleanly in their persons, and generally appear at church and market in substantial fine clothes.' In 1837 there were two surgeons operating in the parish. These were John Morrison and John Syme. John Syme was married to Anne Wallace (d. 4 August 1841 aged 37).

On 11 November 1843 Rev James Boyd gave some evidence to the Poor Law Inquiry Commission for Scotland, in which he states that a nurse was employed to look after some of the fatuous poor. He also noted that 'there is a medical man in the village who attends the poor, and he is sometimes paid by the session, but not generally'.

In June 1881 a Convalescent Home was established in Ochiltree for patients of Ayr Fever Hospital (later Ayr County). Established at Gallowlea Cottage, located at the top of the Main Street, this home was purchased by Flora Campbell Whiteside (1834-March 1913), wife of Charles George Shaw, and converted into the home. Mrs Shaw was the daughter of Dr Whiteside. The first superintendent was Miss Veitch. It was proposed that the home should mainly be used by the Ayr Nursing Association and Ayr County Hospital for giving patients some time of rest and recuperation within the country before returning to work. The home was

7.1 Ochiltree Convalescent Home from the South East *(Author's Collection)*

maintained by various subscriptions. On the death of Mrs Shaw in 1913, the home was bequeathed to the Ayr Nursing Association, and was continued by them for some time.

When initially established, it had been the proposal that some of the patients would pay for their care, whereas others would be free. However, it was found more difficult to get paying patients than expected. In its first year only 29 patients were seen and in its second, 59 – 30 males and 29 females, of which seven were children. Originally, there were six beds, but this was soon increased to eight. In 1882 a new dining room was added to the home. In 1883 it was noted that the convalescent home was a success, the beds being in big demand. Payment of one shilling per day was required. Further extensions were added in 1890 and 1892, a dormitory for males in the latter year. In 1892 112 patients had been admitted and a surplus of £29 was made.

Miss Elizabeth Morton was appointed as matron of the home in 1892 and held the position for 23 years. She died at the home on 9 July 1915 aged 55. Jane Dempster was matron for 25 years and died on 2 September 1941. The home was closed in 1942, the trustees petitioning the Court of Session for power to transfer the property and funds.

Ochiltree parish had its own Medical Officer, Dr A. D. Dunn, appointed in 1889. In 1895 the Parish Council raised the salary for the medical officer to £25. Dr Montgomery JP was the Medical Officer from 1897 until his resignation in

September 1908, following his move to a Glasgow practice. He was replaced by Dr Thomas Winning MA MBChb of Ty Clyd, Hirwain, Glamorgan, but he remained for only a short time. In 1910 the new Medical Officer was Dr Stuart Jackson Farries. He was followed by Dr John Jago, of Eskdalemuir, in 1911, followed by Dr Jane Boyes, the first female doctor in the parish, appointed in 1911. She had studied at Queen Margaret College, Edinburgh, and previously served as Medical Officer for the island of Coll, Argyll. Paid a salary of £40 per annum, she resigned in March 1913. In April 1913 Dr John Lindsay Boyd was appointed as Medical Officer. In November 1913 Dr H. Gilbert Bruce was appointed, but in 1915 he left Ochiltree to serve in the First World War. In 1915 Dr William Donaldson was appointed as the new Medical Officer for the parish. He belonged to Flotta, an island in the Orkney archipelago.

Dr John Morrison was the doctor in Ochiltree from 1836 until his death in 1888. He was born at Black Farden in New Cumnock parish. After qualifying, he settled in Ochiltree and became a well-respected member of the community, 'greatly like, trusted and respected,' according to his obituarist.

Dr James Morrison died at Blackbush Cottage in October 1911. He was the son of the late Dr John Morrison. Blackbush was placed on the market in 1912 at offers around £300. It was bought by William Kerr, builder, who died on 28 December 1918 aged 76.

In 1924 Dr James Morrison retired and he was replaced by Dr Donald MacLennan MC ChB of Stornoway. However, Dr MacLennan resigned in July 1924 as he claimed there was insufficient income to maintain his position.

7.2 Ochiltree Convalescent Home from the West *(Author's Collection)*

In 1962 a clinic was erected in Gallowlee Avenue at a cost of £4,831 for the local doctors. This was opened in 1963.

Other medical services were provided across the parish, some by charity. The Ochiltree unit of the British Red Cross was formed on Friday 24 February 1911 after a public meeting was held in the James Angus Memorial Hall at the parish church. Ochiltree Nursing Association was formed in 1931. It was taken over by the county council around 1950.

At Drongan Dr George Bryden took up practice in 1936. Over time, the practice was extended and with a variety of partners passing through, became Taiglum Medical Practice. In 2019 there were eight doctors working at the practice. The practice moved into new premises in Mill of Shield Road.

CHAPTER EIGHT

INDUSTRY

Being a rural parish, Ochiltree historically had little or no industry of any great size within it. It was only with the arrival of coal-mining on a larger scale that any industry of any significance came to the parish.

The manufacture of snuff boxes was carried on in Ochiltree, though it was eclipsed by the makers in Cumnock and Mauchline. There have been a number of different box makers in existence in the village. These were Hugh Kay, John Murdoch, Alexander Murdoch, and Mungo Peden. Alexander Murdoch had his finger in a number of pies, for he is listed in 1837 as a grocer, spirit dealer and snuff-box maker. Also in 1837 Matthew Colville and David Hutchinson were snuff-box painters, applying decoration to the exterior.

Ochiltree was at one time famous for the manufacture of 'toddy-ladles'. This was regarded as being a branch of the snuff-box manufacturing business. The ladles were used to mix toddy, which had whisky, water, honey and spices blended to form a drink. However, toddy went out of fashion and the demand for ladles died with it. An unusual bottle stamped 'Ochiltree 1727' exists and it was claimed to be a whisky bottle, but it is doubtful if there was ever a whisky distillery in the district. What did exist, however, were a number of illegal whisky stills, often located in hidden places. The *Caledonian Mercury* of 1806 makes reference to one of these:

> We hear, that a few days since, Mr Gillies, Supervisor of Excise, Ayr, and Mr Erskine, Officer, discovered an illegal distillery in the house of Polquhairn, parish of Ochiltree. They seized and carried off the still and utensils, together with a quantity of aquavitae, which they found secreted in the drawing-room and in the chaise.

The village was also noted for its sickles and hand-made nails which were exported throughout the country. From 1837-1851 James Brown, James Findlay (1812-1862) and Hector Walker are listed in trade directories as shearing hook manufacturers, the latter also noted by Aiton in 1811. They also made reaping hooks and other agricultural tools. It was noted that those manufactured by Hector Walker were sent across the country and were held in high regard for their quality. With the advent of the scythe, followed by the reaper and binder, the demand for reaping hooks plummeted, resulting in the business folding. Hector appears to have been unlucky in his domestic life, for on 17 August 1826, Sarah Johnston, his wife, died at the age of fifty. He must have remarried, but he lost at least seven children, some to consumption, including Sarah, died 17 April 1830 aged twenty; on 14 December 1833 his seventeen-year-old son, also Hector, died, the sixth of his children to die young. A seventh child, Helen Walker, died on 5 December 1834. James Brown's son, Robert Brown, was appointed as schoolmaster of the Free Church School in Cumnock in 1863.

Many other small businesses operated over the years. In 1837 we have notes of John Duncan, who was a cooper in the village; James Kay, who was a joiner and cartwright; William MacClure, saddler; James MacKennah, cartwright; Hugh Morton, mason and builder; Mungo Pedden (or Peden), fishing rod maker; David Rowan, slater; and William Sloan, cartwright. By 1850 we also have Alexander Gregg, cooper.

In the village of Ochiltree weaving became a major cottage industry in the nineteenth century. In 1837 there were normal weavers as well as cotton weavers. The cotton weavers were employed by the manufacturers of Paisley and Glasgow.

8.1 Gravestone of James Findlay, hook maker *(Dane Love)*

There has probably been a mill at Ochiltree since the twelfth century, the meander of the Lugar Water being ideal for a lade across its waist. The present Ochiltree Mill building dates from the early nineteenth century. It comprised of a four-storey building with machinery driven by a breast-paddle wheel. There was a large kiln. The mill had four pairs of stones, one for shelling, one for oatmeal finishing and two for grinding provender.

8.2 Ochiltree Mill *(Author's Collection)*

Ochiltree Mill was rebuilt in 1859, when the low-breasted waterwheel was used to power four or five pairs of millstones. It had recently become the property of Andrew Paterson (1803-1876) of Carston. He was born at Dalleagles, New Cumnock, and trained as a land surveyor. He also served as Provost of Ayr from 1861-1863. Also in 1859 a new Sawmill was erected, downstream from the main mill.

8.3 Ochiltree Mill *(Author's Collection)*

Following Paterson's death, Ochiltree Mill was operated by David Murdoch. At a later date the mill was purchased by Messrs MacGill & Smith, grain merchants in Ayr.

Burnock Mill was located by the side of the Burnock Water, two miles to the south of Ochiltree. The building was three storeys in height and had a medium sized kiln within it. The mill workings were driven by a bucket-type wheel which could produce around ten horsepower. Within the mill were three pairs of stones, one for shelling oats, one for finishing oatmeal, and the third for provender. In the 1920s the mill received new workings, provided by Messrs George MacCartney & Co. of Cumnock. These were of the bevelled gear type. The building survives, having been converted into a house.

There were a few other mills that formerly existed in the parish. One of these was located by the side of the Drumbowie Burn, near to Hayhill. Known as Polquhairn Mill, the mill had virtually disappeared by the twentieth century. Clydenoch Mill is shown on General Roy's map of 1747 as 'Claydonogh Mill'. This would have been located near to Clydenoch farm, using the Taiglum Burn as its source of power. The burn hereabouts is not significant, its lack of power probably significant in the mill disappearing soon after, not appearing on the 1856 Ordnance Survey.

A lint mill was established to the north of Ochiltree sometime in the eighteenth century. Located to the west of the larger corn mill, the lint mill used the water in the same lade as the corn mill. The mill may also have operated as a waulkmill either simultaneously, or at different times. At a later date, the mill was used for dyeing cloth, and it became known as the Dye Mill thereafter. David Reid (1757-1817), known as 'Reid the Dyer', second cousin of William Tennant in Ochiltree MIll, operated the mill at the turn of the nineteenth century. In 1829 John Murdoch (1770-1844) was a flax, or lint miller and mason in the village. A gravestone in the old churchyard marks the burial place of his son, William, who died in 1811.

The Dye Mill was later converted into a sawmill On the gable of the mill, at the north end, was a waterwheel, comprising six spokes, twelve feet in diameter. This may have been manufactured by George MacCartney of Cumnock. The mill was apparently rebuilt in 1857 for Thomas Cuthbert (1793-1870) of Burnockholm. The joiner at the sawmill for many years was James MacIntyre (died 1861), followed by his son, also James MacIntyre (1810-1885) who was succeeded by his son, Charles MacIntyre (1851-1928). He operated the mill for almost fifty years. In September 1928 the sawmill was taken over by Hugh Morton of Low Carston, who set up in business with a joinery, undertaker and cartwright. He remained at the mill until 1980. In the 1950s, during Morton's time, part of the mill building was rebuilt to improve the accommodation. The mill was sold in 1991, when it was converted into a house.

The manufacture of curling stones took place in Ochiltree for many years. In the late nineteenth century James Peden was a curling stone manufacturer in the village. He presented a pair of stones to Ochiltree Curling Club for competition in 1888. Often the stone used for making curling stones at Ochiltree was quarried from the headwaters of the Burnock Water, the 'Burnock Stone' curling stone gaining an international reputation. The manufacture of curling stones appears to have ended around the time Peden had presented the curling stones, the business being described as defunct in 1890.

In the second half of the eighteenth century a pottery works was established on Drongan estate. Located at Coalhall, the Drongan Pottery was originally leased by Peter Moir. He obtained a contract in 1790 to make clay pipes through which water was piped to the house of Kaimshill and the ironworks from the Cairntable Cauldron, a distance of around five miles. The minute book of the Muirkirk Iron Company makes reference to them:

> Mr Gillies and Mr Gordon represented to the meeting that, when they were here in the month of June last, they saw a necessity of finding good water for the use of the family at Kaimshill and of the people at the Works, and there being none of good quality known to be nearer than a spring of water of excellent quality above the Canal from the Garple called 'Cairn Table Cauldron', they wrote to several Potters for estimates of what they would furnish and lay 2-inch earthen pipes for. Peter Moir, Potter at Drongan, having offered to do it at 6d per yard, which was lower than any of the others, they accordingly agreed with him for it, the Company to be at the expense of cutting the tract for them and filling it up.

When some of the pottery pipes were discovered at Muirkirk in the 1920s, they were noticed to have spigot and faucet ends. The pipes measured around thirteen inches long, tapering from around 3 to 3¼ inches internal diameter at the wide end, to 2 to 2½ inches at the narrow end. Major Dugald Baird of Kaimshill donated two of the pipes to the National Museum of Antiquities in Edinburgh in 1929.

The business was acquired by John Boyle, but he died on 10 April 1829 aged 64. His wife, Elizabeth MacCosh, died at Taiglum on 16 February 1845, aged 84.

In 1832 Drongan Pottery was taken over by Boyle's sons, Robert and John, but within a few years Robert Boyle was the sole proprietor. He made many improvements to the works, installing a new claymill, boilers and sifters. Boyle is noted for having improved a patent tile machine originally invented by the Marquis of Tweeddale. It was described as a 'Ayrshire Double Acting Patent Tile Machine'. This doubled the production rate by allowing tiles to be extruded at two ends. Boyle patented this machine and it is known that he sold at least one to the Island of Arran. Boyle lived at Ronaldshaw Park in Ayr, in which town he also had a pottery shop in Fort Street. However, his speculative developments in Ronaldshaw Park led to his bankruptcy in 1866. The strain was also too much for him, and he died the same year.

The pottery at Drongan manufactured a variety of items, including black and brown ware, chimney cans and garden pots. The proximity of the clay pit to the works, and the ready supply of coal from Drongan pits, meant that the wares produced were often cheaper than the competitors. Drongan ware was sold across south-west Scotland, from Glasgow to Dumfries and Stranraer. It is also known to have been sold in the Highlands and some was exported to America.

In August 1843 Robert Boyle announced in the local press that he had made various improvements to the pottery and enlarged the works there. As a result the pottery was able to supply a wider variety of items for sale. He introduced a new kind of flower pot, 'highly approved of by gardeners and others'. He was also using some of the finer clays to produce teapots and kettles, described as being 'furnished in a style which cannot but give satisfaction'. The *Ayr Advertiser* sent a reporter to investigate the new works, and he gave a fairly detailed account of the produce:

> In making pipes for the carrying of water from the soil, the workmen fit them into one another by a peculiar method which prevents either the chance of the water leaking, or of their being choked by sand.
>
> [The table kettles and teapots were manufactured in great variety and because of their] handsome appearance, and extreme cheapness, [he thought they would be in general use.]
>
> Mr Boyle has also introduced a new species of flower pots. Formerly the surface of those articles being very uneven, it was almost impossible to remove plants from one pot to another, without destroying the ball, and causing much unnecessary labour, and danger of injury to the plants; it was also a complaint that instead of sloping downwards to the hole in the centre of the bottom, they generally were deeper round the sides, whereby the water was allowed to collect, and the plants destroyed from over moisture. These objections are completely obviated by Mr Boyle's new construction, which very much resembles in shape the half of an egg, sloping gently downwards, in an even surface from the mouth, so that no over moisture is allowed to remain, and the earth easily removed unbroken. We have been informed by competent judges, that they are of a more porous nature than those formerly in use, and consequently much more favourable to the health of the plant.

Robert Boyle appears to have used the newspapers to promote his wares, in some cases doing this in a roundabout way. For example, the following report from the *Ayr Observer* in October 1844 was syndicated to newspapers across the country, and appeared in some as far away as Inverness and Hull:

> On Monday, some stalks of corn, which had been grown upon a small piece of land at Drongan Pottery, were sent to our office by Mr Boyle. In length they were upwards of six feet, and in thickness some of them measured fully an inch; while the heads are proportionally strong. This extraordinary growth is the more wonderful when we take into consideration the nature of the soil on which they were raised. It was neither more nor less than a portion of the clay field, which, after being denuded of its proper surface, had lain exposed to the action of the atmosphere for some four or five years, and was thus converted into a friable state. Mr Boyle had it, in the first instance, thoroughly drained – the tiles being laid at a depth of a couple of feet. He next ploughed it, and gave it a slight top-dressing with lime, which he harrowed in with the seed. After the braird had appeared an inch or so above the surface, he caused a small quantity of guano to be thrown broad-cast over it. This was all the culture which it received, and so luxuriantly did the crop come away, that it attracted very general observation from the passers by. This experiment, though upon a small scale, disproves the opinion which generally prevails, that tile-draining is altogether inoperative and inefficient on stiff clayey land; and shows that good coarse clay, when divested of moisture, becomes as productive as any other description of soil.

Many farmers preferred to use a bottom slate under the inverted U-shaped drainage tile, and to satisfy demand Robert Boyle brought slate back when exporting pottery to Wales.

When the Ordnance Survey visited the district in 1854, they noted that 'only a coarse kind of pottery ware is made at these works – red and black'. The works comprised of a kiln, drying houses, and a single-storey dwelling house attached. It was said that the pottery produced here was not particularly robust and was easily broken. It is said that James Keir Hardie lived at the pottery for a time.

Drongan Pottery was then taken over by the Nichols, probably the same Nichols as those at Cumnock Pottery. The Nichols gave up the let in 1874 and the pottery was offered for lease in September 1874, alongwith the clay pits, workmen's houses and grass fields. There appears to have been no takers, and it was closed in 1878. The kiln was demolished, but some of the buildings were converted into cottages, used by miners employed in the local pits.

To the east of Ochiltree, on the road to Cumnock, stood Ochiltree, or Burnfoot Tileworks. These works were located on Dumfries House Estate and were established in 1835 by Lord John Crichton Stuart, 2nd Marquis of Bute. The first proprietor was Robert Taylor, son of James Taylor (d. 1825) of Cumnock Pottery. Initially, Robert Boyle of Drongan Pottery advised, but Taylor appears to have given up the lease in 1838. In 1838-39 the tileworks were run by lawyer, Alexander Hamilton of Mauchline, as part of the Cumnock Pottery & Tile Company. He died in 1839 and his heirs and trustees continued the business until 1856. There had been an issue with the lease, which compelled Taylor to supply any quantity of tiles each year to Lord Bute at a fixed price of 20 shillings per 1,000 of common drainage tiles; 40 shillings for five-inch drainage tiles and 50 shillings for eight-inch tiles. Taylor and Hamilton were permitted to make a further 150,000 free of royalty which they were allowed to sell to anyone, and for any above this figure, a royalty payable of one shilling per thousand, or two shillings per thousand for drain soles or bricks. Various managers ran the Cumnock Pottery and Ochiltree Tileworks during this time, including James MacGavin Nichol (1819-1886). He purchased the business in 1856, paying Dumfries House Estate £48 half-yearly at Martinmas and Whitsun. Burnfoot tileworks were sold on when the Cumnck Pottery business grew, and the tileworks were acquired by Hugh Meikle. It was then occupied for many years by the Edgar family. The Duncan family took over the lease. Alexander Duncan (1819-1902) was born in Ochiltree parish, and worked at Ochiltree Tileworks. He later took over the tileworks at Failford, before moving to Shawneuk Tileworks at Catrine. He then operated the tileworks at Auchinleck, followed by Cronberry. He died in 1902 aged 83. His son, John Syme Duncan, took over at Cronberry, enlarging the works there. In the 1850s, the Ordnance Survey described the works at Ochiltree as comprising 'a number of drying sheds built of wood and thatched, 2 kilns and grinding and rolling engine, 1 cottage house also 1 storey thatched, all of which are in good repair and working order.'

James MacLennan (c.1809-1899) became the proprietor of Ochiltree tileworks. He was born at Bonnyton and started a tilework in Galston, before taking over the works at Ochiltree. He retired to High Lugtonridge farm, near Beith.

In 1906 John Syme Duncan took on the lease at Ochiltree Tileworks and soon after he fitted modern machinery. He became a noted member of the local community, so much so that his friends called him the 'Provost of Ochiltree.' John Syme Duncan died in 1925 aged 73.

In 1927 the tileworks were taken over by Robert Waddell Martin of Carluke. He was the youngest son of Hugh Martin, engineer, Carluke. Martin lived at Midsands, Ayr, and died on 29 June 1943. When he took over the works they were almost dormant, but he resurrected, extending the clay pit.

In 1937 the tileworks became the property of Ochiltree Tile Works Ltd., a company incorporated that year. Electricity was introduced to the works in 1953.

The company was dissolved on 13 March 1980. The kilns were demolished in April 1984. The former clay pit used as a landfill site by the council for dumping rubbish. It is now totally filled in and the site partially planted with trees.

A second tileworks existed in the parish, located immediately to the north of Killochside farm. A clay pit on-site was used as a source of material for making field drains. The tilework had been a fair-sized enterprise, but by the time the Ordnance Survey visited in 1856 it had been abandoned. In the 1851 *Ayrshire Directory* a James MacClownan is listed as a tilemaker - perhaps this is where he was based.

The Drongan Brick Company Ltd was established in 1934 to carry on the business of manufacturing and dealing in bricks, slates and pottery. It had £2,000 capital in £1 shares. The proprietors were John Boyde, Roclincourt, 112 Ayr Road, Prestwick, and William Cuthbertson Jr., Stranleur, Ayr. The company was dissolved in 1939 and the works were dismantled soon after. Bricks made by the firm had the word 'Drongan' within the frog.

In 2014 initial proposals were made for a wind farm to the south of Sinclairston on Polquhairn lands by Brookfield Renewable UK. This would have up to nine wind turbines with a maximum tip height of up to 470 feet. The turbines could produce up to 22.5 MW of electricity when in full motion. Planning was initially refused, but in September 2018 planning was approved. The company proposed increasing the turbine sizes in February 2020.

OTHER TRADES

The manufacture of clothing has taken place in Ochiltree on a small scale over the centuries. In the first half of the nineteenth century Hyndford Aitken was a stocking, or hosiery, manufacturer in the village. Other hosiery makers included Andrew Galbraith. In 1945 the former Free, or South Church of Ochiltree, was converted into a hosiery factory.

In 1837 there were three boot and shoe makers running businesses in the village - James Fisher, David MacMillan and Thomas Watson. In addition, William MacDill was a shoemaker. At the same time Andrew Hamilton and James Kerr were tailors and David Reid was a dyer. By the 1850s, tailors and clothiers included James Gray, Andrew Hamilton, George Hillhouse and Andrew Smith.

Old trade directories give us the names of some folk employed in different industries, usually on a small scale. In 1851 we have note of John B. Andrew, bookbinder; and William Miller, cartwright.

The Smithy at the foot of the Main Street was long in existence. Smiths over the years included William Weir (1757-1829) John Weir (also a farrier - 1837), and William MacCurdie (1868-1927).

Another smithy existed at Mote Toll. In 1851 this was run by Hugh Strathern, and by 1863 by John Strathern. He also owned a joiner's shop adjoining, which was newly-built and offered for let in 1863. In 1890 the smiddy was taken over by the

Burton family. Hamilton Burton died in 1919, after which the business was taken over by his sons, William, John and Thomas. The smiddy building was demolished in 1968.

A smithy also existed at Taiglum. In the first half of the nineteenth century the smith was James Simson (1791-1860). At Bent, on Auchencloigh farm, there was a smithy for a number of years. James Smith (1800-1862) was the blacksmith there in the 1820s until the 1850s, after which he moved to Glasgow where he continued to work as a master blacksmith. He was followed at Bent by William Hislop, after which the cottage was occupied either by ploughmen or shepherds.

COALMINES

Mining has taken place within the parish for many years. When it was first worked cannot be ascertained, but one of the earliest confirmed references to coal in the parish dates from 1710, there being an old map dated 18 May that year depicting the Drongan Coal seams. The coal was developed by the Earl of Stair, owner of Drongan estate.

Local tradition claims that one of the oldest mines in the parish was located at Coalhall, hence the community's name. The pit mouth is thought to have been positioned near to the roadend into Drongan House. It is said that the men dug the coal in the seams underground, but that women were engaged to carry creels of coal on their back up the ladders to the surface.

A 'coal work' is indicated on Taylor and Skinner's survey of roads at what would be Coalhall. These maps were surveyed in 1775. By 1784 Drongan coal was undercut in price by coal from Lord Dumfries's works in Old Cumnock, which was sold across Ochiltree and 'Caltown' parishes.

At Coalhall, for many years, were the remains of a stone-built colliery works. One of the earliest atmospheric pumping engines used in coal mines in Ayrshire was located here. The pumping engine may have been the one that was purchased by Mungo Smith of Drongan around 1750-60 from Robert Reid of Auchenharvie, Stevenston. In the 1770s the customs officer at Ayr harbour noted a ship loaded with coal from Smith's Drongan works was of a 'superior quality'.

The older mines were located in the middle part of the parish, in a belt from Burnton through Sinclairston to Drongan. When the first Statistical Account of the parish of Ochiltree was compiled in 1792, Rev Thomson stated that there was only one coal mine in the parish, located at the western end. This produced a 'kind of coal without much smoke, used for drying oats.' This may have been a mine established by the Earl of Stair, who owned Drongan estate prior to 1760.

By 1837, when the *New Statistical Account* was compiled, mining for coal appears to have halted in much of the parish, this not being commercially viable due to the difficulties of transporting it to the markets. The pit at Drongan, however, still appears to be working around this time, for Rev William Rorison, writing in

8.4 Old Coal Pit, Coalhall *(Author's Collection)*

1841 in the *New Statistical Account* of the parish of Stair (in which Drongan was located at that period), makes reference to the pit:

> Coal abounds in the parish. The colliery mentioned in the former Account, as having been wrought on the estate of Drongan, for above a century, is still in full operation.

The minister continues with a table, indicating the depth of seams in the Drongan pit: Under a 'strong red clay, generally running from 24 to 54 feet, according as the ground rises or falls,' there is a seam of strong grey freestone, eighteen inches thick. Below this is a 3 feet thick seam of soft whitish till, below which is 3 feet 9 inches of freestone. Eight feet of light blue till follows, under which is a seam of eight inches of crow coal. Under this is seven feet of fine white freestone, then five feet of light blue till. Sixteen inches of soft black stone follows, then three feet four inches of 'very fine coal, almost unequalled'. Four feet of a blackish freestone lies underneath, and below again is twenty feet of sandy till. A layer of two feet of limestone follows, then 30 feet of freestone. Another four feet of freestone is very hard and fine white. Six feet of black till follows, then six feet of a very hard black till, which 'burns when put into the fire'. Six feet ten inches of very fine coal, called top coal follows, under which is ten inches of soft marl. A layer 22 inches in thickness of coal, the 'bottom coal' follows, then fourteen inches of coal 'eft for a pavement'. Six feet of till lies below, followed by 24 feet of gray freestone. Another seam of coal, five feet nine inches follows, and below thirty feet of soft white till is a two-foot seam of coal.

Rev Rorison also notes that in Stair parish there were 32 colliers, of which around twenty were employed at Drongan pit; in addition the colliery engaged a master blacksmith. A cartful of coal could be 'laid down at [any cottager's] front door for 5s.' Rorison noted that the Drongan colliers 'have not constant work throughout the year. The output of coal is not allowed to exceed 20 creels (which is something short of three tons) per day'.

In 1841 the pit at Drongan was leased by Messrs Robert and John Duncan. They also leased a pasture field and the colliers' houses attached. In 1842 the company had morphed into J. & P. Duncan.

In 1842 Drongan Colliery was working three seams of coal: the first seam was 48 feet below the level of the ground. The second was eleven feet thick and was 132 feet below ground. The third seam was five feet thick and was 168 feet below the ground. At the time the pit employed 27 adults, plus three boys aged from 13 to 18. There were also five lads under 13 years of age working at the pit. It was noted that boys could start at the pit at age eight, and that there were no girls employed in the pit. Each hutch had a gross weight of 2½ hundredweight, which had to be hauled on average 100 yards. The engine hauling the hutches up to the surface was 32 hp.

The 'Children's Employment Commission' reported on conditions for the youth working at various pits, including Drongan. The report resulted in the passing of the Mines and Collieries Act 1842, after which the age at which a boy could work underground was raised to ten, and no women or girls were allowed to work below ground.

Coal from Drongan was being sold across the county. James Gemmell was selling Drongan coal from his yard in Ayr's Green Street in 1863 at 8s 4d per ton, delivered, or 5½d per hundredweight collected. An advertisement of August 1864 for the Prince of Wales Inn in Ayr's High Street noted that the landlord, John Park, was also an 'Agent for Drongan Coal', in addition to providing hot dinners on market days.

It is claimed that the first Newcomen engine to be erected in Scotland was used to pump water from the Drongan coal mines. This engine was located at Coalhall and even by the mid nineteenth century it was known locally as the 'auld engine'. It appears to have survived until the 1950s.

Drongan Colliery was operated by John Smith & Sons in the mid 1800s. When the Ordnance Survey made maps of the district in 1856 the largest coal pit in the area was referred to as Drongan Coal Pit, located in a field almost opposite Hannahston farm road-end. The map indicates two buildings positioned to either side of the shaft. All other contemporary pits in the area were little more than openings in the ground, probably bell pits, with little, if any surface buildings. Messrs Merry & Cuninghame operated the Drongan and Rankinston Works in the late 1800s. The manager at the work, John Muir, retired in 1879. In March 1880 the mineral field and colliery, which had two pits working at the time, were offered for lease, the present tenants giving it up.

Drongan Colliery was taken over by J. & J. Gilmour soon after, who also ran the mines at Garrochhill and Duchray. George Sharp served as manager during the period of Gilmour's lease.

In November 1883 the proprietors of the Drongan coal field gave up their lease and it was placed on the market. It was offered either as a whole, or in divisions. At the time it had five workable seams of coal, within its 1,780 acre extent. It was reckoned that there was also blackband ironstone and shale available. In addition, 77 miners' houses were included.

A new pit was sunk around 1890-91. On 16 December 1896 an explosion of firedamp occurred in Drongan Pit, injuring two brothers who were working underground. One of them was taken to Ayr Hospital where he died on 17 December, aged 39.

SHIELDMAINS

The mineral rights at Shield Mains were owned by A. G. Moore & Co. Ltd. of 156 St Vincent Street, Glasgow. This business was owned by Alexander George Moore, and appears to have started with the Duchray and Garrochhill pits in neighbouring Coylton parish, A. G. Moore being the manager of these pits in 1896. Moore was a civil and mining engineer, as were his brothers, Ralph D. Moore, and Robert T. Moore (1860-1938). Their father, Ralph Moore, was Her Majesty's Inspector of Mines. Duchray and Garrochhill were closed in 1898 and work at Shieldmains commenced. James Allan of Kilsyth was tasked with developing the new pits, as well as laying a mineral siding or tramway from the pit to join the main railway just to the north of Drongan Pottery. This siding was around one mile in length, the hutches drawn by an endless wire rope worked by a fixed engine.

The first pit, No. 1, was sunk immediately to the east of Shield Mains farm in 1898. James Allan was the first manager, having commenced working with Moore's at Duchray in 1893. Allan's father was manager of the Haugh Colliery, Kilsyth. In 1901 Allan moved on to Moore's Blantyreferme Colliery at Uddingston. In 1898 there were 35 men employed at Shieldmains pit. By 1901 the number employed had increased dramatically, with 252 men working in the pit, of which 215 worked below ground, the remaining 37 on the surface. Pit No. 1 was abandoned on 8 September 1926.

Shieldmains No. 2 was sunk almost next to No. 1, due east of Shield Mains steading. It was often referred to as the Siding Mine. By 1918 there were only eight men working underground here, plus a further two on the surface. The manager here in 1923 was Peter Paterson, at which time there were eight miners below ground and six employees on the surface. It was abandoned on 8 September 1926.

Shieldmains No. 3 was operated in tandem with Shieldmains No. 2. Pit No. 3 was abandoned on 24 December 1927. Similarly Shieldmains No. 4/5 was abandoned on 1 May 1928.

Shieldmains No. 6 was sunk around 1900. In 1933 there were 57 men employed underground and a further sixteen on the surface. Pit No. 6 was closed down in 1950.

Shieldmains No. 7 was often referred to as Drongan Station Pit. It was located at Hannahston farm road-end, very close to the site of the older Drongan Coal Pit. During the miners' strike in March 1912, A. G. Moore wished to start a number of Polish miners who had arrived in Coylton. This resulted in a crowd gathering at the pit, the picketing miners trying to persuade them not to start work. The strike ended on 4 April 1912 when 34 of the 70 miners employed at the pit returned to work. In 1913 there were 64 men working underground, plus a further 33 on the surface. In 1921 A. G. Moore had three pits in operation – No. 7, and Siding Nos. 1 and 2 pits. Pit No. 7 and Siding No. 1 were treated as a single pit by Moore's, but they were taken to court in 1921 for failing to adhere to the mining regulations. They lost their case, and each of the pits were declared to be independent. Whether or not this was a factor, but Pit No. 7 was abandoned on 14 December 1922. The pit also suffered from serious subsidence, which may have been another deciding factor. It may have reopened, being listed in 1947 when the pits were nationalised. On 2 December 1908, James Muirhead was accidentally killed at the pit, aged 43. He was married to Elspeth Calder (1858-1946) and he was interred in Coylton cemetery. In 1918 there were 47 men working underground, with 19 surface workers. The Siding Mine had 67 underground miners plus 20 surface workers.

Shieldmains No. 8 did not last very long. It only employed a few miners and was abandoned on 27 October 1927. The shaft was to be linked with No. 9 and Shieldmains No. 8/9 operated until the Second World War. In 1936 there were seventeen men employed at this pit, ten of which worked underground. In the following year this increased to 21 underground and eight on the surface, before dropping once more, to 14 underground workers and seven surface workers in 1938.

Shieldmains No. 10 and No. 11 were short-lived attempts at finding coal. Shieldmains No. 12 was abandoned on 24 December 1927. Shieldmains No. 13 was unsuccessful and didn't last long. Shieldmains No. 14 was located south of Drongan Mains, accessed by a railway siding that struck south from near Carston. Sinking of the pit commenced in 1943. Producing household coal, the mine didn't last too long, for it was closed in 1950. In total, there were fourteen different shafts bearing the Shieldmains name.

A late mine sunk by A. G. Moore & Co. Ltd. was the Barbeth Pit, located at Coalhall, just east of the Gateside Inn. Sinking of this pit commenced in 1945 and the first coal was brought to the surface in 1950. In 1948 it was reported that the pit produced around 25 tons of coal per day, a quantity that was increasing. The pit had a workforce of around 137, but by 1948 only had 21. The coal was screened and washed at Shieldmains. The pit was closed soon after nationalisation, in 1955.

The managers of the Shieldmains pits over the course of their operations were James Allan (1898-1901), Peter Paterson (1901-1927), Hugh MacLeod (1927-1928) and John Watson (1928-1950). John Watson, a native of Benquhat, moved to the Edinburgh area to take up a post as Area Education and Training Officer for the National Coal Board.

On 1 January 1947, at the time of nationalisation of the coal industry, Shieldmains pits were still owned by A. G. Moore & Co. Ltd. At that time pit Nos. 6, 7, and 14 were producing coal. In 1946 the mine employed 57 miners, with a further 16 workers on the surface. In 1947 the annual output was around 60,000 tons of coal.

Robert Brown, aged 49 years, was killed at Shieldmains Pit when the cage fell 180 feet to the bottom of the shaft on 30 January 1905. He and George Dyer, who was injured, had been clearing the air courses whilst the pit had been idle for a few days. Another death took place on 30 March 1920 when John Peebles, aged fourteen, who was employed in wheeling empty hutches at the pit, fell down the shaft. He plummeted around 130 feet to the pit bottom. Other events in the history of the colliery include the case in May 1902 when George Martin of Whitletts, a miner at No. 4 Pit, was found guilty of part-loading hutches with dirt and stones then covering this with coal, in an attempt at claiming a greater output. He was fined £4, failing which he would have been imprisoned for 21 days.

DRONGAN CASTLE COLLIERY
The Drongan Castle Colliery was sunk to the south-west of Reidston farm in the early 1890s. A railway siding was laid from a junction to the south of Drongan Station, passing Drongan Mains, and skirting round Kayshill to the colliery. The original owner was George Cameron Black of Drongan, son of coalmaster, John Black of Airdrie. The business headquarters was located at 18 George Square, Glasgow, and Black's residence was Viewbank in Airdrie. The manager was John Keirs. The pit mined household coal, and in 1894 employed 108 men underground plus a further twenty on the surface. Within a few years the owner was William Black & Sons who operated it until it was closed in 1899. This company was incorporated on 16 October 1895 to take over works at Airdrie, Slamannan, Paisley and elsewhere. During William Black's ownership of the mine, fewer miners were employed there – in 1897 just 22 in total, fourteen of which worked below ground. In 1898 seventeen worked below ground and a further seven on the

surface. William Black & Sons Ltd was wound up on 17 October 1902, and in that year former employees from the colliery sent a donation to Ayr County Hospital of £7 7s 0d.

BURNOCKHILL

Burnockhill No. 1 Pit was sunk on the lands of Burnockhill farm, two miles south of the village, in July 1902 and it started producing coal in 1903. The pit was initially operated by Messrs. A. Simpson & Sons, based at Knockterra Cottage, near Cumnock. The mine was later sold to William Baird & Co. Ltd. A second shaft was sunk, in addition to the first - these shafts were 290 fathoms (1,740 feet) deep, and the company were hoping to extract 1,000 tons of coal per day. By 1918 the mine was managed by George Bryson, with Andrew Brown as under-manager. The mine employed 95 men below the surface, with a further 22 above ground.

As with most mines in the country, there were a number of fatalities. An explosion on 14 May 1908 severely burned William Thomson. He was to die on 27 May 1908. James Crawford was squashed between a cage and the roof in April 1911. He lived at Garrallan, Old Cumnock. On 20 November 1919 Andrew Strachan, aged 25, of Trabboch was killed in the pit by a fall of stone from the roof. Jose Blanco, a Spaniard, was killed on 20 January 1920. Hugh Mitchell of Trabboch was killed on 29 March 1923 by the fall of stone from the roof. He was 40 years of age and was buried at Stair. On Tuesday 4 September 1923 Hugh Reid of Skares was entombed for eighteen hours behind a fall of rock. The mine was closed in 1928.

DRUMSMUDDEN

In 1869, the building of the railway across Ochiltree parish, resulted in various landowners seeing this as an opportunity to exploit their minerals. On 12 May 1869 an advertisement appeared in the *Glasgow Herald*:

> To let, coal and ironstone fields in Ayrshire. The coal in the estate of Drumjoan, in the parish of Ochiltree, measuring about 753 acres, is to be let, in two lots, both of which are intersected by the Ayr and Cumnock Railway, now being made. The blackband and other ironstone also on the whole estate, with one of the tin coal seams for the supply of engine and fire coal, to be let, on proving leases, either in one or two lots. Offers may be made for the coals and ironstone separately, or for both conjoined. The lands will be shown by Mr George Brown, tenant of Drumsmodden Farm; and further particulars may be learned on application to A. Gillies Smith, Esq. C.A., 59 George Street; or to Messrs Landale, Frew & Landale, M.E., 6 Forth Street, Edinburgh, and 160 Hope Street, Glasgow – with

either of whom offers may be lodged, stating fixed rents and optional lordships. – Edinburgh, 7th May 1869.

The Drumsmudden Colliery was established in 1882 by the Dalmellington Iron Company. It stood on what had been a green field lying between two low hills on the farms of Drumsmodden (as it is spelled today) and Crawsland. The Ayr and Cumnock branch railway was constructed between these hillocks, providing a ready opportunity to export the coal mined from below the green fields, and a series of sidings with 'lies' and loading hoppers for the waggons were built. Two shafts were sunk into the ground and the usual group of surface buildings and horrals were constructed to service the pit. The shafts, which were 40 yards apart, were 202 fathoms (1,212 feet) in depth. Two managers served the pit, William Prentice from 1882, followed by William Howat. The pit produced coal of a top quality from the Lugar Main seam, but it was hampered by many faults. Often miners working at a face would discover that the coal disappeared, to be replaced by rock. Many hours and days were lost in prospecting up and down these faces

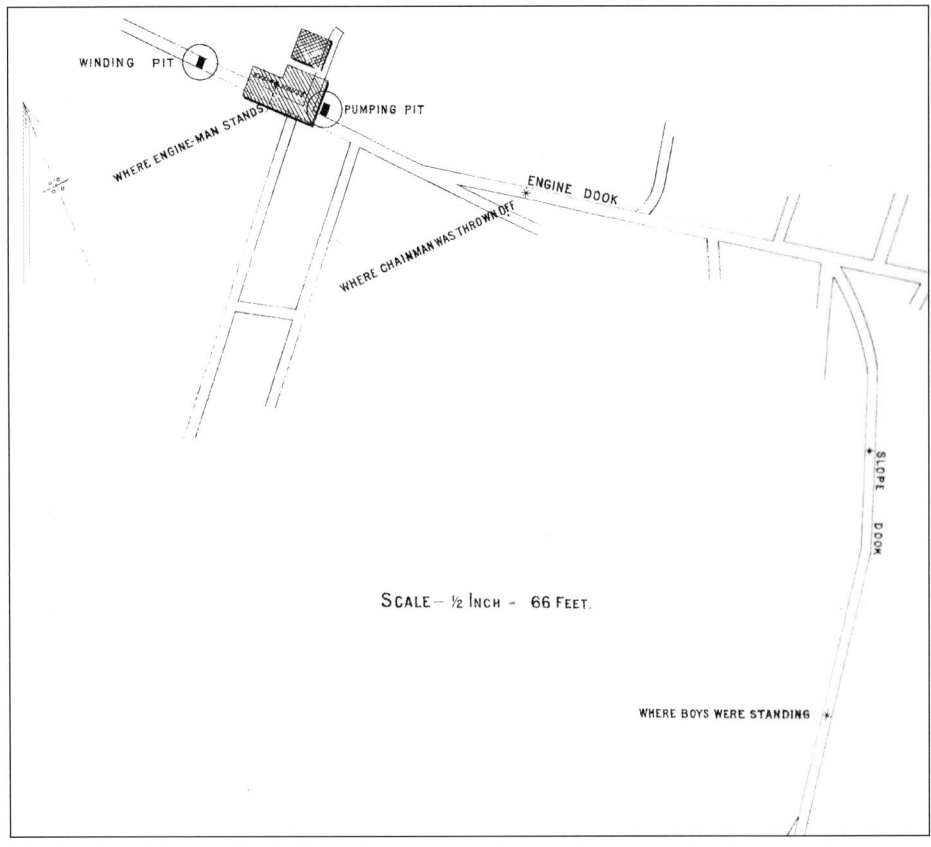

8.5 Plan of Drumsmudden Pit *(Author's Collection)*

to try to find the seam once more. This cost the company thousands of pounds, and the pit had only really covered the expense of sinking itself by the time it was closed in 1904. Maps of 1908 indicate that the surface buildings were quickly removed, leaving only three bings to indicate the existence of the colliery.

As with almost every colliery in the country, accidents far below the ground resulted in deaths that left the local community devastated. Drumsmudden was no different, although there appears to have been fewer deaths there, compared with other mines. Nevertheless, in September 1882 two men were killed whilst the pit was being created. They were at the bottom of the shaft and wished to send a beam to the surface. They sent a message to the signalman, surnamed Bennett, to send down a 'kettle' to collect it. Somehow, the kettle was not stopped at the proper place, and it struck the platform where the two men were standing, causing them to fall headlong to the bottom of the shaft, killing them instantaneously. One was Thomas Milroy, who was married with three children; the other was William Smith, unmarried. Bennett was charged with culpable homicide – he claimed his attention was diverted from his charge by some water escaping from a boiler. On 15 April 1886 James Paterson was squashed when the roof and sides of the area where he was working collapsed. He was only 26 years of age.

An unusual occurrence took place in Drumsmudden pit on the morning of Wednesday 21 November 1888. A severe thunderstorm broke out in the area, and a large flash occurred when the ascending cage was almost 20 yards from the surface. The engineman was made powerless by the electricity, but was able to throw himself on the brake lever, stopping the engine. On recovery, he felt pains in his arms, neck and shoulders. A report in the *Transactions of the Mining Institute of Scotland* gives details of the further problems:

> A heavy charge descended the conductor on the stalk, uplifting the earth and ashes at the bottom, but otherwise doing no damage. The pit bottomer of the winding pit heard a loud, cracking noise, and saw a clear, bluish flame on the crowns on the roof at the pumping pit. The signal boy was terrified, seeing fire running and leaping between the haulage rope and the rails. The chainman was engaged at the time taking down the empty race, and was sitting on the last hutch, with his feet on the chain. When about 40 yards down he felt a shock through his legs, and was pitched on to the road, and lay stunned for a time. Twenty yards beyond the foot of the slope dook, or 320 yards from the pumping pit bottom, and 240 fathoms from the surface, two boys were standing, one having his feet on the rails and his head almost touching the electric bell wires. He got a shock, turning him round about and both were terrified by seeing fire flying between the rails and wire. They ran off to find the oversman. When they found

him they were white with fear, and said fire was flying all through the pit. Fortunately, no serious injury was done to any of the workmen or property by the above strange occurrence.

Drumsmudden Pit was a good three miles from Ochiltree, and slightly farther from the nearby community of Coylton. To provide a ready workforce, the firm created its own small village, two rows of houses built alongside the pit. These were the Skerrington and Drumsmudden Rows. Built of brick, the houses were small.

POLQUHAIRN
To the south-east of Old Polquhairn coal was extracted from some small coal pits sunk into the moorland. These pits were worked intermittently, probably sequentially, and were abandoned before 1855. However, the presence of coal on Polquhairn estate was noted, and proposals for a larger mine was made.

In 1895 the Polquhairn Coal Company was established with capital of £10,000 in £1 shares, in order to acquire the mineral rights to the Polquhairn estate. Polquhairn Colliery was sunk within the year. The owner of the mine was Alexander Wilson Waddell and in 1918 his offices were located at 52 Newmarket Street, Ayr. The firm took over George Taylor & Co. of Ayr in 1916, and also acquired the ownership of Mansfield Colliery at New Cumnock (before 1918), but that colliery was closed in 1926. By 1947 the registered office had moved to 45 Dalblair Road in Ayr.

Up to 1896 the manager was Joseph Dyer, successor to a Mr Barrie. In 1896 Polquhairn mine was managed by Robert Barr, with William Davidson as under-manager. The mine employed 33 men below ground, plus further 11 on the surface.

From 1906 until 1916 the colliery manager was James Allan, and he encouraged the miners to have an annual gala day. In 1908 four hundred people attended the gala, taking part in the various fun activities. In that year the pit had 86 men working underground, with a further 24 working on the surface. He moved to take over management of the Drumley and Mairburn pits at Annbank, following their acquisition from George Taylor & Co. The next manager was Andrew Managhan, with James Whyte as under-manager.

The two shafts at Polquhairn were No. 1 and No. 2, these being 250 and 130 feet deep. In 1918 the mine had 111 men working below ground, plus a further 36 on the surface. Other managers included Mr MacArthur and James Adair, who died suddenly at the colliery on 20 October 1934, aged 55. By 1950 the manager was J. MacLucas. In 1940 the Miners' Welfare Commission proposed the construction of pithead baths, capable of taking 250 men. Thus, Polquhairn Pit was one of the first to have pithead baths installed.

In 1946 the colliery produced around 44,000 tons of coal, at which time there were 142 miners below ground, plus a further 36 on the surface. Polquhairn Coal Company Ltd. was taken over by the National Coal Board on 1 January 1947 in accordance with the terms of the Coal Industry Act of 1946. A report in 1948 noted that Polquhairn produced 46,500 tons per year of house coal, mainly from the Main and Ell seams. The miners used the stoop and room method of extraction. In March 1952 miners at the pit went on strike over budget cuts.

In 1955 the National Coal Board reconstructed Polquhairn, sinking two more shafts, referred to as No. 5 and No. 6. These were sunk adjoining the existing pit. At the time, new pithead baths, cycle stores and offices were added.

Despite the peak year of production at Polquhairn being in 1960, in 1961 Polquhairn Colliery was under threat of closure. At the time over 360 miners were employed there, producing an average output of 310 tons per day. The last coal was raised at Polquhairn in August 1962, and the last man employed there, a nigh watchman, finished up on 16 February 1963.

A number of deaths have occurred at the colliery. An explosion of fire-damp took place in November 1909, killing James Clark (aged 32) and seriously burning Hugh Hamilton. In December 1911 an explosion took place seriously injuring four miners, two of whom subsequently died. Robert Heron, pit roadsman, and William Withers (aged 14), both of Drongan, died in Ayr County Hospital. An outburst of gas occurred whilst a new road was being developed, and this was ignited by a lamp carried by one of the miners. The explosion caused a fall from the roof of stone. In December 1924 James Parkin was killed when he fell down the mine shaft, a total of 330 feet. He had only started work at the pit a week earlier. On 4 February 1929 James McGarvie was killed.

In 1936 the Greenhill Colliery was sunk just under a mile south-east of Polquhairn Colliery. The shafts there were officially known as Polquhairn No. 3 and No. 4. Located higher on the moor, the drift mine worked the coal seams for house coal. An average of 70 miners worked there, the peak number being 74. In 1948 the mine produced around 80 tons of coal per day, equating to 21,000 tons per year. The coal from Greenhill was sent in buckets carried by aerial ropeway to the sister mine at Polquhairn, where it was screened. The mine was amalgamated with Polquhairn around 1952. It was closed in 1958. After closure, the aerial ropeway was dismantled and re-erected at the Butlin's Holiday Park near Ayr.

KILLOCH COLLIERY

In the 1930s the coal industry in Scotland was going through a period of major change. The old mining methods were being abandoned, and it was decided that it would be better to create a number of large, deeper mines in productive coal-seams and close down the older, smaller collieries, which could only reach comparatively shallow seams. In Ayrshire, one major development that came about as a result of these plans was the sinking of Killoch Colliery. A survey compiled prior to 1942 discovered that there were four major seams, varying in thickness from three to four feet, containing 200 million tons of coal, described as 'perhaps the best house coal in the world'. The war caused difficulties with developing this field, but £1 million was allocated for the building of the pit. In 1947 it was anticipated that 500 council houses would be built at the 'as yet un-named' town (to be Drongan).

A new deep mine was sunk at Killoch from 1952 onwards, though this took many years to develop from the original proposals. In 1877 a local mining company had attempted to find coal here, but their four bores were insufficiently deep to reach the seams. In 1890 further boring took place from an underground position in Drumsmudden Colliery, and these were successful in finding that there was coal present. Around 1939 more boring took place, six bores being sunk over a period of years. These were finally completed by 1942, proving that there were eight seams of workable coal.

8.6 Killoch Colliery under construction *(Author's Collection)*

Built for the National Coal Board, the mine was designed by the industrial architect Egon Riss, chief architect to the NCB. Initial projections were that the pit would be able to produce 6,000 tons of coal every day, and that the reserves below ground were in the region of 150,000,000 tons, claimed to be sufficient to keep the pit in production for over one hundred years. The area to be worked by the Killoch Colliery was to the north of the Kerse Loch Fault, and east of a large fault which lay to the east of Coalhall, extending to around ten square miles. The area had not been worked before, mainly due to the depth needed to mine before the coal was reached, due to the height of the overburden over the seams. In 1955 two headframes were constructed to allow the sinking of two shafts, and a number of temporary buildings were erected for the workers.

8.7 Killoch Colliery *(Author's Collection)*

As time passed, two tall concrete-built towers were constructed, known as Koepe towers, which housed the winding motors over the two shafts. The shafts were 400 feet apart, concrete-lined, and measured 24 feet and 20 feet in diameter respectively. The principal shaft (No. 1) was used for coal-winding and upcast. The pair of skips, capable of holding eighteen tons, were hauled up on steel ropes, powered by electric motors. These were 6.6 kV, 1,875 hp AC motors. Each winder had a capacity of 300 tons output per hour from 385 fathoms. Shaft No. 2 was the downcast shaft, mainly used for transferring men up and down, as well as stone and other materials. The three-deck cage could transport 150 men per wind, plus additional coal if required. This shaft was powered by a 6.6 kV, 1,250 hp AC motor.

Additional facilities and buildings were constructed on the surface and on the pit bottom. A Car Circulation Hall was located at the foot of Shaft No. 2, as was a compressor house, where the compressed air used by many of the machines was produced. On the surface were pithead baths, an administration block, canteen, lamp-room and first aid office. The pit was designed so that miners could enter the baths and remain under cover until they emerged at the end of their shift. A coal preparation plant was to have a turnover of 500 tons per hour. A branch railway was constructed by the British Railways Engineering Department, leaving the main line near to Drongan Station. This meandered across the countryside, passing Macquittiston, and Chipperlagan, on a slope of 1 in 85 in favour of the load.

The Killoch scheme was expected to be the largest mining unit in Ayrshire at the time. There were eight seams of coal worked, the deepest being over 2,000 feet below the level of the pithead. The seams workable are tabulated below:

Seam	Thickness of coal in inches	Depth in feet	Quality/Type
Ell	36	1,710	First-Class House
Main	80	1,800	First-Class House
Major	50	1,840	Industrial
Diamond	33	1,930	House
Maid	54	2,040	House and Industrial
40 Fathom	36	2,270	House
Bonanza	60	2,350	Industrial
20 Fathom	33	2,390	First-Class House

It was reckoned that the pit could produce an annual output of 1½ million tons of coal, produced by two shifts. It was reckoned 3,500 men would be employed, working out on average at 35 hundredweight per manshift.

Killoch operated a modified version of horizon mining, working on an easterly and westerly direction from the pit bottom. Cross-cuts were set off to the south to intersect the seams. The seams had an average inclination of 1 in 10 on a south to north direction. It was proposed to work the Ell seam firstly, and as it was worked out, to work the seams below it in turn.

The first coal was produced in 1960. By August 1964 the mine was still aiming to become the first pit in Scotland to produce over one million tons of coal per annum, this being achieved in 1965. Much of the produce was exported to Northern Ireland for use in electricity power stations. At the time it produced 4,000 tons per day, meaning that it was heading for a total of 1.2 million tons. In 1968 estimates were made that the pit had reserves of 100 million tons. The faults below ground at Killoch resulted in coal production being erratic, and at times the pit output was often only half the Scottish average per miner. In 1972 an underground tunnel was dug to create a link with Barony Colliery at Auchinleck.

A number of miners were to lose their lives in various accidents in the Killoch Pit. Among these were a mine driver, Livingston Forsyth, of Coronation Road, Drongan, who was struck by a girder which fell on him at the pit on 6 July 1960. He died at Ayr County Hospital seven days later. A mine driver, William Rutherford, was struck by an overturning mechanical shovel at the pit on 21 May 1963 and was killed. He was forty years of age and lived at Glenramskill Avenue in Cumnock. John Brown Stewart of Holmburn Road, Cumnock, was found dead on 2 March 1964 when he became entangled with the mechanism of a conveyor belt. James Ross, of James Street, Tarbolton, was a colliery locomotive driver. He was crushed between a locomotive and a mine car and was taken to Ayr County Hospital but died on the same day, 27 September 1964. Antonio, or Tony Cano, of Shawlands Street, Catrine, was killed on 18 January 1965 aged 21 when he was struck by a runaway bogey. He was buried at Catrine Cemetery. Charles Forsyth of Queenzieburn, Kilsyth, was injured by a fall of stone and debris at the pit on 15 June 1966. He was a coal mine supervisor. He died of his injuries at Ayr County Hospital later that day. John Brodie, a power loader in the pit, was seriously injured on 26 September 1967 when a fall of debris from the roof of No. 4 East Section struck a steel girder which fell on him. Brodie, who lived at Boswell Drive in Auchinleck, was taken to Ayr County Hospital but he died the following day. James Corrigan O'Hara of Mauchline Road, Mossblown, was killed when his head was crushed between two power supports in the pit on 1 October 1968. Andrew Brown, coalminer of Hannahston Drive, Drongan, was killed on 12 August 1970, aged 57, when he was struck by a runaway mine car. He was buried in Ochiltree Cemetery. William Brown Hammond Carswell, a coal miner, was thrown from a runaway mine car on which he had been standing on 7 October 1970. He was eventually sent home from hospital, to Ballochmyle Avenue in Mauchline, but he died on 29 October. A trainee miner, Thomas Drysdale Wallace, was caught between a moving conveyor belt and a pulley at the Preparation Plant on 8 January 1973. Wallace belonged to Dalleagles, New Cumnock. Thomas Walker Grozier was killed when a large fall of stone from the roof of the Stable Section North 22 fell on him and crushed him on 22 June 1974. He was the colliery deputy, aged 34, and lived at Castlemains Avenue, New Cumnock. Andrew Beaton Spiers of Coronation Road, Drongan, was struck by a piece of falling coal in the pit on 18 November 1977. He was 22 years of age. Jared Woods Shearer MacFadzean was killed by a fall of stone from the roof which resulted by the breaking of a batten above him on 13 December 1978. He lived at Bonnyton Avenue, Drongan.

The number of miners employed at the pit in 1980 were 1,817 underground workers plus 332 on the surface. Employee numbers in 1985 was 1,650, but in 1984-85 the miners across the country went on strike, led by their union leader,

Arthur Scargill. The strike lasted for twelve months (6 March 1984-3 March 1985), and by early 1985 the workers at Killoch decided to return to work. The National Coal Board decided to close the unprofitable mines, and Killoch and Barony were among those selected for closure.

The colliery was closed in 1986, but much of the site was retained as a coal preparation plant, treating coal excavated in various local opencast mines. The main buildings were sold to Barr Construction and were converted into a concrete works and offices. A new concrete mixing plant was installed, and developments took place over the years. A Barr subsidiary, Solway Steel, also operated at the site, but was closed in 2012 with the loss of forty jobs. In 2014 the business of Barr Quarries was sold to Breedon Aggregates for £20.8 million. This included the Killoch site, and eleven quarries operated by the company.

In 2017 permission was granted for the construction of an 'energy recovery park' at Killoch. This was to be operated by Barr Environmental Ltd. and would recover recyclable materials from municipal waste, plus produce fuel derived from non-recyclable waste. The gasification plant would take non-recyclable materials and produce fuel which would be burned to create electricity. It was expected that up to 120,000 tonnes of waster per annum could be turned into up to 12 MW of electricity plus 25 MW of heat energy. A new chimney 180 feet in height was to be erected. In 2021 further plans were made to erect a larger 'moving grate' facility, which would burn up to 166,000 tons of non-recyclable waste and convert it to electricity, capable of supplying the equivalent of 40,000 houses.

CARSTON COLLIERY

The National Coal Board sank a coal mine at Carston, east of Drongan, in 1950. The pit was never very successful, and it was closed in 1956 and finally abandoned the following year. Producing house coal, the pit had an average workforce of 39, the maximum number of employees at the pit reaching 44. The largest output occurred in 1952.

AUCHLIN MINE

A private colliery was established in 1977 under licence by James R. MacLellan. Auchlin Pit was in danger of closing in the eighteenth week of the miners' strike, July 1984. There were only eleven men employed at that time but it was closed due to picketing. The mine operated until 1991.

The mine at Auchlin was latterly owned by Fairclough Parkinson Mining Ltd. The area was surface mined for a time. In 1990 the company wished to use the former mine as a dump for rubble, road planings and broken concrete. The proposals were not accepted by the council.

The former mine area and surroundings were acquired by Portcullis Developments Ltd. in 2001 and, working with East Ayrshire Woodlands, the

Forestry Commission and the Woodland Trust, it was developed as a habitat for wild birds. It covers 48 acres and includes a lochan with hide.

MINERS, STRIKES, ETC.

Miners have gone on strike for better wages and conditions over the years. One of the earlier references to a major strike occurred in October 1842, regarded as the first Ayrshire coal strike. Miners across the country had been on strike for some time, but in many areas had agreed to return to work, signing up for a full year. At the time a large meeting of miners took place at Coalhall, 200 colliers attending. The men from Crawfordstone, Springs and Gadgirth pits agreed at the meeting to join the strike. The Drongan miners, however, refused.

Other significant early strikes took place in 1880, and in 1881 a strike lasted for ten weeks. Shortly after this, miners banded together to form the Ayrshire Miners' Association in 1886, under the guidance of James Keir Hardie.

In the twentieth century there have been various outbreaks of industrial action in the coalmines. In 1920 the miners went on strike, and the laying down of tools continuing until the following year. At this time many miners living in Drongan had no income, and the Public Hall was set up as a soup kitchen.

In 1926 the miners joined the General Strike. The Drongan Public Hall was again set up as a soup kitchen. The strike started on 3 May 1926 and lasted ten days. However, the miners did not return to work, and remained out for many more months. As winter drew in, the miners were getting nowhere, and some drifted back to work. By December the strike was over.

Many Ochiltree and Drongan men worked in collieries furth of the parish. In November 1962 there was a major collapse at Barony Colliery in Auchinleck. Four men were trapped underground, including John MacNeill, aged 49, who

8.8 Drongan Miners' Memorial *(Dane Love)*

lived at Hannahston Avenue, Drongan. Their bodies were never to be recovered. A memorial stone was subsequently unveiled at the Barony A-Frame in 1989.

A memorial to the miners of Drongan was unveiled at the Drongan Centre around 2006. Made from a block of Portland stone, it bears the legend, *A TRIBUTE TO THE MINERS DRONGAN*, surrounding a carved scene depicting miners working below ground.

SURFACE MINING
In more recent years opencast mining has taken place of pits. A small opencast existed at Hannahston, near Drongan, from the early 1990s until around 1998. The site, which covered 49 acres, was latterly operated by ATH Resources. In 2004 part of the site was restored and sold to a developer who built 36 houses on part of it. The ATH Resources company went into liquidation in May 2013. When the site was closed, there was an insufficient bond for full restoration, so the land was converted into woodland, with paths and lochans. The work was carried out by East Ayrshire Woodlands in 2000-4. The wood was formally opened on 4 August 2006 by Cathy Jamieson MSP. The site became the property of Hargreaves Land, part of an opencast operator company, which proposed selling the woods in 2020. However, locals set up a group with the intention of raising the £75,000 needed to buy the site. This was achieved by December 2020, with the assistance of donations from the Scottish Land Fund (£55,000) and Cumnock and Doon Valley Minerals Trust (£14,000).

In the mid 1990s a large opencast mine was established at Piperhill, mining coal below the ground between Belston Loch and the Plyde. Coaling was carried out by SB Minerals of Uddingston, Lanarkshire, a subsidiary of Law Holdings. It was later operated by Fenton. The coal was hauled by road to Killoch Disposal Point. By September 1995, when the mine closed, 850,000 tons of coal had been extracted by SB Minerals. The site was not restored fully and in 2018 work commenced by Hargreaves to make the land suitable for forestry. Part of the ground was sold to local farmers.

The Chalmerston North open-cast coal mine was located at the southern end of the parish, but is more readily associated with Dalmellington and the Doon valley, to which access for workers and the extraction of coal was made to Chalmerston rail head. The coal was blended and sent by train to electricity generating stations. A haul road also existed northwards, through the Piperhill site, allowing coal to be taken to the KIlloch Coal Preparation Plant. The site was located in the midst of the Kyle Forest, between the headwaters of the Water of Coyle and the Black Water, south of Stannery Knowe. Owned by the Forestry Commission, then Forestry and Land, as it was renamed, the site was run by Scottish Coal. The last coal was extracted in 2010-11, and when Scottish Coal went bankrupt in 2013, the site was abandoned.

GAS WORKS

A gas works was established in Ochiltree, supplying its first coal gas to the village on 1 May 1862. The gas company had offered shares at £1 each and managed to raise the £800 required to construct the equipment. A site in Mauchline Road was acquired and there a gasworks was constructed. Work commenced in November 1861, the engineer being James Munn of Ayr and Newton Consumers' Gas Company. Andrew Murdoch of Ochiltree did the masonry work and Messrs Orr, Muir & Co. of Kilmarnock did the engineering work. At the first annual general meeting held in Morton's Inn in 16 July 1862 the chairman, John Greenshields, reported that the business was now well established. The sale of gas was never great in the village, resulting in many annual meetings recommending that there should be no dividend payable to the shareholders. In 1891, 'in view of the state of affairs' it was proposed that the gas company should be dissolved and wound up in liquidation, but this proposal was averted.

On Wednesday 30 December 1908 the gas manager at the time, Wiliam Bartholomew, was accidentally poisoned with coal gas at the works whilst engaged in cleaning out a purifier. He was found by a villager who had been sent to inquire as to the poor supply of gas. When he found Bartholomew, he sent for Dr Winning who immediately arranged for him to be transferred to Ayr County Hospital. Unfortunately William Bartholomew died in hospital on Monday 4 January 1909.

Another manager was James Beresford, who was at Ochiltree from 1913 until 1915. He moved in 1915 to manage the gas works at Lochmaben. He later moved to Lochgilphead Gas Works (Argyll) and in December 1918 returned to Ayrshire to Auchinleck Gas Works. The cost of gas varied over the years, in 1913 being sold at 6s 3d per 1000 feet.

The demand for gas in Ochiltree was never too great, and many residents did not take up the opportunity to join to the supply. As a result, the works only supplied some residents in the town, and had to charge more than other local gas works. The company went through various owners, all of whom had difficulty in making the business pay. Eventually on Tuesday 27 May 1924 the gas works were closed. The machinery was sold to a Kilmarnock scrap merchant, and the site of the gas works was sold to Mr Aird for a motor garage.

QUARRYING

By the side of the Lugar Water, below Slatehole farm, a sandstone quarry operated for many years. A newspaper advertisement of 1 September 1834 lists the 'stone quarry' as part of the lands of Slatehole, 'Balturck, or Barturck, Auchinbay or Auchinbaig, and Dejore' which were offered for sale. By 1899 the property belonged to Andrew Kirkwood MacCosh, an ironmaster who lived at Gartsherrie, Lanarkshire. The quarry was leased to Elizabeth Kerr Morton and William Kerr, builders.

In May 1794 one man was killed whilst working in a quarry within the parish when a huge block of rock fell onto him. The rock also bruised a second man. The deceased left a wife and five children behind.

In addition to the quarry at Slatehole, the working of stone was only carried out in a small scale in the parish. Old maps indicate disused quarries, often indicating that they were for whinstone. These were probably only used to supply building materials for houses and farms, and when the work was completed, the quarry abandoned. Some other quarries were for limestone, used in limekilns to create lime for building and for use on land.

At the former Drongan Station, Edenrock opened a concrete mixing plant on 8 May 1975. Employing six people, the works produced ready-mixed concrete.

FOOD

At Drongan a meat processing factory was established by Hodgmac, opening in June 1972. The firm was owned by Kenneth Hodge and Andrew McCallum, hence the name. This proved to be successful, and extended soon after, a larger factory being erected in 1975. The business produced cooked and processed meats, including sausages and bacon. By 1978 it employed around thirty people. In 1988 it became Nimmo Quality Meat Produce Ltd. The business was taken over by Glanbia Fresh Meats Ltd in 1999. In March 2003 Glanbia closed the meat processing factory and laid off 120 workers. Grants of Galston took over the factory and work commenced in July 2003.

Lynch Quality Meats was established in 2005. The business, which was operated by the Lynch family, grew to employ 45 at its factory in Drongan. In February 2014 the business was sold to Dunbia, based in County Tyrone, Northern Ireland. In 2018 the factory was considered for closure, with the loss of 64 jobs.

CHAPTER NINE

COMMERCE

As with all small villages, a number of shops existed to supply the needs of the residents. Most of the names of the premises are long-since forgotten, the original shops being little more than rooms in houses where one went to purchase various goods. Buildings erected as commercial premises, or what we would recognise as shops today, did not come about until the early nineteenth century.

In 1837 shopkeepers and traders in the village included Thomas Cuthbert (grocer, cheese factor and spirit dealer), John Greenshields (baker), John Howatson (grocer), David Kirkland (grocer), Andrew MacGregor (flesher), Alexander Murdoch (grocer and spirit dealer) and John Murray (grocer and spirit dealer). There were nine grocers and shopkeepers, according to the 1831 Census. In 1831 a Savings Bank was established in the village.

Around the middle of the nineteenth century, tradesmen and businesses in the village included William Wyllie, horse dealer (1862). A Mrs Clement was an elderly shopkeeper who seems to have specialised in the sale of cheese. She had at least two sons, Andrew and Thomas, who established themselves elsewhere as cheesemongers, still in business at the time of the First World War, as Andrew Clement & Sons. They were the largest wholesale dairy produce supplier in Scotland. Andrew's son was knighted, becoming Sir Thomas Clement KBE. He received his knighthood for services to cheese, being responsible for the distribution of butter and cheese to the nation during the First World War. He erected a small country house for himself, known as Barcapel, on the outskirts of Newton Mearns, in 1912. The architects were Watson & Salmond.

At the turn of the twentieth century were J. MacLean, clothier, and Mrs Polly Steven, draper and fancy goods merchant, both located in Main Street (1911). In 1907 Mrs William Simpson opened a new drapery in Burnock Street. In 1908 James Gibson opened as a tailor and clothier in Mill Street. In June 1905 William Crawford (1865-1928) opened a new bakery in the village, taking over an older business – he was later to move to that shop previously occupied by the baker, William Probert (d. 17 January 1895, nephew of John Greenshields, baker in the village) and latterly by Mr MacQueen at the Cross. Crawford retired as baker in 1927.

Charles Wyllie opened a new butcher's shop around 1875. Taken over by his son, also Charles, it was subsequently run by Mrs Wyllie up to 1924, when it was taken over by Sam Hendry. Hendry had previously run a small butchery at the Crown Inn for over twenty years. James Hendry began trade as a butcher in the early twentieth century, travelling around the countryside with his butcher's van. He died on 17 November 1927. Hendry the butcher continued to operate in the village until 18 February 2012, the business having been taken over by Donald in 1988. However, by 2012 competition from larger outlets and the need to upgrade his equipment led owner Donald Hendry to retire.

In 1897 a new grocer's shop was erected at the corner of Mauchline Road with the Cross by John Jamieson Probert (1849-1944), who lived in the house above. Probert also served as the Registrar for Birth, Marriages and Deaths in the village from 1876 until 1935.

In 1899 a branch shop was opened by the Auchinleck Co-operative Society Ltd. in a building at the foot of the Smithy Brae. This building had been owned by John Gemmell (1831-1886) of Glencairn Cottage, Main Street, but by the time the co-op rented it, it was the property of his widow, Sarah Gemmell, nee Colville (1832-1901). The building was then acquired by John Purdie, saddler. In the 1920s, Auchinleck Co-operative Society purchased the shop. The Ochiltree branch of the Auchinleck Co-operative Society was closed around 1962 when the shop was taken over by Gilbert WIlson.

A bootmaker, C. S. Alexander, had premises at 22 Main Street in 1914. John Barclay moved to a new shop adjoining the Commercial Hotel in 1926 where he operated as a boot and shoemaker.

In 1951, at the time of the *Third Statistical Account*, Ochiltree had seven shops in the village – a grocer, baker, draper, butcher, confectioner, fish and chip shop and a newsagent.

Agnes Davidson MacIlwraith had a small shop at the top of the Main Street, on the south side of the road. She emigrated to Canada, selling the shop to John Smith. He moved across the road to larger premises in the newly-erected Crown Buildings, where he remained until January 1963. At that time the business was bought by James Brown, who remained proprietor for many years. In 2013 the House with the Green Shutters building was converted into a pharmacy.

DRONGAN

At Taiglum and Drongan there were a number of smaller early shop premises, some of which were located in the old miners' rows. Among these were Aggie Gray's Shop, opposite the smithy; Willie Drain's Shop and Mrs Taylor's Shop, both in the lower Drongan Cottages Row; and Mrs Boyd's Shop, in the middle Drongan Cottages Row. Also in this row was Martha Brennan's chip shop. On the opposite side of the road from Drongan High Row was Hammy Barr's Shop, next to Will

Reid's Garage. Hammy Barr sold fish and chips and ice cream in a large timber hut. At the back of the hut was a room with two billiard tables.

In April 1875 advertisements appeared in local newspapers looking for tenders for 'the erection of a grocery store at Drongan Colliery, near Ayr, for Messrs. Merry & Cuninghame Limited.' Consequently, Drongan Store was erected at the corner of Lane Road and Main Road. Built of sandstone, it had a slate roof and a couple of chimneys. The door and two windows were located at the gable end, facing Littlemill Road. The store was managed from 1876 by John Hunter, formerly store manager at Overton Store, near Dreghorn. Hunter was able to get a grocer's license for Taiglum in November 1875. It was later owned by J. & J. Gilmour, coalmasters. At a later date the store was owned and run by James Davidson, selling everything from groceries to clothing, miners' equipment to alcohol. In 1933 George Hannah Sturgeon was granted a grocer's certificate for the Store on condition that he built a partition to separate the alcohol sales.

When the new community of Drongan was established, new commercial premises were erected in Glencraig Street in 1951 and Mill of Shield Road in 1954. In Glencraig Street there were eight shops built, originally occupied by the Kilmarnock Equitable Co-operative Society Ltd. (founded 1860), being a butchery and grocery, a relocated post office, a pharmacy, Matheson's ice cream shop, William MacGregor's butcher's and Glencraig Baker. The first pharmacist was Bruce Wilson, who also owned the chemist in Patna. In 1963 Gavin Clyde purchased the Drongan shop and in 1971 extended to Coylton. The shops were

9.1 Drongan shops in Mill of Shield Road *(Author's Collection)*

designed by Stevenson & Ferguson. In Mill of Shield Road there were two blocks of shops, built in two phases. The first phase had four shops (with a fifth added) and a second phase of six premises was added to the east. These were originally occupied by Tom Bone, grocer; Edna Sturgeon, draper; Ken Hodge, butcher; Gordon Webster, dentist; King's sweet shop; Sandy Gourlay, baker; as well as a chip shop, barber and hairdresser, fruiterer, doctor's surgery and a hardware store. The shops have been rebuilt and extended over the decades.

POST OFFICE

In 1808 the Post Office nationally decided to introduce penny post offices in villages across the United Kingdom. According to an 1813 map of *Post Roads in Scotland*, Ochiltree is not covered, the nearest post office being in Cumnock, but by 1838, a *Map of the Circulation of Letters in Scotland* shows a pedestrian post existed from Catrine, to Ochiltree, and thence to Cumnock. The post office in Ochiltree was established in a building at the bottom of Smiddy Brae, three along from the Manse Road corner. In 1837 the postmaster was John Murray, and letters arrived in the village at half past twelve during the day. They were delivered by a penny-post runner from the post office in Cumnock, and this postman also lifted the mail to take on his return route. Around 1850, Thomas Cuthbert, who lived at Burnockholm, was listed in trade directories as the postmaster.

There were also three independent carriers who were able to transport goods. John Lammie took goods to Ayr every Tuesday and Thursday. James MacCrae did the same route on Tuesdays and Fridays. Goods for Glasgow were taken by Mary Bryan every Monday, and on Mondays and Tuesdays John Lammie transported goods to Muirkirk. In 1884 Robert Brown was a carrier who brought mail and parcels from the Whip Inn in Ayr to Ochiltree on Tuesdays and Fridays.

Early postmasters and mistresses included John Andrew (until 1858). By 1896 the post office had moved to the building at the corner of Burnock and Mill streets. Postmasters there included Jeanie Weir (in 1899); Mrs Jamieson (until 1920); Charles Murdoch (from 1920-1949, when he died); Alexander Samson and Annie Samson (1921-2011), then Steven Preston for a short period. In 1985 the post office was taken over by James S. Brown, and it was moved to Brown's shop in upper Main Street. In 2012 the post office was closed, and the post office agency was moved to the former Auchinleck co-operative shop lower down Main Street. However, by this time the term postmaster had been discontinued.

At Taiglum a post office was established in the late nineteenth century. The actual office was located in a number of different buildings in the rows and then Drongan over a period of time. These locations included the Smithy House (late 1800s), the actual office being in the kitchen to the rear. In the 1890s this was operated by the smith, Sam MacCulloch.

The post office was relocated to the end house of the row of houses on the east side of the Main Road. At a later date, the Post Office was moved into the old Toll Cottage. When the new shops were erected in Glencraig Street in 1951, the post office moved there. The postmaster for many years was George Sturgeon, who was succeeded by his son, also George Sturgeon, and latterly his daughter. Ian Mitchell ran the post office from 2015-2016.

INNS

There have been a number of inns in the village. In 1837 Pigot's *Directory* lists four innkeepers, but unfortunately does not identify with which inn they were associated. Their names were Andrew Edgar (1764-1843), Alexander Gemmel, Agnes Haddow and John Lammie. Around the same time, the *New Statistical Account* states that there were six inns and alehouses in the parish, all of which were located in the village.

The Head Inn (often referred to locally as the Head Inns) stood on the south side of the Cross. This was tenanted by Andrew Edgar, but when he died in 1843 it was continued by his widow until she retired in 1849. In 1875 the building was owned by John MacGregor, dealer, but the innkeeper was Andrew Muir (1851), then Hugh Morton (1862-1891). Other landlords included Agnes Park (1865-1929), William Probert (1901-1921) (although the building was the property of his father, John Jamieson Probert). In the early twentieth century it was run by Hugh Morton, of Burnockholm, builder. In the 1940s, the old stone porch leading to the hotel was demolished to aid traffic flow and the sightlines on the main road.

9.2 Commercial Inn *(Dane Love)*

On the porch was a carved stone lion, later to be positioned in a garden in Main Street. In 1994 permission was sought to convert it into houses. This work was subsequently carried out, and the inn now only survives as dwelling houses on the side of the road.

The Commercial Inn stands on the opposite side of the road, at the corner of the Cross with Mauchline Road. In the 1860s-1870s the landlord was George Wallace (1827-1878). In the late nineteenth century the landlady was Agnes Park (1865-1929), who was also licensee at the Head and Star inns for a period. She later moved to become the hostess at the Black Bull Hotel in Dalmellington, before dying in January 1929. William Wilson was the landlord in 1921. In 1926 the licensee was Mrs Morton, the tenant at the time, but the inn had recently been purchased by Miss Fullarton from Kilwinning. From 1929 the licensee was Martha Bryan. In 1939 William Dykes was given permission for new additions to be made and for the grant of a hotel license. Another proprietor was the Gilmour family. Hugh Morton was the licensee in the 1950s until the 1970s. By 1979 the owner was James M. Somerville of Ayr. In recent years it has passed through various hands, and has been closed for extended periods.

The Crown Inn was located at the top end of Main Street, on the northern side. The landlords over the years included Edward Holmes (*1894*-1912). He was followed by Joseph Smith (1877-1923) and his wife (*1909-1923*). Heather Holmes (nee Reid) demolished some old cottages on the top side of the Crown Inn and there

9.3 The House With the Green Shutters *(Dane Love)*

erected a new block, known as the Crown Buildings. These were erected 1905-6 in sandstone, rising over two storeys. The building contained four properties. The Crown Inn was placed on the market in 1925 and was closed around that time.

The Star Inn was located in Main Street, just a few doors up from the smithy. Late nineteenth century landlords included Agnes Park. John Crichton Stewart was the landlord from around 1882 until 1929. He was born at Cooperhill farm, the son of Charles Stewart, and was landlord of the Inn for around fifty years. He died on 29 September 1929 at the age of 81 years. He was succeeded by his son, Alexander Stewart.

The birthplace of George Douglas Brown, the 'House with the Green Shutters', was sold in 1960 by Ayr County Council to the Royal British Legion for £60 and converted into a club. The building suffered from a fire in December 2004. The building was not insured, and the British Legion branch could not raise sufficient funds to restore it. The club was sold in 2006 and was reopened in August 2007 by Norman Wylie as a pub known as the Green Shutters. It has since been converted into a pharmacy.

On 4 February 2006 The Green Shutters Festival of Working Class Writing took place in the village with the aim of bringing the work of George Douglas Brown back into the public consciousness. Organised by Spartacus Arts and Music Management Services, the first festival was supported by writers, Janice Galloway and Tom Leonard.

The Gateside Inn was located at the junction of the Drongan road with the Ochiltree to Ayr road. In 1899 it was part of Drongan estate. Landlords included John MacWhirter (*1899*) then Thomas MacWhirter (*1914-1930*), both of whom owned a number of cottages in the locality. It became a Dryburgh's inn and lay

9.4 Gateside Inn *(Dane Love)*

empty for a time before it was purchased by Robert Blair (d. 2020) and his wife, Marion Blair (d. 2019), who took over in 1970. The Blairs sold the inn and bought the Dumfries Arms in Cumnock in 1985. Gateside was purchased by the Spence family, followed by Dave and Catherine Finlayson. The inn was closed in the 1990s and remained empty for a number of years, before being converted into a private house in 2019.

There were no inns or public houses in Drongan or Taiglum until 1954, when two premises opened on the same date. The Welcome Inn was erected at the corner of Mill of Shield and Littlemill roads. The first landlord was James Stodart Robertson, of the Doon Hotel, Patna. It closed down in 2017 and the building was demolished in January 2019.

Also on Littlemill Road, at the corner with Watson Terrace, the Toll Bar was erected, on the opposite side of Watson Terrace from the site of the old Taiglum Toll. The first proprietors were Douglas and Bessie Montgomery, of the Finlayson Arms, Coylton.

9.5 Toll Bar, Drongan *(Dane Love)*

Historically, there were one or two other public houses in the parish. At Littlemill Bridge, where the road to Dalmellington crosses the Water of Coyle, a public house existed on the east side of the road, on the north side of the bridge, certainly operating in the mid-nineteenth century, but closed by 1900.

CHAPTER TEN

AGRICULTURE

The rural nature of Ochiltree parish has meant that agriculture has been an important industry for centuries. This has changed and developed over the decades, as new methods of farming have been introduced. Of the parish's approximate 24 square miles, over ten thousand acres are in cultivation. The remainder, which is rougher and less-productive, have been in recent years used for forestry, but in the past were little more than rough grazing.

Farming has also played a very important part in the commercial history of Ochiltree parish. For many years there were two fairs held for the sale of cattle. These were certainly in existence in 1837, when they were held on the second Wednesday of May and on the first Tuesday in November.

Originally, many farms in the parish were leased on a life-time tack, but as the tenants died, new leases were originally made for nine years at a time. This length of tack soon became unpopular amongst farmers, as they were only getting settled in and beginning to make improvements to their farms when the lease expired. By the middle of the nineteenth century leases of nineteen years became more common.

With developments in agriculture taking place in the eighteenth century, many wet or mossy stretches of farmland were drained, bringing the unproductive areas into use. No longer in existence were the mossy stretches of Ha' Moss, Holehouse Moss and Finlaystone Moss.

A rental book for the farm of Palmerston long existed, and an extract from it can give an indication of how things were at the time. The oldest rental receipt, which was payable annually, dates from 1714:

> Ochiltree, 16th Jany. 1714 – Then received from James Duncan in Ffynlaystone, compleat payment of his year's rent, One thousand seven hundred and fifteen years, and all former payments are allowed him.
> Charles Cochrane.

Cochrane was the factor on Ochiltree estate at the time – his last receipt is dated 13 January 1736. The estate changed hands about then, and the next receipt is dated 1739. The rental varies slightly:

> Received by me, John Gairdner, Wryter in Ayr, as factor for Governor MacRae, from James Duncan, now and formerly satisfaction for the rent of Finlayston for cropt, seventeen hundred and thretty-eight years, in which the meal laid into the garnel is allowed, with the coals laid into the place of Ochiltree. Therefore, I discharge the said year's rent; as witness my hand, at Ochiltree, the Twenty-seventh day of October, Seventeen hundred and thretty-nyne years.
> J. Gairdner

General Roy's map of 1747 includes a number of farms that had disappeared by the time the Ordnance Survey made their maps in 1856. These include Parkend (near Corselet), Tarbeghill (near Tarbeg), Hags (near Lessnessock), Fauldhead (near Ravenscroft), Auchingee (near Ravenscroft), Thornyside (near Reidston), Dickstown (near Drongan Mains), Peeshill (near Mill o' Shield), Glengibber (near Treesmax), Windyhills (near Drumsmudden), Kerrstown (near Treesmax), Boghead (near Knockshiffnock), and Barebelly (near North Palmerston).

Farm houses at this time were meagre buildings, little better than those of the cottar in the villages. They were 'built of rough whin stones, with clay as mortar, and roofs of thatch. In many cases the fire was in the centre of the floor, with an opening in the roof to let out the smoke; the floors being of earth, and the windows very small'. David Rowan recalls the farms of his childhood in the latter years of the eighteenth century:

> There was no green crops nor sown grasses; no vegetables but green kail; oats, bere or barley, and beans and peas were the cereals. Of turnips, carrots, cabbages, cauliflowers, apples, pears, plums, cherries, gooseberries, or strawberries there were none. Potatoes became common only towards the end of the century. Tea is a modern luxury. There were no carts. Successive crops of oats were taken from the same field as long as it continued to produce anything beyond the seed sown, after which it was allowed to remain perfectly sterile. The cattle were starved in the winter, and when spring arrived could scarcely rise without assistance. They were often incapable of performing the ordinary function of their nature.

The agricultural revolution took place in the second half of the eighteenth century, at which time many of the older holdings were merged together to form larger farms. A lot of rural steadings were demolished at this period. Similarly, the old small fields were merged into larger fields, or else unfenced areas of ground were enclosed for the first time. The landowners were often keen to carry out these improvements, for it showed that they were progressive, and also the new farms were more profitable. To encourage tenants, leases were usually now of nineteenth years extent, allowing farmers longer to work their farm, and see the benefit of any improvements that they made. In addition, landowners offered inducements to the new tenants to enclose their property, straighten fences and plant trees and hedges. An example of this is found in the tack of nineteen years from the Earl of Glencairn to Andrew MacCowan of the farms of Burnockmiln and Hillhead:

> … the said Earle [of Glencairn] shall be obliged to allow the Expence of lnclosing out of the said Andrew his Rent or advance the same, the said Andrew being obliged on the said allowance or advance to pay at the rate of six per cent tor the same yearly and his Receipt thereof shalt be sufficient for appertaining the money Extent of the said money for inclosing, and the said Andrew shall be obliged to make the Dykes sufficiently Finuble at the sight of two skilled men one whereof to be chosen by each partie, and also shalt be obliged to take care of and preserve the Hedges, and plant Trees in the Hedge Rows and prune and take care of the same, The Earl furnishing young trees for planting and to Leave the whole in good condition and sufficiently Finuble [protected?] at his Removal and the said Andrew shall be obliged to straight Marches with his neighbours when required, He choosing one of the Judges for straighting the same, and the said Andrew obliges him not to keep any more sheep in the winter than he does in the summer and to answer to the said Earle, his Barren Courts, and obey the acts thereof…

Tenancies on the farms often lasted only for a fairly short period, farmers moving on in a regular basis. Some families remained on the same farms for generations, however, an example being the Sloans, who spent five generations as tenants on Plotcock farm up to 1905, when Hugh Sloan moved to Carbello farm, Auchinleck parish. Family tradition claimed that the Sloans of Plotcock were a branch of the Sloans of Cawhillan, and took on the tenancy at Plotcock around 1695, remaining for around 210 years.

Palmerston farm was tenanted by the Duncan family for almost four hundred years. The family initially took on Finlayston, which at the time included the lesser farms of Netherton of Finlayston, North Palmerston, South Palmerston, Stamley and Barebelly. The Duncan family appear to have moved around each of these tenancies, various sons occupying the farms for a period of time. In 1758 they gave up the lease to all but North Palmerston and Barebelly. At the time, the rental of this farm was £10 14s 6d, compared to £14 payable for the same property plus Finlayston, Netherton and South Palmerston in 1714. By 1879 the rental of the farm was in the region of £90. The eighth generation of Duncans took over in 1928, however by that time the family had purchased the farm from the Marquis of Bute. The family have remained in possession for another century.

A number of other long tenancies existed in the parish. At High Carston, the Murrays were tenants for many years. An Ayrshire cow, 'County Maggie' was bred there by John Murray (1804-1903). It was walked to Ayr, taking two days to reach the town, for show, where it won its class. The Duke of Buccleuch offered £80 for it, but he refused to sell. Various other cattle won at the Highland show, and John Murray was noted judge at the Highland and Royal shows.

10.1 Lease of Carston farm from Earl of Glencairn to Hugh Murray
(Author's Collection)

Sometimes tenants were evicted from their properties against their will. An example was George Douglas Brown, who was removed from Drumsmudden in 1892 by the landlord. He had been the tenant for 32 years, and the only real reason for evicting him was his age – 82 at the time. To show support for Brown, 'and the feeling and indignation for such an injustice, on the 18th March upwards of 100 people proceeded with torch-light to a field on Drumsmudden farm, carrying the effigy of a gentleman whom they named a "Scotch Landlord's Patent Evicting Machine," where they erected a large bonfire, the object of which, the chairman of the meeting said, was to show our respect and heartfelt sympathy for Mr Brown'.

There are various glimpses of how agriculture was practised in the parish at different times through the centuries. In 1778 Andrew Wight compiled a couple of volumes of the *Present State of Husbandry in Scotland*, in which he refers to farming on Drongan estate. Wight passed from Cumnock towards Ayr, and en route passed over the heights of Killoch, which he described as being:

> ...exposed to stormy weather, a poor thin Moorish soil, and little done to make it better. In the midst of a scene so dispiriting, I was refreshed by the inclosures of Drongan. Perceiving the hand of an intelligent and bold enterpriser, I learned that all was done by Mr Smith, whom I unluckily missed. The soil cannot be boasted of; but this gentleman, by a singular effort of genius and application, has made a wonderful change. I begged of him in a letter to favour the public with particulars. His answer follows:

Drongan, Sept. 3, 1778.
I had some time ago the pleasure of receiving a letter from you. I am sorry I was so unlucky as to be from home when you intended me the honour of a visit; but, had you examined more particularly the state of my farm, and manner of cultivation, you perhaps would not have had so high an opinion of my knowledge as a farmer as you seem to have at present; though it is certain my farms wears a very different aspect now from what it did in the year 1770, being

10.2 Harvesting Ryegrass Seed at Clydenoch *(Author's Collection)*

the first season I had it in my power to get any quantity of manure brought to it worth mentioning, on account of having no made road till that time; and as, since that time, I have had too many things to do to attend to the minutiae of farming, my methods of cultivation have been very simple. In the first place, most parts of my land were outfield long rested, at least fifty years, and covered with a mixture of short flowering heath, bent and spret, in which case my way has been to lay on the sward at the rate of 160 bolls of five Winchester bushels of lime in powder per acre; sometimes more, but never less on old rested land. But though I say at the rate of five Winchester bushels of powdered lime to the boll, I do not mean that my lime is reduced to powder before it is laid on the land, as I always lay it on so soon as I can from the kiln, and it is often too much slaked by the weather before I can get it led out. This lime I sometimes let ly on the ground three years before ploughing, as I am convinced the longer it lies the better, and never plough any that has not lain at least one year, unless some small part of a field that has not been finished for want of lime, or some other circumstance. From that land I commonly take three crops of oats running, the last always the best; and I always find the crops best where the lime has lain longest on the sward, but most remarkably so in the first crop. After the three crops of oats, I generally sow gray pease; but, as the soil and climate are unfriendly, it is frequently late in the season before I can sow them. I seldom have many pease, but always a great quantity of straw, equal to any crops of hay I can expect; so that I do not think myself disappointed. After the pease I sow bear, with about eighteen bolls of red and white clover, and three bushels of ryegrass to the acre, giving betwixt forty and fifty double carts of dung to the acre, and two or three ploughings, as the season, and my other operations, will permit. This is my method when the land is well swarded, and the ridges narrow, and of course, flat or even, so that I can easily make them straight, without burying any of the manure; but, when the ridges are broad and raised in the middle, or any bare places that have been made so by the storms, I then summer fallow the land, if I may use that expression, before I lay on the lime; but it almost as properly deserves the name of winter fallow; for I give it the first ploughing in the winter, when, on account of the stiffness of the sward and bent roots, I am obliged to take as large a furrow as four oxen or four good horses can draw, to make it turn over.

In that state it lies all next summer, the following winter and spring; for, was it to be attempted sooner, which I have done, no plough, with ever so sharp irons, could cut it to plough it cross; as ploughing it in the same direction as first time, before the furrows get time to grow together, would make every one of them turn over whole. In the course of the second summer, I get it reduced to a proper tilth, the ridges made straight, and the lime, about 100 or 120 bolls an acre, laid on, and sometimes spread and ploughed in, and sometimes I do not get the whole lime on until I get it on in time of frost, and then use it in the same way as when limed on the sward; which method I rather prefer, though my experience is not such as enables me to decide which is best. I have sometimes tried pease first after fallowing and liming, but never had a crop equal to the seed and labour, allowing only for one ploughing; and some gentlemen not far from me have tried it with no better success. I also sometimes give dung for the pease, after three crops of oats, and make bear afterwards without any, which answers tolerably well; but I think it best to give the dung to the bear.

You will be perhaps be surprised that I mention nothing of wheat, beans, and barley. I have tried them all; and though I have had tolerable crops, yet I am convinced, that, in such a climate as Ayrshire, oats, gray pease, and bear are more profitable. I should have mentioned that my land is generally a strong red clay, besides lime, I have laid on, at different times, 300 or 400 tons of sea-shells, at the rate of 15 tons to the acre; but I think lime answers fully as well; and on one field of twenty-one acres, after treating it as already mentioned with the bear crops, I harrowed in 860 barrels of horn shavings, and had a very indifferent crop. What effect they may have when the field is broke up again, I know not; but I shall not be in haste to purchase any more of them. Thus far I have sat down, in a very bad forenoon, to answer your letter; and if you have the occasion to be in this country, will be happy to see you at this house, I am, &c.

P.S. Since the year 1769 l have laid on near 100,000 bolls of lime.

Soon after, in 1792, Rev William Thomson gives a short description of the state of agriculture in Ochiltree parish. He wrote that 'the land is mostly employed in tillage, and feeding black cattle, there being only 3 or 4 sheep farms upon the higher ground towards the south. The farmers chiefly cultivate and depend on an oat crop; they sow also a little bear, but no wheat or rye. The land consists of a strong clay soil, spouty in some places, but producing good crops. Black cattle thrive very well, and considerable quantities of butter and cheese are made for sale.'

In 1797-98 a Farm Horse Tax was applied across the country. A list of all horses in the parish was compiled, for which two shillings was payable for each animal. The roll found that there were 244 horses in the parish, of which 210 were liable to be taxed. The remaining 34 horses weren't liable. The total raised by this tax was £21. The list of farms and 'Masters and Mistresses Names and Designations' makes interesting reading, and from the roll we find that Rev William Thompson, the minister, had one horse. John Tennant of Auchinbay had seven horses, as did Robert Smith in Barlosh. These were the farmers with the most horses. Farmers with six horses were William Sloan in Plotcock, John Steil in Tarelgin, William Mearns in Auchencloigh, John Colville in Bardarroch, George Muir in Lessnessock, David Guthrie in Drumsmudden, John Hood in Hoodston of Trabboch, George Reid in Barquharrie and William Sloan in Gargowan. All other farmers had fewer than six horses.

In 1811 William Aiton published his important *General View of the Agriculture of the County of Ayr*. He makes a number of references to Ochiltree within the volume, from which we can assemble a bit more detail on agriculture in the parish. He makes reference to the largest farm in the county at the time, Girvanmains, at 500 acres, which was tenanted by John Tennant. He goes on to report that Tennant also 'holds two or three large farms on the estate of Ochiltree'. Aiton also mentions Mungo Smith of Drongan, who, 'by [his] persevering industry … an extensive tract of that soil [clay], round his house, has been converted into loam; and much more of his lands is under a train of improvement, which if persisted in, will change them from stubborn clay, into rich loam—A change the more meritorious, when it is considered, that Mr. Smith's estate is farther from lime, than any other estate in the county of Ayr.'

In the first half of the nineteenth century farmhouses in the parish were generally roofed in thatch. A few had been improved by having new roofs of slate, regarded as far superior, as they were less likely to house mice or rats. The principal produce in the parish was white crop, with pease and beans. There was also some green crop grown, and hay. In 1837 there were 1,043 cows in the parish, 140 fat cattle, 1,089 young cattle, 3,448 sheep and 167 pigs.

In 1862, William Wilson, farmer in Laigh Tarbeg, gave a short speech on the state of farming in Ochiltree in centuries past. He noted that 'then, only the crofts, or strips of land near the houses were cultivated, and the manure was carried out in baskets on the backs of the farmers' wives. Potatoes for long remained a rarity, being used at but two meals in the year – at the kirn and on New Year's Day – while half a dozen for seed were suspended in an old stocking above the fire-place. The first turnips grown in the parish were on the farm of Ochiltree Mains.'

In 1837 it was noted that there were 14 proprietors in the parish who owned lands raising over £50 in yearly rent. There were 101 farmers who held leases on their farms. A total of 121 families found their principal income from agriculture. Of the total acreage of the parish, it was reckoned that around one third of this (5,145 acres) was hill pasture, woodland or waste ground. It was thought that around 1,000 acres of this could be brought into cultivation or tillage, but that the cost was prohibitive. Land was rented at 10 shillings to £2 per acre for arable ground. Over the whole parish the average rent was 15 shillings per acre.

10.3 Knockshiffnock farm in 1966 *(Author's Collection)*

In 1837 men-servants working on farms earned around £12 10s per annum, whereas female servants earned around £7. In addition, the servants were fed and received lodgings on the farm. Day labourers were paid 1s 8d without food in the summer, and 1s 3d per day in the winter months.

Most of the farms in the parish kept sheep or cattle. The sheep were mainly black-faced, with some smaller herds of Leicester, Bakewell, Southdown and Cheviot breeds. At Burnton farm there was a herd of black Egyptian sheep, noted for their wool. Cattle grazed tended to be Ayrshires, and there were improvements being made in the milk returns. Alexander Baird was a cattle dealer in 1850, based at Sinclairston.

The buying and selling of grain took place over the years. In 1851 Mathew Bryson is listed as a grain-dealer in the village.

John Tennant of Creoch was one of the first farmers to introduce a new method of draining his fields. He was one of the first to use what was known as furrow-draining. Trenches about twenty inches in depth were dug, and these were part-filled with small broken stone. The soil was replaced over these, the gap between the stones forming space where the water could drain more readily. About one hundred acres of land were drained this way and it was soon noticed that the crops grown thereon were usually better and ripened earlier.

After the First World War many estates and landowners across the country sold off their properties in order to pay off death duties and other debts. This made a significant difference to the agricultural face of the parish, for in November 1919 the 4th Marquis of Bute sold many farms on Dumfries House Estate. Within Ochiltree parish twenty-six farms were sold by the estate to the sitting tenants. Other farms followed. Ochiltree Mains, for example, was sold in 1923 to the tenant, Hugh Brown, for £3,000. The price was determined by multiplying the annual rent by twenty.

The new owner-occupiers of the farms were keen to improve them, but often things beyond their control prevented this. In 1924 there was a major outbreak of Foot and Mouth disease in cattle across the country. Among the farms affected was Slatehole, where in February 1924 it was among the first in Ayrshire to have its stock of cattle slaughtered.

When the New Statistical Account was produced in 1950, it was noted that there were 57 farms in the parish, those on the lower ground averaging about 130 acres each. In addition to this there were five small holdings of ten acres of less, and eight large farms in the southern, higher parts of the parish, Auchencloigh being the largest, at almost 2,000 acres. Of these farms, there were only two which were not owner-occupied. Each farm had on average 35 to 40 dairy cattle, most of the Ayrshire breed, but one farm had Friesian cows. An average farm of 130 acres was reckoned to have 28 acres of oats, five acres of beans and oats, five acres of turnips, one acre of marrow stem kale and one acre of potatoes. The remainder, about ninety acres, were pasture.

At Lessnessock, Adam Wilson Montgomerie was awarded the OBE on 1 January 1945 for his services to the promotion and export of the Ayrshire breed of cattle. At one time Ayrshire cattle from Lessnessock held the world record price. The herd had been established in 1860. Montgomerie himself was born on 24 August 1873 at Hall of Caldwell, Neilston, and lived at Lessnessock with his parents. He died on 18 March 1955 at Maybole.

By the twenty-first century, there had been considerable decline in agriculture, and many farmers were struggling to survive. A number sold off their ground to adjoining farmers, the steadings being converted into private houses or else redeveloped as groups of cottages. One such example was Barlosh steading, divided into houses in 2004. In 2007 proposals were made to divide the lands of Bonnyton farm into eight 'Lowland Crofts', but this did not materialise.

Many farmers have branched out into other areas of commerce in order to support their farms. At Auchinbay, in 2020 David Morton introduced a self-service milk supply and farm produce shop.

Ochiltree Farmers' Society was founded in 1846 by 28 members and soon organised an annual show, the first held in April 1847. One show had to be cancelled due to rinderpest. It was later determined that the date of the show should be

10.4 Carston farm in 1966 *(Author's Collection)*

the Wednesday nearest 15 May. The location for the show was often close to the village, to attract as many people as possible. It has been held in various fields around the villages, including Ochiltree Mains, Ochiltree House, etc. Connected with the annual show was a horse race, though entries at this varied over the years. In 1874 there were only two horses taking part, the winner being that owned by Mr Wyllie. In 1883 there were more entries. By 1890 there were 55 members. In the late nineteenth century, the society also organised an annual ploughing match in February, or thereabouts. In 1947 a new ladies' committee was established, and in that year handicrafts and baking was displayed for competition. Long-serving secretaries included John Murray of Low Carston (1846-1878) and Robert Wilson in Auchencloigh, who served from 1878 until at least 1903.

Ochiltree Agricultural Discussion Society was founded in 1898, the only one of its kind in the district. Early presidents included Thomas Drysdale and Adam Montgomerie. In addition to meetings where agricultural papers were discussed, the society had an annual ball. The society may have only lasted a few years.

Smaller scale market gardening took place in Ochiltree for some time. The Samson family were nurserymen for many years, their nursery being located opposite the old kirkyard, in a piece of ground known as the 'Tenrood'. In 1725 the business was operated by John Samson, listed as 'gardiner' in the birth notice of his son. He was married to someone with the initials M. M. The business was taken over by John Samson, younger. This John Samson died in June 1793, aged 73, having had married Jane Good (died December 1767 aged 45). The second son, Thomas Samson, became an acquaintance of Burns, moved to Kilmarnock where he set up a market garden and seed merchants' business of his own.

CHAPTER ELEVEN

RECREATION AND LEISURE

Many of Ochiltree's societies are long-lived. Probably the oldest known club to continue in the village is Ochiltree Curling Club. It was founded on 9 February 1841 by the merger of four smaller clubs. These were the Belston Curling Club, Burnock Water Curling Club, Boswell Curling Club and the Killochside Curling Club. Initially it was referred to as Ochiltree Senior Curling Club. Members had to be nominated by two others, pay an annual subscription of one penny, and own two curling stones. The annual general meeting was held in the first week of November, and this was announced in the parish church from 1849 until 1884, after which postcards were sent out. The meetings were initially held in the hall of John Lammie's inn, but in 1849 was held in the schoolhouse. In 1852 it was held in Andrew Muir's inn, then randomly within other inns, such as James Findlay's in 1855 and then Hugh Morton's. In 1909 it was agreed that the meeting should rotate around the four inns that existed in the village at that time. In 1918 the annual general meeting did not take place due to the influenza epidemic that was spreading across Europe.

From 1865 Ochiltree Curling Club played at a rink known as 'Palmerston Flush', or Palmerston Loch, which was located immediately west of South Palmerston farm. The creation of a pond here was arranged 'at considerable expense' by the factor of Dumfries House Estate. It was given to the club to use, so long as they dammed the pond on 1 November each year, then drained the water on 1 March. The club was responsible for keeping the embankment and the dam in good repair. Being almost five hundred feet above sea level helped the water to be colder and more likely to freeze. The club presented the factor with a pair of curling stones with engraved silver handles as a token of thanks. Further improvements were made in 1883 when the embankments were repaired.

In 1852 the winning curler was presented with a curling stone. A Parish Medal had been presented for annual competition, as well as a silver cup, presented by James Wilson in Finlayston. Captain H. G. Fallowfield of Ochiltree House presented a Jubilee Medal for annual competition and in 1888 presented a second medal to the Junior section of the club for competition on Palmerston Loch. The club also held the Boswell Medal for conpetition. J. J. Probert presented a jug for competition in 1904, and Mrs Angus's Cup and Barometer were competed for in the early 1900s. A Centenary Medal was presented by the president in 1941.

In 1891 an Ice Stones House was erected at Palmerston Loch by the club, costing £5 12s 6d, in which the club's stones could be stored. Some years, perhaps depending on the amount of ice available, the club played at Belston Loch. In 1932 the Robb family at Palmerston announced that they were no longer willing to allow the club the use of the loch, and a new curling pond was created near to the Ochiltree Tileworks.

11.1 Eglinton Jug - the Morton Rink *(Mungo Howat)*

The club have won the leading Ayrshire curling trophy, the Eglinton Jug, on a number of occasions. The silver jug, one of the most valuable trophies in the country, was presented to the Ayrshire curlers in 1851 by Archibald, Earl of Eglinton and Winton. Members were encouraged to take part, but originally they had to fund their own entry fee. By 1897 five shillings of club funds were allocated towards this, paying for the club's most successful rink to take part. In 1958 Mungo Jamieson's rink came second in the competition. In 1962 the club won the trophy for the first time, with the unique fact that the players in the rink were all Morton brothers – William of Gargowan (skip), Hugh (Sawmill), David (Hazelbank Cottage) and John (Broom Crescent). They beat J. P. Gibb's Fairywell rink by 10 - 8.

It was the brothers' fourth attempt at the trophy. On 28 October 1966 the Ochiltree Number 2 Rink won the jug, defeating a team from Sorn. The rink comprised Mr Willie and Mrs Nessie Mair, Alex Brown and Jack Brown. In 1979 the club won the title again, the rink comprising George Connell, David Brown, Jack Brown and John Caldwell. In 1981 the same four won the trophy again. Following each occasion, the club held a celebration dinner. As late as 1941, when the Centenary Medal was presented, it was stipulated that it should be played for outdoors, up to 15 February, after which indoor ice could be used. In 1944 four nights were booked at the indoor rink in Ayr, and in 1950 the full season was played indoors, after which outdoor curling has died. On 12 February 2016 a celebration dinner was held to mark the club's 175th anniversary. The first lady president was appointed in 1976 (Nessie Mair). Other presidents of the club included James Lyons (1883), J. D. Boyd (1904), Edward Holmes of the Crown Inn (1906), A. Howat (1921), and R. W. Martin (1941). The club still exists, playing at Ayr Ice Rink.

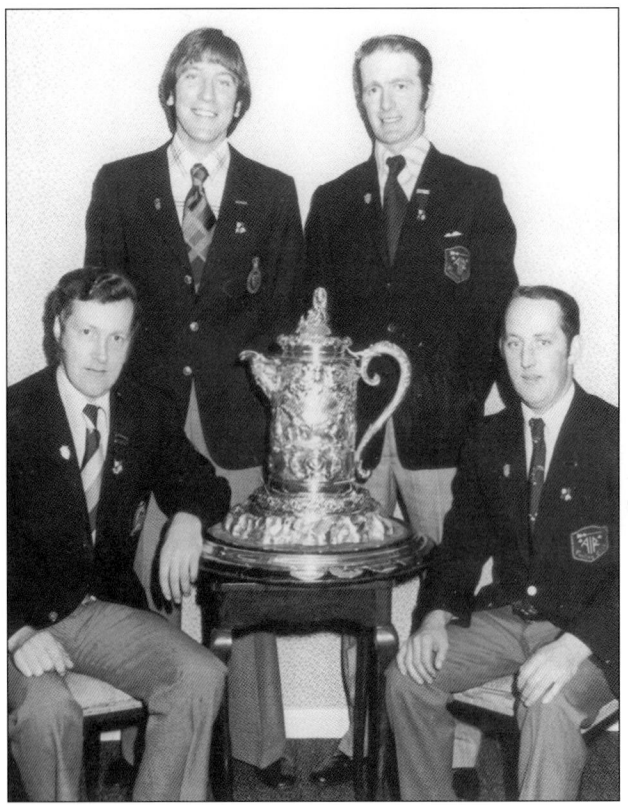

11.2 Eglinton Jug winners *(Mungo Howat)*

Information on the other curling clubs in the parish is mostly lost, however we do have a few details. In 1882 Ochiltree Water of Lugar Curling Club existed, John Stewart being president. They competed in the Eglinton Jug tournament as usual that year. The Killochside Curling Club was formed in January 1881, the first president being William Wallace in Killoch. The club played on a new pond created at Killochside for a silver medal.

The sport of bowling was for many years popular in the village. In the early twentieth century bowlers used a field belonging to M. Hannah, but in 1923 they started to look for a site on which to create their own bowling green. The plans were dropped in 1924. The present Ochiltree Bowling

Club was founded in 1980 and plays on a green located on the site of the football pitch at the Kay Park in Mill Street. The president for the first three years was R. Grierson.

Drongan Miners' Welfare Bowling Club was founded in 1960 and survived until around 2016. It leased the land from Cumnock & Doon Valley District Council from 5 January 1995 at a rental of £500 per annum. In 2002 the club purchased the land from the council. After the club folded the green was converted into a small football pitch and the clubhouse was converted into The Boolers, a community hub, opening on 19 October 2019.

An old Scots past-time was handball, which was usually played against a wall. Ochiltree took part in the sport in the 1870s.

In 1923 two new badminton courts were laid out on the corner of a field immediately behind the U. F. Manse, belonging to Robert Lennox of Hill farm. Soon after, in July 1923, Ochiltree Badminton Club was formed. Ochiltree Tennis Club was formed in 1927 and by 1928 had its own tennis courts laid out over the fence from the U. F. Church Manse. The new courts were opened on 4 May 1928 by Colonel William Collins, of Grey Gables, Monkton, and his two sons, Scottish tennis champions Ian and Billy, who demonstrated their skills on the court with Hon. Miss Corbett and Mrs W. A. R. Collins.

Football has been a major form of recreation in the parish since the mid nineteenth century. Around 1878 a senior club called Ochiltree Football Club existed, playing in the Ayrshire Cup. References to the club continue until around 1881, when it probably folded. A public meeting held on 2 July 1909 was called with the intention of forming a new football and recreation club. At the start of the twentieth century, there was a football team in the village known as Ochiltreeonians Football Club. They played at juvenile level and existed in 1917. On 19 March 1919 a meeting was held at the Smiddy with the intention of forming yet another new football club. The first president was William MacCurdie. Around 1950 Kay Rovers Juvenile Football Club was formed, playing in the public park.

Drongan Rangers F. C. played in the junior leagues. In 1902 they won the Land o' Burns Cup. The Drongan Football Club existed for a number of years, often referred to as 'The Buffs'. In 1917-18 the club won the Ayrshire Consolation Cup, one of only fifteen clubs still operating during the war.

Drongan Carson Thistle Football Club existed at the start of the twentieth century. It seems to have folded around 1910, for the former secretary, Michael Colrain, wrote to the Scottish Referee in 1911 indicating that there were efforts taking place to restart it. According to Colrain, 'Carson Thistle at one time was one of the best junior combinations in the country'.

Drongan United Amateur Football Club were founded in 1960. On 11 May 1985 the club beat Motherwell Miners A. F. C. two goals to nil to win the Scottish Amateur Tennent Caledonian Cup at the final played at Hampden Park in Glasgow.

Scoring for Drongan were Lex O'Hara and Martin Lynch. They won the Ayrshire Cup in the same season. The club were the Ayrshire Amateur Football Association Division 2A Champions 2018/19, moving to the First Division the following season. Drongan Academicals Boys Club formed a football team in 1987.

A number of residents of the parish went on to play at higher level in football. John Graham (d. 1927) played for Annbank and also Preston North End. Whilst playing with Preston he was part of the team that won the English Cup in 1882. In Preston his demeanour was such that he was known as 'Preston's Safety Valve'. In 1884 he was capped for Scotland. He later returned to Ayrshire and worked at the Barony Colliery. Alex Linwood has already been mentioned with reference to Drumsmudden.

Kirk Broadfoot (b. 8 August 1984) was brought up in Drongan and played for Coyle Thistle as a boy. He played for St Mirren from 2002-2007, followed by Rangers for five years. He then moved to Blackpool (2012-2014), Rotherham United (2014-2017), Kilmarnock (2017-2019), St Mirren (2019-2020) and Kilmarnock (2020-). He was capped for Scotland four times, between 2008-2010, scoring one goal against Iceland in 2008.

The sport of quoiting was at one time very popular in the parish. At the turn of the century this was played in a field adjoing the Star Inn. In 1912 John Stewart, landlord at the Star Inn, presented a new trophy and a prize of £1 for the sport. Ochiltree Quoiting Club was formed on 12 July 1913 at the Star Inn, the first president being John S. Duncan. In 1916 there were sixteen entrants for the cup. In 1917 the Stewart Cup had 49 entries.

During the miners' strike of 1926, the idle workers were active in relaying the five quoiting rinks at Stewart's Green. In addition to improving the rinks, the men also built seating for spectators. The Ochiltree club folded during the war but was revived soon after.

At Taiglum a quoiting pitch was located behind the co-operative shop. The Killoch Welfare Quoiting Club existed from 1968-1975. There was also a quoiting rink at Coalhall at one time.

In the twentieth century cycling became a major past-time and sport. Numerous clubs were formed, and in Drongan the Arran View Cycling Club was established. The club was disbanded in 1936. Another Drongan cycling club was named the Ayrshire Clarion Club (existing around 1936).

Many of the farmers and their sons took part in annual ploughing competitions. Ochiltree ploughing match was held annually for many years around 1880. Also very successful in the 1960s and 1970s was the Drongan Pigeon Club. Drongan Traditional Taekwondo Club was formed in the 1950s and produced over twenty British champions.

At Drongan the Coyle Angling Club fished the Water of Coyle. In 1993 the Coyle Water Fishery was created at Shieldmains farm. A large lagoon, filled with water, was created in a meander of the Water of Coyle, which was stocked with fish. Short piers allowed fishermen to try their luck in catching them. This was later taken over by the Mauchline and Ballochmyle Angling Club. At a later date a café was added. From 2017-19 Coyle Water Fisheries Ltd. was established by Mushfiq Ahmed to operate it.

In 1857 the Forget-me-not Society was established in the village whereby friends and acquaintances belonging to the village would meet up and enjoy a talk from an invited speaker, plus hospitality. The principal founders were Professor James Morton of Glasgow, David Rowan, who lived in Greenock, William Lennox, an ex-soldier with the 79th Highlanders and Superintendent of Kyle Union Poorhouse in Ayr, and John MacRae, headmaster of Newton Academy in Ayr. The group awarded prizes to schoolchildren in Ochiltree, notably the annual dux medals. The society survived for a number of years, with events held in Morton's Inn in August 1864, when William Lennox spoke, and August 1867 when William Stevenson was the speaker. The society appears to have become defunct thereafter, perhaps due to the popularity of the following organisation.

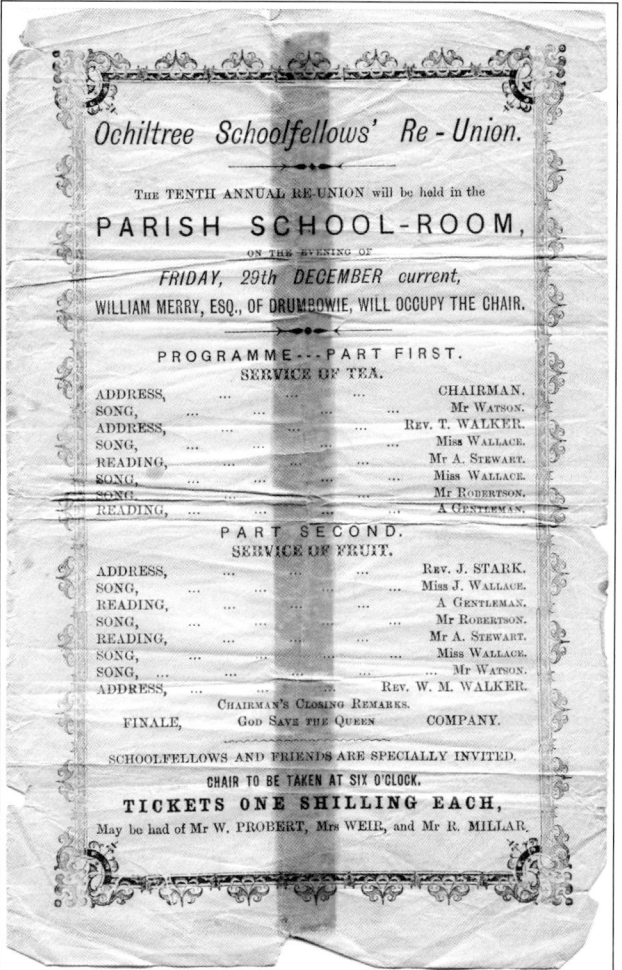

11.3 Programme for fourth Schoolfellows' Reunion 1871 *(Mungo Howat)*

This long-established institution is the Ochiltree Schoolfellows' Reunion. The association was founded in 1862, and took over the presentation of the dux prize to the school. In 1864 they also donated prizes to the Ochiltree Rifle Corps for a shooting competition, held at Palmerston.

The first annual dinner took place in the Free Church schoolroom on 30 December 1862. The date was selected as a 'large ... proportion of the young leave home in pursuits of a literary, or a mercantile character; and who, on their return to spend the Christmas holiday, are thus doubly glad to have the opportunity of shaking hands with most of their former associates'. At the first meeting it was agreed to meet annually, the requirement being that the guest speaker was educated in Ochiltree parish. The meeting continued to meet in the Free Church School until around 1870, when it is known to have been held in the Parochial School. The parochial, or public school remained the normal venue, but at Hogmanay 1908 it was held in Mr Holmes' Hall (Crown Inn) as the school was being rebuilt that year. More recently, the dinner has been held within the British Legion Club, followed by the Bowling Green clubhouse.

The Reunion has taken place every year, including the war years, a guest speaker being invited to reminisce about life in Ochiltree in days' past. In 1923 there were complaints that only farmers were invited to serve on the committee, and as a result only they were in the platform party at the annual dinner. In 1927 one of the farmers who attended the reunion announced that he was wearing the very same pair of trousers that he wore when he first made an appearance at the reunion 54 years earlier. The story was reported in newspapers all over Britain!

Sometimes difficulties occurred which caused the committee some consternation. One happened in 1944 when Mr Probert was asked by a delegation of committee members to supply the whisky and beer for the concert. The minute book reads: 'It was a great surprise to everyone when they returned to the room and told them there was neither Whisky or Beer to be had; it was a serious problem at this time. After discussing it for a few moments, some of the committee agreed to

11.4 Schoolfellows' Reunion - 100th dinner *(Mungo Howat)*

11.5 Ochiltree Schoolfellows' 100th dinner speakers *(Mungo Howat)*

surrender their Ne-erday bottle to uphold the tradition of the Reunion.' Similarly, on 16 January 1945, at the post-reunion committee meeting, the 'committee having made it customary to finish up with a supper and a 'sing-song' and a 'wee bit hawf', but for the first time in the history of the reunion, they were to have no whisky from Mr Probert, but to the astonishment of the committee, Mr H. Brown stated he had spoken to Mr Dykes of the Commercial who said he could manage to supply the needful, so it was agreed to transfer across the road and hold the supper on the following Tuesday evening at 5 p.m., the farmers agreeing to supply roasted hens and scones if the villagers supplied the dishes and knives and forks, a very good offer. This was by far the best meeting of the 81st Reunion and we were very reluctant to stop on the call of 'time up'.

Chairmen, or speakers, at the re-unions over the years have been:

1	1862	Robert Brown, teacher, Gartmore (30 December 1862)
2	1863	
3	1864	John Boyd, headmaster of Free Church Institution, Dingwall (30 December 1864)
4	1865	
5	1866	Rev John Sloan (28 January 1866)
6	1867	
7	1868	Rev Thomas Walker, Dalmellington
8	1869	James Hutchison, Kirkoswald (31 December 1869)

9	1870	Thomas Gemmell, banker, Girvan (30 December 1870)
10	1871	William Merry of Drumbowie (29 December 1871)
11	1872	
12	1873	
13	1874	
14	1875	
15	1876	
16	1877	
17	1878	
18	1879	
19	1880	
20	1881	Rev Matthew Dickie, Sanquhar (30 December 1881)
21	1882	Alexander Murdoch, Gallowlea, Paisley (December 1882)
22	1883	
23	1884	
24	1885	
25	1886	
26	1887	John MacMillan, Glasgow
27	1888	
28	1889	Robert S. Steel, merchant, Glasgow (December 1889)
29	1890	William Murdoch, merchant, Glasgow (31 December 1890)
30	1891	J. S. MacLennan, schoolmaster, Glasgow (31 December 1891)
31	1892	
32	1893	Jacob Sloan, Clydenoch (December 1893)
33	1894	M. M. Osborne, editor, *Kilmarnock Standard* (31 December 1894)
34	1895	
35	1896	
36	1897	
37	1898	Thomas Wallace, Edinburgh (30 December 1898)
38	1899	
39	1900	
40	1901	
41	1902	
42	1903	Robert Miller, Sen., Ayr (30 December 1903)
43	1904	Robert Miller Sen., Ayr, (December 1904)
44	1905	
45	1906	James Montgomerie, Tarelgin
46	1907	
47	1908	Hugh Sloan, Carbello (31 December 1908)
48	1909	John MacCosh CA, Glasgow (31 December 1909)

46	1909	Alexander Green, headmaster, Sinclairston Public School
49	1910	William Sloan, Shawsmuir, Closeburn (30 December 1910)
50	1911	M. O. Osborne, editor, *Kilmarnock Standard*
51	1912	
50	1913	John Jamieson, Langholm
51	1914	John Brown, Garleffan, Cumnock (January 1915)
52	1915	
53	1916	
54	1917	Alexander Murdoch MA, Paisley (January 1918)
55	1918	James Hillhouse, solicitor (January 1919)
56	1919	John P. Smith, Thirdpart
57	1920	John Ferguson
58	1921	Peter Duncan, Ayr
59	1922	David Weir MRCVS, Ayr
60	1923	William Kelly, Ayr (January 1924)
61	1924	William Wyllie, Ayr
62	1925	David Millar, poet, Ayr
63	1926	Jacob S. Murray, Dalgig, New Cumnock
64	1927	Quintin Aird FEIS, Paisley
65	1928	John P. Dickson JP, editor, *Kilmarnock Standard* (31 December 1928)
66	1929	Andrew Sloan (31 December 1929)
67	1930	John Urquhart MA, Dumbarton (31 December 1930)
68	1931	John Thom, Black Bull Hotel, Cumnock (31 December 1931)
69	1932	William L. Ferguson, East Cairnweil, Stranraer (30 December 1932)
70	1933	William Montgomerie, Castle Douglas (1 January 1934)
71	1934	Mungo L. Jamieson, Langholm (31 December 1934)
72	1935	James Kirk, Kirkpatrick, Closeburn (31 December 1935)
73	1936	John N. Watson, Tarelgin (31 December 1936)
74	1937	John Gemmell, Steelpark (31 December 1937)
75	1938	David S. Taylor, Craiglea, Ayr (30 December 1938)
76	1939	Hugh Brown Sr., Ochiltree Mains (1 January 1940)
77	1940	Alex Stewart, Ochiltree (31 December 1940)
78	1941	Mungo L. Jamieson, Langholm
79	1942	John Baird, Treesmax (31 December 1942)
80	1943	Charles Murdoch, Post Office, Ochiltree (31 December 1943)
81	1944	James A. Watson, High Tarbeg (1 January 1945)
82	1945	Mathew Auld, Glenhead, Ardrossan, ex-Elymains, (31 December 1945)
83	1946	Hugh Dick, Ochiltree

84	1947	James B. Anderson, Riccarton, poet – 'Knockarton' (31 December 1947)
85	1948	James S. Henderson, Schoolmaster, Ochiltree (31 December 1948)
86	1949	William Dick, Tollcross, Glasgow (30 December 1949)
87	1950	David Brown, Plotcock (1 January 1951)
88	1951	David Orr, Galashiels (31 December 1951)
89	1952	James K. Murdoch OBE, High Corton (31 December 1952)
90	1953	Mungo Howat, Auchencloigh (31 December 1953)
91	1954	Alex MacLaren, Hawkhead House Farm, Paisley (31 December 1954)
92	1955	John Burton, Moat Toll
93	1956	Edward Connelly, Hamilton (31 December 1956)
94	1957	John Duncan, North Palmerston (27 December 1957)
95	1958	D. Smith, Ayr Road, Cumnock (30 December 1958)
96	1959	Robert Walker, Burnock Street, Ochiltree (30 December 1959)
97	1960	John Reid MA, Schoolmaster (29 December 1960)
98	1961	Dr Alistair Bruce Wallace, Cheltenham (29 December 1961)
99	1962	John Jamieson, Glenhead, Ochiltree (28 December 1962)
100	1963	Hugh D. Brown, Ochiltree Mains (30 December 1963)
101	1964	John Wilson, Waterside Creamery
102	1965	Alan Davidson, Schoolmaster
103	1966	Hugh Morton, Main Street, Ochiltree
104	1967	Robert Lammie, Low Drumore
105	1968	John MacGarvie, Darntaggart
106	1969	John Caldwell, Pennyfadzeoch
107	1970	Dick Wills, Lessnessock
108	1971	Mungo L. Jamieson, Hill of Ochiltree
109	1972	Jim Brown, Digby, Lincolnshire
110	1973	Dr Angus MacLeod, York
111	1974	James Hendry, Butcher, Ochiltree
112	1975	John Murdoch, Barlosh
113	1976	James Wallace, formerly in Clydenoch
114	1977	William Farrow, Dalkeith
115	1978	George Murchie, Massachusetts
116	1979	Mrs Jean Jamieson, Belmont Road, Ayr
117	1980	Jim Brown, Post Office
118	1981	Hamilton Burton, Ayr
119	1982	Alex Brown, Woodleigh
120	1983	J. Graham, Cumnock
121	1984	Mrs Jean Logan, Bargenoch, Ayr

122	1985	D. Watson, Kilmarnock
123	1986	James Watson, Creoch
124	1987	Andrew Niven, Annbank
125	1988	John Fleming, Ochiltree
126	1989	Mrs Jean Murdoch, Ayr
127	1990	Mrs Helen Blythe, Ayr
128	1991	Gordon Anderson, Mill Street, Ochiltree
129	1992	Drew Brown, Coylton
130	1993	Mrs Jean Morrison, Ochiltree
131	1994	John Fleming, Ochiltree
132	1995	Andrew Rankin, Ochiltree
133	1996	James Fitzsimmons, Ochiltree
134	1997	Mrs Nancy Kennedy, Hookhead, Strathaven
135	1998	William Brown, Ochiltree
136	1999	Mervyn Hendry, Dalblair, Cumnock
137	2000	William Mair, Drumfork (1 December 2000)
138	2001	Mrs Nettie Harvey, Steelpark (7 December 2001)
139	2002	Mrs Isabel MacDicken, New Cumnock (6 December 2002)
140	2003	Alexander Black, Irvine (5 December 2003)
141	2004	Tom Bain, Lanarkshire
142	2005	Hugh Brown, Mauchline (2 December 2005)
143	2006	John Reid, ex-headmaster, now resident in Lochmaben
144	2007	Jack Brown, Pointsfield, Slatehole (7 December 2007)
145	2008	Tom Robertson, Drongan (5 December 2008)
146	2009	James Friedlander, Sandwick, Shetland
147	2010	Barbara Weir (nee Corrie), Home Farm, Auchterarder (3 December 2010)
148	2011	Sally Brown, Ochiltree
149	2012	Jean Gemmell, Dumfries
150	2013	Jim Morrison, Auchinleck (6 December 2013)
151	2014	Ian Howat, Ochiltree
152	2015	Helen Welsh, Dunfermline
153	2016	Donald Hendry, Ochiltree
154	2017	Ella Burns, Ayr
155	2018	Allan Hope, Carluke (7 December 2018)
156	2019	David Reid, Ochiltree
157	2020	

In 1862 a number of former Ochiltree residents in Canada decided to form a club in a similar vein to that in Ochiltree. A newspaper report of the time gives a little more information:

It appears that a number of people from Ochiltree and the neighbourhood have been situated for several years at Guelph, Canada West, and are occupied mostly in the farming way. Their farm steadings are placed at such convenient distances from each other that, during the winter season, when little work can be done, they can and do visit each other's houses, and enjoy themselves after the manner of the 'Rockings' so popular in Scotland in the days of yore. Well, those worthy people, hearing of the 'Forget-me-not' Society of Ochiltree, their home feelings swelled up with a warmth known only to Scottish men and Scottish women who have left the dear land of their birth, and settled on some foreign shore, and so they resolved to form a branch 'Forget-me-not' Society in Canada West, and to hold their meetings at the same time – the same day and the same hour – as the parent Society at Ochiltree held theirs, so that they could exchange reminiscences and pledge each other in cups of kindness across the broad Atlantic.

The organisation that was to become the Glasgow Ochiltree Society was founded on 15 October 1860, again in a similar way to the Canadian 'Forget-Me-Not' Society. Initially it was known as the Glasgow-Ochiltree Young Men's Association, but on 29 November 1861 the name was changed to the Burnock Society. The first reunion took place in the Tontine Hotel, Glasgow Cross, with Hugh Howatson presiding and around thirty in attendance. Around 1866 it changed its name to the Glasgow Ochiltree Reunion. This was often later referred to as the Natives of Ochiltree Reunion. The object of the society was 'the maintaining and promoting of good fellowship amongst the young men of Ochiltree and neighbourhood now resident in or connected with Glasgow, and holding an annual meeting to associate with old friends'. In 1877 ladies were allowed to attend the meetings. At a committee meeting on 6 October 1898 there was a proposal to rename the society the Ochiltree and Coylton Reunion, but the motion was later withdrawn.

The first meeting of the Glasgow reunion took place on Friday 30 November 1860 within the Tontine Hotel in Glasgow. Other locations for the dinner included the South Side Assembly Rooms. Initially, the meetings were very successful. Among those giving talks on their home community were James Gibson (d. 1883) in 1883, son of John Gibson, who left Ochiltree and set up a successful potato merchants in the city. At that event over 500 attended. Many of the meetings were held in the Trades Hall, Glassford Street, Glasgow, as in 1898, after which a 'Grand Assembly … with dancing to Mr George McCorquodale's Quadrille Band' took place. However, in 16 October 1899 it was noted that it was 'inadvisable in the meantime to proceed with the arrangements for the Reunion … the committee … have not been able to make ends meet, but on the contrary have been losing money

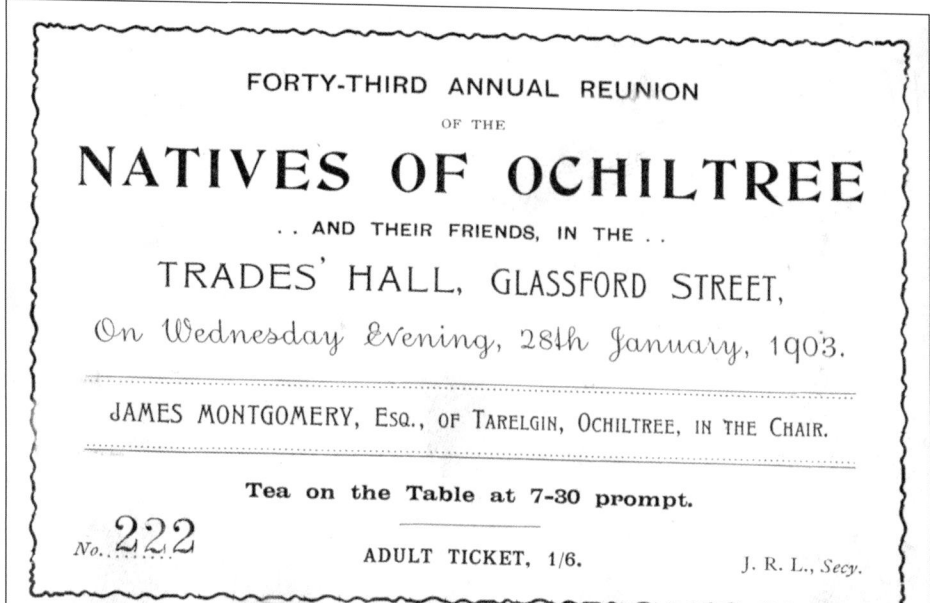

11.6 Ticket for Glasgow Ochiltree Reunion *(Mungo Howat)*

steadily.' A leaflet was issued to possible members to try to drum-up more support. In 1901 there were plans to change the reunion to a conversazione, to be held in Glasgow's Grand Hotel in December. John MacmIllan was to preside, but many of the older members were unhappy at the change and refused to attend. In 1902 the meeting was held in the Trades Hall, and a trip to Ochiltree was held in May. In January 1903 James Montgomerie of Tarelgin proposed changing the name of the society to the Glasgow Ochiltree Society, which was agreed. The society survived for a number of years, still exisiting in 1904.

In addition to the annual reunion, the Glasgow society also had a supper around March time, but in 1900 this was changed to a picnic. These often took place in Ayrshire, with buses booked to take the members around places like Ayr, Alloway, and up to Ochiltree, where the food was supplied by a local inn. Often, on that day, races and games were held on the field at Burnockholm.

Funds from the society were gifted for the erection of a public clock in the village, to be situated at a suitable site near the Cross. When Jacob Sloan of Clydenoch died on 28 October 1913 he left £50 to assist with the erection of the clock, which had been stored at his farm, and which would 'be handed over by my executrix when the clock is erected in a substantial manner and guaranteed by a practical clockmaker to keep good time'. By 1935 the clock was still not put up, and the £50 was offered to Cumnock District Council if they would arrange the erection.

Speakers at the Glasgow Re-union were as follows:

1	1860	Hugh Howatson (30 November 1860)
2	1861	Robert Brown, Cumnock
3	1862	James Gibson
4	1863	
5	1864	
6	1865	Thomas Gemmill, banker, Girvan
7	1867	Prof. James Morton, Andersonian University, Glasgow
8	1868	
9	1869	
10	1870	
11	1871	
12	1872	
13	1873	
14	1874	Robert Brown, Cumnock
15	1875	George Lammie
16	1876	
17	1877	
18	1878	
19	1879	Alexander Murdoch, Neilson Institute, Paisley (January 1879)
20	1880	Andrew Stewart, schoolmaster, Kirkintilloch
21	1881	
22	1882	John MacMillan (27 January 1882)
23	1883	James Gibson (1841-1883), potato merchant, Glasgow (26 January 1883)
24	1884	David Wilson, Writer, Glasgow
25	1885	WIlliam Murdoch (19 March 1885)
26	1886	Thomas McCosh
27	1887	
28	1888	Robert S. Steel, merchant, Glasgow
29	1889	
30	1890	James R. Wilson, Sanquhar
31	1891	Robert Kennedy (30 January 1891)
32	1892	
33	1893	
34	1894	David Andrew, schoolmaster, Old Kilpatrick
35	1895	Robert S. Steel, merchant, Glasgow (January 1895)
36	1896	William Murdoch, potato merchant
37	1897	
38	1898	(28 January 1898)

39	1899	M. M. Osborne, editor, Kilmarnock Standard
40	1900	
41	1901	John MacMillan
42	1902	Thomas Wallace, Edinburgh (23 January 1902)
43	1903	James Montgomerie of Tarelgin (28 January 1903)
44	1904	W. G. Wallace, editor of the Ayrshire Post (January 1904)

Ochiltree Mutual Improvement Society was established in 1858 and survived for over a decade. Presidents included William Young, teacher at the Free Church School (1862), John Andrew (1863) and Robert Montgomerie of Lessnessock (1868).

The Ochiltree branch of the British Legion was formed in 1929. A number of ex-servicemen from the village and surrounding district met in the Star Inn where it was agreed that they should apply to the British Legion to form a branch. The minute book reads: 'It was unanimously agreed to form a branch of the British Legion (Scotland) as contained in application form in the hands of the secretary and that the branch be named Ochiltree Branch.' The application was quickly granted, for the poles supporting the legion's colours have a plate engraved, 'Formed 19th November 1929'. The first official meeting as a British Legion was held in the Star Inn some months later, and the minute then noted, 'Next meeting to be held when Secretary thinks business and communications require same. Three months passed before the next meeing was held in the Star Inn, by which the treasurer could report that the branch had £1 4s 4d. The branch ran dances and 'go-as-you-please' meetings, the funds raised being used to assist families in hardship. During the Second World War it raised funds and sent gifts to the soldiers serving abroad.

On 6 November 1958 the branch almost closed, a meeting held in the Head Inn considering a proposal that it should be wound up. However, it was decided to continue until the next annual meeting, again held in the Head Inn in March 1959. Although only a few members attended, it was resolved to continue. By 1960 the branch began its search for premises, and it was agreed to negotiate with Ayr County Council to purchase The House with the Green Shutters at 90 Main Street. At the time the building was in a poor condition and was threatened with demolition. At a meeting held in the Bowlers' Hall on 8 May 1960 it was announced that the Green Shutters house would be saved, and the council would sell it to the branch once the title deeds had been found. In July 1960 a letter was received from the council informing the branch that the building could be sold to them for £60. The branch only had £30 to its name, but it was agreed to purchase the building. This was subsequently restored, and in 1962 a license was granted, allowing the sale of alcohol. The premises were soon regarded as being too small, so an extension was added to the rear. A larger extenson was added in 1973-74.

In June 1972 the Legion had new colours dedicated, at the same time as a plaque was erected within the vestibule of the club premises. On the plaque were the name of 46 men of the parish who had fallen in the two world wars. The British Legion club closed in 2004 and the building suffered a fire in the same year. The building was sold and converted into a public house, known as the Green Shutters.

In 1886 the Ochiltree Horticultural Society was founded, one of the early patrons being Captain H. G. Fallowfield of Ochiltree House. The society held an annual exhibition each August, the 19th in 1906. Ochiltree Apiarian Society was established in 1863 and held a number of shows in the following years, often held in Morton's inn, where honey was displayed and commented on.

An Ochiltree Burns Club was formed in the late 1880s, but it appears to have folded within a short period, and by Burns' Night in 1889 was closed. The *Ardrossan and Saltcoats Herald* reported, 'Where is the Ochiltree Burns Club? Echo answers, where? It is our sad duty to record the demise of this club. The little infant was ushered into the world with a feeble and delicate constitution, but it was thought that with suitable stimulants and good nursing it would have gained strength and lived to a good old age'.

A public meeting was held in the school on 7 February 1928 which resulted in the formation of a new Ochiltree Burns Club. The first president was Hugh Brown, of Ochiltree Mains, with M. L. Jamieson as vice-president and William Watson, Burnock Street, as secretary and treasurer.

Other Burns Clubs have existed in the parish. The Winsome Willie Burns Club was formed in 1939. The club held their Burns' suppers in the Commercial Arms. Presidents included Robert Fleming (1941). The Drongan and District Working Men's Burns Club was formed in 1980.

The Picture House was located at 102A Main Street. In 1956 a new frontage was added to it for the proprietor, James Young.

In 1925 the Men's Guild at the parish church fell out with the authorities and decided to separate from the church. They held a meeting in the Crown Inn on 9 February 1925 and decided to rename and reconstitute the club. This was to be the formation of the Burnock Recreation Club, which grew to have a considerable membership. There were forty members when the club commenced, the first president being Robert Lennon. At the annual general meeting held on 26 March 1926 it was proposed to acquire their own building. By November 1928 the building fund had reached £304 and a site had been identified for a hall opposite the public school. The village hall was maintained by the Burnock Recreation Club. Despite its poor facilities it had an average membership of eighty just after the war, and the hall could accomodate 200 folk. The hall was used for whists, carpet bowls, dances and other functions.

Ochiltree Recreation Ground was opened in 1921. The Kay Park was gifted to the community and officially opened on 19 May 1934 by John Kay, of Pettoch, Ayr. John Kay had been the original owner of the land on which the park was created.

Total abstinence from alcohol was something which grew in popularity in the Victorian years. Ochiltree Total Abstinence Society existed from 1859. The Rechabites established what were called 'Tents' throughout the country, and promoted good living without drink. The Burnock Water Tent (No. 3359) was formed in Ochiltree on 4 February 1905 and a Star of Burnock Juvenile Tent in 1906. They promoted the ideals of 'abstinence and thrift'. When the new school opened in 1909 the tent met there one night per fortnight. In 1913 the organistaion had fifteen state and seventeen order members, two members' wives, one honorary member and 44 juveniles.

Fleeting references are found to numerous organisations within the parish. The Ochiltree Unionist Association existed from at least 1902 until at least 1913, often meeting in Mr Holmes' Crown Inn. Ochiltree International Order of Good Templars existed in 1907. Ochiltree Flute Band existed in 1859. Ochiltree Friendship Club existed in 2014.

In 1960 the first discussions took place on the formation of Ochiltree Community Association. For over ten years the association met in an old hall as it organised fundraising events towards the erection of a community centre. In 1968 a site on Main Street was acquired. By the 1970s funds from councils and other bodies made the erection of a new community centre possible, and work began on this in 1971. The centre measured 3,200 square feet. It had cost £28,000 to build, the cost spilt between Cumnock District Council (£10,000), Ayr County Council (£10,000) and the Coal Industry Social Welfare Organisation (£8,000). The building comprised of a timber building supported by a steel frame externally, all resting on a brick base. It was designed by Ayr County Council architects. The centre was officially opened on Friday 24 March 1972 by County Convener William Paterson.

The Ochiltree Women's Rural Institute was formed in April 1955 when seventeen ladies met in Ochiltree school to propose the establishment of a new group. Among those present were members of the Ayrshire Central Council and Mrs Agnew, chairwoman of the Ayrshire Federation. The meeting proved to be fruitful, and the institute was founded soon after. The first president was Jenny Brown, of Ochiltree Mains, and Jean Murdoch was appointed as secretary. It was agreed that there should be a maximum membership of seventy, limited to ladies from Ochiltree and surroundings. Mrs Brown remained as president for 21 years, and in 1956 had presented a silver salver for annual competition. The institute held many social events, including the first Scots night in 1963, and a long-running entertainments group. The institute met to start with in the old school, using the 'Boolers' Hall' across the road when larger events were held. They were later to move to the community centre. Amy Kinnaird, a long-standing member, contributed numerous articles to the institute's national magazine, Scottish Home and Country. The institute celebrated its golden jubilee on 25 April 2005.

On 4 February 1910 a meeting was called of all Freemasons who lived within Ochiltree parish with the intention of celebrating Burns' birthday. On that occasion eighteen freemasons attended, and there were proposals for establishing a masonic lodge in the village.

In 1916 Ochiltree Musical and Amateur Dramatic Association was founded. The members practised their music and sketches and entertained the public at their first concert, held in the school on Hogmanay, 1916.

The Ochiltree Yeomanry Rifle Club existed in 1913-1923. The Rifle Club used the rifle range at Langholm, the president of the club for a time being John Jamieson, farmer there. In 1913 the club proposed erecting a second target on the range.

The members of Stair Parish Church started a collection with the intention of erecting a hall at Taiglum to serve the parishioners of the Drongan area. As the collections proceeded, there appears to have been some dispute over the naming of the hall, which was to be Drongan Public Hall, resulting in some people withdrawing support. Residents of Drongan took over, and continued to fundraise, eventually being able to erect a public hall in Mill of Shield Road, adjoining the Gospel Hall. Known as the 'Iron Hall', from having been constructed of timber covered with corrugated iron, the building was officially opened on 4 December 1903 by Sir William Arrol of Seafield, Ayr. It was he who was the engineer for the Forth Bridge and many other major civil engineering works. Once opened, the hall was well used by the community, including the church which insitgated its erection. In addition to Sunday School classes, it was used for lectures, weddings, public meetings, concerts, dances and whist drives. In later years it doubled as a cinema.

Drongan Public Hall resulted in more community groups being established in the village. These included the Drongan Amateur Dramatic Society, established in 1952 by John Davidson; and Drongan and District Pipe Band.

Drongan Working Men's Club was erected in Lady's Walk in 1965 at a cost of £15,000. The club was successful for many years, but with a dwindling membership it was closed in 1997.

William Houston was instrumental in establishing Drongan and District Horticultural Society in 1988 and the first Drongan Flower Show was held in the primary school in 1989.

YOUTH GROUPS

In 1909 Ochiltree Scouts were founded, the first scoutmaster being Archibald Andrew, headmaster at the school. They met in the school on Friday evenings. In 1910 the scouts under Troop Master Lorimer constructed a footbridge across the Burnock above the village. They still existed in 1914.

In 1927 there were proposals to start a new troop of Boys Scouts and Brownies in the village. The Brownies started in July 1927. A group of Girl Guides was also formed in 1927, with Etta Lennox as the first captain. The Brownies were led by Lieutenant A. Maclaren. The Boy Scouts were formed in 1927, meeting in the laundry room of Ochiltree House, by permission of the Marquis of Bute. The first Scoutmaster was William Watson.

At Drongan the 104th Ayrshire (Drongan) Scout Group was established. In 1986 there were 23 Beavers, 23 Cubs and 13 Scouts. Scout Leaders included the brothers Patrick and Philip McGhee, Craig MacCubbin (1986) and Rosalie McCluskey. The Scout group became a charity in 2004 but was removed from the register in 2012.

The 1st Ochiltree Company of the Boys' Brigade was affiliated to the parish church. In 1950 it had thirty members. Captains of the company included Hugh Brown (1980s-1992), and Mrs Catherine Harvey (1992-1995). After Mrs Harvey the company had no captain, and only survived for a short time, closing in 1996.

At Drongan a company of Boys' Brigade associated with the Schaw Kirk was formed in 1961, the first captain being William Morgan, assisted by his brother, Robert Morgan. This company folded in 1976 due to a lack of leaders.

1st Ochiltree Girls' Guildry was formed in 1926 under the guidance of the minister's wife, Mrs Rutherford. The Guildry presented the font and hymn boards to the church. In 1964 the Guildry became part of the Girls' Brigade, at a national amalgamation. In 1976 a set of colours were purchased to mark the golden jubilee of the Brigade. The Girls' Brigade celebrated its 70th anniversary at a church service on 27 October 1996.

At Drongan a Girls' Guildry was formed in 1961, becoming 1st Drongan Company. The company celebrated its fiftieth anniversary in May 2012 with a service led by Rev David Whiteman. The company still exists in 2020. Leaders included Rena Robertson and Allison Bradford.

Ochiltree Gala Day ran for many years until 1985. After a gap of 22 years it was revived in 2007, with a Gala Queen and King, live bands and dancers, helicopter fly pass, battle re-enactment and other events. The gala survived until 16 June 2012.

CHAPTER TWELVE

SONS AND DAUGHTERS

GEORGE DOUGLAS BROWN (1869-1902)

George Douglas was born on on 26 January 1869 in Ochiltree's Main Street at the house known as the 'House with the Green Shutters', though at the time it did not bear this name. He was the illegitimate son of Sarah Gemmell (named on the certificate as 'Gammell', but sometimes known as Sarah Gemmell Hare) and a local farmer, George Douglas Brown of Drumsmudden (d. 28 September 1897). Sarah, an Irishwoman, had been a dairymaid at Drumsmudden, working for Brown, but fell pregnant to him. It is said that Brown would have married Gemmell, but local tradition says that his sister dissuaded him from this. As a result, Gemmell left Drumsmudden and moved into Ochiltree. She soon found work on other farms, and she and the young George seems to have spent most of his youth moving from farm to farm. Among those known where she worked were at Ochiltree, Coylton, Ayr and Cronberry. At Coylton, Gemmell worked at Duchray farm.

Although born into difficult circumstances, he received a better education than most. He was able to attend Coylton School from 1875. There, the schoolmaster, John Smith, recognised his ability, and recommended him to the rector at Ayr Academy, William Maybin. In 1884 he enrolled into the Higher Fourth Class Ayr Academy, his education there being sponsored, the school Fee Book noting that his school payments were 'Reduced to £1 per quarter by masters'. Maybin is known to have subsidised Brown's fees personally, and it is known that he also provided Brown with a holiday in Ireland one summer. In 1886, with Maybin's encouragement, Brown was able to win the Scripture Medal. In 1887 he won the Hamilton Silver Medal for Classics and the Cowan Bursary

12.1 George Douglas Brown
(Author's Collection)

which allowed him to study at Glasgow University.

In 1887 the Scotch Education Department made the first reports on classworks in Ayr Academy, and by chance Brown is mentioned in it. In a test on English literature, he was fourth out of seven. He was first in the essay examination. He was second of five in Latin and Greek, and third in Greek Testament. Dr John Birrell, the school inspector, noted, 'It has seldom been my good fortune to revise such full and accurate papers as those of Currie and Brown.'

In October 1887 Brown was enrolled at the University of Glasgow, studying Classics. He graduated as a Master of Arts in 1890 with First Class Honours. He obtained the Eglinton Classical Fellowship, which allowed him to study at Glasgow for a postgraduate year.

It was during this postgraduate period that Brown won the Snell Exhibition, which allowed Ayrshire students to attend Balliol College at the University of Oxford with a considerable bursary. His time in the city wasn't a particularly joyful one. He did make some friends, but he was older than most of the other students, and his Scottishness made it even more different. In 1893 he took a First in Mods. In 1893 he took a Third in Greats.

In 1895 Brown's mother took ill, and he gave up part of his education at Oxford to nurse her back in Ayrshire. She had been discharged from hospital, but it was literally to die to at home. She passed away on 13 May 1895 at the age of 62, according to the memorial stone in Holmston Cemetery, Ayr, but 60 years according to the death certificate, signed by George Douglas Brown.

George Douglas Brown returned to England and commenced work as a journalist in London and a publisher's reader. He contributed articles to numerous magazines and journals, including the popular *Blackwood's Magazine, Morning Herald, The Speaker*, and *Sandow's Magazine of Physical Culture*. Some of these articles have been described as being rather poor, whereas others had some merit. He was offered a permanent job by the publisher, and his friend, Andrew Melrose, which would have earned him £600 per annum, but he turned this down, instead believing that he could make it on his own, and allowing him to concentrate on his novel-writing.

Whilst in London, Brown lived with his publisher, Andrew Melrose, at Hornsey. He met an Ayrshire lass, Isabella MacLennan, but after some time they fell out of love. She was the daughter of James MacLennan (1839-1899), a wine and spirit merchant in Glasgow, who had been born in Coylton. He then began dating her sister, Elizabeth Smith MacLennan, who was living in Glasgow, and they became engaged in early 1902.

In between writing for periodicals, Brown was working on a novel set in the Alfridi War, *Love and a Sword*, which was published in 1899 by Macqueen. This was issued under a pseudonym, Kennedy King. The novel was a fair success, keeping him in pecuniary comfort for a period.

His next work, appearing in 1901, was to be his greatest achievement. He wrote the novel *The House with the Green Shutters* as an antidote to the kailyard school of writing, which it killed virtually stone dead. The novel was dedicated to the headmaster at Ayr Academy who had guided him in his youth, William Maybin. Originally a longish short story, extending to 20,000 words, Melrose and other publishers suggested to him that it should be expanded. Published under the pseudonym, George Douglas, it appeared from the publishing house of Macqueen in London. It was also issued by MacClure, Phillips in New York.

Success for *Green Shutters* was quick. It has been suggested that it may have sold 12,000 copies in its first year and by 1902 was issued in its seventh impression. Following the novel's success, Brown was invited to be the guest speaker and chairman at the Ochiltree Schoolfellows' Reunion in 1901.

Brown started a third novel, *The Incompatibles*, but by this time he was seriously ill of pneumonia. As he was making his way back south from Glasgow by rail, he became seriously ill. He spent some time with friends, eventually going to Melrose's house in London's Highgate, where he died on 28 August 1902. The death certificate stated that he died of cardiac failure following upon laryngitis and congestion of the lungs.

Brown's body was transported by rail to Glasgow, where it was taken to the home of his fiancee in Dowanhill. He was buried in the Holmston Cemetery, Ayr, the headstone being erected by Miss Maclennan. In his will, he is known to have stated that 'any money that is left (it won't be much) may be given to the Coylton poor'. Thus, the George Douglas Brown Trust was established.

A few unfinished works by Brown were known to exist. He was writing a study of *Hamlet*, and it is said that he was working on a historical romance, set in the Cromwellian period. Another work of fiction, *The Novelist*, was still in draft form.

A committee was formed to create a memorial to Brown. The secretary and treasurer was D. E. Edward of the Carnegie Library in Ayr. On 1 November

12.2 George Douglas Brown's gravestone, Holmston Cemetery, Ayr *(Dane Love)*

12.3 George Douglas Brown's plaque, Ochiltree *(Dane Love)*

1919 a plaque was unveiled on the 'House with the Green Shutters' in his memory. This was sculpted by Robert Bryden (1865-1939), a native of Coylton. On the day the eulogy was delivered by Andrew Melrose, publisher of *The House With the Green Shutters*, London, and a second speech was given by Sir Howard Handley Spicer (1872-1926), stationer and editor. Also in attendance were Duncan Mackay, master of modern languages at Ayr Academy, who had instigated the plans to have a plaque erected, and D. E. Edward. After the plaque was unveiled, the party moved across the street to the school, where a series of speeches were given and refreshments were served. The plaque contains the inscription:

> Born 26 Jan 1869. Died 28 Aug 1902. The birthplace of George Douglas Brown, author of 'The House With the Green Shutters'.

A similar plaque in bronze, with a circular disc bearing a bas-relief of Brown's head, was presented to Coylton School. It reads:

> Born 26 Jan 1869. Died 28 Feb 1902. Here as a pupil 1875-1883 was George Douglas Brown, author of 'The House With the Green Shutters'.

JOHNNY CYMBAL (1945-1993)

John Hendry Blair was born on 3 February 1945 in the back room at 2 Broom Crescent, Ochiltree, the son of John Blair and Jean Hendry. His father was a miner, and was separated from his wife, subsequently moving to Ayr, where he remarried. Jean Hendry moved to Canada in 1952 where she ran a store at Sudbury, Ontario. She was married to Nicky Cymbal, a Polish national and member of the Free Polish Forces stationed in Scotland during the Second World War. Johnny was adopted by Nicky Cymbal, hence him taking the name. Nicky Cymbal died in a mining accident in Green River, Wyoming, in 1967, when he was knocked off a platform in the shaft by an air hose.

Johnny Cymbal was married three times, firstly to Carol, by whom he had two children, John and Kimberly. Whilst living in Nashville he was married and divorced twice.

Johnny, as he was known, became infatuated with music whilst in his teens. He moved to Cleveland, Ohio, U.S.A., where in 1960, aged just fifteen, he received a recording deal with MGM Records. Early releases included 'The Water is Red', in which his girlfriend is eaten by a shark! He moved to Knapp Records in 1963. He released 'Mr Bass Man' that year, which reached number 16 in the American charts and number 24 in the U.K. He performed the song on 19 April 1963 on Dick Clark's American Bandstand, after which it remained in the charts for thirteen weeks. It reached number one in Japan and Argentina. It was a popular novelty record. His follow-up record was 'Teenage Heaven'. He became the lead singer and producer for the group 'Derek', with whom he had a million-seller with 'Cinnamon (Let me In)'.

Johnny continued writing songs, composing 'Mary in the Morning' in 1967 for Al Martino, also covered by Elvis Presley, Glen Campbell, Percy Faith and Eddy Arnold. It was featured in the movie, 'Elvis: That's the Way It Is'. He produced several records for David Cassidy ('Rock me Baby'), and Gene Pitney ('Nobody's Child (Somewhere in the Country)'). Other titles include 'I'm Drinkin' Canada Dry', recorded by the Flying Burrito Brothers, 'Fire in the Sky' by the Wright Brothers and 'Growing Pains' by Frankie Ford. Other acts who have recorded his songs include Mae West, Bette Midler, Reba McIntire and Terry Gibbs. In 1968 he wrote a song entitled 'Ochiltree', but this was not successful.

Johnny Cymbal recorded a number of songs, but used pseudonyms to release them, such as 'Brother John', 'Dallas' 'Derek' and many others. In total, it is reckoned that he had published over 200 songs, but he kept copious notebooks, filled with ideas for other titles.

Johnny Cymbal was musical director for a number of television shows, including the popular 'Partridge Family' and a cartoon series entitled 'Catanooga Cats'.

Johnny Cymbal moved to Nashville in 1980 to concentrate on country material. He died in his sleep of a heart attack on 16 March 1993.

John C. Wilson, a cousin of Cymbal's, also emigrated to Canada and his son, Dr Jason Wilson, is also in the music business, having performed and recorded with acts such as UB40, Percy Sledge, Dick Gaughan, Alanis Morissette and many others.

GEORGE MACCARTNEY (c.1790-1868)

Some accounts claim that George MacCartney, the well-known agricultural engineer from Cumnock, was born in Ochiltree parish. He was certainly buried in the old kirkyard. Most accounts claim that MacCartney was born around 1790 at Roadside, to the south of Cumnock, his mother claiming descent from the Covenanting minister, Rev Alexander Peden. He learned much of his trade as a boy from Walter Galbraith, millwright at Roadside. He obtained the use of Clocklownie barn as a workshop, where he made numerous items. From 1812 he started redesigning the threshing mill (invented by Meikle in 1787). MacCartney's first mill was used at Auchincross in New Cumnock parish, where it was a great success. In 1832 he acquired a site on the side of the Glaisnock Water in Cumnock where he erected a workshop. This was built by David Reid, father of David Reid of Milzeoch. MacCartney designed various bits of machinery, including an engine lathe. He is also known to have designed the interior layout of the old Free Church, Ayr Road. Mills manufactured by MacCartney won medals as far afield as Australia (gold), and the London International Exhibition of 1851 where he won bronze. John Drummond became a partner, but this was dissolved in 1858, Drummond setting up his own works elsewhere in Cumnock. He and George Moore skated from Cumnock to Ochiltree along a frozen Lugar. MacCartney died on May Fair day, 1868, aged nearly 80 years. He had remained a bachelor all of his life.

PRIMROSE MACCONNELL (1856-1931)

Primrose MacConnell was born at Lessnessock farm on 11 April 1856, the son of Archibald MacConnell (1821-1898) and his wife, Agnes Milroy (1830-1897). He attended Ochiltree Free Church School, followed by Ayr Academy before being apprenticed to a Glasgow engineering company. In the 1870s he attended the University of Edinburgh, passing the diploma offered by the Highland and Agricultural Society. When the university started to offer degrees in agriculture, MacConnell returned, being the second student to pass. He and his father were to rent the 636-acre Ongar Park Hall farm, twenty miles from London. His father returned to Scotland in 1893. In 1905 Primrose MacConnell moved to 500-acre North Wycke farm, near Southminster, Essex, which he purchased. He retired from farming in 1928, his son-in-law, James Kelly, taking over.

In 1880 MacConnell was appointed as Professor of Agriculture at Glasgow Veterinary College. He excelled in agricultural matters and in 1883 wrote *The Agricultural Notebook*, which became a standard reference work for farmers and agricultural colleges across Europe, being repeatedly reprinted. Other works included *The Elements of Farming* (1896), *The Elements of Agricultural Geology* (1902), *The Diary of a Working Farmer* (1906), and *The Complete Farmer* (1908). He contributed a number of articles on agricultural matters to the *Encyclopaedia Britannica* 1911 edition. He edited *Farm Life* for a time and was dairy editor for the *Agricultural Gazette*. He was a member of the Royal Agricultural Society. He devised improvements to the hay sweep and experimented with a hay-cocking machine. MacConnell lived much of his life in England, including at Dial House, Epping Forest, and North Wycke, Southminster, both Essex.

MacConnell died on 7 July 1931 and was buried at Southminster Congregational Church burial ground. MacConnell was married in 1884 to Katherine Anderson, the seventh daughter of Rev George Anderson, New Cumnock Free Church minister. She died in March 1930. They had a son, Archibald MacConnell. Their youngest son, Captain Primrose MacConnell MC, RFA, was killed in Salonika (Thessaloniki), Macedonia, three days before the Armistice. A daughter was married to James M. Kelly.

'QUINTIN MACCRINDLE' (1860-1950)
'Quintin MacCrindle' was the nom-de-plume of Rev David Stewart, the minister of Currie in Midlothian. He took the pen-name from his father's Christian name and his mother's surname. He was a son of Ochiltree. He wrote a series of articles in the Church of Scotland magazine, *Life and Work*, entitled 'Jock'. These were humorous sketches of Scottish country life. In 1916 the stories were collected and published in book form by Alexander Gardner of Paisley. The stories were believed to have been set in Ochiltree parish.

JOHN MACRAE (1804-1891)
John MacRae was born in Ochiltree on 5 October 1804, the son of James MacRae (1782-1859) and Christina Forgie. He was educated in the village. He was married to Agnes Paterson (d. 24 April 1871) on 20 October 1838, by whom he had six children, Anna, Jane, Robert Paterson (1839-1892), James Fergus (1841-1872), Andrew Paterson (1843-1887) and John T. (1847-1870). He was to become a teacher, for a time working at New Cumnock school before he was appointed as parish schoolmaster at Newton-upon-Ayr in 1845 on a salary of £34. When it opened in 1846, he became headmaster of Newton Academy. He was described as 'an energetic and successful teacher'. In 1820 he published a text-book on *The Principles of Writing*. Another work, a *Brief Introduction to Astronomy* was published in 1837. He devised a perpetual calendar, by which the day of the week on which any date can be calculated. He died at his home in Charlotte, Street, Ayr, on 12 December 1891.

PROFESSOR JAMES MORTON (1819-1889)
James Morton was born in Ochiltree on 12 December 1819, son of Hugh Morton (d. 1848), builder, and his wife, Margaret Hair (1789-1825). He was the brother of Hugh Morton (1823-1891), landlord of the Head Inn and a prominent building contractor and mason in the village. James was an educated child, and he acted as an

12.4 James Morton, painted by T. Corsan Morton *(Royal College of Physicians and Surgeons of Glasgow)*

assistant to Patrick Simson at the village school for a time. In 1841 he started studying at Andersonian Institute in Glasgow, remaining for three years. He moved to Edinburgh for a short period before continuing his studies at St Andrews, where he graduated as a Doctor of Medicine in 1845. By 1855 he had worked himself up to become Professor of Materia Medici at Anderson's College. He held the position for 33 years. At the same time, from 1859 until 1885, he was surgeon to Glasgow Royal Infirmary. Morton also did research into medical issues, and published a number of articles in medical journals. In 1877 he wrote *The Treatment of Spina Bifida by a New Method*, published by James MacLehose, which brought him great acclaim, and which gave him the reputation of being one of the most advanced medical theorists of the period. In 1881 the Clinical Society recommended Morton's method as being the only treatment they could support. The Royal College of Surgeons in Edinburgh preserves a letter written by Morton in their archives in which he writes to Professor John Chiene regarding the treatment of spina bifida. Morton was President of the Faculty of Physicians and Surgeons of Glasgow from 1886-89. In 1888 he was made an honorary Doctor of Laws by the University of Glasgow.

Although Morton was praised and recognised for his work into spina bifida, he was less successful in his opinions regarding the work of Joseph, 1st Lord Lister, on antisepsis, being a leader of a group of surgeons in the city which tried to ridicule his theories. Morton also tried to debunk the germ theory work of Louis Pasteur. Professor Morton died in Glasgow on 31 December 1889 and was interred in Ochiltree's old kirkyard.

JANE MORTON

A minor poetess who lived in Ochiltree at the turn of the century was Jane Morton (*fl.* 1903). In 1903 she wrote 'To Mr A. B. Todd, on attaining his Eighty-First Birthday'. Todd was a local poet, Covenanter historian and editor of the Cumnock Express.

JAMES MURDOCH (1807-1829)

James Murdoch was the son of John Murdoch, lint miller in the parish, and Janet Murdoch (1765-1840). James became an accomplished portrait painter. James died young, on 16 August 1829, aged 22.

THOMAS REID (D. 1831)

Andrew Smith (1797-1869), of the Mauchline box-making firm of William & Andrew Smith, is often credited with inventing the Apograph, a device for copying drawings. It comprised of a metal frame which supported a drawing board and pens, allowing the user to copy an illustration, reducing it in scale from 1/8 to ¾ in size. This was an important device in the boxworks, which made numerous items with small engraving representing landmarks on them. Although Andrew Smith took out a number of patents for his various inventions, the creation of the Apograph was disputed by Thomas Reid of Ochiltree, who laid claim to it. According to William MacCarter's 1832 Ayrshire directory, Reid 'so far as originality goes to settle the point, is supposed to have the best of the argument. He died in 1831, but before his death a great improvement was made on it.'

DAVID ROWAN (1822-1898)

David Rowan was a successful businessman in Glasgow. He was born in Ochiltree in 1822, the son of David Rowan, slater in the village, and Elizabeth Smith. Rowan appears to have been an apprentice slater initially, but he moved to Glasgow in 1840 where he became an engineer with John MacAndrew at the St Rollox Foundry Company. He later moved to Greenock where he worked for the Caird & Company shipbuilding business, moving up to become the manager. He then removed to Glasgow, having accepted the position of managing partner for James Aitken & Co., which became Messrs. Murdoch & Aitken. There he was responsible for establishing the Langloan Ironworks, building the blast furnaces. At the time, these were regarded as one of the greatest triumphs of engineering skill in the west of Scotland. He was also responsible for the pumping engines which were used to supply water to St Petersburg. Rowan left Murdoch & Aitken in 1866 to establish his own business, David Rowan & Sons, in Glasgow's Elliot Street. This was involved in the manufacture of marine engines and other machinery. David Rowan designed a number of improvements to marine engines, especially the propelling machinery for steam vessels. He held a number of important positions in the city, including the Institute of Engineers and Shipbuilders in Scotland (serving as president from 1870-72), Glasgow Mechanics Institution (becoming president), and Clyde Navigation Trust (1872-1885, serving as deputy-chairman).

David Rowan wrote a book about his birthplace, entitled *Memorials of Ochiltree*. This was published in 1879 for private circulation. He was instrumental in establishing the 'Forget-me-not' Society.

David Rowan was married to Agnes Gallacher (b. 2 July 1828) on 8 September 1850. They had twelve children - David Rowan the younger (b. 1858) was to become a director of the Ayr Steam-Shipping Company and of the Laird Line Steam-Shipping Company of Glasgow. James Rowan (1854-1906) took over David Rowan & Sons in 1888. In July 1875 his other three sons were to drown when a boat in which they were sailing overturned. They were William (b. 1864); Frederick (b. 1865) and Charles Todd (b. 1867). They had seven daughters – Agnes Maria (b. 1856); Elizabeth Smith (b. 1859); Janet Pender (b. 1861); Ellen Margaret (b. 1863); Janet Pender (b. 1867); Florence Jane (b. 1871); and Alice Rowena (b. 1873).

David Rowan died at his Glasgow home at 22 Woodside Place on 30 July 1898 after a lingering illness. He left an estate of £25,032 6s 2d. The business, David Rowan & Co. Ltd., continued for a number of years, becoming part of Lithgows. In 1963 the business was merged with the Fairfield ship-engine building division to form Fairfield Rowan Ltd. This business was closed in 1966, following the collapse of Fairfield shipbuilders.

12.5 David Rowan Baillie as depicted in 'The Baillie' *(Author's Collection)*

12.6 Brass Plaque from engine manufactured by David Rowan *(Author's Collection)*

TAM SAMSON (1725-1795)

Thomas Samson was born in Ochiltree on 17 November 1725, the son of John Samson, market gardener in the village. He moved to Kilmarnock and there established a seed merchant's business and a forest nursery in 1759, known as Wm. & T. Samson. This was located behind his house of Rosebank at the corner of London Road and Braeside Street. He sent seeds from Kilmarnock to Burns' farm at Ellisland. A plaque was erected on this building and unveiled by Thomas Amos, Honorary Secretary of the Burns Federation: *Tam Samson's House. Marked by Winsome Willie Burns Club, Kilmarnock, April 1928.* Rosebank has since been demolished and the plaque relocated on a wall. Tam's daughter married Sandy Patrick of the Bowling Green Inn in Kilmarnock. His nephew was Charles Samson. Both were also friends of Burns. Two of Tam's sons succeeded to the business, the eldest, William, being noted for standing 6 feet 6 inches in his bare feet. Tam Samson was buried in the Laigh kirkyard, Kilmarnock, where his gravestone survives. It bears the inscription, with an epitaph by Robert Burns:

> Thomas Samson, died the 12th December 1795, aged 72 years.
> Tam Samson's weel worn clay here lies,
> Ye canting Zealots spare him,
> If honest Worth is Heaven rise,
> Ye'll mend or ye win near him. – Burns

Burns wrote a poem about Tam's exploits, but the final line of each verse was 'Tam Samson's dead!' Tam met the poet on one occasion, and berated him for the lines, stating that 'I'm no' deid yet; in fact, I'm worth ten deid men. What wey should you aye keep sayin' I'm deid?' Burns noted that Samson was quite hurt by the poem, and after a few moments recited the final verse:

> Per contra
> Go, fame, and canter like a filly,
> Through a' the streets and neuks o' Killie,
> Tell evry social, honest billie,
> To cease his grievin',
> For yet, unskaithed by death's gleg gullie,
> Tam Samson's leevin'!

JAMES SMITH (1759-1847)

James Smith was a noted Ayrshire botanist. He was born at Bonnyton. He lived at Monkwood Grove, near Minishant, for over fifty years. During that time he collected numerous foreign and indigenous plants, having over 600 varieties growing at his nursery. His son in law often travelled abroad, to the likes of Russia, to bring back specimens. It was Smith who named the *primula Scotica*, being the first to detect it as a new British plant around 1808. He is also credited with having created the original Kilmarnock Willow, which was propagated and sold commercially by Thomas Lang of Kilmarnock. Smith's daughter, Margaret Dunlop Smith, was married in 1815 to James Goldie, who explored much of east Africa. James Smith died on 30 December 1847. He is buried in the kirkyard surrounding Ayr's Auld Kirk, where his gravestone describes him as 'the father of Scottish botany'.

JOHN TENNANT (1760-1853)
Auchinbay Farm was in the latter half of the eighteenth century the home of John Tennant, second son of John Tennant of Glenconner. He and Burns attended Ayr Grammar School together, lodging with John Murdoch, the schoolmaster. John seems to have gifted the poet a crate of whisky, for on 22 December 1788 Burns wrote to him care of Mr. Robb, innkeeper, Ayr, thanking him for it. John Tennant acquired Steelpark farm, Shield farm at St Quivox, and Girvanmains at Girvan. He later purchased the small estate of Creoch in Ochiltree parish.

Burns refers to John Tennant in his 'Epistle to James Tennant of Glenconner'. At the time Tennant's wife was in labour, and someone had come into Mauchline in search of a midwife to assist:

> And Auchenbay, I wish him joy,
> If he's a parent, lass or boy,
> May he be dad, and Meg the mither,
> Just five and forty years thegither!

THOMAS WALKER (1750-1833)
Thomas Walker was a minor poet who lived at Poole, which was located near to Watston farm, Ochiltree. Some say that he was born in Sorn parish, but this is unconfirmed. He was a tailor to trade, but spent much of his time writing verses, becoming known as the 'Poetical Tailor'. He became friendly with William Simson (1758-1815), schoolmaster in Ochiltree and Cumnock, better known to Burns aficionados as 'Winsome Willie'. When he heard that Simson received verses from Burns, he thought he would try the same. Accordingly, he wrote a 26-stanza poem to him, but Burns appears to have ignored this:

> O, but my heart would be fu' licht
> In Ochiltree to get a sicht
> O' your braw rhyme, sae trim and ticht,
>   An ye can 'dite it;
> So, sit ye doon a while, some nicht,
>   An' rhyme an' write it.

When the poet's Kilmarnock edition was published, Walker tried again, writing a sermon of 21 stanzas to him – again ignored. This annoyed Walker, and he wrote scathingly to Burns, attacking his moral standing, in a poem with the first verse:

> What woefu' news is this, I hear?
> Frae greetin' I can scarce forbear,
> Folk tell me ye're gawn aff this year
> > Oot o'er the sea,
> And lasses wham ye lo'e sae dear,
> > Will greet for thee.

Walker continued, commenting on Burns' affair with Jean Armour and his intention to leave Scotland. This goaded Burns into writing the poem 'Reply to a Trimming Epistle received from a Tailor', around August or September 1786:

> What ails ye now, ye lousie bitch
> To thresh my back at sic a pitch?
> Losh, man, ha'e mercy wi' your natch!
> > Your bodkin's bauld:
> I didnae suffer half sae much
> > Frae Daddie Auld.

This poem, which extends to 12 verses, despite its remarks, was treasured by Walker, who believed it to be by the poet. However, no manuscript of the poem survives, and it has been claimed that the reply was composed by none other than Simson himself. This theory was noted by James Paterson in his *Contemporaries of Burns*, in which he relates how Simson told Burns that he had replied on his behalf, and that the poet replied, 'You did well. You thrashed the tailor much better than I would have done.'

A poem by William Simson refers to Walker, who is known to have struggled to finish some pieces of work. In the verses, Simson commiserates with him:

> Ye Muses, why leave ye Tam Walker so long?
> > His rhymes unconnected
> > Show he's disrespected
> By you, ye inspirers of elegant song;
> > For to his vexation
> > His versification
> Runs frequently wrong.

Thomas Walker later wrote a religious pamphlet, *A Picture of the World*, which was distributed widely and brought him some degree of fame. Patrick Simson described him, stating that he 'maintained a respectable character for sobriety, honesty, and glee.' He later moved to Bridgend Cottage at Sorn, where he died in 1833 aged 82 years. His remains were interred in Sorn kirkyard.

APPENDIX I

FARMS AND SMALL LAIRDSHIPS

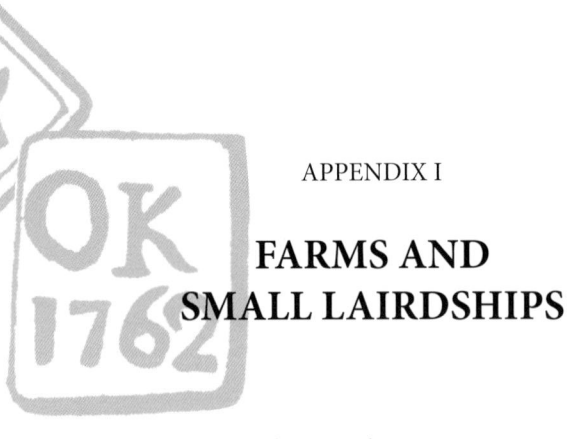

1899 – dates in Roman type are known dates.
1900 – dates in Italic type are known, but are not necessarily terminal.
c.1895 – indicates approximate dates.
Ordnance Survey six-figure Grid References are shown after the farm name to indicate its location.

Auchencloigh (NS 493166)
Originally spelled Auchincloigh. 360 acres of arable land and 600 acres of hill ground in 1851. Farmstead demolished when Piperhill opencast coal mine extended onto grounds.

1619	Ochiltree Estate –
1696	Ochiltree Estate -
1797	Ochiltree Estate – William Mearns
1825-1846	Ochiltree Estate - James Wilson (1799-1846)
1846-1878	Dumfries House Estate – David Wilson (1813-1878)
1878-1904	Dumfries House Estate – Robert Wilson (1844-1904)
1904-1909	Dumfries House Estate – D. Wilson
1909-1911	Dumfries House Estate – H. Wilson
1914-1920	Dumfries House Estate – David Howat (1868-1940)
1920-1940	David Howat (1868-1940)
1940-1971	Mungo Howat (1898-1971)
1971-	David Howat
1979	Ian Logan
	Scottish Coal

Auchinbay (NS 486235)
120 acres in 1861. 345 acres in 2013.

1619	Ochiltree Estate –
-1782	Ochiltree Estate - James Colvil (d. 1782)
1782-	Ochiltree Estate - Charles Colvil
c.1797	Ochiltree Estate - George Colvill
c.1790	Ochiltree Estate - William Lees

1793-1797	Ochiltree Estate - John Tennant (1760-1853)
1836	- Charles Sloan (1784-1862)
1841	- Adam Dickie
1851-1855	Auchinleck Estate – George MacKerrow
1857	Auchinleck Estate – George Brown
1861-1899	Andrew Kirkwood MacCosh – John Ferguson (1830-1900)
1911-1920	Auchinleck Estate – James Sloan Ferguson
1930-1940	James Sloan Ferguson
c.1950	Smith
-1988	James Hair (1967-2011)
1988-	Wilson Morton
2009-2020	Quintin David Morton (1972-)

Auchingee (NS 464137)
Abandoned and merged with other farms to form Ravenscroft (q.v.).

1841	Bonnyton Estate – James Clement
1851	Bonnyton Estate – John MacMurray
1853	Bonnyton Estate – John Campbell in Rankinston

Auchlin (NS 498170)
600 acres in 1861, 1,600 acres in 1881.

c.1780-1788	- John Sloan (1734-1791)
1797-1843	- William Sloan (1776-1843)
1843-1851	- Robert Cowan Wilson Sloan (1819-1851)
1851-	- Mrs Sarah Sloan (1780-1864)
1854-1861	Dumfries House Estate - David Blackburn (1806-18)
1868-1890	Dumfries House Estate – John Brown (1813-1890)
1890-1901	Dumfries House Estate – William Brown (1850-1901)
1901-1919	Dumfries House Estate – Quintin Brown
1919-1959	William Brown
1959-2014	John Craig
2010	D. & M. Craig

Auldbyres (NS 429190)
84 acres in 1871. 100 acres in 1881.

1855	Drongan Estate –
1871	Drongan Estate – Robert Steele (1798-18)
1878	Drongan Estate – John Smith FEIS (d. 1909)
1881	Drongan Estate – Thomas Beattie (1830-)
1891	Drongan Estate – James Cameron (1835-)
1899-1914	Drongan Estate – James & David Mair

1925	James Mair (1865-)
1930	Helen M. Mair (1875-)
1940	James Mair (1901-)

Back o' Hill (NS 502198)

85 acres in 1881.

1700	Ochiltree Estate - Andrew Strawhorn
1797	Ochiltree Estate - Robert Wright
1832-1851	Dumfries House Estate – George Muir
1875-1905	Dumfries House Estate – William Muir (1830-1922)
1905-1919	Dumfries House Estate – Alexander P. Rorison (d. 1959)
1919-1940	Alexander P. Rorison (d. 1959)
-1987	William Grierson (1897-1987)
2015-2016	J. MacLeish

Barbeth (High) (NS 443194)

Originally known as South Barbeth. 40 acres in 1851. Converted into housing, known as Henry's Place, in 2006.

1841-1850	Drongan Estate – James Murdoch (1786-1850)
1850-1896	Drongan Estate – John Knox (1828-1896)
1914	Drongan Estate – Sarah Knox (1851-1918)
1925-1956	James Wyllie Knox

Barbeth (North) (NS 442200)

1841	Drongan Estate – Margaret Brown (1808-)
-1854	Drongan Estate – MacCartney Boyd (1792-1854)
1861	Drongan Estate – John Currie (1795-18)
1878-1891	Drongan Estate – William Cowan (1837-1891)
1891-1914	Drongan Estate – Henry Cowan (1865-)
1953	Ruth Cowan

Bardarroch (NS 471185)

264 acres in 1844. 335 acres in 1894.

1607	William Cathcart
1797-1813	John Colville
1841-1844	Craigie Estate – James Colville (1789-18)
1851-1854	Drumjoan Estate - James Colville (1789-18)
1861-1875	Drumjoan Estate - John Colville (1851-)
1879-1894	Drumjoan Estate – Matthew Steel (1824-)
1894-1897	James Kenneth of Buckreddan – Matthew Steel (1824-)
1897-1914	James Kenneth of Buckreddan – Hugh Sloan (1866-1945)

1925-1940	James Kenneth (trustees) – Hugh Sloan (1866-1945)
c.1991-2004	John Dunlop
2004-*2019*	Edward Musson

Barlosh (NS 481193)

Barlosche in 1619; Barloish in 1654. 150 acres in 1851. 200 acres in 1871. First floor of farmhouse added on 1928. Redeveloped as housing 2009.

1619	Ochiltree Estate -
1797	Ochiltree Estate - Robert Smith
	Dumfries House Estate - David Smith (1788-1857)
1837	Dumfries House Estate - William Smith
1841-1861	Dumfries House Estate - John Brown (1813-1890)
1871-1899	Dumfries House Estate – Mungo Howat (1817-1899)
1899-1914	Dumfries House Estate – Mungo Howat (1845-1914)
1914-	Dumfries House Estate – Mungo Murdoch (d. 1921)
1925-1962	Mungo Murdoch (1881-1962)
c.1970-2004	Mungo Murdoch and John Murdoch (1922-)
2004-	*Redeveloped as housing in 2009*

Barquharrie (NS 503190)

41 acres in 1851. 50 acres in 1881. 65 acres in 1922. Also spelled Barwharrie (1851-1881).

1619-1686	Ochiltree Estate – George Craufurd
1725	Captain Hugh Campbell (b. c.1660)
1778-1786	Rev George Reid (1696-1786)
1786-	George Reid
-1790	- John MacKerrow (d. 1790)
1841-1881	Dumfries House Estate – David Brown (1806-18)
1888	Dumfries House Estate – Robert Brown (1859-)
1891-1919	Dumfries House Estate – John F. MacFarlane (1858-1920)
1919-1920	John F. MacFarlane (1858-1920)
1920-1922	Trustees of John MacFarlane
1922-	J. R. Aitken
1925	Jane Aitken
1930-1940	William Wilson
1980-2020	James Wilson

Barturk (NS 495221)

72 acres in 1909.

1619	Ochiltree Estate –
1625	Ochiltree Estate – John Kay

c.1780-1784	Ochiltree Estate - Patrick Murdoch
1797	Ochiltree Estate - Robert Smith
-1812	Ochiltree Estate -
1841-1844	Auchinleck Estate - William Smith (1768-1844)
1861	Auchinleck Estate – Andrew MacLelland (1806-18)
1875	Auchinleck Estate – William Wyllie
1899	Andrew Kirkwood MacCosh – David Brown
1911-1914	Auchinleck Estate – John W. Murdoch
1920	Auchinleck Estate -
1925-1930	John W. Murdoch
-1939	Charles Murdoch (1856-1939)
1939-1940	John W. Murdoch
-1949	John Armstrong (1877-1949)
2013-2020	Quintin David Morton of Auchinbay (1972-)

Belston (NS 475171)

-1831	- John Murdoch (1743-1831)
<1834	- Patrick Murdoch
1851-1861	- Hugh Auld (1806-18)
1891	- Robert Brown (1837-)
1901	- James Murdoch (1876-)

Boghead (Approximately NS 509184)
Between Crofthead and Knockshiffnock. Became part of Knockshiffnock.

1687	Ochiltree Estate - Bessie Strathearn

Bonnyton (NS 455159)
In some accounts referred to as Bonnyton Mains. 100 acres in 1861.

1632	Polquhairn Estate – Hugh Watt
1725	John Chalmers
<1830	- William Guthrie
1835-1851	- John Reid (1806-18)
1851-1854	Bonnyton Estate – James Murdoch
1861	Bonnyton Estate – James Bowman (1815-)
1871-1901	Bonnyton Estate – William Jardine
-1914	Bonnyton Estate – William Jardine (1871-1941)
1925-1941	William Jardine (1871-1941)
1941-1981	Archibald Jardine (1902-1981)
1981-	

Burnfoot (NS 522207)
Abandoned by 1895.

Burnockhead (NS 517147)
1,010 Scots acres in 1798.
1619	Ochiltree Estate -
1797	Newton Don Estate - James Mitchell
	Newton Don Estate - William Campbell (1747-1814)
1798-	
-1827	- Andrew Mitchell (1744-1827)
1837	- William Gillespie
1841	- William Crawford (1801-18)
1851	- Peter MacMurray (1781-18)
1851	Dumfries House Estate – Thomas MacMurray (1814-18)
1854	Dumfries House Estate - Robert Riddle
1865	Dumfries House Estate – Ivie Campbell
1875	Dumfries House Estate – John Brown
c.*1880*-1919	Dumfries House Estate – William Brown in Auchlin – Archibald Wilson (1841-1929)
1919-	William Brown of Auchlin – Archibald Wilson (1841-1929)
1923	Howat & Brown

Burnockhead, Little (NS 524149)
Referred to as East Burnockhead (1861). In ruins by 1957.
1837	- John MacCulloch
1841	- James Weir (1796-18)
1855	Dumfries House Estate –
1861	Dumfries House Estate – James Morrison (1809-18)

Burnockhill (NS 501179)
119 acres in 1882. In ruins by 1957.
1751-1770	Ochiltree Estate – Andrew McCowan
1797	William Campbell
1828	- John Merrie
1841	- William Brown
1851-1855	Captain MacDermott - Agnes Brown (1816-18)
1861-1871	- Agnes Brown (1816-18)
1875-1891	James MacCosh, Dalry – William Brown, Glenconner – Robert Brown (1851-)
-*1896*	James MacCosh, Dalry – James Allan
1896-*1899*	Andrew Kirkwood MacCosh – Robert Orr

1901	- William Gibson (1850-19)
1925	Thomas Howat -

Burnock Mill (NS 505177)
Burnockmiln in 1751. 132 acres in 1851. 127.9 acres in 1925. Former mill restored as a house with half of land separated from steading.

1687	Ochiltree Estate – James Thomson
c.1710-c.1740	Ochiltree Estate – James Samson (d. 1741)
1751-1770	Ochiltree Estate – Andrew MacCowan
1772	Ochiltree Estate – George Mearns
1797	Ochiltree Estate - Andrew Mearns
-1803	Ochiltree Estate - John Mearns (d. 1803)
1803-1809	Ochiltree Estate –
1809-	Dumfries House Estate -
1840-*1851*	Dumfries House Estate – Patrick Mearns (1796-18)
1861-1892	Dumfries House Estate – John Murdoch (1816-1892)
1892-1918	Dumfries House Estate - John Murdoch (1849-1918)
1918-1925	Dumfries House Estate – John Murdoch (1877-1929)
1925-1929	John Murdoch (1877-1929)
1929-1962	William Watson (1904-1968)
1962-	

Burnockstone (NS 502186)
Also spelled Burnockston. 120 acres in 1851. 180 acres in 1871. 215 acres in 2011.

1619	Ochiltree Estate –
1658	Ochiltree Estate –
1658-	Robert Fergushill
1744	John Fergushill
1797	Rev John MacDermeit Fergushill – William Brown
1841-1862	Captain Robert MacDermeit Fergushill (1775-1862) – John Brown (1778-1865)
1862-1865	Dr Andrew Fergushill-Crawford (1798-1867) – John Brown (1778-1865)
1865-1867	Dr Andrew Fergushill-Crawford (1798-1867) – Quintin Brown (1822-1898)
1867-*1881*	James MacCosh, Dalry – Quintin Brown (1822-1898)
1891-*1930*	Andrew Kirkwood MacCosh of Rochsoles – Andrew Howat (1863-19)
1951-1958	- John Drummond
1967-2005	John Drummond (d. 2008)

2005-2011	Hadfield
2011-	MacWhirter

Burnside (Drongan) (NS 455162)
5 acres in 1861.

1851-1861	Drongan Estate – William Smith (1793-18)
1914	Drongan Estate – Marion Smith
1918	Drongan Estate – Adam Campbell
1920	Adam Campbell
1927	James Fleming – Adam Campbell
1931	James Fleming - Thomas Lockhart
1941	James Fleming - George Spreadbury

Burnton (NS 494179)
154 acres in 1851.

1578	Polquhairn Estate – William Bell
1656-1663	Polquhairn Estate – William Wallace
-1792	- Andrew Muir (d. 1792)
1828-1836	- William Muir (1770-1836)
-1840	- Andrew MacCosh (d. 1840)
1841	- Andrew Muir (1806-1883)
1851-1854	Robert MacDermid - Hugh Brown (1821-18)
1861-1871	- Robert Brown (1817-18)
1875	James MacCosh, Dalry – William Brown (d. 1882)
1899-1914	Andrew Kirkwood MacCosh –Thomas Howat (1861-19)
1920-1930	Thomas Howat - Thomas Howat & Mungo Howat (1893-1974)
1940-1974	Mungo Howat (1893-1974)
1974-	

Cairnston (NS 432185)
42 acres in 1861. 110 acres in 1871. 181 acres in 1881. 3 acres in 2018.

1772	Drongan Estate – William Semple
1781-1785	Drongan Estate – William Murdoch
1797-1830	Drongan Estate – John Smith (1741-1830)
1844	Drongan Estate – Adam Hillhouse
1851	Drongan Estate – David MacFadzean
1861	Drongan Estate – Andrew MacGill (1819-18)
1871-1881	Drongan Estate – Henry Cowan (1811-1891)
1891	Drongan Estate – John Wilson (1851-)
1899-1901	Drongan Estate – John Lymburn (1857-19)

1914	Drongan Estate – John Lymburn
1925-1940	John Lymburn
	Alexander Lymburn

Carlaverock (NS 435189)
1816	Drongan Estate – James Cowan
1840	Drongan Estate – Henry Cowan
1855	Drongan Estate -

Carston (Drongan) (NS 453182)
Known as Kerrston up to 1919. Incorporated Dickston before 1855. 187 acres in 1871. 210 acres in 1881. 411 acres in 1919. 190 acres in 1959. 160 acres in 2010.
1797	James Murdoch
-1853	Drongan Estate – John Douglas (1771-1853)
1871	Drongan Estate – Hugh Douglas (1819-18)
1878	Drongan Estate – James Mair
1881-1901	Drongan Estate – William Mair (1842-19)
1914	Drongan Estate – James Mair (1886-19) &
	Hugh Mair (1890-19)
1919	Drongan Estate - James Mair (1886-19)
1920-1930	James Mair (1886-19)
1940	Daniel Wilson
-1959	Peter Wilson
1959-	W. Mortimer
-2010	
2010-	

Carston (High) (NS 514186)
Believed to have been Murrays in Carston since around 1500. 90 acres in 1861 and 1881.
1774	Ochiltree Estate - Hugh Murray
1791-1797	Ochiltree Estate - James Murray
-1809	Ochiltree Estate - James Murray (1755-1838)
1809-1838	Dumfries House Estate - James Murray (1755-1838)
	Dumfries House Estate - James Murray (father of below)
1841-1903	Dumfries House Estate – John Murray (1804-1903)
1903-1914	Dumfries House Estate - John Murray (1834-1914)
1914	Dumfries House Estate – Annie Smith Murray (1877-19)
1925-1940	James Kirk
-1971	Jacob S. Murray (1884-1971)

Carston (Low) (NS 499217)

Kerrstown in 1747. Carstoun in 1775. 74 acres in 1881. 40 acres in 2013.

c. 1780	Ochiltree Estate - James Murdoch
-1857	Alexander Ross heirs
1857-	Thomas Cuthbert -
-1876	Andrew Paterson (1803-1876)
1875-1881	Andrew Paterson – John Murdoch (1816-18)
1899-1911	Trustees of Andrew Paterson – John Sturgeon (1845-19)
1914	Eleanora Guthrie Johnston – Robert Sturgeon (1877-19)
-1919	Dumfries House Estate – Robert Lennox
1919-*1925*	Robert Lennox – William Murdoch
1930-1940	Robert Lennox – Quintin Brown Morton
1954	J. C. Jamieson
-1979	Quintin Brown Morton (1905-1979)
1979-	David Wilson Morton (1940-)
-c.1995	Morton
c.1995-	

Cawhillan (NS 492219)

Cowquhallane in 1619; 56 acres in 1851. Cowhallan in 1875. 165 acres in 1871.

1619	Ochiltree Estate –
1686	Ochiltree Estate – William Cochrane
	Ochiltree Estate - John Sloan (1673-17)
c.1780	Ochiltree Estate – William Campbell
1786-1789	Ochiltree Estate - James Murdoch (d. 1789)
-1812	Ochiltree Estate –
1812-	
-1828	- John Calderwood (1784-1828)
1838-1841	- David Ross
1851-1861	John Douglas Boswell - John Smith (1812-18)
1865-1875	Belmont Estate – Robert Watson (1842-)
1881-1891	- William Watson (1846-)
1901-1921	Andrew Kirkwood MacCosh – John Neill Watson (1876-1958)
-1922	- William Watson (1879-1943)
1922-1943	William Watson (1879-1943)
1947	William Watson
c.1970	Robert Patterson
-2018	
2018-	

Closs (NS 506168)

-1793	- Robert Gibson (d. 1793)
1855	Dumfries House Estate -
	- Beaumont (Bowman)

Clydenoch (NS 472192)

Claignoch in 1619, Klaignoch in 1654, Claydonugh in 1747, Clydeneuck, 1895-1914. 120 acres in 1861. 150 acres in 1881.

1619	Ochiltree Estate -
-1787	Ochiltree Estate - Andrew Straehorn (d. 1787)
1789-1812	Ochiltree Estate - John Strahorn
1812-*1828*	Dalblair Estate - John Strahorn
1832	Dalblair Estate - James Richmond
1839-1844	Dalblair Estate – Hugh Sloan (1801-1882)
1844-1882	Dumfries House Estate – Hugh Sloan (1801-1882)
1882-1913	Dumfries House Estate – Jacob Sloan JP (1849-1913)
1913-1919	Dumfries House Estate – Hugh Wallace (c.1866-1945)
1919-1945	Hugh Wallace (1867-1945)
1965	Wallace
	Wallace
2015-*2021*	Hugh Wallace

Cooperhill (NS 519196)

Incorporates Stamley or Stamleyparks. 140 acres in 1851. 176 acres in 1861.

1755	Ochiltree Estate – Andrew Gibb
c. 1790	Ochiltree Estate - John Mitchell
1797	Ochiltree Estate - John Samson
-1809	Ochiltree Estate -
1809-	Dumfries House Estate –
1841	Dumfries House Estate – David MacCulloch (1821-18)
1848-1881	Dumfries House Estate - Charles Stewart (1818-18)
1885-1891	Dumfries House Estate – Robert Stewart (1845-)
1898-1919	Dumfries House Estate - Robert Wallace (1859-1928)
1919-1928	Robert Wallace (1859-1928)
1928-1932	Andrew Wallace
1932-1966	Hugh Sloan (1909-1966)
1966-1974	James Stevenson (1910-1974)
1974-1990	D. Murray Stevenson
1990-*2021*	Matthew Gemmell

Corselet (NS 484217)
92 acres in 1881.

1619	Ochiltree Estate -
-1812	Ochiltree Estate - James Sloan (1777-1850)
-1834	- William Pagan (1750-1834)
1840-1854	Mrs Hamilton Boswell - William Pagan (1796-18)
1861-1898	Belmont Estate - William Gemmell (1823-1898)
1914-1930	Andrew Kirkwood MacCosh of Rochsoles – Elizabeth, Jane & Margaret Gemmell
1940	Elizabeth Gemmell and Jean Gemmell

Craigbrae (NS 450166)
185 acres in 1919.

-1854	Drongan Estate – William Mair (1781-1854)
1871-1907	Drongan Estate – Archibald Mair (1826-1907)
1914-1919	Drongan Estate – Agnes Knox Mair (1863-19) & Mary Mair (1870-19)
1925-1940	Agnes Knox Mair (1863-19) & Mary Mair (1870-19)

Creoch (NS 476210)
288 acres in 1864.

c.1780	Ochiltree Estate – Robert Wallace (1757-1829)
1837	Ochiltree Estate - James Paterson
1838-1841	- William Paterson
1851	- Andrew Bell (1815-18)
1854	John Tennant (1795-18) - James Veitch Yr.
1861	John Tennant (1795-18)
1871	George Tennant - Joseph MacQuaker (1841-)
1875	George Tennant
1881-1895	- James Howie
-1909	- William Mair (1841-1909)
1914-1925	Andrew Kirkwood MacCosh of Rochsoles – William B. Mair
1930	James Watson
1940-1959	James Watson Jr.

Crofthead (NS 506188)
Incorporated Bogbrae from at least 1790. 125 acres in 1871. 100 acres in 1861, 1881.

1619	Ochiltree Estate -
-1783	Ochiltree Estate - Andrew Strawhorn (d. 1783)
1797-1809	Ochiltree Estate - James Dalziel (1754-1832)

FARMS AND SMALL LAIRDSHIPS

1809-1832	Dumfries House Estate - James Dalziel (1754-1832)
1841-1855	Dumfries House Estate – David Wilson
1861	Dumfries House Estate – Catherine Wilson (1787-18)
1871-1881	Dumfries House Estate – David Wilson (1823-18)
1891-1899	Dumfries House Estate – David Wilson (1856-)
1901-1905	Dumfries House Estate – David Murdoch (1862-1905)
1905-1919	Dumfries House Estate – Sarah Murdoch (1866-1923)
1919-1940	David Murdoch (1896-1969)
1952-	William McHarg (1929-)
2012-2015	William McHarg (1929-) & [William] Martin McHarg (son)

Darntaggart (NS 512170)
300 acres in 1881.

1619	Ochiltree Estate –
c. 1780	Ochiltree Estate – John Gemmill
1797-1852	- William Howatson (1757-1852)
1852-1861	- William Howatson (1792-1870)
1875-1881	Dumfries House Estate – Robert Howatson (1848-)
1891-1914	Dumfries House Estate – Henry Howat
-1919	Dumfries House Estate
1919-1930	James MacGarvie – Henry Howat (d. 1934)
1930-1945	James MacGarvie (1879-1945)
1945-	
1995-	*Abandoned for opencast mining, demolished 1998.*

Dickston (NS 452179)
Once a farm, became part of Carston prior to 1855.

1855	Drongan Estate -
1919	Drongan Estate -
1925	James Mair

Drongan (Drongan House) (NS 450196)
Incorporates Lochmark. 128 acres in 1879

-1879	Drongan Estate – John Smith (d. 1879)
1879-	Drongan Estate –
1882-1901	Drongan Estate – James Sloan (1852-19)
1914	Drongan Estate – Henry Knox
1925-1940	Drongan Estate - James Lymburn
2020	David M. Gemmell

Drongan Mains (NS 450179)
64 acres in 1862.

-1827	Drongan Estate – William Grieve (1759-1827)
-1862	Drongan Estate - Adam Grieve (1807-1880)
1862-	Drongan Estate – William Grieve
1878-1879	Drongan Estate – Robert Wilson (1825-1879)
1879-*1899*	Drongan Estate – James Mackie
C 1900-1912	Drongan Estate – James Mackie (1858-1912)
1912-*1914*	Drongan Estate – Mrs Mackie
-1921	- Archibald MacCallum Mackie (1889-1921)
1925-1926	- Richard Mackie, Duncan Mackie & Adam Mackie
1930	Duncan and Adam Mackie
1940-1943	William M. Craig
2019	W. & M. Craig

Drumbowie (NS 466153)
Drumbuie in 1632; 183 acres in 1851. 250 acres in 1880.

1632	Polquhairn Estate –
1800-1855	Bonnyton Estate – John Colville (1775-18)
1861-1871	Bonnyton Estate – William Merry (1834-18)
1880-1881	Bonnyton Estate – Malcolm Jardine (1841-)
1891-1910	Bonnyton Estate – William MacHarg (1840-1910)
1910-*1914*	Bonnyton Estate – James MacHarg & William MacHarg
1925	James MacHarg & William MacHarg
1930-1940	James MacHarg and Mary G. MacHarg – Mungo & Henry Howat
c. 2020	A. Fergusson

Drumjoan (NS 463173)
127 acres in 1797. 209 acres in 1878. 200 acres in 1993.

c. 1530	Drumjoan Estate – Allan Cathcart
-1797	Drumjoan Estate – David Guthrie
1797	Drumjoan Estate – William Guthrie
1827-1854	Drumjoan Estate – James MacCosh (1781-18)
1871-1878	Drumjoan Estate – James MacCosh
1878-1892	Drumjoan Estate – Robert Osborne (1853-1929)
1892-*1901*	Drumjoan Estate – David Purdie (1857-1910)
1914-1925	Drumjoan Estate – David Purdie reps.
1930-1940	Drumjoan Estate – David Purdie
1940-1999	David Purdie (1905-1999)
1999-2019	David Purdie (1935-2019)

Drumsmodden (NS 475175)

Drumsmoda in 1654. Drumsmiding in 1725. Drumsmudden in 1930. 160 acres in 1725. 230 acres in 1871. 330 acres in 2010.

1517	William Cathcart
1523	William Cathcart (son)
1730	Thomas Guthrie
1770	David Guthrie (1730-)
1797	David Guthrie (1770-<1837)
1841-1861	- Robert Guthrie
1861-1892	Drumjoan Estate – George Douglas Brown (1811-)
1899-1901	Drumjoan Estate – John Murdoch (1871-19)
1914-1940	Drumjoan Estate – Hugh Rorison
1990	Andrew Rorison
1997-*2010*	Ian & C. Morrison

Elymains (NS 459159)

Name has been spelled variously as Lee Mains, Le Mains, Elie Mains (1921) or Liemains (1654, 1868). 145 acres in 1871. 166 acres in 1921.

1832-1837	- John Black (1786-1837)
1841-1871	Polquhairn Estate - James Mair (1809-18)
1875-1881	Polquhairn Estate – William Howie
1887-1891	Polquhairn Estate – William MacKerrow (1832-)
1899-1914	Polquhairn Estate – Robert Auld (1853-19)
-1921	Polquhairn Estate – John Main
1921-	Polquhairn Estate – Robert Smith
1930	Bellsbank Estate – Robert Smith
1940	Polquhairn Coal Co. – Robert Smith
-1965	Robert Smith (1892-1965)
-2002	
2002-	

Fauldhead (NS 461138)

Abandoned and merged with other farms to form Ravenscroft (q.v.).

1841	Bonnyton Estate – Andrew Clement
1851	Bonnyton Estate – Thomas Riddell
1853	Bonnyton Estate – John Campbell in Rankinston
1861	Bonnyton Estate – George Walsh
1871	Bonnyton Estate – David Young

Finlayston (NS 502205)
81 acres in 1861. 216 acres in 1881.
1619	Ochiltree Estate –
1714-1747	Ochiltree Estate – James Duncan (d. 1747)
1747-1750	Ochiltree Estate – Bessie Scott, or Duncan
1750-1758	Ochiltree Estate – John Duncan
c. 1780-1797	Ochiltree Estate – John Samson
1805-1809	Ochiltree Estate - John Samson (1783-1833)
1809-1833	Dalblair Estate - John Samson (1783-1833)
1833-1841	- James Roxburgh (1783-18)
1851-1874	Dumfries House Estate - John Bowman (1811-1874)
1874-1903	Dumfries House Estate - Mary Wilson, nee Bowman (1842-1901) and James Wilson (1848-1920)
1903-	Dumfries House Estate – James Wilson (1848-1920)
1914-1919	Dumfries House Estate – Andrew Wilson (1879-1957)
1919-1957	Andrew Wilson (1879-1957)
1957-	

Gargowan (NS 474223)
60 acres in 1851.
1619	Ochiltree Estate -
1774-1790	Ochiltree Estate - James Sloan (1744-1790)
1790-1812	Ochiltree Estate - William Sloan (1771-1837)
1812-1837	Ochiltree Estate - William Sloan (1771-1837)
1837-1886	Polquhairn Estate - James Sloan (1801-1886)
1886-	Polquhairn Estate - Wilhelmina Sloan (1840-1926)
1899	Polquhairn Estate – Jane Kerr & John Kerr (1858-1939)
1914	Walker of Bellsbank – John Kerr (1858-1939)
1925-1930	Walker of Bellsbank – James S. Ferguson
1940	Walker of Bellsbank – James S. Ferguson
-1976	
1976-2011	James Hunter
2011-*2017*	Ann Hunter

Glenconner (NS 495193)
130 acres in 1769. 234 acres in 1851.
1619	Ochiltree Estate -
	Ochiltree Estate - James Sloan (1734-1791)
1769-1810	Ochiltree Estate - John Tennant (1726-1810)
1841	- Charles Crichton
1851-1881	Dumfries House Estate - William Brown

1885	Dumfries House Estate - John Brown
1891-1919	Dumfries House Estate - Quintin Brown (1857-1940)
1919-1940	Quintin Brown (1857-1940)
1940-1966	John Brown (1903-1967)
1966-2010	Robert Logan Montgomerie
2010-2016	Gordon Lindsay (1971-2016)
2016-*2020*	Sue Lindsay

Greenhill (NS 494136)

c. 1780	- John Canan
1841	- Wilson
1855-1859	Dumfries House Estate - William Clement (1813-1859)
1875	Dumfries House Estate – David Wilson
1899	Dumfries House Estate – Robert Wilson – William Cunningham
-1920	Dumfries House Estate – David Howat -
1920-*1923*	David Howat -
1950	*Empty*

Greenside (NS 464145)

200 acres in 1851. Abandoned and merged with other farms to form Ravenscroft (q.v.).

-1600	- John Murdoch
1615-	- Agnes Murdoch
	- John Murdoch
1664	- Catherine Murdoch
1841	- William Baird
1851-1855	Bonnyton Estate – Gilbert MacKerrow
1871	- Archibald Cameron
1881	- William Miller

Hannahston (NS 441190)

Originally Hannaston; also Hannieston. 438 acres in 1919.

1855	Drongan Estate –
1878-1890	Drongan Estate – Robert Mair (1820-1890)
1890-*1914*	Drongan Estate – John Mair (1864-1935), David Mair & James Mair
1919	Drongan Estate - John Mair (1864-1935)
1925-1935	John Mair (1864-1935) – Robert Mair & James Mair
1935-*1940*	Robert Mair (1897-1977)

Hayhill (NS 461163)
1797   - James Dempster
1841-1895   Polquhairn Estate – William Kay
1899-1925   Polquhairn Estate – William MacMillan
1930   Bellsbank Estate – William MacMillan

Headmark (NS 498124)
1672   - James Cannon
1826   - Thomas Gemmel
1855   - Alexander Gemmel
1899-1901   Hon. Augustus Murray Cathcart of Brockloch –
                              Polquhairn Estate – Alexander Bell (1858-1931)
1914   Hon. Augustus Murray Cathcart of Brockloch – Adam Smith
1923-1925   Maj. Frederick Adrian Cathcart – Polquhairn Estate –
                              Mungo Wallace
1945   Polquhairn Estate –

Hillhead (NS 510176)
1687   - William Murray
1751-1770   Ochiltree Estate – Andrew MacCowan
1855   Dumfries House Estate -
1875-1888   Dumfries House Estate – William Miller (1853-1916)
   -1919   Dumfries House Estate – James Russell & J. R. Miller
1919-   James Russell & J. R. Miller
   -1971   John MacGarvie (1910-1971)
1971-

Hill of Ochiltree (NS 500213)
Incorporates Pool. Steading rebuilt 1849. 145 acres in 1862.
1619   Ochiltree Estate -
c.1780-1786   - William Paterson (d. 1786)
<1826   - James Campbell
1857   Alexander Ross heirs
1865-1868   Dumfries House Estate – William Steel
1875-1916   Dumfries House Estate – William Wallace (1827-1916)
1916-1919   Dumfries House Estate – Robert Lennox
1919-*1940*   Robert Lennox
   -1960   Mungo Lennox Jamieson (1887-1960)
   -2017   James Gatherer (1929-2017)

Holehouse (NS 496199)
Holhaus in 1654. 105 acres in 1861.

1770-1812	Ochiltree Estate - James Murdoch (1737-1825)
1812-1825	Dalblair Estate - James Murdoch (1737-1825)
1825-1832	- John Reid (d. 1832)
1841	- William Wilson
1851-1855	John Breadon - Alexander Steel
1871-1881	Dumfries House Estate – Alexander Steel
1891-1919	Dumfries House Estate – James Steel (1861-1942)
1919-1942	James Steel (1861-1942)
1942-	

Kayshill (NS 453173)
18 acres in 1851.

1841-1861	Drumjoan Estate – John Reid
1870	Drumjoan Estate – William Frew (1786-1870)
1871	Drumjoan Estate – Margaret Lindsay
1905	Drumjoan Estate – Robert Purdie (1866-1932)
1930	Drumjoan Estate – John Paterson

Killoch (NS 479202)
90 acres in 1861, 80 acres in 1871.

1619	Ochiltree Estate –
1689	Ochiltree Estate - James Dalrymple
1774-1800	Ochiltree Estate - Hugh Wallace (d. 1800)
1800-1809	Ochiltree Estate –
1809-	
1831-1857	Alexander Ross heirs – John Wallace
1857-	Dumfries House Estate - John Wallace
1861-1874	Dumfries House Estate – William Wallace (1799-1874)
1874-*1899*	Dumfries House Estate – William Wallace
1901-*1905*	Dumfries House Estate – David Howat
1914	Dumfries House Estate – William Montgomerie
1915-1920	- John Montgomerie (1884-1920)
1925-1944	William Samson (1855-1944)
2016-	Barr Environmental Ltd.

Killochside (NS 473201)
63 acres in 1861.

1797-1812	Ochiltree Estate – Robert Osborne (1761-1840)
1812-1840	Dalblair Estate – Robert Osborne (1761-1840)

1840-*1841*	Dalblair Estate – James Osborne
1843	Thomas Ross heirs -
1851-1857	Thomas Ross heirs – Hugh Meikle
1857-*1861*	Dumfries House Estate – Hugh Meikle
1871-1884	Dumfries House Estate – Peter Ballantine (d. 1884)
1891	Dumfries House Estate – James Moir
-1912	Dumfries House Estate – Munro
1914	Dumfries House Estate – James Montgomerie – Thomas Inglis
1930	John Neill Watson (1876-1958)
1940	- James Watson

Knockguldron (NS 481135)

1795	- Andrew Lennox (d. 1799)
1841	- William MacAdam
-1845	- Alexander Gemmell
1845-	-
1851-1861	- James Weir
1871	Jean MacAdam of Craigengillan – Polquhairn Estate - William Miller
1881	- James Kelly
1886-1901	Hon. Augustus Murray Cathcart of Brockloch – Polquhairn Estate – Alexander Bell (1858-1931)
1914	Hon. Augustus Murray Cathcart of Brockloch – Adam Smith – John MacMillan
1923-1925	Maj. Frederick Adrian Cathcart - Mungo Wallace
1937	- David Welsh
1940	- Archibald Pyper
1945	Polquhairn Estate –

Knockshiffnock (NS 512182)

133 acres in 1871.

1619	Ochiltree Estate -
-1750	Ochiltree Estate - James White (-1750)
1797-1809	Ochiltree Estate - Andrew Key (1743-1825)
1809-1825	Dumfries House Estate - Andrew Key (1743-1825)
1825-1836	Dumfries House Estate - John Kay (1781-1836)
1841-1861	Dumfries House Estate - William Guthrie (1811-1880)
1868-1875	Dumfries House Estate – Adam Colville & John Colville
1881	Dumfries House Estate – John Colville (1840-)
1891	Dumfries House Estate – Samuel Murray
1899	Dumfries House Estate – John Murray

1914-1919	Dumfries House Estate– Jacob Smith Murray
1919-1927	Andrew Howat of Burnockston – Jacob Smith Murray
1930-1934	Andrew Howat & Alexander Howat (d. 1934)
1934-1940	Andrew Howat
2010-2014	Leslie Harvey
2014-	

Lane (NS 443180)

Farmhouse erected in 1846. 130 acres in 1861, 106 acres in 1947. Now demolished and covered by Drongan Primary School.

1851	Drongan Estate – John Douglas
1855	Drongan Estate –
1861-1871	Drongan Estate – John Lindsay
1881	Drongan Estate – Elizabeth Lindsay
1891-1895	Drongan Estate – James Dalziel Gibson
1899-1905	Drongan Estate – John Knox
1914	Drongan Estate – David & John Knox
1925-1930	David Knox
1940-1947	David Murchie
1947-1954	Ayr County Council - David Murchie
1954	*Farm demolished*

Lawershill (NS 481168)

Laurshill in 1855. 64 acres in 1851.

1825	- William MacCosh (1780-18)
1841-	- John Pearson (1805-18)
1855-1875	Dumfries House Estate – John Pearson (1805-18)
1899-1915	Dumfries House Estate – John Pearson (1839-1915)
-1919	Dumfries House Estate – William Jardine
1919-*1920*	William Jardine
1925	Andrew Curragh
1930-1940	Hugh Main
	Demolished for opencast coal mine.

Lessnessock (NS 481196)

Farmhouse burned down in 1806. 200 acres in 1851, 260 acres in 1863.

1619-	Ochiltree Estate – William Colville
-1642	Ochiltree Estate - Robert Colville (d. 1642)
1642-1677	Ochiltree Estate – William Colville (d. 1677)
1677-1698	Ochiltree Estate – Robert Colville (d. before 1698)
1698-	Ochiltree Estate – William Colville (1662-1707)

-1792	Ochiltree Estate - Alexander Murdoch (d. 1792)
1797	Ochiltree Estate - George Muir
-1812	Ochiltree Estate –
1812-	Dalblair Estate -
1841-1851	Alexander Ross - John Paterson
-1857	Alexander Ross heirs
1857-1863	Dumfries House Estate - Archibald MacConnell (1821-1898)
1863-	Dumfries House Estate – Robert Montgomerie (1840-1904) & John C. Montgomerie (c. 1845-1933)
1899-1904	Dumfries House Estate – Robert Montgomerie (1840-1904)
1904-1919	Dumfries House Estate – Adam Wilson Montgomerie (1873-1955)
1919-1943	Adam Wilson Montgomerie OBE (1873-1955)
1943-1974	Robert Wallace Montgomerie (1916-1990)
1974-2009	Adam Wilson Montgomerie (1944-2017)
2009-	Adam Wallace Montgomerie & David Kay Montgomerie

Lochmark – *see Drongan*

MacCoshton (NS 438196)

-1828	Drongan Estate - James Paterson (1750-1828)
-1851	Drongan Estate - William Munn (1821-1851)
1878	Drongan Estate – Edward Courtney
1899	Drongan Estate – Thomas Hutchison
1914	Drongan Estate – Alexander Thomson
1930	William Lang Smillie
1940	David MacCubbin
1946-1954	John MacCubbin

MacQuittiston (NS 460192)

Whitiestown in 1747. 102 acres in 1851. Around 112 acres in 2018.

-1812	Ochiltree Estate –
1812-	Dalblair Estate - Murdoch
1832-1842	Dalblair Estate - John Steele (1764-1842)
1842-1844	Dalblair Estate – John Steele (d. 1871)
1844-1871	Dumfries House Estate - John Steele (d. 1871)
1871-	Dumfries House Estate – Janet Steele
1885-1913	Dumfries House Estate – Robert Steele (1850-1913)
1914	Dumfries House Estate – Heirs of Robert Steele
-1919	Dumfries House Estate – William Hutton
1919-*1930*	William Hutton

1940-1958	John Neill Watson (1876-1958)
-2018	[John] Neil Watson Mackie (1940-2017)
2018-	William Robb

Mill of Shield (NS 438178)

Miln o' Shiel in 1791, Mill of Shiell of Drongan in 1844. 70 Scotch acres in 1844. 446 aces in 1919. Conversion into courtyard development granted.

-1791	Drongan Estate – James Gibson (d. 1791)
1797-1818	Drongan Estate – John Murdoch
-1844	Drongan Estate – James Kerr
1844-	Drongan Estate –
1851-1866	Drongan Estate – George Anderson (1813-1866)
1866-*1899*	Drongan Estate – William Mair & David Mair
1914	Drongan Estate – David Mair
1919	Drongan Estate -
1925-1942	James Wilson (1880-1955)
	Steel
	Douglas
-2007	Dunlop
2007-	

Muirston (NS 468162)

125 acres in 1851. 196 acres in 1921

1626	Polquhairn Estate -
-1786	Polquhairn Estate - Alexander Murdoch (d. 1786)
1796-1827	Polquhairn Estate - William Gemmell (1760-1827)
1827-*1841*	Polquhairn Estate – David Gemmell
1851-1860	Polquhairn Estate – Mungo Howat (d. 1860)
1860-*1861*	Polquhairn Estate – John Howat
1865	Polquhairn Estate – John Purdie
1871-1893	Polquhairn Estate – David Purdie (1819-1893)
1893-*1901*	Polquhairn Estate – Hugh Purdie (1869-1949)
1914-1922	Polquhairn Estate – John Purdie
1922-	Polquhairn Estate –
1925	Polquhairn Estate – Hugh Sloan (1895-19)
1930	Bellsbank Estate – Hugh Sloan
1940	Polquhairn Coal Co. – Hugh Sloan
1992	Robert Wyllie (1939-2020)
2002-2015	Robert William Wyllie

Netherton (NS 505517)

Nether Finlayston in 1831-1871. 44 Scots acres in 1797. 52 acres in 1871.

c. 1780	John Scott
1797	Ochiltree Estate - Adam Scott
-1812	Ochiltree Estate –
1812-	
1830-1843	- John Hyndman (1776-1843)
1851-1855	John Bryden heirs - George Connell
1871-1881	Dumfries House Estate – George Connell (Connal) (1797-18)
1899-1919	Dumfries House Estate – William Wallace (1832-1922)
1919-*1929*	Andrew Wilson
2008-*2020*	Spark of Genius Training Ltd *(children's home)*

Ochiltree Mains (NS 510208)

181 acres in 1851. 237 acres in 1871.

1797	Newton Don Estate - Jacob Smith
1838-1841	- William Murray
1851-1861	Dumfries House Estate - George Paterson
1863-1890	Dumfries House Estate - Hugh Brown (d. 1890)
1899-1914	Dumfries House Estate - Ann Douglas or Brown
-1918	Dumfries House Estate – Robert Brown (1893-1918)
1918-1923	Dumfries House Estate – Hugh Brown (1883-1942)
1923-1942	Hugh Brown (1883-1942)
1942-1965	Hugh Brown (d. 1965)
1965-1986	Hugh Brown (1942-2020)
2010	Gatherer

Ochiltree Mill (NS 508215)

1700	Ochiltree Estate - John MacRae
1792	Ochiltree Estate - Andrew Murdoch
	Ochiltree Estate - Samson
-1812	Ochiltree Estate -
1812-	
	- William Tennant
-1835	- James Tennant (1754-1835)
1838-1847	Alexander Ross - David Reid
1851-1855	Alexander Ross - John Murdoch (1788-1859)
-1857	Alexander Ross heirs - John Murdoch (1788-1859)
1857-	Thomas Cuthbert- John Murdoch (1788-1859)
1859-1869	- Andrew Murdoch (1829-1869)
1871	Dumfries House Estate - Jane Murdoch

1895-1899	Dumfries House Estate – David Murdoch
1911	Dumfries House Estate – John Gemmell
1925	Dumfries House Estate – MacGill & Smith Ltd.
1940	- Robert Martin

Palmerston (North) (NS 507200)

Had been Duncan family for c. 400 years by 1950. Incorporates the farm of Barebelly.

1619	Ochiltree Estate –
1680-1747	Ochiltree Estate – James Duncan (d. 1747)
1747-1750	Ochiltree Estate – Bessie Scott, or Duncan
1750-1789	Ochiltree Estate – John Duncan (d. 1789)
1789-1829	- James Duncan (1742-1829)
1841-1851	- John Duncan (1777-1868)
1855-1868	Dumfries House Estate - John Duncan (1777-1868)
1868-1893	Dumfries House Estate – John Duncan (1807-1893)
1900-1919	Dumfries House Estate – Edward Duncan
1919-1938	Edward Duncan – John Duncan
1938-*1940*	John Duncan

Palmerston (South) (NS 508195)

Also known as Laigh Palmerston. 112 acres in 1871.

1619	Ochiltree Estate -
1680-	Ochiltree Estate – James Duncan
-1758	Ochiltree Estate – John Duncan (d. 1789)
-1838	- James Gibson (1754-1838)
1841-1855	Dumfries House Estate - William Robb
1861-1906	Dumfries House Estate – David Robb (1830-1906)
1914-1919	Dumfries House Estate – John Robb (1864-1940) & David Robb (1869-1960)
1919-1940	John Robb (1864-1940) & David Robb (1869-1960)
1940-1960	David Robb (1869-1960)
1960-*2015*	D. & W. Robb

Pennymore (NS 488219)

Dennymore in 1654. 105 acres in 1851. 132 acres in 1861. 125 acres in 1881.

1619	Ochiltree Estate -
1791-1797	Ochiltree Estate - John Key
-1812	Ochiltree Estate –
1812-	

FARMS AND SMALL LAIRDSHIPS

	- William Chalmers (d. 1827)
-1835	- James Kay (1744-1835)
1841-1855	Mrs Hamilton Douglas Boswell - Robert Murdoch
1855-	Mrs Hamilton Douglas Boswell – John Hunter
1865-1901	Belmont Estate - John Sloan (1835-1907)
1904-*1925*	Andrew Kirkwood MacCosh – Hugh Ross (1862-1935)
1925-1940	Alexander Ross
-1947	
1947-1981	James Hunter (1919-1984)
1981-2011	James Hunter & Mungo Hunter (1956-)
2011-2017	Mungo Hunter (1956-)
2019-	

Piperhill (NS 484164)
125 acres in 1844. 166 acres in 1945. The site of the farm was obliterated by surface coal mining in the 1990s.

-1786	- John Guthrie (d. 1786)
1797	- Thomas Guthrie
1838-1843	Polquhairn Estate - Andrew Templeton (1775-1843)
1851-1894	Polquhairn Estate - James Wallace (1823-1894)
1899-1918	Polquhairn Estate – James Taylor
1925	Polquhairn Estate – Archibald Pyper
1930	Polquhairn Estate – John Jardine
1945	Polquhairn Estate -

Plaid, High (NS 489177)
Also spelled High Plyde

1619	Ochiltree Estate -
1782	Ochiltree Estate - John Murdoch
-1792	Ochiltree Estate - Patrick Gibson (d. 1792)
-1812	Ochiltree Estate –
1812-	Dalblair Estate -
1841-1844	Dalblair Estate – John Miller (1806-1889)
1844-*1871*	Dumfries House Estate – John Miller (1806-1889)
	- James Miller (1844-1923)
1881-1891	- Thomas Clark
1920-1940	David Howat
-1998	
1998-2001	
2001-	

Plaid, Laigh (NS 487180)
Part of Rottenrow farm since before 1855.

1619	Ochiltree Estate -
-1792	Ochiltree Estate - Andrew Gibson (d. 1792)
1797	Ochiltree Estate - Allan Gibson
-1809	Ochiltree Estate -
1809-	Dumfries House Estate -
1841	Dumfries House Estate – David Smith
1851	Dumfries House Estate – Helen Henderson
1861	Dumfries House Estate – Allan Gibson
1881	Dumfries House Estate – John Miller
1899	Dumfries House Estate – Robert Wilson – Mary Clark
-1917	- Allan Millar (1845-1917)
1940	Hugh Howat - *uninhabitable*

Plotcock (NS 480223)
90 acres in 1851. Steading converted into five houses c.2000 – renamed Gowanpark.

1619	Ochiltree Estate -
1695-	Ochiltree Estate - John Sloan (1673-17)
	Ochiltree Estate - William Sloan (1703-17)
1791-1807	Ochiltree Estate - William Sloan (1753-1807)
1807-1812	Ochiltree Estate – Hugh Sloan (1780-1861)
1812-1861	Polquhairn Estate – Hugh Sloan (1780-1861)
1861-1891	Polquhairn Estate - Andrew Sloan (1811-1891)
1891-1908	Polquhairn Estate – Hugh Sloan (1857-1932)
1914-1921	Walker of Bellsbank – William Lammie
1925	Walker of Bellsbank – David Brown
1940	Walker of Bellsbank – David Brown
-1961	David Brown (1887-1961)
1961-*1965*	A. Brown
-2004	David Brown
2004-*2020*	Hugh Watson of Laigh Tarbeg (1960-20) *(land only)*

Polquhairn (Home Farm) (NS 474162)
c. 1,900 acres in 2021.

1797	William Crawford
1825	- Thomas Guthrie
1854-1875	Polquhairn Estate -
1914-1925	John Walker
-1930	Archibald Pyper (1859-1930)
1930-1961	Archibald Pyper (1904-1963)

1961-2011	Walter Young (1927-2011)
2011-*2021*	Grant Young (1961-)

Pool (NS 496212)

c.1770	Ochiltree Estate - Thomas Walker (1751-1833)
-1784	Ochiltree Estate - James Paterson (d. 1784)
1797-1812	Ochiltree Estate - William Paterson (1764-1837)
1812-1837	Dalblair Estate - William Paterson (1764-1837)
1855	Alexander Ross heirs -

Ravenscroft (NS 460142)

New steading erected in 1860s to replace three former farms – Auchingee, Fauldhead and Greenside (q.v.). 750 acres in 1871.

1871-1875	Bonnyton Estate – Thomas Hunter
1878-1879	Bonnyton Estate – William Wilson (1841-1879)
1881-1885	Bonnyton Estate – William McClure
1899	Bonnyton Estate – John Howie & Robert Wallace Howie
1905-1914	Bonnyton Estate – John W. Campbell
1923-1949	John Purdie (1876-1949)
2010-2015	James Purdie

Reidston (and Kayshill, q.v.) (NS 455171)

Reidstown in 1784; Reidstone in 1940.

-1784	- William Straehorn (d. 1784)
-1831	- Thomas Guthrie (1760-1831)
1841-1843	- David Guthrie
1851	Drumjoan Estate - William MacCosh
1861-1891	Drumjoan Estate – Thomas Lindsay (1829-1915)
1899-1901	Drumjoan Estate – Philip Arthur Solomons
1914	Drumjoan Estate – Robert Purdie
1925-1936	Drumjoan Estate – John Paterson (1869-1936)
1936-1943	Drumjoan Estate – Susan Paterson
1943-*1951*	Susan Paterson

Rottenrow (NS 489190)

Sometimes spelled Rattan Raw. 148 acres in 1844.

1619	Ochiltree Estate -
1797	Ochiltree Estate - John Smith
-1809	Ochiltree Estate –
1809-	Dumfries House Estate –
1841	Dumfries House Estate – Mrs A. Smith

1851-1854	Dumfries House Estate - Mungo Howat
1861-1891	Dumfries House Estate – Henry Howat
1899	Dumfries House Estate – Mungo Howat
1901-1908	Dumfries House Estate – William Howat (1849-1908)
1908-1919	Dumfries House Estate – Robert Howat (1857-1928)
1919-1927	Robert Howat (1857-1928)
1930-1942	Mungo Howat (d. 1942)
1942-	
2010	Converted into housing

Shield (NS 452199)
Scheill in 1779. 279 acres in 1919.

1518-1522	Peter Rankin
1522-	William Rankin
1705	Stair Estate -
c.1780	Drongan Estate - William Ferguson
1855	Drongan Estate –
1865	Drongan Estate – James Osborne
1899	Drongan Estate – James Sloan
1905-1919	Drongan Estate – Hugh Wallace
1919-	Hugh Wallace
1930	William Wallace
1940	James Wallace
c.1952-2009	Robert Paton (1937-2009)
2009-*2021*	John Paton (1965-)

Shield Mains of Drongan (NS 433194)
66 Scotch acres in 1843.

1878	Drongan Estate – John Weir
1899	Drongan Estate – Henry Cowan
1914	Drongan Estate – Henry Cowan
1925-1965	James Wallace (1879-1965)
1965-	
2003-2013	John C. Fergusson

Sinclairston (NS 469169)

1797	- James MacCosh
c. 1820	Drumjoan Estate – William Aird (d. 1830)
1851-1854	Drumjoan Estate - James Kay
1894	In ruins

Slatehole (NS 491231)

Originally spelled Sclaithol (1654) or Sclatehole (at least to 1864). Approximately 100 acres in 1861. Roup in 1864. 153 acres in 1909.

1774-1797	Ochiltree Estate - Charles Colville
-1812	Ochiltree Estate –
1812-	Auchinleck Estate -
1832	Auchinleck Estate - James Colville
1841-1851	Auchinleck Estate – Charles Colville
1857-1861	Auchinleck Estate – William Hillhouse
1871	Auchinleck Estate – Alexander Muir
1874-1886	Auchinleck Estate – William Wyllie (1833-1896)
1892-1895	Auchinleck Estate – David Brown
1914-1915	Auchinleck Estate – John Brown
1920	Auchinleck Estate -
-1922	Andrew Kirkwood MacCosh - David Morrison Brown (1870-1922)
1922-1945	John Brown (1869-1945)
1945-1968	Quintin Brown (1913-1968)
1968-2005	John Brown (1941-20)
2005-	Cameron Brown (c. 1973-)

Steelpark (NS 485225)

108 acres in 1851. 157 acres in 2020.

	Ochiltree Estate - John Tennant
-1791	Ochiltree Estate - James Hill (1713-1791)
-1812	Ochiltree Estate –
1812-	Polquhairn Estate -
1827-1854	Polquhairn Estate – James Wyllie
1861-1871	Polquhairn Estate – David Gibson
1881	Polquhairn Estate – Isabella M. Gibson
1885	Polquhairn Estate – Robert Wallace
1891	Polquhairn Estate – William Wallace
1895-1899	Polquhairn Estate – James Sloan
1905-1914	Polquhairn Estate – Thomas Lammie
1915-1930	Polquhairn Estate – John Gemmell
1930-	Bellsbank Estate – John Gemmell
1940	John Galbraith
-1964	Thomas Galbraith
1964-1966	James Harvey (d. 1966)
1966-2020	George Harvey

Tarbeg (East) (NS 489208)
58 acres in 1851. In ruins by 1908. Site now occupied by Tarbeg Cottage.

1619	Ochiltree Estate –
c. 1780	Ochiltree Estate – William Inglis
1819	Ochiltree Estate – John Strawhorn
-1829	- Christian Ingles (1759-1829)
1841	- John Strathern
1855	Mrs Hamilton Boswell – John Strathern
1861-1871	- William Strathern
1875	Belmont Estate – William Strathearn
1891	Belmont Estate - William MacMillan
1885	John Morton – Robert Sloan
1915	Andrew MacCosh
1925-1940	James A. Watson

Tarbeg (High) (NS 487207)
Formerly known as Mid Tarbeg, or just Tarbeg. 73 acres in 1861.

1619	Ochiltree Estate –
C1790	Ochiltree Estate – John Wallace
	Ochiltree Estate - James Wilson (1799-1846)
1841	- Andrew Sloan
1851-1855	Mrs Hamilton Boswell - Andrew Sloan (1809-1886)
1861-1875	Belmont Estate – Robert Sloan (1817-1891)
1888	Belmont Estate – James Sloan
1913-1921	Andrew Kirkwood MacCosh – William Watson (1846-1921) & James Andrew Watson (1883-1954)
1921-1954	James Andrew Watson (1883-1954)
1954-2011	Hugh F. Watson (1928-2011)
2011-	James Watson

Tarbeg (Laigh) (NS 487204)
99 acres in 1851. 120 acres in 1861.

1619	Ochiltree Estate -
1785	Ochiltree Estate - Robert Wallace
1797-1812	Ochiltree Estate - John Wallace (1747-1841)
1812-*1830*	Dalblair Estate - John Wallace (1747-1841)
1838	- Thomas Kilpatrick
1851	- Mrs Adam Wilson (Janet)
1861	- Mrs Adam Wilson (Janet)
1862-1868	- William Wilson
1871-1881	Dumfries House Estate – John Montgomerie

1891-1919	Dumfries House Estate – George Connell (1881-1951)
1919-1951	George Connell (1881-1951)
1951-1983	George Connell (-2011)
1983-1986	J. A. Watson
1986-*2020*	Hugh Watson (1960-)

Tarbeg (West) (NS 483208)
In ruins by 1894.

1619	Ochiltree Estate –
c.1780	James Osburn
-1834	- David Robb (1754-1834)
1841	- James MacKinna
1851	- John Sloan
1855	Mrs Hamilton Boswell – Hugh Wallace (1776-1860)
1861	- James Rodger
1871	- Bernard Murray

Tarelgin (East) (NS 466198)
Terrelgin in 1619.
In eighteenth century, Steele. 150 acres in 1851. 192 acres in 1871. 250 acres in 1881.

1619	Ochiltree Estate -
1778	Ochiltree Estate -
c.1780	Ochiltree Estate – Mungo Smith
-1812	Ochiltree Estate –
1812-1844	Dalblair Estate – James Wills
1851-1853	Dumfries House Estate - James Montgomerie (1782-1853)
1861	Dumfries House Estate – John Montgomerie
1865-1899	Dumfries House Estate – William Montgomerie
1901-1922	Dumfries House Estate – James Montgomerie
1922-1958	John Neill Watson JP (1876-1958)
1958-1979	James Watson (1906-1979)
1979-1997	William Ramsay Watson (1944-1997)
1997-*2020*	Gavin J. Watson (1970-)

Tarelgin (West) (NS 461200)
Known also as Westtown. 140 acres in 1851. 194 acres in 1861.

1778-1800	Ochiltree Estate – Steele
1800-1812	Ochiltree Estate –
1812-	Dalblair Estate -
1841-1844	Dalblair Estate - Hugh Wallace (1777-1860)

1844-1860	Dumfries House Estate - Hugh Wallace (1777-1860)
1860-1877	Dumfries House Estate - Hugh Wallace (1817-1877)
1877-1928	Dumfries House Estate - Hugh Wallace (1857-1928)
1899-1919	Dumfries House Estate – Hugh Andrew & James Wallace
1919-*1930*	Andrew Wallace & James Wallace
1935-1940	James Wallace
-c.1952	James Montgomerie (1918-1966)
c.1952-c.1991	Robert Paton (1937-2009)
c.1991-	
2000-2020	Peter Webb

Tobergill (NS 425188)

1855	Drongan Estate –
1878	Drongan Estate – Robert Smith
1892-1920	Drongan Estate – Thomas Beattie (1822-1920)
1925	Thomas Hamilton

Treesmax (NS 460185)
110 acres in 1851.

	Ochiltree Estate - James Cuthbert
-1809	Ochiltree Estate –
1809-	Dalblair Estate -
1841-1844	Dalblair Estate – Robert Sloan (1782-1851)
1844-1851	Dumfries House Estate - Robert Sloan (1782-1851)
1855	Dumfries House Estate -
1875	Dumfries House Estate – W. Sloan & James Sloan (1829-)
1881-1901	Dumfries House Estate – James Sloan
1914	Dumfries House Estate –
-1919	Dumfries House Estate - John Baird
1919-1931	John Baird
1931-*1942*	John Baird
1944	David Murdoch
c.2000	Alan Watson (1965-2013)
James Sloan	

Waterton (NS 454150)
130 acres in 1851.

1797	- William Smith
-1839	- Ronald Good (1768-1839)
1839-*1871*	Bonnyton Estate - John Merrie
1880-*1881*	Bonnyton Estate – James Henderson

1899-1906	Bonnyton Estate – David Henderson & James Henderson (1851-1906)
1906-*1915*	Bonnyton Estate – John Henderson (18 -1926)
1925-1926	John Henderson (18 -1926)
1926-	
1930	Mary, Margaret and Mary Adamson Henderson
1940	Mary Henderson & Mary A. Drummond

Watston (NS 496210)
57 acres in 1851. 63 acres in 1861. 85 acres in 1862.

	- William Wyllie (d. 1792)
1797	- William Wyllie
1841-1857	Alexander Ross heirs - Robert Baird
1867-1875	Dumfries House Estate – Robert Baird
-1884	Dumfries House Estate – William Baird (1848-1884)
1899-1919	Dumfries House Estate – Robert Baird
1919-1943	Robert Baird (d. 1943)
1943-	

Whitehill (NS 461178)
84 acres in 1851. 110 acres in 1871. 140 acres in 1881.

1786	- William Reid (d. 1786)
1797	- Adam Currie
-1802	- Thomas Symington (1753-1802)
1802-1860	Drumjoan Estate - James Smith (1774-1860)
1860-1881	Drumjoan Estate – Robert Smith (1808-1881)
1881-1914	Drumjoan Estate – Hugh Smith (1851-1914)
1914-*1940*	Drumjoan Estate – John Smith
1948-	James Harvey (d. 1966)
2010-2014	James Harvey

APPENDIX II

COAL MINES

The following list is not an exhaustive list of all the coal mines that existed within Ochiltree parish. Many smaller and earlier mines must be unrecorded. In the lists, a, b, c, etc. after the name is only used to identify the individual shafts, and are not their official mine numbers, which is identified by No. 1, No. 2, etc. In addition, the names of some pits are not confirmed, and their names are indicative of the area in which they were located. This applies to Coalhall, Drongan, Polquhairn, Shieldmains and Windmillhall pits with letter indicators.

+ = After   < = Before

Name	NGR	Date Opened	Date Closed	Original Owner
Auchlin	NS 507167	1977	1991	James R. MacLellan
Barbeth	NS 444200	1945	1955	A. G. Moore & Co. Ltd.
Burnockhill No. 1	NS 502175	1923	1928	A. Simpson & Sons
Burnockhill No. 2	NS 502175	1923	1928	Wm. Baird & Co. Ltd.
Carston	NS 450183	1950	1956	National Coal Board
Coalhall a	NS 448199	+1856	<1910	
Coalhall b	NS 445199	+1856	<1910	
Coalhall c	NS 444198	+1856	<1910	
Coalhall d	NS 448198	+1856	<1910	
Coalhall e	NS 449199		<1856	
Drongan a	NS 446185	<1856	<1896	
Drongan b	NS 447186	<1856	<1896	
Drongan c	NS 449187	<1856	<1896	

Drongan d	NS 448194	+1856	<1910	
Drongan e	NS 442193	+1856	<1909	
Drongan f	NS 445184	<1856	<1896	
Drongan g	NS 445186	+1856	<1910	
Drongan h	NS 443187	<1856	<1896	
Drongan i	NS 445188	<1856	<1896	
Drongan j	NS 442189	<1856	<1896	
Drongan k	NS 446188	<1856	<1910	
Drongan l	NS 447188	<1856	<1910	
Drongan m	NS 449185	<1856	<1896	
Drongan n	NS 448188	<1856	<1910	
Drongan o	NS 445190		<1856	
Drongan p	NS 442187	<1856	<1896	
Drongan Coal Pit	NS 446190	<1856	<1897	
Drongan Castle	NS 454169	<*1894*	1899	G. C. Black
Drumsmudden	NS 470176	1882	1904	Dalmellington Iron Co.
Killoch	NS 480204	1953	1987	National Coal Board
Polquhairn a	NS 484154	<1856		
Polquhairn b	NS 485154		<1856	
Polquhairn c	NS 485153		<1856	
Polquhairn d	NS 486155		<1856	
Polquhairn No. 1	NS 470160	1894	1962	Polquhairn Coal Co. Ltd.
Polquhairn No. 2	NS 470160	1894	1962	Polquhairn Coal Co. Ltd.
Polquhairn No. 3	NS482153	1936	1958	Polquhairn Coal Co. Ltd.
Polquhairn No. 4	NS482153	1936	1958	Polquhairn Coal Co. Ltd.
Polquhairn No. 5	NS 469159	1955	1962	National Coal Board
Polquhairn No. 6	NS 469159	1955	1962	National Coal Board
Shieldmains a	NS 435198		<1856	
Shieldmains b	NS 434197		<1856	
Shieldmains c	NS 432196		<1856	
Shieldmains No. 1	NS 435194	1898	1926	A. G. Moore & Co. Ltd.
Shieldmains No. 2	NS 434195	*1908*	1926	A. G. Moore & Co. Ltd.
Shieldmains No. 3	NS 430193	*1908*	1927	A. G. Moore & Co. Ltd.
Shieldmains No. 4	NS 430193	*1902*	1928	A. G. Moore & Co. Ltd.
Shieldmains No. 5	NS 438190	*1908*	1928	A. G. Moore & Co. Ltd.
Shieldmains No. 6	NS 438190	c.1900	1950	A. G. Moore & Co. Ltd.

Shieldmains No. 7	NS 444192	*1908*	1950	A. G. Moore & Co. Ltd.
Shieldmains No. 8	NS 444192	*1908*	1927	A. G. Moore & Co. Ltd.
Shieldmains No. 9	NS 446191	*1908*	1937	A. G. Moore & Co. Ltd.
Shieldmains No. 10	NS		1928	A. G. Moore & Co. Ltd.
Shieldmains No. 11	NS		1928	A. G. Moore & Co. Ltd.
Shieldmains No. 12	NS	*1927*	1927	A. G. Moore & Co. Ltd.
Shieldmains No. 13	NS		1928	A. G. Moore & Co. Ltd.
Shieldmains No. 14	NS 450174	*1943*	1950	A. G. Moore & Co. Ltd.
Windmillhall a	NS 447202		<1856	
Windmillhall b	NS 448202		<1857	

BIBLIOGRAPHY

REFERENCE BOOKS
Ayrshire Directory, Ayr Advertiser, Ayr, 1851.
Statistical Account of Scotland – Chapter on Ochiltree Parish by Rev William Thomson, E. P. Publishing, East Ardsley, 1982.
New Statistical Account of Scotland - Chapter on Ochiltree Parish by Robert Pettigrew of Polquhairn, William Blackwood, Edinburgh, 1837.
Third Statistical Account of Scotland: Ayrshire, by John Strawhorn and William Boyd, Oliver & Boyd, Edinburgh, 1951.
Burke's Landed Gentry - various volumes.
Burke, Sir Bernard, *A Genealogical History of the Dormant, Abeyant, Forfeited and Extinct Peerages of the British Empire*, Harrison, London, 1883.
Dictionary of National Biography - various volumes.
Pigot & Co.'s National Commercial Directory, J. Pigot & Co., London, 1837
Scottish Biographies 1938, E. J. Thursdon, London, 1938.
Fasti Ecclesiae Scoticanae, volumes 3, 8, 9, 10, 11.
The Register of the Great Seal of Scotland, (11 Vols.) edited by John Maitland Thomson, Clark Constable, Edinburgh, 1984.
Scotland - Owners of Lands and Heritages, HMSO, Edinburgh, 1874.
Ordnance Gazetteer of Scotland, edited by F. H. Groome, 6 volumes, 1882-1885.
Valuation Rolls for Ochiltree Parish, various years, 1875-1974.

BOOKS
Aiton, William, *General View of the Agriculture of Ayrshire*, A, Napier, Glasgow, 1811.
Bailey, Clementine, *A History of the House of Ochiltree of Ayrshire, Scotland, with the Genealogy of the Families of those who came to America and of some of the allied families*, 1124-1916, Bulletin Printing Company, Sterling, Kansas, 1916.
Barber, Derek, *Steps Through Stair – a History of Stair and Trabboch*, Stair Parish Church, 2000.
Blow, Simon, *Broken Blood – the Rise and Fall of the Tennant Family*, Faber & Faber, London, 1987.
Boyd, William, *Education in Ayrshire Through Seven Centuries*, University of London Press, London, 1961.

Children's Employment Commission, Section 30, p. 318-9, 1842.

Davidson, James R., *Footsteps – History of Schaw Kirk Drongan*, Schaw Kirk, Drongan, 1994.

Dickson, Neil T. R., *Brethren in Scotland 1838-2000*, Paternoster, Milton Keynes, 2002.

Ewing, Rev William (Editor), *Annals of the Free Church in Scotland*, 2 vols., T. & T. Clark, Edinburgh, 1914.

Fullarton, Col. William, *General View of the Agriculture of the County of Ayr*, John Paterson, Edinburgh, 1793.

Gibson, John, *A Contemplation of Lugar Water, descriptive of the scenery of Ochiltree and Auchinleck*, David & Co., Ayr, 1817.

'Innes, John' (Miller, Rev Edward), *Till a' the Seas Gang Dry*, J. M. Dent, London, 1924.

Ives, Edward D., *The Bonny Earl of Murray: the Man, the Murder, the Ballad*, Tuckwell Press, East Linton, 1997.

Johnson, Christine, *Scottish Catholic Secular Clergy (1879-1989)*, John Donald, Edinburgh, 1991.

Lamb, Rev John Alexander (Editor), *Fasti of the United Free Church of Scotland, 1900-1929*, Oliver & Boyd, Edinburgh, 1956.

Lennox, Cuthbert, *George Douglas Brown*, Hodder & Stoughton, London, 1903.

McClure, David, *Tolls and Tacksmen: Eighteenth Century Roads in the County of John Loudon MacAdam*, Ayrshire Archaeological and Natural History Society, Ayr, 1994.

Ayrshire in the Age of Improvement, Ayrshire Archaeological and Natural History Society, Ayr, 2002.

MacCrindle, Quintin, *Jock*, Alexander Gardner, Paisley, 1916.

Maxwell, *Old Coylton, Drongan and Dalrymple*, Stenlake Publishing, Catrine, 2015.

Morrison, Alex., *The Bronze Age in Ayrshire*, Ayrshire Archaeological and Natural History Society, Ayr, 1978.

Morton, Dr James, *The Treatment of Spina Bifida by a New Method*, James MacLehose, Glasgow, 1877.

Murdoch, Alexander, *Ochiltree, its History and Reminiscences*, Alexander Gardner, Paisley, 1921.

Murray, Jacob S., *Jacob's Ladder: the Life, Work and Philosophy of Jacob S. Murray*, Jacob S. Murray, Ayr, 1966.

Paul, Sir James Balfour, *The Scots Peerage*, David Douglas, Edinburgh, 1904-1914.

Potter, Harry, *Bloodfeud: the Stewarts and Gordons at War in the Age of Mary Queen of Scots*, Tempus, Strout, 2002.

Quail, Gerard, *The Cumnock Pottery*, Ayrshire Archaeological and Natural History Society, Ayr, 1993.

Retter, Janet, *Drongan: the Story of a Mining Village*, Cumnock & Doon Valley District Council, Lugar, 1978.
Riddell, Jean Oliver, *There's Wind on the Heath*, Hodder & Stoughton, London, 1924.
Sunlight and Salt, Hodder & Stoughton, London, 1927.
Miss Murchie's Holiday, Hodder & Stoughton, London, 1930.
Clerk Maxwell of Glenlair: a Centenary Booklet, Adam Rae, Castle Douglas, 1930.
Pyperhill: a Galloway Story, Hodder & Stoughton, London, 1932.
Rogers, Rev Dr Charles, *The Scottish Branch of the Norman House of Roger*, Privately Printed, London, 1872.
Rowan, David, *Memorials of Ochiltree and Neighbourhood, in a Letter to a Friend*, Aird & Coghill, Glasgow, 1879.
Sanderson, Margaret H. B., *Ayrshire and the Reformation, People and Change 1490-1600*, Tuckwell Press, East Linton, 1997.
Strawhorn, John, *750 Years of a Scottish School: Ayr Academy 1233-1983*, Alloway Publishing, Ayr, 1983.
Tranter, Nigel, *The Fortalices and Early Mansions of Southern Scotland*, The Moray Press, Edinburgh, 1935.
Veitch, James, *George Douglas Brown*, Herbert Jenkins, London, 1952.
Walker, Frances H., *Vignettes from Scottish Parish Life*, Arthur H. Stockwell, London, 1926.
About 'The Old Place', Kilmarnock Standard Press, Kilmarnock, 1927.
Morning Musings: On Things New and Old in Scottish Life, Kilmarnock Standard Press, Kilmarnock, 1929.
Wodrow, Rev Robert, *The History of the Sufferings of the Church of Scotland, traced from the Restoration to the Revolution* (4 vols.), Blackie & Son, Edinburgh, 1839.
Young, Alex F., *Old Ochiltree*, Stenlake Publishing, Catrine, 2012.

PERIODICALS
Ardrossan & Saltcoats Herald (various editions)
Ayr Advertiser (various editions)
Ayrshire Post (various editions)
Cumnock Chronicle (various editions)
Kilmarnock Standard (various editions)

JOURNALS
Archaeological and Historical Collections Relating to the Counties of Ayr and Wigton:
MacDonald, James, *Notices of Ancient Urns Found in the Cairns and Barrows*

of Ayrshire, Vol. 1, Edinburgh, 1878.
MacDonald, James, *Illustrative Notes of the Ancient Stone Implements of Ayrshire*, Vol. 3, Edinburgh, 1882.

Ayrshire Archaeological and Natural History Society:
Fowler, James J., *The Presbytery of Ayr: Its Schools and Schoolmasters, 1642-1746*, Vol. 6, 1958-60, Ayr, 1961.
Historic Mauchline, Ochiltree, Catrine and Their Surroundings, Monograph No. 46, Ayr, 2019.
Livens, Robin, G., *A Cinerary Urn from Ochiltree*, Vol. 4, 1955-57, Ayr, 1958.
Sleight, George E., *Ayrshire Coal Mining and Ancillary Industries*, Vol. 7, 1961-66, Ayr, 1966.

Bannatyne Club:
The Original Letters of Mr John Colville 1582-1603, Edinburgh, 1858.

Discovery and Excavation in Scotland:
Hendry, T. A., *Ochiltree, 1964.*
Finlayson, W. L.; and Alexander, D., *Skares Road, near Cumnock (Ochiltree & Old Cumnock parishes)*, evaluation, 1995.

Scottish History Society:
Romanes, Charles S. (editor), *Selections from the Records of the Regality of Melrose*, Edinburgh, 1917.
Scott, Andrew Murray, *Letters of John Graham of Claverhouse*, Vol. 11, 1990.

BOOKLETS

Auchinleck Co-operative Society Limited 1890-1940, Auchinleck Co-operative Society, Auchinleck, 1940.
Ayrshire Burials Index: Parish of Ochiltree, Troon Ayrshire Family History Society, Troon, 2006.
Killoch Colliery, a New Major Sinking in Ayrshire, National Coal Board, Edinburgh, 1959.

MAPS AND PLANS

Coila Provincia, Timothy Pont, 1654.
Geological Survey of Scotland, Maps of Scotland, 1928.
Geological Survey Scotland, 6" Map, Sheet No. XXXIV S.W., 1910.
Map of Ayrshire, A. & M. Armstrong, 1775.
Sketch Plan of Drongan Coal, 1710, National Records of Scotland, RHP 3846.
Military Survey, General William Roy, 1750.

Ordnance Survey 25" 1st edition, various sheets, 1855-82.
Ordnance Survey 6" County Series, 1860.
Ordnance Survey 1" Map, sheet 78, 1902.
Plan of Drumsmiding, Bruce, 1725. National Records of Scotland, RHP 1625.
Plans of Ochiltree Parish Church Alterations, Dick Peddie & Mackay, 1897, NMRS, Edinburgh.
Survey and Maps of the Roads of North Britain or Scotland, George Taylor and Andrew Skinner, London, 1776.
The South Part of the Shire of Air, H. Moll, 1725.

UNPUBLISHED SOURCES

Ochiltree Farmers' Society Minute Book and Accounts, 1846-1995.
Ochiltree Parish Church, Poors' Accounts, 1792-1819.
Ochiltree Parish Church Kirk Session Minutes, 1695-1792.
Ochiltree Parish Church Kirk Session Minutes, 1790-1791.
Ochiltree Parish Church Kirk Session Minutes, 1792-1849.
Ochiltree Parish Church Kirk Session Minutes, 1883-1928.
Ochiltree Re-union Committee Minute Book, 5 October 1897-11 January 1904 (Glasgow Re-union).
Ochiltree Schoolfellows' Re-union Minute Book, 1932-1964.
Ordnance Survey Card Index of Antiquities on Maps
Stair Free Church Kirk Session Minute Book, 1844-1908.
Stair United Free Church Kirk Session Minute Book, 1908-1953.
Stair Free Church/Stair United Free Church Deacon's Court Minute Book, 1844-1881.
Stair Free Church/Stair United Free Church Deacon's Court Minute Book, 1881-1923.
Stair United Free Church Deacon's Court Minute Book, 1924-1945
Schaw Kirk Deacon's Court Minute Book, 1954-1965.
Schaw Kirk – Kirk Session Minute Book, 1953-1963.
Schaw Kirk Congregational Board Minute Book, 1966-1981
Schaw Kirk – Kirk Session Minute Book, 1963-1977.
Tombstone Inscriptions from Ochiltree Kirkyard, Ochiltree and Drongan cemeteries, and other on-site examinations.

INDEX

Figures in **bold** type refer to illustrations

Accidents, 51, 72, 142, 235, 239, 245, 249, 294
Adair, James, 240
Afton Reservoir, 62
Airds Moss, 104, 108, 142
Aitken, Rev George, 184, 230, 298, 307
Aiton, William, 27, 36, 222, 266
Alexander, C. S., 252
Allan, James, 234, 236, 240
Allan, Professor, 213
Allan, Rev John, 186
Allison, Private Harry, 51
Anderson, George, 46
Anderson, Gordon, 120, 281
Auchencloigh, 11, 20, 55, 87, 100, 115, 121, 122, **122**, 162, 231, 266, 268, 269, 280, 304
Auchencloigh Castle, 87, 121-2, **122**
Auchinbay, 34, 80, 100, 249, 266, 268, 301, 304, 308
Auchincruive, 83, 84, 119, 131, 133, 134, 143
Auchingee, 260, 305, 331

Auchinleck Co-operative Society, 252, 254
Auchinleck House and Estate, 12, 21, 32, 43, 46, 57, 78, 90, 116, 117, 119, 131, 137, 146, 147, 162, 165, 166, 169
Auchinleck, Alexander Boswell, Lord, 165
Auchinway, 148
Auchlin, 116, 159, 246, 305, 309
Auldbyres, 305

Baird, Alexander, 267
Baird, John (Glasgow), 188
Baird, John, 181
Baird, Rev Andrew, 183
Baird, William, & Co., 237
Baker, Rev Carolyn, 179
Bakers, 251–54
Ballochmyle Hospital, 177
Bannatyne, Rev Ninian, 180
Barbeth, 127, 236, 306, 338
Barbieston, 46, 125
Barclay, John, 252

INDEX

Bardarroch, 75, 80, 147, 163, 266, 306
Barebelly, 260–62, 328
Barlosh, 163, 266, 268, 280, 307
Barquharrie, 33, 34, 87, 99, 146-7, 165, 266, 307
Barr, Robert, 240
Barr Construction, 246
Barskimming, 46, 78, 80, 95, 157, 158
Bartholomew, William, 249
Barturk, 100, 249, 307
Beechbank, 73
Beechland, 73
Beggars, 39, 40, 45
Bellsbank, 138
Belston, 11, 56, 74, 80, 84, 85, 248, 270, 271, 308
Beltane, 27
Blackbush, 220
Blacksmith, 66, 195, 231, 233
Blain, John, 52
Blair, John Henry (Johnny Cymbal), 293-5
Blair, Robert, 258
Bogbrae, 315
Boghead, 162, 186, 260, 308
Bonnyton, 79, 80, 83, 97, 136, 139–44, **141**, **143**, 229, 268, 300, 308
Borland, Father David, 197
Boswell, Alexander, 32
Boswell, Sir Alexander, 116-7, 163, 204
Boswell, David, 146
Boswell, James, 90, 115-6, 137, 147, 165, 166, 169

Boswell, Sir James, 119
Boswell, Colonel John Douglas, 57, 149
Boswell, Lady, 43, 117
Boswell, Thomas, 21
Bothwell Bridge, 103, 105, 161
Bothwell, Lord, 94, 95, 98
Box-making, 298
Boyd, Rev James, 39, 169–70, 218
Boyd, Dr John Lindsay, 220
Boyd, John, 212
Boyd, Rt Rev Mr Joseph, 197
Boyde, John, 230
Boyle, John, 226
Boyle, Robert, 226–29
Boys' Brigade, 289
Bradan, Loch, 66-7, 73
Brethren, 195
Brickmaking, 76, 147, 229, 230
Broadfoot, Kirk, 274
Brown, Andrew, 237, 245
Brown, George, 52, 55
Brown, George Douglas, 197, 257, 262, **290**, 290-93
Brown, Hugh, 46, 52, 268, 286, 289
Brown, James, MP, 57-8, 76, 184
Brown, Robert, 52, 236
Brownies, 288-9
Bruce, Sir Alexander, 110, 111
Bruce of Earlshall, Lt Andrew, 103, 104, 108
Bruce, Dr H. Gilbert, 220
Bruce, King Robert, 20, 89,
Bryden, David, 46

Bryden, Dr George, 143, 221
Bryden, Robert, 293
Bryson, George, 237
Buchan, Colonel, 107–9
Burnett of Gadgirth, Joseph, 186
Burnfoot, 309
Burnfoot Tileworks, 229
Burnock Bridge, 37, **80**, 81
Burnock Mill, 161, 225, 261, 310
Burnockhead, 99, 116, 309
Burnockhill, 237, 309, 338
Burnockholm, **37**, 37, **38**, 38, 50, 180, 225, 254, 255, 283
Burnockstone, 100, 148, 149, 310
Burnton, 135, 231, 267, 311
Butchers, 252, 253, 254
Bute, Marquises of, 36, 42, 43, 50, 116, 118-19, 170, 206, 229, 262, 268, 289

Cairnford, 17
Cairnston, 66, 71
Cameron, Rev Richard, 103, 104
Cameron, William, 50
Campbell, Charles, 94
Campbell, Dugald, 144
Campbell, George, 104
Campbell of Barquharrie, Hugh, 146-7
Campbell of Loudoun, Hugh, 21, 91, 125
Campbell, Sir Hugh, 104, 124, 140, 146
Campbell, John, 84, 125, 144

Campbell, Robert, 73, 145, 153
Campbell, Thomas, 60
Campbell, William, 144-46
Camps, 12, 19, 20, 32, 60
Cano, Antonio, 245
Carlaverock, 312
Carruthers, John 52
Carsgailoch Hill, 159
Carston, 80, 84, 116, 224, 225, 235, 262, **262**, 269, **269**, 312, 313, 316
Carston Colliery, 69, 246, 338
Cassidy, William, 52
Cassillis, Earls of, 100, 103, 125, 126, 147
Cathcart, Sir Alan, 123,
Cathcart, Hon Augustus, 149
Cathcart, Hugh, 126
Cathcart, Robert, 144
Cathcart, William, 22
Cawhillan, 261, 313
Cemetery, 17, **48**, 50, 52, 55, 62, 69-70, 175, 203, 245
Cessnock, 104, 125, 144, 146
Chalmerston open-cast, 248
Cheese-making, 37, 180, 251, 265
Cheyne, Reginald Le, 20, 89
Churches, 20-2, 30-1, 58, 60, 62, 88-9, 95, 143, 150-97, **168**, **173**, **175**, **187**, **188**, **194**, **196**, 198, 200, 286, 288-9
Churchyard, 171, 225
Cinema, 58, 288
Clark, James, 241
Clark, John, 60

INDEX

Claverhouse, Sir John Graham of, 27, 103, 107-9, 160

Clydenoch, 7, 45, 116, 225, 263, **263**, 278, 280, 283, 314

Coachford Bridge, 45

Coalhall, 50, 69, 71-2, 78–80, 83, 189, 226, 231, 233, 236, 243, 247, 274, 338

Coalmines, (see Collieries)

Cochrane, Charles, 111, 148, 259

Cochrane, James, 111-2

Cochrane, Lords, 27, 102–3, 109

Cochrane, Sir John, 103-7, 157, 159, 163, 199-201

Cochrane, Thomas (Earl of Dundonald), 112

Cochrane, William, 110–11, 165

Collieries, 7, 68, 69, 74, 76, 85, 86, 231–34, 236–43, 245–47, 253, 274, 344

Colvil, Charles, 105, 159

Colville, James, 53

Colville, Sir James, 150, 92

Colville, Sir John, 88

Colville, Philip, 87

Colville, Sir Robert, 25, 89, 91–2

Colville, Robert, 90

Colville, Thomas, 88, 90

Colville, Sir Thomas, 89

Colville, William, 88, 92

Colville, Sir William, 91, 124, 135

Commercial Inn, 44, **255**, 256

Community Hub, **63**, 71, 273

Convalescent Home, 218-9, **219**, **220**

Conventicles, 103, 105, 107, 159, 161, 162

Co-operative society, 252–54

Cooperhill, 36, 46, 257, 314

Corselet, 100, 260, 315

Councillors, 45, 50, 70, 124, 137, 213

Couper, Rev Matthew, 164, 199-200

Covenanters, 11, 27, 102, 103–7, 128, 142, 155–64, 198, 295

Coylton, 11, 22, 32, 46, 53, 68, 75, 76, 78, 84, 135, 136, 143, 157, 189, 193, 194, 210, 213, 234, 235, 240, 253, 258, 281, 282, 290–93

Craigbrae, 54, 83, 127, 135, 315

Craigoch, 24, 100

Craufurd of Dalleagles, 123–28, 135–37

Craufurd of Drongan, 21-2, 123-7

Craufurd of Drongan, George, 126

Craufurd of Drongan, John, 124-6

Craufurd of Drongan, Matthew, 127-8

Craufurd of Drongan, William, 126-7

Craufurd of Leifnoreis, 99, 124, 126-8

Crawford of Barquharrie, David, 146

Crawford, James, 237

Crawford, John Stuart, 215

Crawsland, 74, 147, 238

Creoch, 81, 116, 201, 267, 281, 301, 315

Creochill, 51

Crofthead, 162, 308, 315

Cuningham of Polquhairn, 135-6

Cuninghame of Caprington, 23, 94

Cunningham, Lady Elizabeth, 32,

114, 166-7
Cunninghame of Drongan, Charles, 128
Cunninghame of Drongan, John, 128
Cunninghame of Drongan, William, 128
Curling, 226, 270–72
Currie, Rev James, 177
Cuthbert, Thomas, 37, 180, 225, 251, 254
Cuthbertson, Allan, 53
Cymbal, Johnny, 293-4

Dalblair Estate, 116, 132, 149
Dalleagles Estate, 123, 136
Dalrymple, Earl of Stair, 128, 129, 136
Dalzell (or Dalziel, or Dalyell), Thomas, 108, 158
Darntaggart, 15, 99, 280, 316
Davidson, Alan, 210, 280
Davidson, John, 209
Dejore, 249
Dickson, William, 53
Dicksto[w]n, 135, 260, 312, 316
Dobson, Halbert, 160
Doctors, 142-3, 220-1, 254
Don, Sir Alexander, 114–16
Donald, John, 147
Donaldson, Dr William, 220
Donnelly, Canon Gerald, 197
Donnelly, Canon John, 197
Doonholm House, 139, 140
Douglas, Earl of, 90
Douglas, George, 147
Douglas, Hugh, 53
Douglas, Sir James, 95
Douglas, Ralph, 53
Downie, David, 135
Drapers, 251, 252, 254
Drongan, 12, 21-2, 45, 47, 49–55, 58, 61–72, 74, 76, 79, 83–87, 122–36, 143, 185–87, 189–96, 211, 213–17, 221, 226–36, 241, 242, 244–48, 250, 252–54, 257, 258, 260, 263, 266, 273, 274, 281, 286, 288, 289, 338-9
Drongan Castle, 87, 122-4, **123**, 125
Drongan Castle Colliery, 236-7, 339
Drongan Colliery, 233-4, 253, 338-9
Drongan House, 86, 129-32 **131**, 134-5, 187, 231, 316
Drownings, 46, 51, 60, 111, 114, 145, 161, 204
Drumbowie, 13, 142, 225, 278, 317
Drumdow, 113, 127, 190
Drumjoan, 68, 73, 74, 76, 144-5, 237, 317
Drumsmudden, 41, 58, 74–76, 145, 237–40, **238**, 242, 260, 262, 266, 274, 290, 318, 339
Drumsoy Castle, 125
Duchray, 234, 290
Duffy, Mr Francis, 196
Dumfries, Earls of, 36, 129, 231
Dumfries House Estate, 37, 119, 120, 124, 146, 229, 268, 270
Dun, David, 159-60
Dunbar, Sir David, 21

Duncan, Alexander, 229
Duncan, John, 229, 233, 274, 280
Dundee, Viscount; John Graham of Claverhouse, 103, 109
Dundonald, Earls of, 24, 102, 103, 106, 107, 109–12, 156, 157
Dunlop, Rev William, 164
Dunn, Dr A. D., 219
Dye Mill, 225
Dykeneuck, 116
Dykes, 261
Dykes, William, 256

Earlshall, Lt Andrew Bruce of, 103, 108
Edgar, Andrew, 81, 204, 255
Eglinton Jug, 271-2, **271**, **272**
Eglinton, Earls of, 95, 103, 271
Electricity, 48, 58, 190, 229, 230, 246
Elymains, 138, 279, 318
Emigration, 41, 47, 55, 58, 104, 142, 164, 180, 206, 252, 294

Fallowfield, H. G., 119, 270, 286
Farrell, Tommy, 70
Fauldhead, 260, 331
Fergushill, John, 155, 310
Fergushill, Rev John, 148-9, 154-5
Fergushill, Robert, 148-9, 154
Fergushill-Crawford, Andrew, 149, 310
Fergusson, Sir Charles, 57
Feuds, 21, 90, 91, 97, 100, 124-5
Findlay, James, 222, **223**

Finlayston, 32, 50, 80, 82, 100, 114, 116, 259–62, 270, 319, 327
Fishing, 51, 274-5
Flags, 58, 163
Fleming, George, 51
Fleming, Thomas, 199-200
Flodden, Battle of, 21, 25, 92, 93
Floods, 44, 46, 60, 69, 81, 157
Football, 49, 75, 214, 273, 274
Forget-me-not Society, 275, 282, 299
Forsyth, Livingston, 245
Fowler, Alexander, 85
Freemasons, 288

Gadgirth, 136, 186, 247
Gallowlea, 19, 42, 47, 50, 51, 59, 82, 218
Gargowan, 100, 137, 266, 271, 319
Garrallan Estate, 149
Garrochhill, 234
Gasworks, 42, 249
Gateside Inn, 71, 72, 236, 257-8, **257**
Gemmell, David, 46, 135
Gemmell, James, 233
Gilchrist, William, 105, 159, 198, 199
Gillies, Rev Iain, 177
Gilmour, J. & J., 234, 253
Girls' Brigade, 289
Girotti, Abel, 120
Glanbia, 250
Glencairn, Earls of, 28–30, 33, 95, 113–15, 148, 166–68, 204, 211, 261
Glenconner, 32–34, 80, 82, 100, 301, 319

Glenhead, 44
Gold, James, 214
Gordon, John Taylor, 142
Gordon, Major John, 142
Gold, William, 215
Gordon of Earlstoun, 105
Gospel Hall, 195, 288
Gowanpark, 330
Graham of Claverhouse, John, 27, 103, 107, 109, 160
Graham, John, 274
Gray, Aggie, 252
Green Shutters, House with the, 35, 49, **35**, **48**, 195, 252, **256**, 257, 285-6, 290, 292-3
Greenhill, 116, 241, 320
Greenshields, John, 249, 251
Greenside, 320, 331
Greer, John, 45
Greig, Alexander, 213
Grocers, 73, 135, 222, 251-4
Guthrie, David, 41
Guthrie, Rev Thomas, 181

Haddow, Agnes, 255
Haggart, Thomas, 53
Haliburton, George, 91
Hall, James, 53
Halls, 57, 58, 64, 67, 69, 172–74, 176, 189, 190, 192, **194**, 194-5, 209, 216, 221, 247, 270, 276, 285-8
Hamilton, Rev Robert, 153
Hamilton, Sir James, 92-3
Hannahston, 69, 135, 196, 233, 235, 245, 248, 320
Hardie, James Keir, 228, 247
Hardwicke Hall, 194, **194**
Hardwicke, Earls of, 72, 134, 195
Harvie, Patrick, 161-2
Haswell, James, 195
Hawthorn Villa, 44, **44**
Hayhill, 76-7, 79, 138, 225, 321
Head Inn, 255, 285, 296, 204
Headmark, 80, 139, 149, 321
Henderson, Edward, 16
Henderson, James S., 209, 280
Hendry, Alastair, 18
Hendry, James, 82
Hillhead, 161, 261, 321
Hodge, Joe, 70
Hodge, John, 53
Hodge, Kenneth, 250, 254
Hodgmac, 250
Holehouse, 80, 82, 85, 116, 259, 322
Hotels, 44, 83, 120, 252, 255, 256, 258, 279, 282, 283
Houldsworth, Col. William, 57
Houston, Rev David, 161
Houston, Dorothy K., 210
Hughes-Onslow, Captain Oliver, 185
Hunter of Bonnyton, Andrew, 140-1
Hunter of Bonnyton, John, 139
Hunter of Bonnyton, William, 141-2
Hunter, Rev George, 186, 191
Hunter, John, 253
Huntly, Earl of, 97, 98,
Hutton, Rev William, 176
Hyndford Aitken, 230

Ingram, Robert, 174
Inns, 32, 35, 43, 44, 56, 58, 69, 71, 72, 81, 157, 174, 204, 236, 249, 252, 255-8, 270, 272, 274–76, 285-7, 296, 301
Ironstone, 234, 237

Jamieson, Andrew, 44
Jamieson, Cathy, 248
Jamieson, Rev Gordon, 192-3
Jamieson, Robert, 53
Jockstoun, 24
Johnston, James, 105, 159
Johnstone, Capt. John, 116, 118
Johnstone, Robert, 43
Johnstone, Samuel, 215
Johnston, Rev William, 180
Joiners, 223, 225, 230

Kay, Alexander, 46
Kay, John, 168, 286
Kay Park, 273, 286
Kay Rovers J.F.C., 273
Kayshill, 215, 236, 331
Keenan, John, 72
Kennedy of Bargany, 95, 97, 126, 139
Kennedy of Blairquhan, 99, 125
Kennedy of Cassillis, 100, 125
Kennedy, Lord, 93
Kennedy, Major J. C., 57
Kennedy, Rev, 166
Kenneth, James, 147
Keogh, Rev Daniel, 195

Kerrston, 135, 312
Kerrstown, 260, 313
Kerse Castle, 22, 124–26, 136
Killiecrankie, Battle of, 109
Killoch Colliery, 68, 69, 85, 86, 241–46, **242**, **243**, 248, 274, 339
Killoch, 81, 100, 116, 263, 272, 322
Killochside, 53, 116, 230, 270, 272, 322
Kilmein Hill, 159
Kilsyth, 103, 109, 110
Kirkyard, 31–34, 41, 43, 50, 150, 165, 167, 169, 203–6, 269, 295, 297
Knockguldron, 122, 136, 139, 149, 323
Knocklery, 24
Knockshiffnock, 84, 162, 260, **267**, 267, 308, 323
Knox, Henry, 53
Knox, Rev John, 22, 23, 94, 96, 99, 153

Ladles, 222
Lammie, John, 183, 254, 255, 270
Landells, Adam, 153
Lane, 69, 324
Langholm, 288
Lawershill, 324
Leifnoreis Castle, 99, 124–28, 163
Leishman, Rev David, 175-6
Lennox, William, 275
Lesslumnochshill, 24
Lessnessock, 17, 47, 49, 50, 57, 100, 116, 181, 260, 266, 268, 280, 285,

295, 324
Library, 40-1, 64, 70-1
Limestone, 65, 232, 250
Limond of Dalblair, David, 116, 132, 149
Lindsay, Rev George, 169,
Lindsay, Robert G., 215
Linwood, Alex, 75-6, **76**, 274
Littlemill, 211, 213, 216, 258
Livingston, Rev Dr Neil, 187-8
Livingston, William, 103, 109
Lockhart, John, 94
Lockhart, Rev Samuel, 164-5
Loudoun Estate, 21, 91, 103, 124, 125
Loudoun, Earls of, 78, 105, 129
Lugar, 51-2, 54, 119-20, 191
Lugar Bridge, 42, 60, 81-3, **82**
Lynch Quality Meats, 250
Lyons, William, 47

MacAlpine, Rev Duncan Stewart, 176-7
MacArdle, Corporal Philip, 46, 51
MacArdle, William, 51
MacBurnie, Margaret, 79
MacCaig, John, 49
MacCall, John, 41
MacCardle, David, 84
MacCartney, George, 225, 295
Macconnell, Primrose, 295-6
MacCosh, Andrew Kirkwood, 149, 249
MacCoshton, 325
MacCowan, Andrew, 261

Maccrindle, Quintin, 296
MacDermeit, Rev John, 148, 149
MacDonald, Rev A. J. S., 182
MacDonald, James, 14
MacDougall, Allan, 137
MacDougall, John, 81
MacEwan, Lachlan, 54
McFadden, Mr William, 197
MacFadzean, Jared, 245
MacFarlan, Rev John, 186
MacFarlan, Rev Dr Patrick, 187
McGarry, Rev Alexander, 197
McGarvie, James, 241
McGee, Rev John, 197
McGhee, Catherine, 217
MacGill, Rev Dr WIlliam, 166
MacGinn, John, 72
MacGregor, John, 45
McHugh, Rev Frank, 196
MacKay, Captain James, 32
MacKay, Rev Edward, 192
MacKay, Rev Niel, 172, 174
MacKenzie, Rev Kevin, 179
MacKenzie, Rev Raymond, 178
Mackie, Archibald, 54
MacKirdie, Rev Andrew, 190-1
MacLean, Daniel, 51
MacLean, John, 64
MacLellan, James R., 246, 338
MacLellan, Robert, 105
MacLennan, Dr Donald, 220
MacLennan, James, 229
MacLeod, Rev A. A. Gordon, **181**, 181–3

MacLeod, Rev Angus, 174–75
MacMorland, Ralph, 61
MacNeil, Robert, 55
MacNeill, John, 247
MacPherson, Rev William, 192-3
MacQueen, Hugh, 189
Macquittiston, 116, 244, 325
MacRae, Dr Alexander, 142-3,
MacRae, Governor James, 112–14, 144, 260
MacRae, John, 296
McWilliam, W. Allan, 211
Maddocks, Sean, 216
Mair, Archie, 54
Manse, 28, 63, 115, **164**, 164–71, 181, 185, 187, 188, 190–92, 194, 273
Market Cross, 25, **25**, **26**, 27
Masonic lodge, 82, 117, 288
Mercat Cross, 25, 25, 26, 27
Merry & Cuninghame, 65, 142, 234, 253
Millar, David, 54
Miller, Rev Edward, 197
Miller, Rev Robert, 155-6, 163
Millers, 35, 225, 298
Mills, 24, 33, 44, 60, 151, 223-5, **224**, 226, 310, 326, 327
Milroy, Thomas, 239
Mining, 58, 64, 65, 147, 214, 231-48, 338-40
Ministers, 11, 27-8, 30, 32, 36, 41, 45, 79, 94, 114, 147–48, 153–56, 161–83, 185–95, 197, 199, 200, 204, 206, 207, 211, 218, 266, 295, 296
Mitchell, Hugh, 237
Mitchell, Rev John, 163
Mitchell, William, 200-1
Moat (Mote) Toll, 13, 15, 19, 78-9, 81, 83, 230
Moat, 81-2, 116
Moir, Peter, 226
Montgomerie, Adam, 47, 57, 268-9
Montgomerie, James, 50, 283, 285
Montgomery, Dr, 219
Montgomery, Robert, 49-50
Monument, 113, 132, 147
Moore, A. G., & Co., 234–36, 338–40
Moore, Mr, 214
Moore, Rev Douglas, 194
Moray, Earl of, 97-8
Morris, James, 54
Morrison, Dr James, 220
Morrison, Dr John, 218, 220
Morton, Elizabeth, 219, 249
Morton, Hugh, 37, 223, 225, 255, 256, 270-1, 275, 280, 286
Morton, Professor James, 275, 284, 296–98, **297**
Morton, Jane, 298
Morton, William, 46
Morton Rink, 271, **271**
Mote (Moat) Toll, 14, 19, 20, 78-9, 83, 230
Mottes, 17, 19, 20
Muirhead, James, 235
Muirston, 46, 138, 326
Murchie, John, 54

Murdoch, Alexander, 9, 19-20, 42-3, 50, 222, 251, 278-9, 284
Murdoch, Andrew, 42, 50, 82, 249
Murdoch, Charles, 254, 279
Murdoch, James, 298
Murdoch, John, 33, 213, 222, 225, 280, 298, 301
Murdoch, Peter, 105
Murdoch, William, 27, 41, 278, 284
Murray, Hugh, 262
Murray, Jacob, 279
Murray, John, 251, 254
Murray, William, 161-2

Napier, James, 162
Netherton, 43, 64, 80, 261-2, 327
Newall, Adam Craufurd, 136-7
Newall, Margaret, 216
Nichol, James, 229
Nimmo Quality Meat, 250
Noble House, 35
Norman Period, 17-19, 87
Nursery, 34, 269, 300

O'Donnell, Rev Neil, 197
O'Hara, James, 245, 274
Oatmeal, 30, 42, 223, 225
Oats, 21, 225, 231, 260, 264-5, 268
Ochiltree Castle, 12, 23, 87, 90, 94, 96, 122
Ochiltree House, **115**, 115-20, **118**, **120**, 157, 163, 174, 203, 211, 269, 270, 286, 289
Opencast mining, 11, 20, 86, 246, 248

Orchardton, 45
Orkney, 100, 161, 177, 191, 193, 220
Oswald, Alexander, 133-4
Oxnam, 20, 87–91, 150

Palmerston, 39, 99, 259–62, 270-1, 275, 280, 328
Parkend, 260
Parkin, James, 241
Paterson, Andrew, 84, 224
Paterson, James, 239
Paterson, Peter, 235, 236
Paterson, Simon, 159-60
Pease, 264–66
Peden, Rev Alexander, 162, 295
Peeshill, 260
Pennylands Camp, 60
Pennymore, 94, 96, 100, 328
Pentland Rising, 158
Pettigrew, Robert, 170, 206
Pettoch, 286
Piperhill, 138, 139, 248, 304, 329
Plaid Loch, 11
Plaid, 80, 100, 329-30
Plotcock, 81, 100, 261, 266, 280, 330
Polquhairn, 20, 45, 50, 73, 80, 81, 84, 95, 97, 135–39, **138**, 149, 170, 214, 222, 225, 230, 240, 330-1, 339
Polquhairn Coal Company, 73, 240-1, 339
Pool, 15, 116, 301, 321, 331
Poor, 30, 31, 37–41, 43, 45, 49, 50, 170, 189, 206, 213, 218, 275, 292
Porterfield, John, 105

Post office, 47, 64, 66, 67, 135, 253-5, 279
Postmasters 37, 254-5, 279, 280
Pottery, 71, 72, 189, 226–30, 234
Preston, Battle of, 112
Probert, John, 252, 255, 271, 276, 277
Probert, William, 251, 255
Purdie, Adam, 54
Purdie, John, 54
Purdie, William, 55

Quarries, 42, 226, 246, 249-50

Railway station, 83-5, **84**, **85**, 250
Railways, 41, 73–75, 83–86, **84**, **85**, 234–38, 244
Rankinston, 52, 68, 79, 85, 142, 143, 190, 234
Ravenscroft, 142, 260, 305, 318, 320, 331
Rebellion, 105
Rechabites, 287
Reformation, 20, 95, 150, 153, 198
Refugees (Belgian), 56
Reid, David, 225, 230, 281, 295
Reid, Rev George, 33-4, 147, 165-6
Reid, James, 51
Reid, John, 209-10, 280, 281
Reid, John, 61
Reid, Thomas, 298
Reid, William, 55, 70
Reidston, 145, 236, 260, 331
Reservoirs, 43, 47, 62
Resource Centre, 70, **70**

Revolution, Agricultural, 131, 260
Revolution, French, 32
Revolution, Glorious, 107, 163
Richmond, James, 173
Roads, 19, 50, 78–81, 83, 130, 231, 254
Robertson, James, 258
Roman Catholicism, 145, 156, 195-6, 214, 216-7
Romans, 19, 20
Rorison, Rev William, 130, 133, 186, 231, 233
Ross, Alexander, 181, 208-9
Ross, James, 245
Ross, John, 158
Ross, William, 60
Rottenrow, 100, 330, 331
Rowan, David, 43, 119, 260, 275, 298-9, **299**
Rullion Green, 158
Russell, Alexander, 55
Russell, Rev Paul, 193-4
Rutherford, Rev David, 174
Rutherford, William, 245

Saddlers, 223, 252
Sargenson, William, 55
Sawmill, 224, 225, 271
Schaw, 11, 80, 186
Schaw Kirk, 143, 185–94, 289
Schoolfellows' Reunion, 275–77, **276**, **277**, 292
Schoolmasters, 29, 32, 159, 162, 163, 167, 198–217, 223, 278, 287, 280,

284, 301
Schools, 41, 43, 50, 60, 63-4, 69, 70-1, 73, 179, 181, 198-217, **205**, **208**, **210**, **216**
Scott, Sir Walter, 115, 204
Scouts, 69, 288-9
Shaw, Charles, 44
Shaw, David, 208
Shield, 11, 122-3, 135, 205, 332
Shieldmains, 69, 234–36, 274, 332, 338–40
Shoemakers, 41-2, 73, 230, 252
Shops, 64, 67, 73, 251–55, 268
Simson, Patrick, 32, 35, 163, 201, 203-5, 297, 302
Simson, William, 201–3, **204**, 301, 302
Sinclairston, 11, 56, 60, 68, 69, 72–74, 79, 84, 85, 190, 212–16, 230-1, 267, 279, 332
Skeoch, 126
Skeochhill, 127
Skerrington, Lord, 74, 94, 144, **145**, 145
Slatehole, 46, 51, 249, 250, 268, 281, 333
Sloan, Alex, MP, 58, 76
Sloan, Dr Charles, 14-15
Sloan, Jacob, 45, 278, 283
Sloan, Janet, 51
Smallpox, 30
Smiddy/smithy, 65-6, 230-1, 252
Smith & Sons, John, 233
Smith, Adam, 79

Smith, Andrew, 41
Smith, Douglas, 56
Smith, James, 300-1
Smith, Rev James, 193
Smith, John, 129-30, 132-4
Smith, Rev John, 154
Smith, Joseph, 62, 256
Smith, Mungo, 130-2, 231, 263, 266
Smith, William, 214, 239
Somerville, James, 256
Sorn, 162, 178, 207, 301, 303
Stair parish, 11, 45, 64, 87, 113, 189, 233
Stair Parish Church, 178-80, 186, 189, 288
Stair, Earls of, 11, 111, 128-9, 130, 136, 231
Stamley, 261, 314
Stamleyparks, 314
Star Inn, 256, 257, 274, 285
Steelpark, 138, 279, 281, 301, 333
Stevenson, Allan, 50, 76, 119, 254, 314
Stewart of Blackhall, Sir Archibald, 102
Stewart, Alan, 123
Stewart, Andrew, 1st Lord Ochiltree, 93-4
Stewart, Andrew, 2nd Lord Ochiltree, 94-7
Stewart, Andrew, 3rd Lord Ochiltree, 97-9
Stewart, Andrew, Lord Castle Stuart, 23
Stewart, Charles, 257

Stewart, Rev David, 206-7, 296
Stewart, Ellen, 209
Stewart, James, 4th Lord Ochiltree, 99-101, 122
Stewart, John Crichton, 257
Stewart, John, 245
Stewart, Josias, 139
Stewart, Margaret, 23
Stewart, Michelle, 71
Stewart, Quintin, 206
Stewart, William, 198-9
Stewart, William, 5th Lord Ochiltree, 101-2
Stone-age, 13-14
Strachan, Andrew, 237
Straiton, 148, 149, 168, 201, 203
Strathearn, Bessie, 161-2, 308
Strathearn, William, 46
Strathern, Hugh, 230, 334
Strikes, 58, 76, 214, 235, 241, 245–47, 274
Stuart, General, 43
Sturgeon, George, 253–55
Sundial, 28, **28**
Surgeon, 130, 142, 171, 218, 297
Surgery, 142, 254
Syme, John, 218

Taiglum, 64–68, **65**, **67**, 79, 85, 135, 189, 190, 214, 215, 221, 225, 226, 231, 252–54, 258, 274, 288
Tailors, 30, 73, 154, 230, 251, 301, 302
Talbot, Hon Richard, 119
Tarbeg, 15, 20, 46, 83, 100, 116, 260, 266, 279, 334-5
Tarbeghill, 260
Tarelgin, 50, 68, 86, 90, 100, 116, 266, 278, 279, 283, 285, 335
Tarmacadam, 59
Taylor, George, 240
Taylor, Robert, 229
Taylor, William, 72
Tennant, Sir Charles, 27, 34
Tennant, David, 33
Tennant, James, 33, 166, 203, 301
Tennant, John, 32-4, 80, 116, 167, 266, 267, 301
Tennant, Rev William, 33-4, 79
Tenpoundland, 81, 201
Tenrood, 269
Thomson, Alexander C., 49, 207, 213
Thomson, Archibald, 55, 58
Thomson, David, 56
Thomson, James, 161
Thomson, Rev John, 187-9
Thomson, William, 237
Thomson, Rev William, 28, 30, 80, 115, 167-9, 204, 231, 265-6
Tileworks, 229, 230, 271
Tobergill, 60, 336
Toll Bar, 258, **258**
Townhead, 43, 105, 115, 159
Trabboch, 11, 45, 55, 71, 76, 87, 111, 124, 190, 237, 266
Treesmax, 260, 279, 336

Ure, Janet, 211
Urquhart, Adam, 49

Vassal, General, 41, 47, 117

Walker, Frances H., 12, 59, 171
Walker, James, 55
Walker, John, 138
Walker, John Pettigrew, 138
Walker, Thomas, 301-3
Walker, Rev William, 43, 170-1, 173
Wallace, George, 256
Wallace, James, 15-16, 55, 157-8
Wallace, Janet, 23
Wallace, Thomas, 245
Wallacestoun, 24
War Memorial, 52-4, 56-8, **56**, **57**, **61**, 62, 120, 185, 189
Warrick, Rev John, 163, 189
Waterside (Auchinleck), 103–7, 159
Waterside, 85, 196-7
Waterton, 87, 142, 149, 336
Watson, John Neill, 68
Watson, William, 49, 60
Watston, 11, 30, 59, 301, 337
Watters, Thomas, 75
Weir, Jeannie, 254
Weir, John, 230
Weir, William, 230
Welch, Andrew, 160-1
Welch, Rev John, 157
Welcome Inn, 258
Welleyes, 24
Welsh, Rev John, 96
Westwood, Joseph, 68
Whitehill, 75, 145, 337

Whiteman, Rev David, 194, 289
Whyte, James, 66, 240
Wilson, Rev Alan, 197
Wilson, Bruce, 253
Wilson, David, 284
Wilson, Gilbert, 252
Wilson, Hugh, 55
Wilson, James, 65, 270
Wilson, James Pettigrew, 45, 84, 137-8, 149, 214
Wilson, James R., 13, 19
Wilson, Jason, 294
Wilson, John C., 173, 294
Wilson, John Pettigrew, 137
Wilson, Robert, 46, 62, 269
Wilson, Thomas Pettigrew, 50, 137-8
Wilson, William, 46, 256, 266
Windmillhall, 72, 79, 186, 338, 340
Windyhill, 24
Windyhills, 260
Witch Knowe, 17–19, **18**, **19**
Witchcraft, 23, 96
Wither, John, 55
Withers, William, 241

Yorke, Charles, 9th Earl of Hardwicke, 134
Yorke, John, 7th Earl of Hardwicke, 134
Yorke, Rev Kenneth, 178, 179
Young, James, 286
Young, Rev Stephen, 165-6
Young, William, 212, 285